Gulf Security in the Twenty-first Century

GULF SECURITY IN THE TWENTY-FIRST CENTURY

EDITED BY
DAVID E. LONG AND
CHRISTIAN KOCH

THE EMIRATES CENTER FOR STRATEGIC
STUDIES AND RESEARCH

The Emirates Center for Strategic Studies
and Research

The Emirates Center for Strategic Studies and Research (ECSSR), established on 14 March 1994 in Abu Dhabi, United Arab Emirates, is an independent research institution dedicated to the promotion of professional research and educational excellence in the UAE and the Gulf area. ECSSR serves as a focal point for scholarship on political, economic and social issues pertinent to the UAE, the Gulf and the Middle East regions through the sponsorship of empirical research and scientific studies conducted by scholars from around the globe.

The Center seeks to provide a forum for the scholarly exchange of ideas on these subjects by hosting conferences and symposia, organizing workshops, sponsoring a lecture series featuring prominent scholars and international dignitaries, and publishing original and translated books, research papers, translated studies and two occasional paper series. ECSSR also sponsors an active program which provides research fellowships as well as grants for the writing of scholarly books and for the translation, into Arabic, of works relevant to the Center's mission. To support its research activities, ECSSR has acquired specialized holdings for its UAE Federation Library and has created a state-of-the-art Information Center. Utilizing current Internet capabilities and on-line services, ECSSR is establishing an electronic database which will be a unique and comprehensive source for information on Gulf topics.

Through these and other activities, ECSSR aspires to engage in mutually beneficial professional endeavors with comparable institutions worldwide, and significantly to contribute to the general educational and scientific development of the UAE.

Published in 1997 by
The Emirates Center for Strategic Studies and Research
PO Box 4567, Abu Dhabi, United Arab Emirates

Distributed by British Academic Press
an imprint of I.B.Tauris, Victoria House
Bloomsbury Square, London WC1 4DZ
175 Fifth Avenue, New York NY10010

A full CIP record for this book is available from the British
Library

A full CIP record for this book is available from the Library
of Congress

Library of Congress catalog card number: available

ISBN 1 86064 316 7

Contents

Maps, Figures and Tables

Maps

Figures

Tables

ix

Abbreviations

ABIM	Malaysian Youth Movement
ARJ	Arab Radio and Television
ASEAN	Association of South East Asian Nations
CDLR	Committee for the Defence of Legitimate Rights
CENTO	Central Treaty Organization
CFE	Conventional Forces in Europe
CFSP	Common Foreign and Security Policy (EU)
CIS	Commonwealth of Independent States
DRA	Democratic Republic of Azerbaijan
EC	European Community
ESC	Egyptian Satellite Channel
EU	European Union
FAO	Food and Agriculture Organization
GCC	Gulf Cooperation Council
ICJ	International Court of Justice (The Hague)
ICM	Islamic Constitutional Movement (Kuwait)
INC	Iraqi National Congress
KDP	Kurdish Democratic Party
MBC	Middle East Broadcasting Center
MIMI	Ministry of Industry and Military Industry (Iraq)
MRC	Major Regional Contingency
NAFTA	North American Free Trade Agreement
NATO	North Atlantic Treaty Organization
PIS	Islamic Party of Malaysia
PKK	(Turkish) Kurdish Workers' Party
PUK	Patriotic Union of Kurdistan
RCC	Revolutionary Command Council (Iraq)
SAIRI	Supreme Assembly for the Islamic Revolution in Iraq
UNIKOM	United Nations Iraq–Kuwait Observer Mission
UNSCOM	United Nations Commission for the Disarmament of Iraq
WEU	West European Union
WMD	Weapons of Mass Destruction

CHAPTER I

Introduction: Gulf Security in Broad Perspective

David E. Long and Christian Koch

Much has been written about the military aspects of Gulf security since the Iraqi invasion of Kuwait in 1990. While military threat analysis is, and will no doubt continue to be, at the heart of regional security concerns, concentrating exclusively on military threats in the Gulf would ignore many political, social and economic factors that also have a crucial bearing on security. Indeed, a shift towards the latter as primary components of the security dimension has been occurring in recent years.

Military threat analysis is most valid in the short term. Typically, it combines the study of the political-military intentions with the military capabilities of potential adversaries. In the longer run, however, looking to the twenty-first century, both military capabilities and intentions are likely to change significantly in response to changing conditions in those political, social and economic areas that play an important role in the Gulf region. It is these non-military factors that could not only substantially affect the military threat, but that could themselves create and evolve into both internal and external security risks.

An abrupt change in regime could, for example, be such a factor. Successor regimes can have very different sets of national priorities than their predecessors, particularly if the change occurred without a relatively stable transition period. Iran is a good case in point. The United States went from being a close friend of the Shah's government to being the 'Great Satan' in the view of the regime which followed. In seeking to assess the prospects for Gulf security in the twenty-first century, therefore, the focus of this book will be not only and indeed not principally on military threats, but will primarily examine the broader issues of geopolitics and social and economic change. It is a fact that comprehensive security, both in the national and the personal sense, is increasingly defined by such aspects as economic development, social change, population growth and health concerns. All of these represent an integral part of this volume in addition to the traditional geostrategic concerns which continue to dominate much of the academic discussion concerning Gulf security.

The Threats from Iraq and Iran

In terms of geopolitics, the two most powerful states in the Gulf by any measure other than economics are Iran and Iraq. Besides such factors as history, population and geographical size, it is because of the current regime character of the two states that they also continue to pose the greatest external military threats to the six Arab states of the Gulf Cooperation Council (GCC). Moreover, the intentions of these states are unlikely to change so long as the current regimes remain in power. As this is written, neither regime faces any serious challenge in terms of opposition politics. The election of Mohammad Khatami to the presidency of the Islamic republic has sparked renewed hope that some change leading to a more cooperative stance might be forthcoming. At this point, however, it is far too soon to tell how really far-reaching such change might be, in particular, in terms of foreign policy.

Despite Iran's efforts in recent years to appear more 'moderate' in order to end its political isolation and to attract needed foreign capital, its primary long-term foreign policy goal of 'exporting the Iranian Islamic revolution' remains essentially unchanged. As for the future of Iran, Dr Jerrold Green writes that 'Iran is not of a mind either to abandon the powerful ideology that provides the state its doctrinal foundation, or to abandon political activities that it regards as synonymous with these values. Indeed, Iran regards its political canvas as not being restricted solely to its immediate environs.' Green does not equate Iran's ambitions to export the Islamic revolution with a will to dominate the Gulf region militarily, as some would argue, and adds that it does not have the resources to do so at any rate. Nonetheless, he concludes that Iran will not be content to play a minor role in regional affairs, and thus one of the keys to Gulf regional stability in the twenty-first century is to find a constructive regional role in which Iran can be an active partner.

Iran, meanwhile, has a strongly developed national consensus that transcends and indeed strengthens the current regime. For example, the sense of empire goes back in history for millennia, making it essentially fruitless to attempt to distinguish between age-old imperial Persian aspirations and contemporary revolutionary Islamic ideology as the primary motivating factor behind Iran's expansionist foreign policies. It is probably safe to assume that expanding Iran's influence in the Gulf will be a high priority in Teheran during the next century no matter what regime is in power or what its relative military capabilities might be.

The geographical boundaries of Iraq are an artificial creation of Britain following World War I which awkwardly combine Arabs and Kurds, Sunnis and Shi'ites into a single state. While it appeared that over the years a sense of Iraqi identity had emerged, in turn creating the basis for a true nation-state, the old ethnic and confessional differences have remained and have been greatly exacerbated by recent wars and their aftermath. Thus, the question of Iraqi political cohesion is and will indefinitely remain a major factor in the construction of foreign and domestic policies.

In the years since Desert Storm, Iraq's President Saddam Hussein has shown little sign of losing his grip on power, despite international sanctions. Moreover, he remains unrepentant concerning the invasion of Kuwait, and he has not budged from his long-range goal of politically and militarily dominating the Gulf. Rolf Ekeus, the Executive Chairman of the United Nation's Commission for the Disarmament of Iraq (UNSCOM), has said on numerous occasions that Iraqi behavior toward disarmament indicates no change in President Saddam's ambitions for regional hegemony.[1] He also remains very much revanchist in nature.

In her chapter on Iraq, Dr Phebe Marr presents three scenarios for how Iraq might be governed in the twenty-first century. The first, a continuation of the Saddam regime, appears likely for the near-term, but she points out that even Saddam is not immortal. Dr Marr's two other scenarios, predicated on the end of the Saddam regime, are 1) its replacement with another regime; and 2) a collapse of the central government and subsequent collapse of the state, 'either because a new regime fails to consolidate power or because the current dysfunctional political situation persists for so long that a post-Saddam collapse becomes unavoidable.'

While only the second scenario offers prospects for future regional stability, even should this scenario occur, stability is far from assured. A new Iraqi regime will most likely be drawn from the same political circles that have governed Iraq in the recent past – 'the military, remnants of the Ba'ath party, bureaucrats and technocrats, and clan and tribal groups.' Marr concludes that Iraq is crippled politically, economically and socially and that 'the faster a new leadership and different political structures emerge in Baghdad, the sooner recuperation will start.' The debate has already begun over whether the current policy of keeping the entire sanctions regime in place will not prove to be counter-productive in the end, thus ensuring a threat to Gulf security no matter what comes after Saddam Hussein. In turn, it will become important to avoid the creation of a 'Versailles' complex within Iraq and concentrate on viable aspects to reintegrate the country into the overall security structure of the Gulf region.

The Major Powers and Gulf Security

Because of the international strategic importance of Gulf oil, and the resultant political and economic attention to Gulf affairs by countries beyond the region, it is also necessary to look at the impact on Gulf security of geopolitics beyond the region, particularly the West. From a geopolitical standpoint, Western interests are crucial to maintaining Gulf security. US and European participation in the coalition against Iraq in concert with non-Gulf Arab participation was decisive in creating a consensus of collective action.

The United States in particular has become the principal guarantor of external security in the Gulf, a reality that began to form after World War II and reached full maturity with Operation Desert Storm and the post-Desert Storm series of defense cooperation agreements. The driving force behind the US decision to play this role is the strategic importance of oil. Former US President Carter declared Gulf security a 'vital interest' in 1979, a position reaffirmed by every American president since. At the same time, writes Dr Joseph Moynihan in the chapter on US security interests in the Gulf, 'it has always been easier to declare that US security policy must be guided by US 'vital interests' than to achieve a consensus on the specifics of either the 'interests' themselves or the specific security policy to defend those interests.' Moynihan questions the assumption that access to Gulf oil will indefinitely remain a vital interest of the United States. For the present, so long as US forces remain in or readily accessible to the region, the extant military threat to the sovereignty of the GCC states is effectively deterred and contained. The instances in which Saddam Hussein has tested the US commitment to defending the Gulf have been met with immediate and effective counter-measures, causing him quickly to back down.

One should not take for granted, however, that the US security umbrella will remain in place indefinitely. US domestic politics play a large role in the decision by the US government to commit forces abroad, and unless a determination is widely shared by the American public that a proximate and significant danger to US national interests exists, requisite

Congressional support for extended operations can become contentious. Second, domestic political conditions in the GCC states themselves could make a continued US military presence increasingly difficult. The bombings of the US offices for the Saudi Arabian National Guard training program in November 1995 and the US military housing in al-Khobar in June 1996 demonstrate the potential for local dissident groups to use foreign, particularly US, targets to rally opposition against cooperation with the West. US personnel stationed or deployed in the Gulf can themselves unwittingly exacerbate tensions through insensitivity to local customs and mores. Moynihan argues that unless the US military presence in the Gulf maintains as low a profile as possible while protecting the region from external military threats, it could itself become a catalyst for increasing the threat to internal security – a threat exemplified by the Iran-supported bomb attacks in Saudi Arabia.

For the Europeans, Gulf security ranks just behind Europe's security concerns on its Eastern (central and eastern Europe) and its southern flank (the Mediterranean). Moreover, writes Dr Rosemary Hollis in the chapter on Europe and Gulf security, 'member states of the European Union (EU) cannot match the military weight of the United States (US) in the Gulf. In view of this, the Europeans have played a supportive as opposed to a primary role, as witnessed in their contribution to the coalition that liberated Kuwait from Iraqi occupation. This situation, in her view, is likely to endure to the extent that US and European long-term interests continue to coincide. Although Europe is more flexible toward relations with Iran and Iraq than the United States, and these differing outlooks have the potential to result in short-term policy disagreements, Hollis does argue that the principal European concern in the Gulf are in line with those of the US, i.e. the security of energy supplies. Without access to a continuous flow of oil and gas at predictable and manageable prices, Europe's economies and the standard of living of its peoples would be at risk. A related concern is continued access to lucrative markets in the Gulf oil-producing states and the security of European investments there.

Probably no greater geopolitical aspect of Gulf security has changed so drastically in recent years than that occasioned by the collapse of the Soviet Union and the end of the Cold War. Much of the strategic importance of the Gulf to the West was predicated on the threat of the Soviet Union – both external, as a part of the global communist threat, and internal, in terms of subversion supported by the Soviets and their regional surrogates.

That threat is no more. In its place are a number of questions, probably the most important of which in the twenty-first century will be the degree to which post-communist Russia and the newly independent Islamic states of Central Asia will become, or not become, significant players in Middle East and Gulf politics, and whether the roles they play will be on balance stabilizing or destabilizing. There are both opportunities and challenges in seeking ways for the Muslim states of Central Asia to draw closer economically and politically to their co-religionists in the Gulf and the Middle East. At the same time, the Gulf states must consider the impact on security of rivalries among Turkey, Iran and the Arab states for influence with these states.

The most important consideration in this regard is the political evolution of Russian intentions in the region, and the relative ranking of Russian priorities in the Gulf among the many important Russian foreign policy objectives throughout the world. According to Dr Robert Barylski, writing on the security implications of the collapse of the Soviet Union:

> Russian domestic and foreign policy priorities require that the Kremlin demonstrate success at building positive relations with the greater Islamic community. Moscow will want to be friendly with Muslim states even while it keeps the political aspirations of its own citizens of Islamic heritage in check and imposes limitations on the sovereignty of the former Soviet republics of Islamic heritage. The region's basic ethnographic structure simultaneously creates natural enemies and allies for Russia. Democratization tends to increase regional instability and diversity since periodic elections make it difficult for statesmen to maintain a steady course. Political liberalization permits discontented minorities to demand political autonomy and or independence. Even a democratic Russia is likely to be sympathetic to authoritarian regimes which support its policies.

Russia it appears will continue to be politically active in Central Asia and the Caucasus, part of its declared 'near abroad', for the indefinite future. And, as pointed out by Barylski, the key to understanding and interpreting Russia's intentions in this regard will be the close observation of the many Russian relationships – political, economic, social and security – with the Islamic Republic of Iran.

Regional Politics and Gulf Security

One regional trend that actually extends beyond the Gulf to include the entire Muslim world is the rise of Islam as the idiom of political dialogue. This in and of itself could be considered a benefit to the extent that it raises the public's consciousness of Islamic values and heritage. However, with the frustrations that have accompanied rapid Western-styled modernization, the new awakening of Islamic identity has played into the hands of Islamic political revolutionaries, who could be refereed to as 'revolutionary Islamists.' The revolutionaries proclaim most vestiges of Western influence, including science and technology, as antithetical to Islam. Interestingly, these same groups often use modern, Western means of communication – telephone-fax and the Internet – to spread their message. As recent history makes very clear, a radical Islamist message can be attractive to those who are frustrated with the societal discontinuities that tend to accompany rapid modernity, or are truly concerned over the secularization that inevitably accompanies economic and social development. In looking at the issue of Political Islam and Gulf Security, the chapter by David Long concludes:

> Despite the two terrorist attacks in Saudi Arabia in 1995 and 1996, revolutionary Islamism is at present not a major threat to Gulf security. Failure to disarm public disaffection through governmental reform, however, could in the long-run become a self-fulfilling prophecy – a serious threat could easily materialize by the twenty-first century. No state can tolerate open defiance of the established political order; but doing nothing until the threat becomes a crisis ... is bound to be counter-productive. Violence begets violence, and once the cycle has begun, it is extremely difficult to end it. ... The challenge for the Gulf states is to work with their critics in creating evolutionary change or face the alternative of revolutionary change.

Territorial disputes constitute another issue that has threatened regional security for centuries, and one, therefore, that requires scrutiny when looking toward the twenty-first century. In the chapter on 'Boundaries, Territorial Disputes and the GCC States,' Richard Schofield writes that, 'those classic Iranian-Arab cyclical disputes over the Shatt al-Arab and the Lower Gulf islands [the Tunbs and Abu Musa] will continue to fester and periodically explode.' On balance, however, he concludes that the current territorial framework in the Gulf/Arabian Peninsula 'will survive the ravages of time and be with us throughout the next century.'

Schofield states that great progress has been made during the 1990s towards finalizing the political map of Arabia. 'It has been underscored above all by the universal and pragmatic realization that precise and clear boundary delimitations are needed in order for hydrocarbons development to proceed smoothly and securely in border areas.' At the same time, he warns that the continuing absence of Iran and Iraq from any regional forum such as the GCC, in which territorial disputes can be aired effectively, means that 'the region's most serious and historically-entrenched disputes will be increasingly difficult to settle.'

The Middle East peace process initially made solid progress following the 1991 Madrid Conference. The peace treaty between Jordan and Israel and the Oslo Agreement between the Palestinian Liberation Organization and Israel are both solid indicators that the agenda for peace in the Middle East is, or was, strategically on track. The tragic assassination of Prime Minister Rabin in 1995 and the electoral victory of the militantly right-wing Likud the following year, leading to the formation of a new government in Israel under Prime Minister Benjamin Netanyahu, demonstrates the fragility of the peace process, and starkly reminds us all that this process still lacks a conclusion. At the same time, as is currently evident, a breakdown in Arab-Israeli talks has an immediate impact on the Gulf region both politically and economically.

According to Dr Glenn Robinson, the ultimate impact of the conclusion of the Arab-Israeli conflict – when and if that conclusion occurs – on Gulf states is still an open question. In his chapter on the impact of that problem on the Gulf, Robinson speculates:

> containment of the Arab-Israeli conflict will not diminish the importance of that issue in the larger region, particularly the Gulf. Rather, the diminution of the conflict will likely transform (and is transforming) the nature of the engagement from one of arms-length rhetoric to direct entanglement. In short, the regional system of domination that Israel has established militarily in the Levant will likely give way to a geographically larger and more complex pattern of economic and political interaction and hegemony in the Middle East as a whole.

Robinson's provocative but informed speculation reminds us once again that *security* as a term may have economic implications that exceed in criticality the extant regional military balance. Without question, security throughout the world already refers to much more than freedom from military intimidation and aggression, and there is every indication that these non-military connotations will continue and perhaps grow. Indeed, *aggression* can also be thought of as an economic term, and perhaps in the twenty-first century Middle East, aggression as an economic term will increasingly be used to describe the Middle East security environment.

Internal Determinants of Gulf Security

Looking to the future, a major dilemma facing all GCC states is the increasingly visible clash between tradition and modernity as regimes seek to enhance the welfare of their peoples through rapid social and economic development programs. On the one hand, change is always threatening to various segments of the population, particularly those who perceive change as a challenge to their traditional Islamic, Arab and tribal identity. On the other, for those modernists who have taken to technological change, efforts to dictate traditional life styles are seen as stifling creativity and are equally frustrating. At the same time, the more zealous modernizers risk being too far out in front of the general public in pushing for social and political change.

To a great extent, the modernization process and public expectations are economic in nature. The economic mainstay of the Arab Gulf is oil. Its strategic importance is also the basis of the US determination at present to secure Arab Gulf states against external threats. Equally important is the strategy of Gulf economic investment. Over the past three to six decades, the GCC states have become far more sophisticated in their investment strategies, creating detailed five-year economic and social development plans. An underlying assumption of these plans has been the long-term upward growth of oil revenues. Dr Charles Doran argues that the Gulf states are one-third to one-half way through their cycles of revenue generation from oil and must look beyond current strategies for effective economic planning within the next century. Doran looks at various revenue stream optimization strategies, among them – waiting for the next international oil shortage/price hike sequence; increased Gulf foreign investment in the economies of the West; and indigenous investment within GCC economies. These three strategies, he argues however, may raise more problems than they solve. For indigenous investment, for example, the non-oil sectors of the Gulf states' economies are, and will likely remain, too small to realize economies of scale. Doran concludes that it is 'regional development' that offers the best hope for long-term economic prosperity, and by extension, political security into the twenty-first century:

> More pointedly, not only is regional development the key to long-term economic prosperity for the Gulf even after oil revenues enter absolute decline, but regional economic development is also the pathway, perhaps the only pathway, to assured security for the member states. Regional economic development requires more than a plan, it requires commitment politically from the governments that will stand most to benefit on both commercial and structural grounds.

Political stability is far too complex a phenomenon to be linked to only economic determinism. Economic factors, important as they are, are only one of many factors contributing to stability (or instability). Analyzing the long-term impact of modernization on traditional societies is equally important in assessing Gulf security. With new ideas and material comforts obtainable through oil-generated wealth, social mores have changed drastically and expectations have soared. Perhaps the most important test of regime competency in the next century will be their ability to continue to meet public expectations.

The GCC states have nonetheless enjoyed a remarkable degree of internal stability in recent decades, particularly when compared with other regions of the Middle East. Perhaps the most stabilizing institution in the Gulf is not the political systems or even the state welfare programs provided by oil wealth, but the extended family. Tribalism was traditionally one of the greatest sources of political instability in the region, and while tribes today exercise far less political power, Dr Jill Crystal points out in her chapter on 'Social Transformation, Changing Expectations and Gulf Security', that tribal influences remain important. Dr Crystal asserts that in order for social transformations to affect Gulf security, there must be organized groups with articulated grievances, governments or individuals whose policy responses to those grievances are seen as inadequate, and outside powers with an interest in the issue around which conflict has arisen. Crystal concludes that, 'This combination occurs relatively rarely, but each of these components exist at times in each Gulf state. This combination has prompted pressure on both domestic and foreign policy in the past and will doubtless continue to do so as the Gulf enters the twenty-first century.'

Rapidly rising populations throughout the Gulf, accelerated in numerical projections by the reinforcing phenomena of large families and greatly improved health standards and technology, will in all likelihood diminish the ability of Gulf governments to maintain the level of financial distributions and community services to their citizens that have become standard in the last twenty-five years. If populations double in the next 20 years or so, as it appears they might, revenues will have to double for countries just to maintain the same standard of living, and the social and economic infrastructure deemed sufficient now will become woefully inadequate. As a result of these trends, the current population explosion throughout the Gulf, its impact on the labor market and the ability to find a fulfilling job, and gender and health issues arising from shifting demographics and rapid modernization all must be fitted into the equation of long-term Gulf security.

Dr Michael Bonine, writing on 'Population Growth, the Labor Market and Gulf Security,' provides a number of projections for future population in the GCC states which he notes with great understatement '...could be staggering by the mid- and late-twenty-first century.' Many Gulf officials deny that forecast population growth projections indicate a future problem area, believing apparently that as the population grows, local citizens will simply assume those jobs now being performed by foreign labor. Unfortunately, many of these jobs are menial in nature and thus socially undesirable to a great majority of Gulf citizens, and should Gulf citizens be economically coerced to accept a menial position, internal stability could diminish, at least during the transition period. Bonine concludes:

> Twenty-century oil wealth has created a welfare society which cannot easily be weaned from subsidies and social and government benefits. Policies must be formulated – and implemented – which slowly, over time, reduce the dependence on the welfare state, engender a work ethic, educate for skills and trades, and perhaps increase women in the workforce.

Thus far, military, geopolitical and economic determinants of Gulf security have been mentioned. The one determinant not yet discussed, but increasingly prominent in the minds of Gulf citizens, is social cohesion. In the chapter on 'Health, Education, Gender and the Security of the GCC in the Twenty-first Century,' Dr Mai Yamani asserts: 'No country can be secure unless its citizens are safe and well.' This is a changing but increasingly accepted conception of security that in the twenty-first century will require the enhancement of social integration, the reduction of poverty, and the expansion of productive employment. She concludes by stating that:

> It is generally acknowledged in the Gulf region that the long-term prosperity of nations ultimately depends upon the ability of its peoples to manage existing resources and develop new ones. ... New forms and modalities of political participation must be negotiated and implemented between the ruling groups and significant sectors in civil society. ... The future and security of the region will depend on how wisely they choose.

A political analyst once said, 'There are no simple problems, for if there were, they would have already been solved.' A corollary to that assertion is that there are no simple solutions to complex problems, only simplistic ones. The chapters of this book graphically demonstrate that achieving Gulf security in the twenty-first century will be a complex task indeed. The ultimate strategic challenge for the states of the Arab Gulf in the twenty-first century will be not only to deter and prepare to defend against external military threats, but also to insure that change – economic, political and social – remains evolutionary instead of becoming revolutionary. Of one thing we can be certain, there will be change.

On the other hand, however, it is important to acknowledge that while much will change in the Arab Gulf over the coming decades, much will not. The challenges posed by the various forces that have been outlined in this book demand a responsive and flexible public policy within the Gulf. A successful public policy – both substantive and procedural – requires both guidance from above plus action and commitment from below. Such a balancing act cannot be imposed from outside but needs to be built from within, in terms of regional solutions that adequately and comprehensively address the many challenges with which the Gulf is confronted. The age-old traditions that have guided the Gulf countries into the present will also represent the basis from which a course into the future is charted. It is the dichotomy of the demand for change with the longing for tradition that will ensure that the issue of Gulf security will continue to be with us for some time to come.

PART ONE

Gulf Security and Regional Threats

CHAPTER 2

Iran and Gulf Security

Jerrold D. Green

Since the fall of the Shah of Iran in 1979, and the subsequent creation of the Islamic Republic, there has been little agreement among observers of Iranian politics about the character, nature, goals and even legitimacy of the newly reconstituted state. While some have excoriated this new political entity and everything that it represents, others have taken pains to be tolerant of the comparatively new Iranian political order while arguing that Iran's Islamic character and political aspirations have been broadly misunderstood. Despite the contradictions between these extreme views of the Islamic Republic's political behavior, in their most polarized form, these perspectives subsume most prevailing impressions of the Iranian state. And as the twentieth century comes to a close and the twenty-first begins, both the domestic character and the regional role of the Islamic Republic take on particular significance. This is because the Middle East is likely to be transformed into a very different place than it is at this moment. Given the virtual disappearance of the Arab–Israeli conflict, the demonstrated willingness of the USA to intervene militarily to ensure access to petroleum, the political liberalization that is sweeping much of the world and the onslaught of the information revolution from which no state is immune, it is certain that Iran, its neighbors and general understandings about the meaning of regional security are likely to differ profoundly. Thus, the final years of the twentieth century are likely to be particularly critical and indicative, for not only will the world see a new century, but also a new Middle East.

A fundamental assumption underlies this chapter: Gulf security can be achieved only through the collective agreement and involvement of three sets of political actors – the member states of the Gulf Cooperation Council (GCC), the Islamic Republic of Iran, and Iraq. Without explicit cooperation and implicit agreement among these key actors, Gulf security will continue to elude the Middle East. It is the aim of this chapter to analyse the Iranian component of this complicated mixture in order to speculate in an informed fashion about how Iran is likely to influence the question of Gulf security in the twenty-first century.

Current views of Iran can broadly be placed in two categories. On the one hand, we find critics who emphasize such factors as Iran's frequently-discussed attempt to develop a nuclear weapons capability, its sporadic reliance on terrorism in support of its regional and international political aspirations, its aggressive behavior towards its Arab neighbors to the south and west as highlighted by its seizure of Abu Musa and the Tunb Islands from the United Arab Emirates (Sharjah and Ras al-Khaimah specifically), its opposition to the Arab–Israeli peace effort and its ill-conceived *fatwa* condemning Salman Rushdie to death. The litany of policies and actions that constitute the Islamic Republic's abrogation of generally accepted standards of international political behavior has been thoroughly categorized by critics and opponents of Iran. And in this, they have been abetted by the actions and unrepentant tone of the Islamic Republic itself which continues to condone such patently unacceptable activities as the takeover of the American Embassy in Tehran, as well as the occasional use of political violence and economic and logistical support for violent Islamist groups, to accomplish its foreign policy goals. At the same time, the Islamic Republic has done little to improve its own unacceptable human rights record or to modulate its at times horrific political rhetoric and tone.[1]

While critics of Iran are always happy to cite the above deviations from international norms, there is another group of those who favor dialogue with the Islamic Republic and who cite the country's turbulent political history, the unwillingness of its severest external critics (for example, the USA, Egypt and Israel) to come to terms with the fall of the Shah and the creation of a new Islamic-oriented political order in his stead, the inherent anti-Islamic tendencies of the West, Iran's own regional isolation, and the travails of a country that, in the past 15 years, has emerged not only from a massive and broad-based popular revolution, but also managed to survive a brutal eight-year war initiated by Iraq. These challenges have been further exacerbated by ever-present internal subversion in Iran that has as its goal the overthrow of the country's popularly elected and generally legitimate political ruling group.[2]

These two viewpoints are juxtaposed in a somewhat extreme form here, although it would be fair to say that Iran's most vocal opponents generally subscribe to the first set of views, while its supporters tend towards the second. There are obviously differences in nuance, tone and degree of support/opposition between as well as within these two camps.[3] What is particularly noteworthy, however, is the degree to which current views of Iran are determined by the political and/or ideological perspectives of the observer. That is, highly politicized and polarized interpretations of Iranian political behavior, as described above, have become far more ubiquitous than systematic, empirical analyses of Iranian politics. Indeed, dispassionate discussion of Iran's regional role is something of a rarity, particularly in the USA, where this issue has become more politicized than is the case in Europe or Japan where there is considerable scepticism about what many perceive to be an exaggerated American opposition to Iran.[4] Thus, the goal of this chapter is to avoid the broad polarization that characterizes much of the current analysis of Iran, while trying to ascertain how Iran perceives its own regional role and its ties with its neighbors. This chapter is also meant to identify those factors, internal and external, that affect the formation of Iranian policy, and, finally, to speculate about the likely course that Iran's regional policy will take as it enters the twenty-first century.[5]

Understanding Iranian Foreign Policy

Despite surprising internal heterogeneity, Iran's widely varied ideological and political perspectives must be understood as a result of the fact that the Islamic Republic of Iran was forged in the crucible of a bitter and contentious popular revolution.[6] It is impossible to exaggerate the depths of hatred that most Iranians felt towards the Shah of Iran during the Pahlavi period. And thus, many Iranians who held little or no commitment to Islam, or who harbored an active aversion to it, felt no compunction at all in supporting an Islamic-based opposition whose main appeal lay in its broad-based and efficacious opposition to the Shah and the possible likelihood of its success.[7] Although many of those who initially supported Ayatollah Khomeini and his immediate circle of supporters and political allies ultimately came to oppose him, no true meaningful opposition or even serious challengers to the current Iranian government have emerged as the revolution edges towards its twentieth anniversary. This is not to say that regime opposition does not exist in the Islamic Republic, for it does and with great vigor and force in many settings. For example, in a recent interview, the commander of the ground forces of the Iranian Army, Brigadier General Ja'fari, proudly notes how his 'forces have been assigned the duty of tending to the domestic situation and security issues in the south-eastern and north-western areas ... during the past two years'.

The general's willingness to acknowledge publicly the fact that his troops have had to quell domestic disturbances, that in effect the Iranian Army has had to protect the government from its own people rather than from more conventional external military challenges, highlights the degree to which public regime opposition has become a common occurrence in Iran.[8] Yet, despite at times severe fragmentation in the Islamic Republic, there is currently no significant opposition able to mount a meaningful challenge to the ruling group in Tehran.[9]

It is somewhat of an irony to note that, in Iran, supporters of the Islamic Revolution are characterized by insecurity, tinged with an absolute and unshakeable belief in the virtue of the Islamic values underlying the Iranian state. Indeed, their belief in their own system is so strong, and their antipathy to their opponents so profound, that to many of the Iranian revolutionaries it would be inconceivable if the West were *not* fearful of and opposed to the Islamic Republic. And here their insecurity can best be explained, as it is widely believed that the United States in particular is unremittingly committed to the destruction of the Islamic Republic of Iran. It is this sense of ideological commitment that continues to sustain and drive the revolution, although it is significantly undermined by widespread corruption, a decaying economic situation and periodic political unrest compounded by uncertainty about the future of the still fragile Islamic Republic.

The economic dimension of instability in Iran cannot be overstated. For example, Tehran only recently announced a new austerity deficit budget that is almost 44 per cent higher than is the current year's budget.[10] With inflation at the moment running at an officially reported level of 50 per cent, thus indicating that it is probably substantially higher, and unemployment growing, Iran's severe and increasing economic problems cannot be separated from its foreign policy formulation and implementation. There is no reason to expect that, if current conditions prevail, the twenty-first century will treat Iran's economy any better than did the final decade of the twentieth. Indeed, given Iran's rapid population growth and increasing rather than diminishing isolation, pessimistic projections about the economic future of the Islamic Republic are likely to become the conventional wisdom.

Fear of the intentions of the USA is both widespread and genuine in Iran. And although Iran wildly exaggerates US influence, as well as the role that Iran actually plays in American foreign policy, the Iranian government has constructed a case against the USA that holds wide sway throughout the country. For example, America's current Gulf policy of *dual containment* formally precludes the Islamic Republic of Iran from playing any meaningful regional role. Yet, from an Iranian perspective, an unconstrained US military presence in the Gulf is comparable to the Cold War reality of a Soviet-sustained Cuba a mere 90 miles from the US border.

Other US actions also have fuelled Iranian feelings of insecurity, including a recent call by Speaker of the House Newt Gingrich for a special $18 million allocation to the US intelligence budget for the 'covert destabilization of the Iranian government', initiation by Senator Alfonse D'Amato of a secondary economic boycott to augment the already extensive US economic boycott against Iran, the continued freeze of Iranian assets in the USA, the massive US military presence in the Gulf briefly referred to above, and consistent pressure by Washington on US allies to cease their economic and political dealings with Iran.[11] The attempt by the USA to extend Iran's already significant level of international isolation is understandably of deep concern to Iran's political leadership.[12] It has become a virtual article of faith, for example, that at every meeting of the powerful G-7 states, which includes the USA and the world's major industrial powers, President Clinton will raise the thorny issue of US opposition to continued high levels of trade and economic interaction by Japan and Germany with Iran, as well France on a somewhat lesser plane. Such US pressure has also been exerted on Russia and China. Thus, Iran feels, with some justification, that it has been singled out by the USA which is determined to increase Iran's international isolation and economic impoverishment.

Iran's political and regional isolation, as well as its economic debilitation, explain a great deal about its foreign policy orientations and formulation. Both by design and miscalculation, the Islamic Republic is regionally isolated. This results not only from the prolonged and costly conflict with Iraq, a country which is itself isolated, but also because of Tehran's purposefully hostile and aggressive policy towards the member states of the GCC. There are several explanations for this antagonism. These include the fundamentally pro-Western and specifically pro-US orientation of these six states (for example, the United States *did* go to war to liberate Kuwait), the ideological factors that do not automatically divide the Persian, Shi'a Islamic state from its primarily Arab, Sunni political neighbors but that do help to exacerbate the already deep political divisions between them, and the profound disagreement among these regional states about the definitions and implications of Gulf security strategy.

In order to balance these conflictual ties, the Islamic Republic has made a concerted effort to improve relations with its non-Arab neighbors to the north, east and west. Thus, it has worked assiduously with such neighbors as Turkey, Pakistan, the Central Asian states 'north of the Caspian' and others to countervail its insecure and conflictual ties to the south. Iran has conducted highly publicized and successful trilateral talks with the Ukraine and Turkmenistan in which Iran will buy Ukrainian exports while Turkmenistan will increase gas exports to the cash-starved Ukraine, which can then pay for this gas using profits gained through exports to Iran. Other Caspian-related activities include the creation of a Caspian Research Center along with Russia, Turkmenistan, Kazakhstan, Azerbaijan, as well as countless other joint ventures, agreements and collaborative activities with all of Iran's neighboring states.[13]

Iran also organized a major oil conference in which representatives of 120 foreign firms, none American, visited Tehran to vie for ten major and potentially quite profitable joint oil ventures with Iran. Recently, a British engineering firm and a French oil company have each won tenders to do work in Iran. As reported by the Iranians themselves, deals such as this are meant to 'pave the way for advancing foreign cooperation ... contrary to the imposition of a unilateral US trade embargo [as a] warning to American oil firms, which ... will be the major losers to European and other rivals'.[14] Iran's economic divide-and-conquer policy has been partially successful, as evidenced by President Clinton's very limited success in persuading the G-7 states to limit their economic dealings with the Islamic Republic.[15]

In one explanation of Iran's foreign commercial and economic policies, Iran is described as 'stretching its influence over neighboring countries and multinational interests in a flurry of trade deals [as a means to] overpower US isolation efforts'.[16] Indeed, the sheer pace and volume of Iran's aggressive attempts to improve its status within the international community is evident in the steady and heavy flow of visitors to Tehran, meetings held with foreign counterparts by senior Iranian government officials and the significant number of trade and economic agreements entered into by the Islamic Republic. It is the very success of these efforts that has compelled some in the United States to initiate a secondary economic boycott against Iran and its trading partners.

Evaluating the Long-term Iranian Threat

There does seem to be consensus about Iran's dual policy of economic and political engagement with its non-Arab neighbors, combined with hostility towards the states in the Gulf littoral. Nevertheless, the true nature, scope, magnitude and possible impact of this hostility remains a matter of some uncertainty and debate. This lack of certainty is magnified by significant gaps in our ability to estimate Iran's true military capabilities.[17] Such is the case not only for Iran's conventional military capabilities, but also in the realm of its ability to produce weapons of mass destruction (WMD) where 'a large degree of uncertainty surrounds such programs'.[18] Although a detailed discussion of Iran's military capabilities exceeds the scope of this more limited analysis, what is significant is the degree to which uncertainty pervades analyses of Tehran's regional profile.

In an important development described by one journalist as 'the Persian dog that did not bark' (presumably he meant Iranian), it is argued that 'an immense, conventional military buildup by Iran forecast three years ago by Washington and cited ever since as a *major* continuing threat to US interests in the region never fully materialized'.[19] Indeed, in testimony on Capitol Hill, a variety of government and non-government experts alike noted that Iran's acquisition of military equipment declined by 50 per cent 'across the board', billions of dollars of orders in arms purchases have not transpired, the Iranian military is suffering a serious lack of spare parts for much of its equipment and the proficiency of air force pilots is questionable and steadily declining. Despite significant concern when the purchase became public knowledge, it is further noted that Iran is barely able to deploy the two Kilo-class submarines that it acquired from Russia, while the purchase of a third submarine had to be initially deferred.[20] At the same time, Iran's build-up of troops on Abu Musa and the Tunb Islands 'has been scaled back', the acquisition of No Dong ballistic missiles from North Korea has yet to transpire and Iran's acquisition of both planes and tanks has been on a far smaller scale than previously predicted.[21] According to another analysis, Iran 'is in no position to continue signing major arms deals'. Furthermore, despite attempts to portray the Islamic Republic as a major military threat, 'Iran still has a long way to go before its forces approach the strength of those it inherited from the Shah in 1979'. This assertion relies on the work of Gulf military analyst Shahram Chubin, who notes that 'geography and its own growing strength help ensure that Saudi Arabia can also defend itself against an Iranian attack'.[22] Most analysts share this view. Indeed, respected military analyst Thomas McNaugher goes so far as to describe Iran's conventional forces as 'pathetic', while astutely noting that Iran's military build-up, such as it is, reflects a 'desire to complicate U.S. defense planning, more than hegemonic intentions [by the Islamic Republic]'.[23] There is no evidence to suggest that this profile is likely to change dramatically in the twenty-first century.

The above enumeration of the various gaps in Iran's ability to pose a significant military threat to its neighbors should not encourage us to draw the opposite conclusion. Here Iran would be seen as merely an unsuspecting and innocent victim of the machinations of its malevolent neighbors. Iran is neither innocent nor beyond culpability. For example, although it is generally accepted that Iran's reliance on terrorism has diminished in recent years, it is equally possible that Iran would once again turn to terrorism if this would help it to achieve its foreign policy objectives. Iran has relied on terrorism in a largely non-ideological and pragmatic fashion as an unacceptable but occasionally effective foreign policy tool.[24] Although Iran is hardly some sort of 'rogue terrorist international outlaw state' as its least informed yet most vociferous critics would have us believe, Tehran is not completely innocent in this realm either, and thus it bears continued attention in this frequently sensationalized realm.

Iran's WMD Capabilities

It is widely assumed that Iran is heavily involved in the development of weapons of mass destruction (WMD) including nuclear, biological and chemical weapons stocks. Yet these developments have been limited by Iran's relative international isolation as well as by its weak economy. As one analyst notes, Iran's 'nuclear capability remains nascent – even after it signed a deal with Moscow for light-water reactors – expressing distant intentions that must be taken seriously but [that] have little effect on contemporary strategic planning'.[25] This view is supported in a somewhat more nuanced fashion by Middle East strategic analyst Ahmed Hashim. While Hashim agrees that the Islamic Republic would like to acquire nuclear weapons, he also recognizes how difficult this may prove to Tehran.[26] One difficulty lies in developing the appropriate technical expertise, and while some countries, in part due to vigorous US pressure, have been unwilling to provide Iran assistance in its attempt to develop nuclear and chemical weapons capabilities, neither Russia nor China has shown such reluctance.[27] For example, in recent congressional testimony,

Deputy Assistant Secretary of Defense Bruce Reidel talked of Chinese support for Iran's burgeoning chemical weapons program. Although China did agree to suspend an agreement to supply Iran with two nuclear power plants, there has been no such agreement in the realm of chemical weapons. According to Reidel, the Chinese chemical industry has grown so quickly that it may be possible for Iran to be provided with support for its chemical weapons program by Chinese specialists without the knowledge of the Chinese government itself. Whether this is in fact the case, or simply a means for the US government to avoid excessive criticism of the Chinese government, it is apparent that Iran has been the recipient of significant support for its chemical weapons development by China.[28]

In the nuclear sphere, although its officials repeatedly note that 'the Islamic Republic of Iran's sole goal in the atomic sector is for peaceful purposes', it has become a generally accepted principle that Iran is attempting to acquire nuclear weapons.[29] Indeed, such acquisition makes sense from Tehran's perspective given that its long-time adversary, Iraq, made sufficient progress in this realm to invite the 1981 Israeli air attack on its Osirak nuclear reactor outside Baghdad. Iraq is widely presumed to have continued its attempt to develop a nuclear weapons capability despite the fact that intense US pressure and periodic United Nations inspections have made it even more difficult for Iraq to accomplish its goals.[30]

It is also generally assumed that regional actors Israel and Pakistan have nuclear devices, some of Iran's neighboring Central Asian states to the north may have stray, former Soviet weapons on their territory, and Iran's Arab neighbors in the Gulf region are under the protection of the USA which is militarily active all along Iran's Gulf coastline. Thus, although no Western analyst is likely to advocate acquisition of nuclear weapons by the Islamic Republic, the motivation to do this by the ruling circle in Tehran is not difficult to understand and even makes good sense from this group's particular perspective.

In attempting to assess Iran's progress in nuclear weapons development, Hashim notes: 'Iran clearly has not developed a nuclear-weapons capability and reports of secret nuclear sites being built are unsubstantiated.'[31] Having said this, he does not exclude the possibility of Iran becoming a nuclear power although, as is the case with most analysts, he is unable to assign a time-frame within which this capability will emerge. And while the development of a nuclear capability is an important consideration, the issue of a delivery system is of equal importance. Iran's progress in this area has promoted little agreement among Middle East strategic analysts. Thomas McNaugher best sums up our collective uncertainty when he notes: 'there are plenty of reasons ... to doubt what we think we know about Iran's nuclear program'.[32] Vigilance and concern about Iranian nuclear developments are essential, while politically motivated exaggeration must be avoided. More broadly speaking, nuclear proliferation in the Middle East is an issue of such volatility that it is certain to exist as a cornerstone of regional political analysis well into the twenty-first century.

Assessing Iran's Regional Intentions and Capabilities

Given the above uncertainties, we are again left with an unclear portrait of how Iran regards its twenty-first-century involvement within the Gulf. As stated at the outset, true Gulf security can emerge *only* when Iraq, the Islamic Republic of Iran, and the six member states of the Gulf Co-operation Council can agree to agree. That is, genuine security in the Gulf region cannot be achieved as long as any one of the three key regional players is in a position to exercise a veto and is willing to do so. Unfortunately, therefore, true security necessitates a degree of collabora-tion and consensus that has never been achieved and that may be beyond the capabilities of the Gulf states both in this century and the next.[33] Certainly, Iran is not of a mind either to abandon the powerful ideology that provides the state with its doctrinal foundation, or to abandon political activities that it regards as synonymous with these values. Indeed, Iran regards its political canvas as not being restricted solely to its immediate environs. For example, the Islamic Republic's involvement in Bosnia highlights both the global scope of Iran's commitment to Islam and the potential for the USA and Iran to find yet another arena for disagreement.[34]

Perhaps the best policy option for those committed to future Gulf security is offered by Zalmay Khalilzad who notes that the United States 'needs a long-term vision' for an Iranian regional role, as well as an Iraqi one, that will at the same time deter attempts by Iran to attain regional hegemony.[35] Although Khalilzad presupposes a greater regional ambition for the Islamic Republic than that posited here, his policy recommendation is both realistic and non-ideological. In a sense, whether or not Iran seeks regional hegemony is largely irrelevant as it does not have the capability to dominate the region nor is it ever likely to attain it. It is significant that virtually all well-informed analysts agree to some measure that these limitations exist. Still, there are those who nonetheless perceive the Islamic Republic as aspiring to a dominant regional role. Rather, what is argued here is that Iran does not wish to play a *minoritarian* role in its own region. This, then, is the crux of the issue and one that will occupy the Middle East as it enters the twenty-first century. It is also with this question that this chapter began.

Visitors to Iran are struck by the apparent normalcy of a society whose rhetoric and occasional political behavior speak to anything but 'business as usual'. Yet, the latest of these visitors, Milton Viorst writing in *Foreign Affairs*, is hard pressed to perceive Iran as being anything other than a country trying to deal with severe economic problems, isolation, uncertainty and a continuing quest for its own identity.[36] Despite its aggressive behavior, objectionable rhetoric and at times idiosyncratic world-view, there is no evidence to suggest that Iran truly is seeking to dominate its region. Certainly, this case could be made in an even more compelling fashion if Iran were to work harder to improve its ties with its Gulf neighbors, although here the same question can be raised about the political orientation and behavior of these states themselves. Conflict is rarely a one-way street. While the Middle East is likely to look quite different, the Gulf region of the twenty-first century is likely to remain susceptible to the same challenges and uncertainties that bedevilled it throughout the twentieth.

CHAPTER 3

Iraq Faces the Twenty-first Century: Potential Challenges for Gulf States

Phebe Marr

Twice in the decade between 1980 and 1990, Iraq initiated wars with its neighbors, unleashing years of conflict and inflicting on itself and others a toll in human life and economic destruction unprecedented in modern Gulf history. Can Iraq again challenge the GCC states in the twenty-first century? Is it likely to do so? And if so, in what ways?

Among all the Gulf states, Iraq's future is the most difficult to predict. Yet any attempt to address these questions must begin with an analysis of what kind of Iraq we are likely to face in the twenty-first century. As a point of departure for such an inquiry, one issue that must be examined is what, if any, evolution will take place in Iraq's domestic political situation. What social, economic and political structures will emerge within Iraq after the impact of wars and sanctions? What important domestic trends can be identified and how are they likely to affect Iraq's posture towards the Gulf in the next century?

Iraq's future foreign policy direction depends, to a very large extent, on the nature of its leadership and the domestic political situation it faces. Various domestic political outcomes are possible in Iraq and these may be grouped into three broad scenarios. It is not the purpose of this chapter to develop these scenarios in detail (all are speculative), but simply to outline them at the outset of the discussion, since they will determine the parameters within which Iraq's future can be addressed.

The first scenario is the continuation of Saddam Hussein's leadership into the twenty-first century. Its chief feature is Saddam's overwhelming political dominance, with some reliance in differing degrees on family and clan loyalties, party and military institutions and the secret police apparatus. It is unlikely there would be any basic shift in Iraq's long-term strategic goals or in the regime's *modus operandi*. Although, over time, sanctions will most likely be eased and contacts with regional and European countries may grow, as long as Saddam and his immediate family remain in power, a wide array of economic and military constraints are likely to continue, stunting its ability to achieve full recovery and leaving Iraq's future stability open to question.

A second scenario posits the removal of Saddam Hussein from power. How this might be accomplished is highly speculative, ranging from a peaceful transition (highly unlikely) to more violent means, including assassination, a coup or even a popular uprising. Whatever the means, those who would follow would most likely be drawn from the same political circles that have governed Iraq in the recent past: the military, remnants of the Ba'ath party, bureaucrats and technocrats, and clan and tribal groups including the 'Takritis' that are currently at or close to the center of power.

Continuity with the past would undoubtedly be strong, but there would be some prospects for more participation in the political process. How much, would depend on personalities and the mix of regime constituencies. The most desirable outcome in this scenario is a more responsible regime in Baghdad leading to a lessening of repression at home and of isolation abroad, and an end to sanctions and other constraints on Iraq leading to economic and social reconstruction. None of these contingent outcomes would be certain, however, and a change of regime by insiders could lead to a long period of instability or another highly authoritarian and repressive government.

A variant of this scenario is the coming to power of some of Iraq's exiled opposition leaders who espouse a more pluralistic political system and a more open society. While this prospect is conceptually attractive, it is difficult to envision the concrete steps that would plausibly bring outsiders back to power in Baghdad. If more cooperation between outsiders and insiders became possible, it could result in some of the exiles in opposition returning to Baghdad once a regime change had taken place. It is far more likely, however, that those who replaced the current regime would seek to retain power for themselves.

The third, more drastic, scenario involves the collapse of the central government in Baghdad and a disintegration of the state, either because a new regime fails to consolidate power or because the current dysfunctional political situation persists for so long that a post-Saddam collapse becomes unavoidable. Disintegration scenarios include a weakened and factionalized central government unable to maintain control over the Kurdish north or the Shi'ite south; the resurgence of tribalism and/or regionalism leading to civil war; and the inability of the central government to control Iraq's borders. While the potential for disintegration exists, particularly if the current situation persists far into the twenty-first century, this is not the most likely outcome in Iraq. It would, however, be the most dangerous for the GCC. If it should occur, regional instability could be greatly exacerbated for much of the early portion of the new century as the reorganizing and restructuring of the polity in Iraq takes place.

Of these three potential scenarios, only the second offers prospects for future stability in Iraq and security for other Gulf states. This does not mean that a change of leadership assures such stability; far from it. But neither of the other two outcomes offers much prospect for any degree of long-term stability.

The key to Iraq's future lies where it has in the past – in the quality of its political management. Despite its promising resource base, educated middle class and strategic location, Iraq's leadership has since its inception as a state in 1920 consistently failed to manage these assets in a way that realized Iraq's potential. Few past leaders, however, have squandered Iraq's patrimony to the extent of the current regime. Mending Iraq's crippled economy and society, dealing with domestic political alienation and improving relations with deeply suspicious neighbors will all be far harder after the record of war, rebellion and sanctions that have marked the last decades of the twentieth century. The faster a new leadership and different political structures emerge in Baghdad, the sooner recuperation will start.

What then are the chances of Iraq moving towards stability and moderation in the next century? And what challenges will the Gulf states face if it does not? To gain some perspective on these prospects, this chapter will assess the impact of the Gulf War and its aftermath on Iraq, identify some long-term trends in progress and conclude with some tentative projections on what these may mean for future Iraqi challenges to the Gulf.

The Impact of the Gulf War on Iraqi Capabilities

Any assessment of potential challenges from Iraq must begin with Iraq's capabilities following the Gulf War. After the damage suffered in the last decades of the twentieth century, what sort of political, military and economic challenges will Iraq be able to mount? Assessments of the

damage to Iraq's infrastructure have been revised downwards since the
Gulf War and lead to the conclusion that while the destruction was
serious, it was not as devastating as was first thought. In addition, much
of what was damaged has since been repaired. The sanctions, in the
meantime, have caused more harm than the fighting, and the human and
psychological impact of these events may have taken a higher long-term
toll than the war-created physical and material damage. The following is
a rough estimate of war damages which, on balance, should give some
sense of Iraq's potential capacity to raise challenges to Gulf security in
the future.

HUMAN RESOURCES: To gain perspective, Iraq's human losses from
the Gulf War must be added to those of the eight-year war with Iran.
In both cases, earlier high estimates have been revised downwards over
time. Losses in the Iran–Iraq War were estimated at 135,000 to 150,000
killed – roughly 4 to 5 per cent of the population of military age.[1]
Figures for the second Gulf War ranged more widely with some sources
estimating between 50,000 to 120,000 fatalities.[2] In retrospect, these figures
appear highly inflated. It is now clear that early estimates did not take
account of the massive desertions that occurred before the ground war
took place. The USA has never published official figures, but soon after
the war a figure of 100,000 killed was cited, a number that was almost
immediately challenged by seasoned analysts. One US defense analyst
who has studied the matter carefully and based estimates on POW
interviews, has put the number killed as low as 10,000. Because wounded-
in-action generally number about three times as many as killed-in-action,
the total casualty figure, using this projection, would be around 40,000.[3]
At the same time, civilians killed in the war have been estimated at fewer
than a thousand.[4] Even if these numbers are doubled or tripled, the
estimates would still be well under 100,000.

Casualties suffered as a result of the armed rebellions which followed
the war must be added to these figures. While there exists no accurate
count of such, the figure of 20,000 or more is possible. One must also
add the thousands of victims of the Kurdish exodus to the mountains
if one is looking at overall casualties.[5] An estimate, then, of the total
killed in both Gulf wars, the rebellions and the Kurdish flight to the
mountains could range from 50,000 to 100,000, or about 6 to 8 per cent
of the military-age population.

The death toll from sanctions is more difficult to estimate. The greatest
number of casualties have been among the very old and infirm and the

very young, particularly among the poorer classes where malnutrition and water-borne diseases are more common. A 1995 Food and Agriculture Organization (FAO) report states that since 1990, 109,000 persons a year may have perished from disease and malnutrition, but this figure was given by the Iraqi Ministry of Health and the authors of the FAO report acknowledge that it could not be independently confirmed.[6] Like other such claims, it is almost certainly exaggerated for propaganda purposes.

By any standards, Iraq has suffered a substantial depletion of its working-age population, which can only adversely affect its ability to regain its productive capacity. How much of Iraq's skill level has been lost is open to interpretation. During the Iran–Iraq War, Iraq continued to educate its young people, thus reproducing its national skill base to an extent. But all elements of the population had to serve in the war with a concomitant and significant loss of human resource capacity. Even more skills were lost during the Gulf War and its aftermath. This loss of human capability is far more difficult to replenish owing to the sanctions regime and the isolation enforced upon Iraq following the war. For example, few students are now travelling abroad for education while education inside Iraq is experiencing a slow, steady decline. Many of Iraq's youth have spent the last two decades of the twentieth century either at war or in an education system isolated from the outside world and permeated by anti-foreign attitudes. These are hardly the occupational preparation experiences requisite to compete within the global economy of the twenty-first century.

Iraq's travails have depleted its population in other ways as well, including substantial refugee outflows. The migrations have been heavier among some groups than others, but all of Iraq's communities have been affected. Moreover, the Baghdad government began expelling Iraqi Shi'a in the 1980s, particularly those inhabiting the holy cities of Najaf and Karbala, on grounds of their reputed 'Persian origin'. To these groups have been added persecuted Shi'a supporters of the Islamic parties who left during the Iran–Iraq War, and Shi'a POWs from that war who decided to stay in Iran. Many southern Shi'a fled into Iran as a result of the failed rebellion of 1991. The subsequent unrest in the marsh areas around Amara and Nasiriyya and the draining of the marshes by the government to root out dissidents deprived many local Shi'a of their livelihood. Some Shi'a POWs from the Gulf War remain in Saudi Arabia while others have emigrated to Europe and the USA. Most of the Shi'a refugees, however, are in Iran. They number between 250,000 and one million; one source put the number at 650,000.[7]

Most of the Kurds who fled to neighboring Turkey following their aborted rebellion in 1991 have returned to Iraq. However, a large number of returning Kurds, possibly over half a million (mainly those uprooted during Saddam's earlier 'anfal' campaign), remain in camps awaiting the rebuilding of their villages. Many of these displaced Kurds and Shi'a are farmers and their displacement has certainly disrupted agricultural production.

Even more serious has been the outflow of Iraq's skilled middle class. Emigration from Iraq has been continuous since the onset of revolutionary regimes in 1958, but the flow has greatly intensified since the Gulf War and the imposition of the sanctions regime. Many have migrated to neighboring Arab states, Europe and the USA. Figures are unreliable, but estimates of the exiled Iraqi population range from 1 to 2 million or 5 to 10 per cent of the total population. This segment represents Iraq's most creative and productive resource, but the loss transcends the economic sphere. It is this more experienced, sophisticated element of the population that represents the best hope for political stability and reform in Iraq, and one that could serve as a bridge between the outside world and its isolated political culture. Those Iraqi *émigrés* in the West are developing a different political culture and outlook and are gaining skills that will be needed by Iraq if it is to make the necessary adjustment to the global environment of the twenty-first century.

While these population losses will greatly hamper Iraq's ability to rebuild, they should not be exaggerated. The losses must be compared with the rapid increase of population due to natural growth. Between 1980 and 1990, Iraq's population grew at an annual rate of 3.6 per cent, although it has since declined to less than 3 per cent due to recent disasters.[8] Since Iraq has a high fertility rate (5.8 per cent in 1991) and a young population, rapid growth will most likely resume once sanctions are lifted. By the year 2010, Iraq could therefore have a population of 35 million.[9]

The outcome of these developments has been to skew Iraq's population profile in certain directions. First, Iraq has suffered severe although not irreparable losses among its youth, particularly its military and working-age population. These losses will hamper its development, as well as its military capacity, and they may not be replaced until well into the twenty-first century. A second result has been to deplete large numbers of the population that fall into the 'minority status' category, namely the Kurds and the Shi'a. (The Shi'a actually form a majority of the population although they are often treated as a minority in Iraq.) Failure to assimilate

Shi'a and Kurds into the mainstream of Iraqi life has not only weakened and alienated these groups but also stunted prospects for development in the north and south of the country. These were also the areas worst hit by war and rebellion. This differential damage may be a contributing factor in retarding the emergence of cohesive leadership in these communities. Lastly, these developments have also deprived the country of large numbers of its best-educated population thereby weakening the middle class and the prospects for political moderation. Meanwhile, Iraq's population is increasing, contributing to a future demographic profile weighted on the side of youth. These burgeoning cohorts below the age of 15 will provide increased pressures on future leadership for education and jobs which can only be met by vigorous development and increased income, unlikely to be forthcoming unless there are substantially changed circumstances and leadership in Baghdad.

ECONOMIC INFRASTRUCTURE: War has also wreaked havoc on Iraq's economic infrastructure and productive capacity, although much that was destroyed in the center of the country has been rebuilt. The telecommunications system, the electricity grid, much of the road and rail network, and bridges across the Tigris and Euphrates have been repaired. Reconstruction, however, was effected through the cannibalization of spare parts from other structures and the ongoing embargo prevents replacement of these critical parts.[10] After years of sanctions, many facilities needing maintenance and spare parts are breaking down.

Reconstruction is less evident in the south, partly because of intentional neglect and partly because the damage has been greater. In the north, the population continues to suffer under a double embargo (the UN embargo on Iraq and Saddam Hussein's embargo on the north) which hampers development, although outside humanitarian aid has helped sustain this region. Electricity, some of it controlled from Baghdad, has been cut off at will in some regions of the north.

Agriculture and industry have been damaged, less through physical destruction than as a result of the sanctions regime. There is a severe shortage of spare parts, seeds and fertilizers, an absence of pest control and poor maintenance of irrigation systems.[11] Instability in the countryside, both north and south, has hampered production in irrigated and rain-fed areas. The massive draining of the marsh areas of the south, ostensibly to expand agriculture but in reality to control insurgency, has resulted in a loss of population and of productive areas. In the north, the razing of villages under the 'anfal' campaign destroyed much livestock and cropland, the latter only slowly returning to life as a result of international relief efforts.

In the area under its control, the government has had some success in instituting policies such as raising food prices in order to encourage agricultural production. Farmers, usually among the poorer elements of the population, are one of the few segments of Iraqi society actually benefiting from economic scarcity with higher farm prices having resulted in some economic and social mobility for this class. Nevertheless, agricultural imports, for which scarce foreign exchange must be used, totalled about $600 to $700 million a year in 1994, according to the Iraqi government.[12]

Heavy industry (steel, iron and aluminum) has been badly hampered by sanctions, but smaller, light industries are producing consumer goods, although with considerable difficulty. Even more than the agricultural sector, industry has been crippled by an inability to import raw materials and spare parts, although some are being smuggled in. According to the Iraqi government, industrial production in 1994 was about 60 per cent of pre-Gulf War capacity.[13] More realistic estimates put it at 30 to 40 per cent of previous output, with a significantly reduced quality of finished products due to an embargo-imposed reduction of foreign components.

HEALTH SERVICES: Health services deserve special mention as the sector hardest hit by sanctions. While the import of medical supplies has been permitted under the sanctions regime, funds are scarce and are made scarcer for the general population by the disproportionate share of these imports going to regime supporters and other protected elements of the population.[14] Recent reports indicate serious shortages of medicine and deteriorating hospital equipment and services.[15] The FAO team cited above found a serious rise in malnutrition among vulnerable elements of the population, resulting in increased infant mortality rates and stunted growth among children.[16] This health/nutritional crisis was expected to improve after 1996. In May of that year, Iraq accepted UN Resolution 986 which permits the sale of $1 billion in oil every 90 days for food, medical and other life-sustaining imports. The provisions of the Resolution call for the close monitoring of the purchase and distribution of these items by the international community. Although the Resolution is renewable, unless the amounts are substantially increased, the relief for the Iraqi population may not be meaningful.

THE OIL INDUSTRY: The regime has lavished much of its attention on the oil industry in an attempt to prepare for the production and export of oil once sanctions are lifted. With the passage of UN Resolution 986, oil began flowing by the end of 1996. Iraq claimed that within 14 months of a full lifting of sanctions it could pump 3.2 million barrels a day (b/d) and within five to eight years could reach a goal of 6 million b/d.[17] Western oil analysts are less sanguine about this goal. Many facilities, such as gas–oil separator plants, storage facilities and the port of Khor al-Amaya, need considerable rebuilding. Neither the Saudi nor the Syrian pipelines are likely to be put back into service while Saddam Hussein is in power. Most important, the 6 million b/d figure is predicated on $25 billion in foreign investment. This level of investment will not be realized without a complete removal of the oil embargo and a more open investment climate in Baghdad; both unlikely without a change of regime or of regime behavior.

FINANCIAL RESOURCES: The most serious impact of sanctions on Iraq's economy has been financial. Iraqi reserves, worth about $4 billion, have been frozen in Western banking institutions and access to these funds may continue to be restricted even after an easing of sanctions. Open sources acknowledge that Iraq's national income has dropped drastically since the inception of sanctions. Income from oil exports, $12 to $15 billion annually before the Gulf War, ranged between $500 million to $1 billion in 1995. (With the export of dates and other commodities, some have put export earnings as high as $2 billion for 1995.)[18] These figures will gradually rise as the oil-for-food resolution is put into effect.

Iraq has also suffered from one of the highest inflation rates in the world. The dinar, officially worth a little over three dollars before the Gulf War, was selling at well over ID 1500 to $1, and, in some cases, ID 2000 to $1 by the end of 1995.[19] After Iraq began negotiations on UN Resolution 986, the dinar recuperated dramatically. In the spring of 1996, it hovered at ID 300 to $1, but by the end of the year had dropped once again to ID 1000 to $1. This has put food and ordinary household goods beyond the reach of all but the very wealthy and those favored and protected by the regime. A substantial number of the latter receive subsidies in the form of housing, cars and supplementary rations which put a floor under their standard of living. Many of the middle class, living on fixed incomes, have suffered; their savings, and even their household goods, have been significantly depleted. By 1995, Iraq's per capita income was roughly what it was in the 1940s.[20]

Merchants and farmers, who live off the market economy, have done better than others. The regime has clearly enriched itself by manipulating exchange rates and by its monopoly on scarce imports. But periodic execution and punishment of merchants indicate that others are profiting from the system as well. However, the dramatic fluctuations in the exchange rate have also hurt the affluent business community and made any investments in the domestic economy highly speculative.

Iraq also faces a major debt burden, as well as potential reparations once the oil embargo is removed. Reparations, if enforced, could take up to 30 per cent of Iraq's revenue, while between 5 and 10 per cent more could be siphoned off to defray the costs of the UN inspection regime. Iraq's debt owed to GCC countries from the Iran–Iraq War, some $40 billion, is not likely to be repaid. The debt to Europe, Japan and other industrialized countries, totalling at least $35 billion (some would put it well over $50 billion) must be met, or discounted against the sale of oil. Service on this debt was running at between $3 and $4 billion a year in the early 1990s and will be a long-term burden.[21] These financial constraints could be relieved if the oil embargo is ameliorated or eliminated, but they are now so demanding that Iraq's development is likely to be hampered well into the twenty-first century. In addition, if there is no regime change, reparations are likely to be fully exacted. Such action will definitely pauperize the country and prevent a revival of the middle class. It may also create a backlash within Iraq against Kuwait, the GCC and the USA as well. A change of regime would make it possible to alleviate this burden; without such a change the cancellation of reparations is unlikely.

MILITARY CAPABILITIES: The key element in Iraq's capacity to pose a threat to its neighbors is its present and future military strength. In terms of manpower, Iraq's military has been severely downsized since 1990, although its armed forces, at 350,000, still constitute one of the largest in the Middle East. Numbers, of course, do not tell the whole story. Much of this standing army may be increasingly hollow. The infantry divisions of the Regular Army, particularly those in the south, have low morale. Republican Guard units are more carefully recruited, trained and equipped and have better morale, particularly those spared the brunt of fighting in the Gulf War. However, sanctions have affected these troops as well, as pay and benefits have been reduced. By the end of 1996, they were reportedly only marginally better off than the Regular Army. In all units, morale is a problem and in many desertions are high.[22] While Iraq's forces can keep law and order domestically, and can protect Iraq's frontiers against Iran and probably Syria, they certainly would not prevail in a contest against Turkey, Israel or the West. A consensus is emerging among military analysts that Iraq's forces are not likely to survive another serious encounter with the West intact, due to poor logistics, readiness and morale.

About half of Iraq's pre-war equipment survived the Gulf War, including over 2200 tanks and 4500 armoured vehicles of various kinds. Iraq has retained some 350 combat aircraft, but these were not all in good condition and lacked spare parts.[23] Still, by Middle Eastern standards, this is a formidable array of armour and manpower, certainly surpassing what the GCC possesses (except for aircraft). In the military – as in its industry – the real problem for Iraq is logistics, including poor maintenance skills among technicians and a debilitating lack of spare parts. Evidence indicates that despite some smuggling of spare parts and equipment, and some domestic military production, Iraq has not been able to prevent a significant decline in operational readiness.[24] The longer the sanctions remain, the higher will be the price paid by the military in readiness and logistic capacity, a decline that will require time to rectify and reverse, even after sanctions are lifted. Should, however, Iraq acquire access to its oil wealth under this, or a follow-on regime, the military is certain to be built back up as rapidly as possible. Even before an easing of sanctions, Iraq's reorganization of its military, its training program and its attempts to consolidate what remained of its force, showed signs of improving military performance based on realistic standards and expectations.

Assessment of the Damage and Prospects for the Future

Given this assessment, what tentative conclusions can be drawn about Iraq's potential capacity to challenge or threaten its neighbors in the early part of the next century? The damage to Iraq's physical plant and infrastructure, particularly in Baghdad, the country's nerve center, while severe, is not irreparable. Much of this infrastructure has already been rebuilt; other sectors are operating but need infusions of capital, materials and spare parts to be brought up to reasonable standards. If oil income and foreign investments were forthcoming to Iraq, Iraq's productive sectors, especially oil, heavy industry and some agriculture, could revive within a period of time.

Iraq's military has suffered severe losses, but it still has formidable assets, especially compared to its Gulf neighbors. Sanctions have, however, eroded the readiness of the military. Even more serious are problems of morale. Until these two issues are addressed, this army will not be able to engage successfully in any major military action, particularly against Western forces, without serious consequences for the regime. A substantial portion of Iraq's (presently) scarce resources is reportedly being spent on the military.[25] If this level of expenditure is continued after sanctions are eased, and spare parts are obtained, Iraq's ground forces could be resuscitated. Iraq's air force and its air defense system may take longer to revive.

Most significant of all, Iraq's weapons of mass destruction (WMD) programs have not in every case been destroyed and could gain momentum in the near term. UN weapons inspection teams, working on documents revealed after Hussein Kamal's defection in August 1995, are convinced that Iraq's extensive chemical and biological weapons and missile programs were mainly indigenous and could be started up within a short period of time if there is any easing of the intrusive inspection regime. By 1996, no report had been issued verifying that Iraq had been cleared of all such weapons, and lingering suspicions persist in the West that some weapons or weapons components may be hidden and never found.[26]

The damage to Iraq's human resources has also been substantial, depleting the best and most skilled elements of Iraq's population. This damage may take longest to repair, both in terms of training and replacement of skills and in terms of changing attitudes and perceptions essential to the creation of a healthy polity in Iraq. Morale in civilian as well as military sectors is the clearest indication of Iraq's human debilitation. While the Kurdish and Shi'a populations in the north and south of Iraq have suffered disproportionate harm from the events of the last decade, war and especially sanctions have now taken a toll on the educated Sunni population in the center as well. Many have emigrated abroad and those that remain have been drained of their savings and now confront an economically bleak future for themselves and their children.

Economically, it has been Iraq's finances that have been hit hardest, and it is in this arena that the current, and future, regimes are likely to concentrate. This will mean continued pressure for full removal of the oil embargo and other trade restrictions, and rapid rebuilding of the country's oil export capacity. Once sanctions fall away, investment priorities within Iraq will depend on the regime in power. Whether Saddam Hussein or a successor regime, both contingencies pose challenges for GCC countries.

The prognosis for Iraq's recovery depends largely on which scenario prevails in Iraq in the early decades of the twenty-first century. Under the first scenario, Iraq's recovery is likely to be slow. The continuance of Saddam Hussein (or his regime) in power will impede any type of solutions in terms of Iraq's financial problems, even if sanctions are eased. Some restrictions on trade and investment are likely to remain; reparations are more likely to be exacted; and the climate for attracting foreign investment will remain poor. In fact, many of the trend lines sketched above, including the brain drain from Iraq, poor morale among the population and low productivity will probably continue. Easing sanctions will merely stave off collapse. UN Resolution 986 is likely to alleviate suffering but not to restore Iraq's health.

Under the second scenario, prospects for economic improvement are better but they are contingent on actions taken by any new regime. Much will depend on the direction of investment and the domestic distribution of resources. If a good deal is spent on the military and security sectors, as well as non-productive enterprises (palaces, subsidies to supporters), investor confidence will lag and growth will be slow. Even with positive actions from a new regime, it will be decades into the twenty-first century before Iraq can approximate the growth rates it saw in the late 1970s, the desiderata of much of the population. An infusion of Iraq's well-educated exile population back into Iraq could speed up Iraq's recovery and its accommodation with the West.

Under the third scenario, the challenges faced in the Gulf will be of a different order: the potential for a spillover of instability. Indeed, the Iraqi state as currently constructed could cease to exist. In this case, growth could be delayed until well into the next century as Iraq struggles to put a new society and polity together.

There is one challenge Gulf states may face under all of the above scenarios, that of a backlash in Baghdad caused by rising expectations from the population. The Iraqi government will very likely be unable to meet these expectations because of slow growth, continued isolation and population pressures that will continue to grow in the course of the decade. An important question is whether such a backlash, if it materializes, will turn against the regime or turn outwards against Iraq's Gulf neighbors.

Prospects for change

If these are the parameters of Iraq's future capacity to challenge Gulf security, the more difficult question is what are the prospects for change in Iraq? War and sanctions have done a great deal to undermine the foundations of Ba'ath society. Have they done much to create anything new to replace it? Are there any portents of change amidst the wreckage? To determine this, one must step back and look at several social, economic and political trends in evidence. Four phenomena are worth examining: the development of a generation gap; the fraying of national cohesion; the erosion of national institutions; and the emergence of political moderation.

THE EMERGENCE OF A GENERATION GAP: Three 'political' generations can be identified in Iraq: the pre-1968 generation, now in its late fifties and early sixties; the post-1968 generation, now in its thirties and forties; and a new, younger generation in its twenties, now coming into its own.

Thus far, the pre-1968 generation – Saddam's cohorts – has yet to relinquish its hold on power. While the circle of power has consistently narrowed, through natural attrition or political purges, many of the same names remain. Two examples will suffice. The first is the personnel of the Revolutionary Command Council (RCC), the chief executive and legislative body in the state and the locus of power for party survivors. In 1980, at the start of the Iran–Iraq War, the RCC consisted of 15 members, in addition to Saddam Hussein. All were long-standing Ba'ath party members, over half of whom had participated in the 1968 revolt that brought the party to power.[27] By 1985, the number of RCC members had been cut in half (all of them participants in the 1968 coup) with only one new member, Taha Muhyi ad-Din Ma'ruf, who owed his seat to the fact that he was a Kurd and a ceremonial 'vice president' of Iraq. By 1990, on the eve of the Gulf War, RCC membership had dropped to six. All were pre-1968 Ba'athists, indicating little breakthrough for the next generation at this level.

The same trend can be seen in key cabinet positions, especially those concerned with security and the economy. Tracking prime ministers, deputy prime ministers and ministers of the Interior, Defense, Foreign Affairs, Industry (or Ministry of Industry and Military Industry/ MIMI), Finance and Oil, we find many of the same names as those on the RCC. In 1980, there were ten such ministers, all pre-1968 Ba'athists.[28] In 1985, there were seven such ministers, five of them pre-1968 Ba'athists.[29] By 1993/94, of the nine key ministers in these fields, three – Saddam Hussein, Tariq Aziz and Taha Ramadhan – had been in previous cabinets. Of the remainder, two were members of Saddam's family: Ali Hassan al-Majid and Hussein Kamal. Out of the total, only Hussein Kamal was a post-1968 Ba'athist.[30]

What these examples show is remarkable stability – or rather resistance to change – in personnel at the top of the political structure. While some new members have been introduced, they usually come from the same age-group as their predecessors and have the same backgrounds. Since 1990, new members of the elite have usually come from Saddam's immediate family. While attention has been focused on the family, the generational phenomenon has been missed.

Of what significance is this generation gap? For the most part, an ever narrower group of the pre-1968 generation has been in power for three decades. They share more than age; they possess a common experience and outlook, best exemplified by Saddam Hussein. This is the group that brought the Ba'ath to power in Iraq and consolidated their hold over the organs of government. As the Young Turks of the early twentieth century, a number served prison terms. Most were underground organizers and accomplished conspirators and they brought this underground mentality with them. They are also the generation that looked to the Communist Party of the former Soviet Union as a model of how to gain and maintain power. The most formative political experience for them was the decade of the 1960s, a period of intense instability in Iraq, which saw four military coups in the space of ten years. It is an experience they were determined to avoid, and they have done so through draconian measures. The pre-1968 Ba'athists know how to survive over the long haul. They have patience, persistence and are young enough to rule well into the twenty-first century, if they can manage to stay the course.

The post-1968 generation, of whom Hussein Kamal was perhaps the best example, is now in its forties or late thirties. The formative years of this age-group have been spent under Ba'ath rule. This generation has little or no effective adult memory of the instability of the 1960s or the experience of being 'out of power'. It takes Ba'ath governance for granted, together with the privileged position society accords to party members. Because they have not had to fight their way to power, this generation may be less disciplined and less willing to make sacrifices for the party and/or the leadership role within Iraqi state and society. Not surprisingly, they appear to be more concerned with their personal futures and privileges than with high-risk adventures.

For this group, the most formative period is probably the late 1970s, an era of burgeoning prosperity for Iraq. The country was gradually opening up to outside influences, the oppression inside had not yet reached the proportions it has reached today, and social mobility was high, especially for the disadvantaged from rural and provincial areas. In return for advancement, membership in and loyalty to the Ba'ath party was required. The late 1970s was also a time when Iraq's aspirations to play a leading role in the Arab and Third Worlds seemed on the verge of realization. It is this era that the post-1968 generation dreams of recreating.

These aspirations were abruptly halted by Saddam Hussein's ascent to the presidency in 1979, an event that has thus far precipitated a decade and a half of war and destruction that could extend to the twenty-first century. In the course of this period, the post-1968 generation saw much of the societal infrastructure they had labored to build destroyed along with their futures. The opportunity to begin reconstruction after the Iran–Iraq War was squandered in a foolish miscalculation in Kuwait. As one member of this generation has indicated, his peers are tired of fighting wars started by older men.[31]

The post-1968 generation is likely to combine a mixture of the old and the new. As creatures of the Ba'ath party, they still embody much of the strong nationalism and independence that is the hallmark of party ideology. Their aim is to create a modern Iraq, with power and influence in the Arab world. They are, however, probably more pragmatic and less ideological than their elders, and their aspirations for the future have been lowered. They recognize (even if they do not like) the new global balance of power, and they have few illusions about the task of rebuilding Iraq. They want to get on with this task and to live to enjoy some of the fruits of their labors. Foolish foreign adventures are not on their agenda. While some members of this generation are currently making their way up the political ladder in Baghdad, few have reached the top. Many have chosen to leave Iraq rather than to stay inside and to await an end to the crisis in voluntary exile. It is this generation who will most likely inherit whatever power is left once the old guard departs, and it is their outlook and motivation which should be of concern to Gulf neighbors and others with equity at risk in the Gulf. There is every indication that, while maintaining many, though not all, of the goals and aspirations of the pre-1968 generation, they are more interested in economic development – and its profits – than war, and would be more amenable to the normal instruments of diplomacy available to the international community than Saddam Hussein and his defiant cohorts. Whether Saddam can accommodate this generation, over time, is an important question. Thus far, despite cosmetic changes, he has not.

The third generation now reaching maturity is difficult to fathom since so much of its normal development has been stunted. It is the age-group that has borne the brunt of a decade and a half of wars and economic hardships and now faces a grim future. One can only guess at the despair and anger that must exist among them. It is not yet clear how this generation will react to its desperate situation. It could prove to be rebellious, or it could manifest its unhappiness in cynicism and passivity. The cause for concern is that this generation has little positive outlet for its early adult years or prospects for advancement in a growing economy. It is also a seriously disadvantaged generation, raised in acute isolation with poor education facilities and little contact with the world outside. Without a realistic measure by which to judge Baghdad's information, this age-group may be much more prone to the 'garrison mentality'. This is a generation that could pose an angry challenge to Iraq's neighbors and to the West now positioned in the Gulf.

THE FRAYING OF NATIONAL COHESION: The war and the subsequent rebellion have had an adverse effect on Iraq's communal cohesion. Both events have strengthened ethnic and sectarian identities at the expense of Iraq's national identity. Erosion of loyalty to the state is farthest advanced in the north, where, as an unintended consequence of the war, a separate Kurdish enclave has emerged, largely free of any control from the central government in Baghdad. Aspirations for Kurdish separatism have been intensified by the brutal repression of the regime, especially the 'anfal' campaign between February and September 1988, which reportedly razed some 4000 villages, uprooted hundreds of thousands of Kurds and killed between 50,000 and 100,000.[32] Protection measures instituted by the West in the aftermath of the rebellion (a secure zone; a no-fly zone), a withdrawal of Iraqi troops and administration from a wide swathe of territory in the north and a free election by the population in that zone in 1992, has encouraged Kurdish separatism.

This Kurdish separatism, however, must be measured against countervailing forces. At least a quarter, possibly a third, of Iraq's Kurdish population remains under Iraqi government control, mostly in Baghdad. Kurds continue to work for the government and a separate Kurdish administration, albeit subservient to the Ba'ath, exists in Baghdad. Even more important, the experiment in Kurdish self-government in the north has collapsed in factional fighting between the two major political parties, the Kurdish Democratic party (KDP) and the Patriotic Union of Kurdistan (PUK). Various Kurdish groups, including tribal contingents, have been engaged in a deadly struggle for power which has obliterated any Kurdish cooperation. This infighting has laid bare the absence of a Kurdish civil society with institutions and loyalties beyond the reach of clan, tribe, region or patronage networks. Meanwhile, the Kurdish administration has fragmented while outside influences (the Turkish Kurdish Workers' Party [PKK]; the Turkish military; Iranian elements) are beginning to fill the political vacuum. Although Kurdish separatist aspirations remain, the reality on the ground has been a growing power vacuum and the re-emergence of a desire by ordinary Kurds for orderly government. Nevertheless, the absence of central government control in the north, which may persist into the twenty-first century, may make future Kurdish reintegration into the Iraqi state more difficult.

No such separatism has taken root in Shi'ite areas, but the brutality with which the regime responded to the post-Desert Storm insurgency has intensified Shi'ite alienation from the regime. An insurgency in the marshes south of Amara continues to be contained by the government, though not totally eliminated. In part by military action and in part by draining large portions of the marsh area, the dissident Shi'a population has been forced from its homeland, and in many cases the response from the dispossessed Shi'as has been a refugee-style migration across the border into Iran. Thus far, Shi'ite alienation has been directed against the regime, rather than the state. Most Iraqi Shi'a (a majority of the population) aspire to dominate the government in Baghdad, not to establish a separate Shi'ite entity.

Some Shi'a, probably a distinct minority, are aligned with movements desirous of establishing a Shi'ite religious state in Iraq. Many of these activists are living in Iran and are organized under the Supreme Assembly for the Islamic Revolution in Iraq (SAIRI) led by Baqr al-Hakim, a cleric and son of a former Chief Mujtahid in Iraq. The Iraqi Da'wa party, severely persecuted inside Iraq, is also religious in orientation but has deeper roots in Iraqi society and a more nationalist orientation than SAIRI. Thus far, the bulk of the Shi'a, even those dissatisfied with the regime, identify themselves as Iraqis first and Shi'a second. The regime itself has always included a number of Shi'a, whose loyalty is clearly to the regime. The upper levels of the Shi'ite community – wealthy merchants, land-owners, tribal leaders and secular bureaucrats – support the state, if not the regime, and are unlikely to rebel. Within the poorer quarters of Baghdad, one finds large, sprawling, semi-modern slums, which over a million migrants from Shi'ite rural areas presently call home. Without question these slums are a potential source of opposition and a potential target for Shi'a activists. So, too, are the holy cities of Najaf and Karbala where the fiercest battles of the 1991 rebellion were fought.

While the rebellion did not sever ties between the Sunni and Shi'ite communities in Iraq, it did strain them. The regime has played on these differences to keep itself in power, while relying ever more heavily upon Sunni elements for its security. Nevertheless, among educated Shi'a and, as far as can be estimated, the bulk of the Shi'ite population in the south, the desiderata are still a change of regime and a better dispensation of power within the state, not separate Shi'ite political status.

While ethnic and sectarian tensions have increased, therefore, they have not yet frayed to the point where national cohesion could not be reconstituted and strengthened under different leadership. The fraying of national ties is, no doubt, a negative outcome of the war; however, it has created a recognition of the need to accommodate all Iraq's communities in Iraq's political structures. Much more will have to be done in the twenty-first century to bring Iraq's diverse population groups together and to create a *modus vivendi* among them if Iraq is to continue as a nation-state. How this issue is dealt with by succeeding governments will greatly influence Iraq's future societal stability.

EROSION OF INSTITUTIONAL STRUCTURES: A third trend can be seen in the weakening of Iraq's institutional structures. Three such institutions are of prime importance: the party, the military and the bureaucracy. While these institutions have been impaired, they have not yet been destroyed. Indeed, prior to the Gulf War, they were extremely powerful. Rather than a sudden disintegration, what is unfolding is a slow process of erosion and decay. In one sense, the decline of the military and the party can be seen as a positive development, allowing for alternative political structures to emerge in the future.

The party, once the backbone of the regime's power base, was estimated to have had members and supporters totalling 1.5 million in the early 1980s.[33] Intensely hierarchical, with a system which carefully vetted recruits, party organization and discipline have provided the regime with a strong institutional base of control and an organization upon which it could rely to keep society in line and to enforce the regime's orders. While greatly weakened, this structure is still functional. Evidence of its effectiveness was demonstrated in part by the October 1995 presidential plebiscite for Saddam, which resulted in the expected 99 per cent support for him. The party's effectiveness was also demonstrated in the administration's rationing system which has provided the Iraqi population with minimal levels of sustenance during sanctions as well as reminding recipients that loyalty to the regime is essential to their physical well-being.

The party, however, has been badly shaken by the Gulf War and its aftermath, and undermined by Saddam's own policy of nepotism. The 1991 rebellions decimated its ranks in the north and the south. Rebels in Shi'ite and Kurdish areas exacted vengeance on party members, depleting their ranks. Meanwhile, in Baghdad, the party has been demoralized by a long-standing process of replacing party stalwarts with members of Saddam's family and an inner circle of Takritis. Patrimonialism and family favoritism have savaged party discipline, including the process of advancement through the ranks based upon merit.

The military as well has undergone a process of fragmentation and compartmentalization, in addition to its degradation as a result of war and sanctions. The Regular Army, an institution that pre-dates the Ba'ath regime, has long possessed an independent professional identity and loyalty to the state quite apart from the party. During the Iran–Iraq War, friction between the Regular Army and the Republican Guard was evident. The Regular Army, especially the infantry, bore the brunt of the Kuwait venture and has been greatly reduced in size and effectiveness as a result. Meanwhile, since the mid-1980s, the Republican Guard has been built up as a competitor to the Regular Army and now constitutes the backbone of Iraq's military force. Presumed to be more loyal to the regime, the Guard has nonetheless been suffering from desertions and poor morale, and the loyalty of some of its units may now be questioned. A crack security force provides for the President's safety and is assumed to be the most reliable for the regime.[34] To this array of organizations has recently been added a new force, the fidayyin al-Saddam (Saddam's commandos) under the control of his sons. The formation of this militia is clear evidence of regime distrust of regular military units.

The military has also become ethnicized and tribalized. While soldiers are conscripted from all ethnic and sectarian communities, the officer corps is overwhelmingly Sunni and specifically recruited from the areas of Takrit, Mosul, Samarra and the smaller towns of the Euphrates. This recruitment pattern, while presumably strengthening loyalty to the regime, has eroded the ethos of the military as a nationalist institution. Recently, officer recruitment patterns have been further restricted to specific tribal groups, further eroding military institutionalism and balanced national representation.[35] Nevertheless, with some 350,000 men under arms, Iraq's military is still an institution to be reckoned with inside the country. And at its upper levels, where rewards and benefits still exist, it continues to support the status quo.

The bureaucracy, including a well-educated core of technocrats and professionals, still functions in Iraq but it has suffered erosion as well. Standards of discipline and efficiency have been undermined by Ba'ath party control which has always placed loyalty above merit. More recently, sanctions have undercut the bureaucracy. Unable to make ends meet, many civil servants have taken additional jobs, leaving little time or energy for serving the public. Reports of corruption, bribery and rampant crime in Baghdad support this conclusion.

Even more important than these factors in eroding Iraq's institutions has been increased reliance on kin and clan ties in appointments in the administration and the military, a process referred to by the regime as 'retribalization', although that term is misleading. Reliance by Saddam on his immediate family for high-level appointments and for his security is so well known that it need only be mentioned in passing. This patronage system suffered a blow with the defection (and subsequent execution) of his sons-in-law, Hussein and Saddam Kamal in 1995 and 1996 respectively, but it has not been a mortal blow. Members of Saddam's Abu Nasr clan continue to occupy key posts in the military.[36] These appointments have been going on for so long and are so widespread that it might be difficult to eliminate them even if the regime should fall.

Designation of tribal leaders to keep law and order in the countryside began during the Iran–Iraq War when the ranks of the Ba'ath party and the bureaucracy were depleted. This process was intensified in the aftermath of the Gulf War and the rebellion; however, it was not senior tribal leaders, but often smaller clan leaders, that were selected. Clan and tribal groups have been played against one another (especially where tribes are split between Shi'a and Sunni sects) to keep them weak. But as numerous reports of plotting among tribal groups in the military, and the recent uprising of the Dulaimis make clear, 'tribalization' is a double-edged sword. While tribes as such are not in a position to play a constructive role in national politics, tribal links, now present in all of Iraq's key national institutions – the military, the party, the presidency and the bureaucracy – weaken not only the institutions and their effectiveness, but also national identity and loyalty. Rather, they strengthen client–patron relationships, and kinship and family ties.

In the spring of 1996, further evidence of tribalism emerged in a report that indicated that tribes were promised additional benefits including the return of previously confiscated land and greater local authority over tribal members.[37] If actually brought to fruition, these would further undermine Iraq's centralized government.

While the institutions of state have been gradually undermined by the forces of ethnicity and sectarianism because of increased reliance on kin and clan, particularly at the top of the structure, it is too early to write off these institutions or their capacity for national governance. Some, like the military and the bureaucracy, pre-date the Ba'ath while others, like the party and the security system, have been built up for more than two decades. These institutions and associations have strength and resilience and are still stronger than the centrifugal forces at work. It is also clear that they have been strong enough to prevent the emergence inside Iraq of alternative political structures and to suppress meaningful opposition to the regime to date. Until such structures can emerge and gain political influence, Iraq will be governed by an authoritarian regime, subject to few checks and balances.

DEVELOPMENT OF POLITICAL MODERATION: The fourth development in Iraq has been some evidence of an ideological and cultural shift on the part of the educated classes, mainly among the post-1968 generation. Intellectual diversity does exist in Iraq, but its expression has been so suppressed and its development so truncated under the Ba'athists, that it is not easily identified. Nevertheless, several schools of thought, vestiges of an earlier period, can be identified.

The first is pan-Arab nationalism, rooted in the Nasser period and epitomized by the Ba'ath party of the 1950s and 1960s. Learning from its failures, Saddam himself transformed this ideology under the Ba'ath. Rather than an amalgamation of individual states into an integral Arab nation, Saddam embraced a concept of a strong Iraq which would become the leader of a reconstituted Arab order. This reformulation allowed Saddam to focus on building up the Iraqi state, while permitting him to pose as a major player in the Arab–Israeli theater, as a bulwark against Iran and as a makeweight in the Gulf. There is little evidence to suggest that Saddam or his pre-1968 cohorts have relinquished this vision.

A second vision that has long existed in Iraq is one espoused by so-called 'Iraqi Firsters'. This school of thought finds its home in a more pragmatic Iraqi nationalism, with a strong basis in secularism, modernization, independence and a strong sense of Iraqi identity. While rooted in the Arab Sunni community, it has much wider appeal to both Shi'a and Kurds. Saddam himself has drawn on this vision by emphasizing Iraq's Mesopotamian heritage. Unfortunately, this school of thought has not had clear or effective intellectual articulation, nor has it made any attempt to appeal to a broad constituency. Nevertheless, it is probably a conceptualization upon which the silent Iraqi majority agree. In the wake of Iraq's recent disasters, starting with the Iran–Iraq War, this tendency has spread. It has become the dominant view among the post-1968 generation. Recently, the concept of 'federalism' has been added to this vision, especially among the Kurds, in an effort to deal with the issue of separatism, while keeping the Iraqi state intact. This idea is still controversial and has been resisted by non-Kurdish communities.

Overlapping with the 'Iraq First' tendency is the 'liberal-left' school which comprises a mixture of movements ranging from the liberal National Democratic Party of the 1950s to the Iraq Communist Party and which focuses on social and political reform in Iraq. While communism managed to inspire support from peasants and workers in the 1950s, its influence reached its apogee under the Qasim regime (1958–63) and then waned. Liberal reform movements never took root in Iraq although they appealed to a small group of intellectuals. All these tendencies, however, have re-emerged among the exile Iraqi community with their main voice located within the Iraqi National Congress (INC), a collection of individuals and groups committed to democratic principles. While these ideas are growing among Iraqis outside Iraq, it is not clear how much of a constituency this group has inside Iraq. The ideas it espoused may have wider appeal, but they may also be evidence of a growing polarization between Iraqis inside and outside the country.

In addition to these mainstream movements, which build on a unified, secular Iraq, there are two counter tendencies which do not. One is Kurdish separatism, embodied in the KDP and the PUK. Both of these movements are moderate, secular and pro-Western, and their programs do not as yet go beyond recognition of a separate cultural identity within the Iraqi state. A more radical Kurdish nationalism, espoused by the PKK, which advocates an independent Kurdish state comprised of Iraqi, Turkish and Iranian Kurds, is taking root in the north as this group settles down in Iraqi Kurdish territory. However, separatist Kurdish tendencies have run aground on the hard rock of Kurdish infighting and political fragmentation, which belie the Kurdish capacity to create a unified movement.

The second is the Islamic vision which is also growing in Iraq. The strongest Islamic movements are Shi'a based and have distinct sectarian overtones. Shi'ite movements, like the Da'wa and SAIRI, envision a unified Iraq, but one with an Islamic orientation. Their failure to seize power during the rebellion of 1991 showed the limits of their appeal and has since caused some soul-searching. Both movements have begun to talk of democracy and a willingness to accommodate other tendencies. Political Islam has made inroads among Sunnis, especially among the younger generation. However, there is no evidence yet to suggest that either the Shi'a or Sunni forms of the Islamic revival have a sufficient constituency to challenge mainstream secular movements.

A key question is whether a more pragmatic 'Iraq First' vision has taken root among the second and third generations of Iraqis or whether the current volatile political climate in Baghdad, based on increasing despair, will generate a backlash against the West and Iraq's neighbors, and strengthen an extreme nationalist ideology and identification.

This latter prospect is strengthened by a strong 'garrison mentality' outlook that has been growing since the 1958 revolution. It has fed on isolation, which intensified during the Iran–Iraq and Gulf wars, and has now reached political significance as a result of the Western containment and sanctions policy. The result has been a well-documented sense of paranoia in Baghdad with its ensuing political misunderstandings and miscalculations (mirrored in the West). In this kind of atmosphere, virulent nationalism flourishes. If more moderate political tendencies are to develop, the isolation that feeds the garrison state mentality must be broken.

These four variables – generation change, national cohesion, institutionalization and ideological moderation – have all been adversely affected by the Gulf War and its aftermath. The post-1968 generation, the future recipient of the mantle of power, has not yet been able to move into power; indeed, members of this generation have been emigrating in large numbers. Meanwhile, national cohesion and sovereignty have been weakened by rebellion and the policies of the regime, creating increased fear and alienation among ethnic and sectarian groups. Nationalist institutions designed to integrate the country – the military, the party and the bureaucracy – have been greatly eroded by war, fragmentation and the re-emergence of kinship and clan politics. However, both the party and the military need to be weakened in order to allow new forces to emerge. The danger is that the ongoing weakening apparent in these institutions will precipitate national disintegration before a healthy Iraqi political restructuring occurs.

Meanwhile, glimpses of pragmatism are emerging among the post-1968 generation, but real moderation and realism are vested in the exile community. Regardless of which political scenario materializes in Iraq, a real change in outlook and behavior is likely to be a long, slow process. It awaits a new generation, greater exposure to outside influences, and the evolution of new national institutions that take account of Iraq's diversity. Managing and responding to these changes are among the most important challenges for the West and the Gulf. If Iraq's economic, military and political capacity is enhanced before the evolution to new leadership and new behavior, Iraq could once again become a military threat. If leadership is changed abruptly without adequate support from outside, national institutions and cohesion could collapse. That, too, would present profound challenges to Gulf security of a different order.

Potential Iraqi Challenges to the Gulf

Given these phenomena, what challenges might Iraq present to the GCC in the coming decade? While the nature and severity of the challenges will depend, to some degree, on which political scenario ensues over the coming decade, some challenges can be expected regardless of regime. One potential challenge that may be anticipated is sharp competition in the oil field. As Iraq begins exporting oil, it will seek to make up for lost time and its need for revenue will be very great. However, it appears highly unlikely that the oil embargo will be lifted without constraints unless there is a dramatic change in Baghdad. Rather, as the application of UN Resolution 986 indicates, Iraq's entrance to the oil market is more likely to be gradual, with a continuation of constraints from the international community rather than a total lifting of the embargo. No matter how Iraq's return to the market is engineered, its revenue requirements over the long term will be extraordinarily high, for reconstruction, for consumer imports, for reparations and for debt service.

If Iraq is not accommodated by its OPEC partners, and its international constraints eased, the GCC could face a variety of challenges. One would be the same sort of threat, driven by exigencies, that led to the invasion of Kuwait. Given Iraq's weakness and the enhanced Western military presence in the Gulf, such an outcome is not likely in the closing years of the twentieth century. There should be little doubt, however, that if the current regime remains in Baghdad, and international sanctions continue to pauperize Iraq, militaristic challenges could emanate from Iraq in the twenty-first century. These could range from intimidation, sabre-rattling and terrorism to military pressures on GCC borders.

As sanctions are eased, a considerable portion of Iraq's income will probably go to arms procurement and quite possibly into circumventing the UNSCOM inspection regime. Recent UNSCOM revelations show no change in Baghdad's intentions to develop strategic weapons. At the same time, continued restrictions on Iraq's trade could produce a backlash among the population in Iraq, directed not just against the West, but the GCC as well. Relative prosperity in GCC countries, coexisting with continued penury in Iraq, is a formula for a poisoned regional atmosphere. A change of regime in Baghdad, with different priorities, could ease the situation; such a regime is likely to meet with more financial accommodation from neighbors and the international community.

However, any Iraqi regime will constitute an economic challenge for the GCC states as it seeks to maximize revenues for post-war and post-sanctions reconstruction and relief. On the economic front, Iraq is likely to seek to gain more revenue in various ways, ranging from selling oil at discount prices, vigorously expanding its markets and rolling over (rather than repaying) its debt. All of these steps were attempted or taken after the Iran–Iraq War. Under Saddam Hussein, as well as some potential successors, Iraq may also resort to political intimidation and military pressure to achieve its economic aims. So long as the West can bring a relatively robust posture of force to bear, Iraq is likely to stop short of military hostilities. Should that Western capacity diminish, a hostile Iraqi regime may be tempted to take such action again.

A second challenge is likely to surface as Iraq seeks to regain its sovereignty over its territory and air space and its freedom of action internationally. Despite an easing of the oil embargo, other restrictions are likely to remain so long as Saddam Hussein remains head of state. These will include the no-fly zones in the north and the south of the country, an intrusive weapons inspection regime, trade restrictions on military and dual-use imports, and arrangements for reparations payments to the victims of its aggression against Kuwait. These restrictions are likely to be eased only gradually as a new regime emerges and Iraq's behavior changes.

There is little doubt that Iraq will continue to mount a campaign to have these restrictions on its sovereignty removed. Once the oil embargo is eased, it will be difficult to enforce import restrictions and Iraq will do its utmost to circumvent them. Even more important will be Iraq's desire to resume air traffic, to regain control over its air space and its borders with Turkey and Iran in the north. Indeed, how the Kurdish problem is to be dealt with is one of the major, unresolved difficulties of the Gulf War. Acceptable arrangements between the Baghdad government, the Kurds and those who guarantee protection for the population of northern Iraq will be extremely difficult to attain with Saddam in power. That problem would be substantially eased if there were a regime change which would be likely to persuade the international community to negotiate new arrangements in the north.

A resumption of Iraq's control over its air space south of the 32nd parallel, and the removal of the current restriction on troop movements south of that line, would be troublesome for military planners in the Gulf. It would make mobilization of Iraqi troops on the Kuwaiti border easier and give less warning time than is now the case.

The issue of Iraq's borders with Kuwait and its access to the Gulf may also pose challenges for the GCC. Most Iraqis, including the opposition, resent the borders drawn by the UN commission following the war. Pressure to renegotiate these borders to give Iraq greater access to the Gulf, including use of Warbah and Bubayan, will probably continue regardless of regime. The sooner some of the personal barriers between Kuwait and Iraq can be dropped through trade and personal contacts, the sooner these tensions can be mitigated. Again, such contacts will be extremely difficult with the current regime in power. Even under a new regime, however, mutual fears, suspicions and resentments will take a long time to dissipate.

Iraq will also seek to alleviate its regional and international isolation, and to reduce the allied presence in the region. This may not be an easy task. Iraq has much work to do to reassure its neighbors of 'better intentions' in the future. Its current behavior, especially with respect to cooperation with UN Resolutions, does not give cause for confidence. Iraq believes and has believed for many years that it has a major role to play in the region – both in the Gulf and in the Arab world. Iraq will continue to seek to restore that position of regional influence, regardless of the regime in power. In particular, it will continue to stress its role as the guardian of the Arab world against Iranian hegemony.

If Iraq is not gradually reintegrated into the region and its isolation continues, pent-up feelings of unrequited nationalism will build up in Iraq, an inauspicious beginning to the twenty-first century. These sentiments could continue Iraq's garrison mentality rather than developing pragmatic policies upon which its economic developmental future depends. Reducing Iraq's isolation and opening the country to outside influences, regardless of regime, will be one of the most important and difficult undertakings for all concerned with Iraq policy.

A third, less likely, challenge lurks in the background. If Iraq fails to solve its domestic problems, if its international position does not improve and, above all, if economic and military sanctions linger into the twenty-first century, Iraq's social and political decline could lead to the gradual disintegration of state institutions. It is impossible to predict how, and to what extent, such disintegration would ensue. It could come in the wake of a regime replacement which failed to stabilize itself, or it could follow a prolonged period of sanctions that eventually causes collapse. Certainly, a significant breakdown of government in Baghdad would confront the Gulf states with a challenge of a different order. Instability in Iraq could spill across borders in the south as it is now doing in the north. The inability of the Iraqi government to maintain law and order in the south, or to control its borders with Iran, Kuwait and Saudi Arabia, could lead to cross-border activities that would be destabilizing. More radical Shi'ite elements, especially those associated with SAIRI and the Da'wa, and supported by Iran, could take root in the south, creating a situation there not unlike that in south Lebanon. Under these circumstances, Iran is likely to increase its influence in this region. Such an eventuality could also put pressures on Iraq's borders with Kuwait. In the event that violence or unrest spreads throughout the south, Kuwait (and Jordan) could experience refugee flows. In short, Iraq's border problems could become more difficult to manage, and, at the same time, groups could take root in southern Iraq inimical to Western and Gulf interests. A weaker Iraqi government and/or a period of instability in Baghdad would also shift the balance of power in the Gulf more decisively in Iran's favor.

Conclusions

The potential challenges from Iraq will not be easy to manage, but they present the GCC and its Western partners with three essential tasks. The first is how to handle the return of Iraq to oil markets in ways that do not destabilize or create serious economic problems for the rest of the Gulf. The gradual easing of sanctions envisioned under UN Resolution 986 will diminish the initial impact of Iraqi oil on international markets, but the international community is likely to insist on some continuous trade constraints to ensure that Iraq does not circumvent the arms control provisions of UNSC Resolution 687. A UN Resolution designed to tighten monitoring of Iraq's imports with this purpose in mind was passed in March 1996. If a change occurs in Baghdad, there is more likelihood that monitoring requirements will be loosened. Whatever the constraints, the problem of accommodating Iraq's economic needs will remain. Iraq's economic losses have been so severe and its reconstruction needs are so high as to generate constant pressures in Iraq to create more revenue. This will keep competition for oil markets and the issue of oil prices at the forefront of Gulf politics. To the extent that Iraq feels that its financial needs are being thwarted by the GCC and the West, the challenge will be intensified. Managing this economic competition for markets and revenue from Iraq will be a critical element in achieving stability in the twenty-first century.

The second will be the restoration of Iraq's sovereignty over its territory and easing the country out of its isolation. Both are problematic if the current regime remains, or if it is succeeded by one like it. Ending the no-fly zone in the north will require appropriate accommodations between the Kurds and the central government. Removing restrictions over Iraq's air space and troop movements in the south will necessitate accommodations with its GCC neighbors, especially Kuwait. Both are likely to be slow in coming. Meanwhile, regional powers, including the GCC, must find a way to reduce the isolation of the Iraqi populace even if this results in a dual-track policy towards the Iraqi government. Only greater and more continuous contact with the outside can strengthen the forces of pragmatism that may be emerging among the post-1968 generation and eliminate the 'garrison mentality' that now prevails in Baghdad.

Lastly, the GCC and the West must be prepared to contain and deal constructively with the instability that may accompany change in Baghdad. While the nature and timing of this change cannot be predicted, it is not likely to be smooth. It is in GCC interests to see that change comes to Iraq, but at the same time to prevent a collapse of government and its institutions, or a disintegration of the Iraqi state. The challenge here will be to balance constraints on Iraq's rearmament with its need for economic revival. If sanctions and containment are continued too long, disintegration could occur. Too little containment, however, could result in an economic and military revival in Baghdad that could threaten the Gulf in the twenty-first century, just as it did at the end of the twentieth.

PART TWO

Gulf Security and Great Power Interests

The Gulf Cooperation Council and the United States: Common and Uncommon Security Interests

Joseph Moynihan

The topic of US security interests in the Arabian Gulf is a large one. Scholars and professionals who focus on this issue are many and the literature is extensive. It therefore becomes important to narrow down the subject-matter and veer away from broad generalizations. Accordingly, this chapter will focus on the evolution of US national security interests in the Gulf, and its accompanying bilateral and multilateral defense and security relationships between the Gulf states and the United States. Although the chapter will comment on the near-term, its purpose is to look at the longer term – well beyond the earliest years of the twenty-first century – and to provoke discussion concerning the shape of a future security relationship between the Gulf states and the United States.

The penchant of defense establishments to plan for the next war in the terms of the last war is well known, and it is a practice that is generally regretted by both security policy analysts and security studies scholars. The current US national security establishment has unfortunately institutionalized this practice to an unprecedented degree. For example, the Clinton administration's security policy planning for regional conflicts is couched in terms of a 'Major Regional Contingency' (MRC), and the associated force structure planning for this MRC is conducted in Desert Storm equivalents.[1] This planning drives day-to-day US military operations, training in and around the Gulf, and often GCC military activity as well, in ways that may not recognize the strategic evolution of potential adversaries in the Gulf, and do not always promote domestic stability.

The Nature of the Relationship

In the early 1990s, a group of prominent US defense and security policy analysts suggested that it would take seven to ten years for the USA fully to discern and articulate a national security policy for the post-Cold War period.[2] As we approach the beginning of that seven-to-ten-year interval in early 1996, only a very few analysts would suggest that a defining national security policy for the US is discernible. Indeed, the consensus that governed US national security decision-making for the Cold War period has vanished, and with it the practice of restricting bipartisan politics to US domestic issues as well. As a result, the absence of consensus within the US national security community has itself begun to affect policy decisions. A Venn diagram might now display only a very small representation of overlap (signifying congruent positions on national security issues) between two circles representing the national security policy positions of the two major competing US political parties.[3] Despite these divergent trends, and while security studies analysts wait for a new consensus to emerge, we should acknowledge that, from the vantage of history, the US has enjoyed only infrequently a real robust national security consensus. In the absence of such an agreement, the security policy of the USA has historically been very selective and circumspect, and indeed event-specific and episodic.[4] New and tougher tests of *vitality* may therefore determine which interests are vital, and which international relationships are integral to the service of those vital interests.

It has always been easier to declare that US security policy must be guided by US 'vital interests' than to achieve a consensus on the specifics of either the 'interests' themselves or the specific security policy necessary to defend those interests. Those who believe that the threat of a nuclear holocaust during the Cold War ensured a consistently harmonious bi-partisan US security policy line need to refresh themselves concerning events associated with the Vietnam War. In addition, the US security policy community's perceived necessity to align the USA with politically unsavoury dictators was often challenged by influential foreign policy elites from both major political parties.[5] Occasionally, specific legislation emanated from Congress that determined such alignments was later found to be unlawful.

There has also been a long ongoing debate among US political and security policy elites concerning the role of US military forces overseas. This aspect of the international security policy of the USA has become even more politically contentious in the post-Cold War era. While US presidents can continue to expect support from the American people and their political representatives in Congress once actual hostilities commence, the executive should expect that their national security policy decisions, other than a firm commitment to use force, will continue to be closely questioned and often constrained by the political opposition. In short, a robust consensus concerning post-Cold War US security policy may never develop.

In light of all this divergence, the prominent US role in Gulf security does currently (1996) enjoy strong bipartisan support. Indeed, there is a remarkable coalition of American Arabs and American Jews, liberals and conservatives, multilateralists and unilateralists, isolationists and globalists, and so on, who would support an aggressive and immediate US military response in the Gulf to any additional instance of Iraqi aggression against its GCC neighbors, Israel or Jordan, or to an overt and unambiguously attributable act of war by Iran against those same states. Such a stout bipartisan coalition is in evidence in very few other important components of current US national security policy.[6] For example, US anti-proliferation policies and policies that require a forward presence of US forces abroad are hotly debated in Congress.[7] Indeed, recent legislative–executive exchanges on national security issues have been vituperative and personal, strongly reflecting narrow partisan views.[8]

The coalition which supports a strong US Gulf security policy persists despite a very limited knowledge or understanding by the American polity of the people and the culture of the Gulf, and despite the non-democratic forms of government that exist in the region which the American people do not admire, and which the Clinton administration has publicly stated need reform.[9] It also persists despite the very limited number of civilian American lives which are placed at risk by Gulf aggression, since there are comparatively few Americans resident in the Gulf at present. Indeed, there is little observable ideological, emotional or familial character to the consensus. The near-unanimous sense among American elites that GCC security is a vital American interest is arguably unemotional, professional and businesslike.

That is not to say that there have been no periodic challenges to strong US support for Gulf security. In 1995 and 1996, for example, domestic political violence flared up in Bahrain and Saudi Arabia, including a terrorist attack on a Saudi National Guard installation in Riyadh that killed several Americans and the bombing of the al-Khobar military housing project in Dahran, Saudi Arabia, that claimed the lives of 19 American servicemen. As a result, the strong counter-measures by Bahrain and Saudi Arabia aimed at controlling domestic dissidence and violence were viewed by human rights advocates as heavy-handed, and the Clinton administration actually proceeded so far as to label the Saudi Arabian government a 'human rights transgressor' (a distinction the Saudi government shares with, among others, the People's Republic of China). However, such challenges have not diminished the strength of the coalition favoring a forward security policy in the Gulf nor have they undermined the policy itself to any significant degree.

Social and Political Change in the Gulf and the US Relationship

Most Gulf observers believe that significant social and political change in this part of the world is inevitable in the years ahead; many believe that this change will be destabilizing as well. For example, one US observer, referring to the process as a likely 'massive wave of realized and yet to come transformations', predicted that strains and fractures in the political and social structure of the Gulf will certainly occur.[10]

Regardless of how optimistic or pessimistic the analyst, predicting the future in the Gulf is at best a highly speculative undertaking.[11] It is one thing to assert that the post-Cold War political transformation of world politics is likely to affect the basic assumptions and the practices of GCC politics; it is quite another to claim that political instability is chronic, increasing or irreversible in the Arab Gulf, or to compare conditions there to the political instability that exists in Algeria or Egypt.[12] In this sense, the people of the Arabian Gulf are likely to disappoint future predictors of political chaos much as they have disappointed present and past purveyors of doom. While significant political and social change in the Gulf is likely to occur, it is important to note that few of the major political changes that have occurred in the Gulf this past century were predicted by analysts much in advance. Moreover, there appears currently to be little evidence of large-scale political discontent in the Gulf, and informal participation in the political process in the GCC states is much greater than observers of formal governmental institutions are likely to observe. It is in this environment that the evolutionary change can be channelled so as not to appear diametrically opposed to the interests of either the existing governments of the Arabian Gulf or of the government of the USA. Given the right amount of foresight and luck, the governments in the region have a very good chance of steering the change that is inevitable into evolutionary rather than revolutionary channels.

Since on balance very few indicators suggest that radical political policies in the Gulf will support US national security interests, the Clinton administration has sensibly backed off its early consideration of assigning the Department of Defense a democratization mission in the Gulf region. There seems to be greater appreciation that attempts to influence domestic political events in the Arabian Gulf are likely to be counter-productive and, much to the relief of most defense establishment professionals, US democratization policy has been substantially moderated and a more realistic mission has evolved.[13]

The United States, the Peace Process and Gulf Security

Unlike the coalition in favor of US support for Gulf security, support for Israeli security policy is backed by a strong, well-financed lobby that draws not only on ethnic ties, but also on the emotional backing of a broad spectrum of the American public. This lobby, most effective in Congress because of its selective support of individual members, has succeeded in providing political and economic support that even the Israeli government occasionally finds excessive. In any case, the United States has consistently elevated Israeli security interests above other major US interests in the region to the extent that it has often produced a predictable backlash within the Arab world, including the Gulf.

The United States has experienced difficulty underwriting Israel's security and at the same time securing its interest in maintaining access to Middle East, particularly Gulf oil supplies. This was particularly evident during the 1973 Arab–Israeli War and accompanying Arab oil embargo. An Arab–Israeli peace offers the greatest prospect for balancing these two incompatible goals and the United States has long striven to promote one. Secretary of State Kissinger's 'shuttle diplomacy' and the Camp David Accords both looked promising but fell short of the mark. After a decade of 'status quo' crisis, peace efforts were again revitalized in 1991 in Madrid, with US Secretary of State Baker a prime mover in getting them restarted. The most dramatic breakthrough, however, was not the result of aggressive US diplomacy, but rather the closed-door, behind-the-scenes bilateral negotiations on behalf of the warring parties, which in this instance culminated in the so-called Oslo I Agreement between then Israeli Foreign Minister Shimon Peres and the leader of the Palestine Liberation Organization, Yassir Arafat, in the summer of 1993.

No one should underestimate the enormous problems that continue to face the negotiators. As this is written in early 1997, the Arab–Israeli peace process has, at best, languished since the election of the Netanyahu government in Israel in mid-1996. While at the strategic level, the opportunity for the peace process to produce lasting and mutually advantageous agreement remains very possible, the willingness of the parties – particularly the Netanyahu government – to take the tactical political risks associated with a peace agreement has clearly diminished from the heady days of 1993/94. At the beginning of the second term of the Clinton administration, newly confirmed US Secretary of State Albright reiterated the preparedness of the United States both diplomatically to facilitiate the peace process and militarily to guarantee further peace agreements in the region. Yet, progress in recent months has not occurred.

The peace process covers a far broader area than political–military relations between the antagonists. In particular, there is an important economic dimension as well. The initial willingness of Arab governments, including Gulf Arab governments, to enter new and creative economic relationships with Israel emanating from the peace process was startling. These increasing economic linkages between private Arab and Israeli businessmen, reportedly including Gulf Arab businessmen, are an important ingredient for confidence-building measures and in time could be more important than government-to-government agreements.[14] That the Gulf Arab governments most willing to enter these economic relationships are also those least endowed with respective oil reserves is probably not accidental. However, on the whole, a changing of attitudes and perspectives was evident while the momentum of the peace process was ongoing.

An Arab–Israeli settlement will have significant ramifications for Gulf security far beyond its restrictive military threat analysis by Israel itself. For example, it will also affect the threat from Iran, most directly on Iranian support for regional Islamist terrorist groups. The Syrian–Israeli track of the peace negotiations have been the most difficult to date, but Syria has acknowledged that a bilateral peace agreement with Israel would include withdrawal of Syria's key and essential administrative and logistical support for the activities of Iranian-financed paramilitary groups in Lebanon. Israel has also acknowledged that a bilateral peace agreement with Syria, and the agreement with Lebanon that would quickly follow, will include the withdrawal of Israel forces and the removal of Israel's key support for indigenous paramilitary forces resident in the Israeli-controlled 'security zone' immediately north of the internationally recognized frontier between Israel and Lebanon. While this move will primarily benefit the security of Israel and Lebanon, it will also undermine ideological Iranian authority in seeking to export Islamic revolution world-wide by denying Iranian support to Islamist groups opposed to both regimes. As long as a comprehensive Arab–Israeli settlement remains elusive, however, there is little possibility of achieving effective strategic cooperation against a commonly perceived threat.

The United States and the Containment of Iran and Iraq

Ever since the United States assumed the role of security guarantor within the Gulf region from the British in the early 1970s, it has sought to maintain regional stability through, among other complementary policies, the maintenance of a rough balance of military power between the two most dominant Gulf states, Iraq and Iran. Initially this meant supporting the Iranian monarchy against socialist, anti-Western Iraq, but this security calculus changed radically with the fall of the Shah and the rise of revolutionary Iran. In order to thwart an attempt for regional hegemony by the Islamic Republic of Iran, and not because either the United States or the GCC preferred, or would ever accept, Gulf regional hegemony by Saddam Hussein's Iraq, the United States and the GCC supported Iraq during its war with Iran. Thus, US and GCC support of Iraq was in effect a textbook, tacit and tactical coalition serving larger strategic interests, much as the one that existed during the Cold War in which members of the 'Free World' coalition submitted to US hegemonic leadership not out of love for the United States but because of greater antipathy towards the Soviet Union. Important to note is that given the inherently temporary nature of such coalitions, the question needs to be asked under what conditions members of the anti-Saddam coalition that drove him out of Kuwait, including the United States, might shift their loyalties in the twenty-first century.

Over five years after the Iraqi invasion of Kuwait, the GCC states have moderated their rhetoric and to a lesser degree their policies towards Saddam.[15] Several GCC states have begun to reassess their relationship with Iraq. In late 1995, Sheikh Zayed bin Sultan al-Nahyan, the President of the UAE, publicly suggested that the existing sanctions policy needed to be reassessed, a view shared by the new ruler of Qatar. Prince Khalid bin Sultan, the Saudi counterpart to General Norman Schwartzkopf during the Gulf War, has expressed similar views.[16] UN confirmation of Iraq's ongoing development and concealment of weapons of mass destruction

(WMD), however, should continue to ensure Iraq's international political and economic isolation, and a continued wariness of Iraqi intentions by the GCC leadership, for at least the short term.[17]

Should the GCC states choose to soften their position significantly with respect to Iraq, it will almost certainly become a source of friction with the United States. It is simply not possible, for a number of reasons, for the United States to accept any normalization of the relationship with Iraq as long as Saddam Hussein remains in power.[18] Nevertheless, it is true that Saddam Hussein's extreme rhetoric and periodic military adventurism, as well as the extensive, expensive and recently increased and enhanced US military presence in the Gulf, continues to politically tarnish the military victory of the Desert Storm coalition.[19] Moreover, the US government, having so effectively demonized Saddam, is currently not politically able to conduct correct, much less cordial, relations with his embarrassingly durable government. In this sense, United States' Gulf security policy is hostage to the pre-conflict rhetoric of the Bush administration.

In the longer term, it is safe to assume that the USA will improve its record of relations with Iraq after Saddam leaves the scene. Iraq is too significant a regional power for the United States to be able eternally to 'contain' it. Further, depending on Iranian politics, there is a realistic possibility that, at a future date, the United States will again see the advantage of checking Iranian ambitions through better relations with Iraq.[20] When and if the Iraqi people choose to replace the Saddam government with one less fond of WMD, and one more prepared to resolve disputes through consultation with the GCC and the US, greater flexibility in security policy is highly likely.

By contrast, it is difficult to overemphasize the depth and durability of the antipathy between the United States and Iran.[21] While control of access to Gulf oil is an important component of the enduring dispute between them, the emotion with which these two countries view each other cannot be fully explained by clashing national interests over energy resources. In the United States, the Iran hostage crisis indelibly colored Iranians in the eyes of the average American as fanatical, terroristic tyrants with little regard for human dignity or the established norms of international political participation. In Iran, the close American support for the Shah, including returning him to the imperial throne in 1953, has colored Americans in the eyes of the ruling elite as self-serving hypocrites with little regard or respect for moral values or the freedom and rights of smaller countries. Thus, even if the USA was totally self-sufficient in oil, it would still politically oppose the revolutionary government of Iran, and even if US military forces departed the Gulf region, Iran would still see the hidden hand of Washington seeking to control events in the Gulf in imposing a secular, materialistic culture on the region.

The frequently vitriolic rhetoric which surrounds the American–Iranian dispute is exacerbated in both camps by politicians seeking office, journalists seeking readership and occasionally by scholars and regional experts who disguise their own ideological preferences in the trappings of scholarship. Since the rise of militant Islamic movements throughout the Muslim world, there has been a trend of thought in the West that the entire Islamic world is inimical to the West and must be treated as an enemy. Indeed, a vigorous academic debate has been produced which attends this perception, and noted scholars within the West have published influential articles in prominent journals with titles such as 'The Clash of Civilizations?' and 'Muslim Rage'.[22] In these instances, Iran's radicalizing influence on Islamist movements throughout the world is often exaggerated.

The Clinton administration insists that it is not opposed to Islam but to extremism. Here, the administration has noted on many occasions that the Islamist foreign policies of Iran are irreconcilable with the ideals of the international community.[23] This condemnation should be viewed in part as an obligatory nod to a stout and enduring US domestic consensus antithetical to Iran. Unlike the antipathy towards Saddam Hussein, this consensus extends well beyond the issue of a single leader. In 1995, years after the death of the Ayatollah Khomeini, the Clinton administration expanded its largely unilateral economic sanctions against Iran and lobbied the Russian and Chinese governments with some success to restrict the transfer of nuclear technology to Iran.

Since in a militarily unipolar world, few states will overtly or casually strain political relations with the United States to gain favor with Tehran on important regional security issues such as the transfer of nuclear technology, the United States has been relatively successful in limiting international arms sales to Iran, particularly involving WMD. It has been far less successful in limiting non-military sales to Iran. In fact, the greatest impediment to non-military trade has been Iran itself. Iran's deteriorating economy and the anti-Western biases of the more doctrinaire members of the government undermine international confidence in Iran as a trading partner. Looking beyond these domestic restraints, Iran remains a significant trading and energy investment partner, in particular for the European powers. European spokesmen frequently suggest that, in striking similarity to the US policy towards China, 'engagement' with Iran will produce better results than 'containment'.[24]

Beyond its universal policy of opposition to nuclear proliferation, the United States justifies its harsh response to Iranian rearmament in general with the contention that Tehran is preparing itself for a course of military action similar to the aggression undertaken by Saddam's Iraq. Given Iran's historical imperial ambitions for regional hegemony, it is certainly prudent for the United States' national security apparatus to train and equip GCC armed forces, and to deploy its own forces to the region to deter un-conventional as well as conventional attacks by Iran. Nevertheless, the nature of the threat should be placed in perspective. Much of Iran's conventional military capability was destroyed during the Iran–Iraq War, and US sanctions on transfers of unconventional weapons materials and technology have realized some additional, albeit limited, success. Most importantly, Iran's economy has declined precipitously in recent years, hampered both by the US-led embargo externally and by a plethora of economic crises internally. Iran is simply not in a position to engage in major regional conflict. Thus, it seems extremely unlikely that Iran will attack any GCC state with overt, attributable military force in the near term. Further, the political inability of the Iranian government to under-take significant economic reform could extend Iran's strategic impotence indefinitely.

The Clinton administration sought to distance itself from the policy of balancing Iran and Iraq against one another, in turn, announcing a policy of 'dual containment'. This policy was intended to quarantine both countries until, in the US view, they demonstrated a willingness to comply with international norms of political behavior. Whether 'dual contain-ment' has furthered US interests since its inception, remains very much subject to debate. In addition, given the historical tendencies of both Iran and Iraq periodically to seek political prominence in the Gulf, it is likely that the utility of a balance of power strategy will again present itself for consideration to strategists within the United States' national security community. In any case, the requirement to protect the security of the GCC states from their more powerful neighbors will continue at least into the early years of the twenty-first century no matter what the ideological proclivities of the regimes in Baghdad and Tehran, or the political preferences of the American administration in Washington. Instead, what may abate in the decades ahead is the national security imperative associated with US access to Gulf energy resources.

Oil as a Determinant of US Strategic Interests
in the Gulf

Since oil is a major determinant of US security interests in the Gulf, long-term changes in the international oil market will have a profound effect on the US security role in the Gulf in the twenty-first century.[25] Within the next 30 years, oil production of some of the Gulf states can be expected to decline drastically, and overall market share generally is expected to shift from OPEC to non-OPEC sources as a result of new finds and new technology. For example, Bahrain's reserves are already greatly depleted and some people argue that this has exacerbated political and social turbulence there. Oman and Qatar are also not expected to be able to maintain current production rates over the next 20 to 30 years. The Emirate of Dubai within the United Arab Emirates will equally lose significant production capability during the same period. In sum, since the economies of all the GCC states are dependent on oil exports, there is a good chance that a significant number of them will not be able to sustain their present gross domestic product based upon revenues generated from oil sales.[26] In addition to a decline in production in some GCC countries, world oil prices themselves, which have actually decreased in real terms in the last 15 years, are expected to remain flat well into the twenty-first century. Not only have advances in technology increased the prospects for greater world-wide supplies, but environmental factors and more efficient use of energy have kept a rein on demand.[27]

Gulf economic prospects are even gloomier than declining production and flat oil revenues suggest. Due to the unusually high birth rates in all GCC countries, per capita income will probably continue to decline for years to come. Moreover, rapid modernization will doubtless result in each new generation demanding a higher per capita energy consumption rate than its predecessor, diverting an increasing amount of production from exports to domestic use. Without doubt, the population increase will in time benefit GCC economies as national workers replace expatriates in many if not most positions within their respective economies. In the meantime, however, GCC governments will be required to provide a full range of social services not only for an expanding population but for a large expatriate workforce as well.[28]

In short, it appears likely that, in the next century, the USA may well re-evaluate the energy assumptions which underpin its strategic policy in the Gulf. At the end of the twentieth century, the focus has been essentially on three major factors: (1) the geo-strategic prominence of

Gulf oil; (2) the very large Gulf petroleum reserves, notably in Saudi Arabia, Kuwait and the UAE, but also in Iraq and Iran; and (3) the relatively low operations and maintenance cost to 'lift' Gulf oil.

Focusing too closely on these factors perhaps allows one to miss three important points. First, the Gulf countries, while still comparatively wealthy, are not nearly as wealthy as they once were, and they are very unlikely to maintain current levels of per capita wealth in the twenty-first century. Second, there is likely to be a greater supply of oil from non-Gulf sources. And third, a relatively smaller increase in demand than has been the case in the second half of the twentieth century will occur in an increasingly environmentally-conscious world. As a result, it is possible that while Gulf oil will remain a major US interest for many decades, the degree to which it is a vital interest – that is, one that justifies going to war to defend – may diminish in the next century. Ironically, there is currently a greater appreciation for this economic reality in the Gulf than in US security policy circles.

There is in addition at least one other important economic factor that relates to Gulf security. All the Arab Gulf states have begun the challenging process of economic diversification, preparing for the day when oil is unable to provide an acceptable level of economic prosperity to Gulf citizens. This economic diversification effort which is taking shape at the end of the twentieth century is likely to become one of the defining components of the future US Gulf security policy. It is already one in which US aerospace firms are prominent. For example, US arms sales to Gulf countries are already extensive and will likely remain so well into the next century. In relation, every Gulf state now insists, or soon will insist, that all arms contracts include provisions for 'offset' programs which require the seller to invest directly as joint minority partners in non-oil-sector, export-related enterprises within the respective country. Offset projects have been materializing slowly but are gathering momentum and in time should increasingly enable participating Arab Gulf economies to diversify and to acquire significant foreign direct investment. This investment should in turn accelerate the development of non-petroleum, export-based industries while the participating country modernizes its military equipment. An important outcome of offset provisions is the resultant additional stake in the security of the Arab Gulf partner, and the stability of the Arab Gulf region. Since the government of the minority partners within the Arab Gulf is often but not exclusively the United States, offset programs ensure that regional stability, national military modernization and economic diversification occur in a mutually supportive, synchronous manner. Importantly, offset programs tend to strengthen the links between GCC governments and their security partners in the West, thus reducing the requirement for a visible military 'presence' in the respective country to provide increased assurance of the West's enduring commitment to regional security.

The United States and Gulf Security: the Military Dimension

At the present time, the operative military components of US national security policy generally and also in the Gulf are *forward presence* and *crisis response*.[29] While these components are likely to remain in place well into the next century, it is important to discuss how they are likely to evolve.

FORWARD PRESENCE: The goal of a forward US military presence in the Gulf is to reduce the potential for regional instability through the prominent reassurance of allies and friends that the United States is prepared to come to their assistance. For many years, it was thought that a forward US military presence had to be tailored to an environment where its high visibility might excite challenges to domestic order and could aid the efforts of hostile powers to subvert friendly Gulf governments. The forward presence component of Gulf security seemed to require a customized show of force – a show not everyone could see, but that regionally important national security decision-makers, friend or foe, could both see and understand. Forward presence needed to be structured in a way that both deterred regional aggressors and reassured regional friends without fuelling and exciting domestic tensions. Thus, the Gulf was generally regarded as a 'maritime' theater for US security planners. US military assets, activities and operations were 'over the horizon'. Highly visible, land-based forces were considered counter-productive.

Since the Gulf War, the concept of an 'over the horizon' or low-profile US forward presence in the Gulf has been abandoned by the United States with the concurrence of the GCC states. The experience of the war and the ongoing concern about Iranian military resurgence combined to produce a far more visible and aggressive forward presence that includes an expanded, quasi-permanent deployment of US military forces on the ground in GCC countries. The US naval and air force presence have become more prominent in recent years with the extensive pre-positioning of US military equipment in GCC states being discussed in the open press.[30]

The prominent forward US presence has served to deter Iran and Iraq from any serious military intimidation of their Gulf neighbors. Moreover, the credibility of US security guarantees has been reinforced by the reality that any attack by Iraq or Iran would of necessity immediately engage US forces in the region, thus ensuring the quick and decisive crisis response of a larger US force structure in the United States. The forward presence is also valuable for operational reasons. Interoperability between GCC forces and US forces has improved as has the sometimes more challenging interoperability between GCC commanders and senior staff members and their US counterparts. Administrative procedures, command/control and logistics methodologies have all been refined. In short, Gulf coalition forces have achieved a higher state of readiness that further enhances deterrence.

A more negative outcome of this increased deterrence is the greatly increased potential for political subversion. The higher the profile of US troops, the easier it is for domestic Islamist activists as well as Iran and/or Iraq to challenge local governments by exploiting nationalistic and religious resentments over what is interpreted by some as foreign encroachment. Recent attacks against US military facilities within Saudi Arabia appear to have been executed by Islamic activists incensed by the US military presence in that country. Iranian and Iraqi propagandists also often and loudly accuse the GCC governments of violating Islamic precepts, if not Islamic law, by permitting foreign forces on their soil. In this environment, an incident involving US forces on liberty within the GCC ports could easily escalate into a major political issue. The lack of US sensitivity to local customs, values and feelings often creates tension, which can assist those politically active groups disenchanted with the decisions of GCC governments. For example, US sailors visiting Arab Gulf ports frequently visit schools and perform repairs in an attempt to be good neighbors. While this is on its own merits a wonderful gesture, it is often resented as patronizing by many Gulf nationals who believe that such practices are evidence that the US considers Gulf countries to be backward, Third World societies, and that in all probability their schools are in better repair than many US schools. Many Gulf nationals are also sensitive to any hint that they should be grateful for US security, often pointing out that the US actually made a financial profit on Desert Storm, and that Gulf treasuries pay the bill for Operation Southern Watch and for the modernization of Gulf military establishments.

CRISIS RESPONSE: Crises can come in all sizes. For contingency planning purposes, the crisis response component of US Gulf security policy is designed for a 'Major Regional Contingency' (MRC). An MRC is a crisis of roughly the magnitude of the Iraqi invasion of Kuwait, and requires a response roughly on the same scale as Operation Desert Storm with more than 500,000 US military members deployed to the Gulf. In other words, the crisis response component of current US Gulf security policy is preparing and equipping US military forces for high-intensity conventional warfare in the Gulf – an unlikely, but possible, worst-case scenario. The credibility of this US Gulf security policy, and the preparation of US forces for its execution, is a major component of the deterrence the USA provides in the Gulf. Moreover, with the current high state of tension between the USA and Iran likely to continue for the foreseeable future, planning for an MRC contingency could be necessary for an extended period of time.

An important criticism of the MRC crisis response policy is its limitations in encountering lesser crises. Its effectiveness in dealing with low-intensity conflict, terrorism and political warfare is problematic, and one should note that the potential/actual occurrence of lesser crises, in the form of non-attributable political violence, could very well be encouraged by the ongoing, high-profile US military forward presence. Such criticism is traditionally countered by military planners who assert that large-scale military operational plans such as those designed to respond to a major regional crisis can also be downsized and 'tailored' to address 'lesser included threats'. There is an underlying assumption that the comprehensive military planning for MRCs in a given region addresses crises at every level.

This is a questionable assertion, particularly in the Gulf where most likely threats do not eminate from the military forces of an opposing state but rather from internal non-military or paramilitary groups seeking to carry out acts of violence in a clandestine or covert manner.[31] Historically, such acts are the preferred tactics of those without the resources to mount a more strategically significant opposition, or of those unlikely to prevail (or survive) in higher-scale conflict, or both. These groups are not deterrable in the military sense, and may in fact be encouraged by traditional military deterrence activity. For many who engage in political violence, death is an acceptable outcome.

An additional factor to consider in the US role in Gulf security is the high visibility of US commercial activity in the Gulf, particularly those ventures linked to regional security, and the near certainty that this commercial presence will continue for the indefinite future. Indeed, despite the advantages of new offset ventures, if a highly visible military presence persists, the offset enterprises themselves could in the long-term become targets of political violence as opposition groups seek to exploit their close linkage to US military assistance and Gulf dependence on the West for regional security. The value of offset projects as a symbolic target could increase even more if the new industries created were directly related to the defense sector, as indeed many of the ones developed thus far are, and if they employed only a small number of Gulf nationals, as many of those developed thus far do.

Assuming a long-term need to maintain a forward presence in the Gulf, the great challenge confronting the US military planners in the twenty-first century will be to maintain a balance between the somewhat incompatible goals of deterring a major regional crisis through forward presence operations, and avoiding contributing to lesser crises that the high visibility of the US forces of the forward presence could stimulate. In sum, the USA must maintain a forward presence in the Gulf of a sufficient size and readiness to deter a potential attacker, while at the same time maintaining a sufficiently low profile to avoid undermining the internal security of the states it is trying to protect. Because these goals are in many ways incompatible, only by maintaining high sensitivity to local feelings and avoiding a proprietary sense of 'squatters' rights' can US Gulf security policy succeed.

Conclusions

It is clear that, from a US perspective, the current set of security relationships with Gulf Cooperation Council (GCC) states serves three important and interrelated interests: the uninterrupted access to the petroleum resources of the Gulf; a potential military base of operations should a regional opponent of the Middle East peace process initiate hostilities against a peace process partner; and, third, the prevention of either Iran or Iraq from attaining regional political–military dominance in a strategically important area of the world.

The degree of confluence of US and GCC national interests will determine the character of the future security relationship, and because of the relatively limited cultural or social linkages between the citizens of the GCC and the US, security relationship changes will respond comparatively quickly to any changes in interests which do occur. Thus, were Gulf petroleum to become relatively less important to the USA, it would over time reassess its Gulf security policy. The same would hold true if the GCC states believed that the political disadvantages of hosting a large US military presence outweighed the benefits.

The long-term military resurgence of an adversarial Iran or Iraq is likely to require an equally long-term US commitment and GCC acceptance of a foreign military presence. The likelihood of a long-term adversarial relationship with Iran is probably greater than that of one with Iraq. The post-Desert Storm dispute between the USA and Iraq is, from the US vantage, a dispute with Iraq's leader. A successor to Saddam Hussein could possess both his ambition and his ruthlessness, but is unlikely to possess them in sufficient quantities in order to survive as long as Saddam has. Meanwhile, the need to check Iran could prompt conciliation if not accommodation efforts from Washington to any Saddam successor willing to negotiate in good faith.

A number of factors suggest that the US and Iran will remain adversarial for the foreseeable future. The near-term tactical focus of this fundamentally ideological dispute will continue to be the presence of a large US military force in the Gulf region. In fact, the US military continues to recommend a significant increase in the strength of Gulf-assigned forces – an eventuality that, should it occur, will further sour relationships between Iran and the GCC states. Unable to confront the stout US–GCC military force structure militarily, Iran may well choose to pursue an agenda of psychological/political tactics in support of its regional political ambitions, for several reasons.[32]

First, Iran is highly competent in these tactics and techniques. Second, the successful deterrence that the US–GCC forces provide against conventional military aggression increases the attractiveness to Iran of engaging in covert acts of political violence. Covert, deniable acts are far less likely to provoke the use of force by the US than overt, attributable military acts. Third, the potential denial of geographic access to Israel will increase the relative attractiveness of a Gulf political–military strategy to Iran. Gulf states will remain geographically proximate to Iran, and in a relative sense will become more attractive as a venue for Iran to claim and demonstrate Islamic leadership through political–military means. Fourth, a continued US forward military presence, particularly as presently configured, will offer attractive, relatively low-cost targets for political warfare tactics – targets with high media value such as ships in port, military aircraft in hangars, military troops allegedly violating Islamic customs, and so on. Fifth and last, Iran's continuing economic crisis is likely to preclude overt military adventurism for many years to come.

In sum, there are many reasons to believe that a major regional crisis is not the most likely form of conflict either the USA or the GCC can expect from Iran in the years ahead. In seeking to prevent such a crisis, therefore, both the USA and the GCC states should ensure that the US military presence in the Gulf maintains as low a profile as possible while at the same time being aware of the cultural sensitivities and national pride of the local populations. Cooperative Gulf security planning should increasingly acknowledge this possibility, and adjust MRC preparedness planning accordingly.

CHAPTER 5

Europe and Gulf Security: A Competitive Business

Rosemary Hollis

In order of priority, Gulf security ranks third for Europe, after security in Eastern and Central Europe, and security along Europe's southern flank, in the Mediterranean. Singly and collectively, meanwhile, the member states of the European Union (EU) cannot match the military weight of the United States of America in the Gulf. In view of this, the Europeans have played a supportive as opposed to primary role, as witnessed in their contribution to the coalition that liberated Kuwait from Iraqi occupation. In so far as European interests in the Gulf overlap with those of the USA, this supportive relationship will endure. However, the interests of the USA and the Europeans do diverge somewhat, especially in relation to Iraq and Iran, and EU members are in competition for Gulf business, both with each other and with the USA.

The Europeans are not altogether happy with the US formula for Gulf security of 'Dual Containment'. While America may be content to cultivate business in the member countries of the Gulf Cooperation Council (GCC), to the exclusion of Iraq and Iran, the Europeans prefer to pursue a wider range of options. Looking to the long term, Europeans anticipate a growing demand for energy resources from the Gulf, and Iraq in particular looks promising for Europe because of its relative geographical proximity. One pipeline already links Iraq to the Mediterranean via Turkey and such facilities can be expanded to obviate the need to bring oil out of Iraq via the Gulf waters. As for Iran, Europeans see this country as such a significant and powerful player in the Gulf that to attempt to exclude it from a say in regional affairs is to court antagonism.

With such considerations in mind, European leaders have warned of the potentially adverse consequences of 'Dual Containment'. The policy could serve to freeze in place unpalatable elements in the northern Gulf, they argue, and it certainly breeds hostility to the West inside Iraq and Iran. They see some value in retaining such leverage as they can with Tehran. On the question of Iraq, while acknowledging the threat posed by the current regime's determination to retain a capability in weapons of mass destruction, they are keen to find a formula for the eventual re-habilitation of the country.

For the time being, though, Europe as a whole, or the EU as such, is only just beginning to think in terms of a comprehensive approach to Gulf security. This is because of more pressing concerns in Central Europe and the Mediterranean. Yet, initiatives taken in these contexts may set the scene for more creative thinking about how to proceed in the Gulf, as and when the EU can act in a unified manner. In the meantime, the role played by the member states of the EU in Gulf security arrange-ments, in terms of their military, political and economic relations there, is overshadowed by that of the USA.

European Thinking on Regional Security Issues

With the end of the Cold War, there has been a fundamental shift of emphasis in European thinking about security issues. Economic depri-vation, population growth rates and environmental pollution are now accorded almost as much attention as traditional military threats.

Not only has the Soviet Union ceased to pose an existential military threat to the West, but the USSR itself has been dismantled. For Western Europe, this has meant the opening up of Central and Eastern Europe to normal relations and, most dramatically, the reunification of Germany. Along with the demise of the Soviet Union, meanwhile, has come the discrediting of the socialist or communist approach to economic develop-ment. States emerging from the old Eastern bloc are pledged, at least in theory, to the principles of liberal economics, free trade and democratic government. The trend towards free market economics has caught on elsewhere and characterizes the restructuring programs advocated for the developing economies of North Africa and the Middle East by the World Bank and the International Monetary Fund.

In financial terms, the world has been turned into a so-called 'Global Village' by the technological advances in telecommunications. At the same time, rapid economic growth in the Far East and some Latin American states has caused a reordering of international investment flows towards emerging markets in these areas. This is not to say, however, that there is a levelling out of the relative fortunes of different countries and regions of the world. On the contrary, the emerging international economic order is characterized by the formation of a handful of major trading blocs, with the EU, along with the North American Free Trade Agreement (NAFTA) and the Asia–Pacific region, in the forefront.

The combined effects of these developments on the strategic military and economic fronts have led to a reordering of European priorities. Freed from the threat of a hostile Soviet Union, European governments have instituted cutbacks in the size of their military establishments. The escalating costs of individual weapons platforms, in the new era of high-tech warfare, meanwhile, has obliged them to choose specialization in a few areas over capability in all, and multilateral cooperation has become compulsory, whether in terms of arms manufacturing or military operations. At issue now is whether the impetus to multilateralism in the defense sector will bind Western European countries closer together, to the relative exclusion of the USA, or strengthen cooperation across the North Atlantic. In this connection, the exact relationship between Europe's defense arm, the Western European Union (WEU), which lacks significant weight as yet, and the formidable transatlantic military alliance of NATO, has still to be agreed upon.

In any case, under the Maastricht Treaty on European Union, the EU member states are committed to devising a Common Foreign and Security Policy (CFSP). This cannot be totally dismissed as a pious wish which will have little real bearing on the foreign policies of EU members. The latter may have singularly failed to achieve a unified approach to the break-up of Yugoslavia, but in other areas, notably Central and Eastern Europe, the Mediterranean basin and the Middle East, the EU has devised something approaching a common policy. The weight of the EU is most significant in the trade and economic sectors and these are crucial to new thinking on regional security.

Poverty and unemployment are critical concerns for most of the states on the periphery of the EU, posing the threat of domestic strife and instability on Europe's doorstep, as well as pressures for migration into the EU. Economic problems are compounded by resurgent nationalist, ethnic and sectarian tensions. A collapse in Russia, meanwhile, could spell environmental disaster, with nuclear, chemical and biological weapons no longer under the control of a strong and unified government. Crime, smuggling, drug-trafficking, gun-running and terrorism are also identified among the new threats to European security from the periphery.

In these circumstances, the EU is faced with two broad imperatives.

On the one hand, in keeping with its *raison d'être*, the EU aims to protect the standard of living and prosperity of its members by promoting internal growth and development and managing external trade. On the other hand, it must prevent damage to those within from adverse developments outside. According to current thinking within the EU, the appropriate formula for reducing security threats from outside is the enhancement of economic development in neighboring regions, thereby generating indigenous prosperity, jobs and political stability. It is this philosophy which has determined Europe's aid and trade policies towards Central and Eastern Europe, North Africa and the Near East.

With respect to the Gulf region, Europe's concerns do not include stemming the potential flow of migrants and the spill-over effects of instability along its periphery. Instead, the principal concern is security of energy supplies. Without access to a continuous flow of oil and gas at predictable and manageable prices, Europe's economies and the standard of living of its peoples would be at risk. Given that some 60 per cent of the world's known oil reserves are located in and around the Gulf, access to this region is very important, and will become more so if and when production elsewhere fails to keep pace with demand growth. A related concern for Europe is continued access to lucrative markets in the Gulf oil-producing states and the security of European investments there.

Europe's Stake in Gulf Security

Europe's material or economic interests in the Gulf fall into three broad categories, namely energy, trade and investments. In 1994, Western Europe consumed 13.7 million barrels of oil per day (b/d) or 20.5 per cent of total world consumption. Of the 9.8 million b/d imported by Europe in that year, 3.7 million came from the Middle East.[1] This latter figure does not include supplies from North Africa and is made up almost entirely of imports from the Gulf. Indigenous oil production in Europe, principally in the North Sea, continues to increase (due to new and ever more cost-effective recovery techniques), but reserves in the North Sea cannot rival those of the Gulf on which reliance will presumably increase in the coming century.

Over the past twenty years, meanwhile, the Gulf has come to represent a major export market for Europe. The oil booms of the mid-1970s to the early 1980s saw demand for major infrastructure projects take off dramatically. The Gulf markets for consumer goods also saw spectacular growth. For the big defense contractors of Europe, led by Britain and France, the Gulf also was home to serious customers, ones able to pay in hard currency for large quantities of sophisticated weaponry and related training and support programs.

The way in which Europe was able to capitalize on growth markets in the Gulf during the 1980s is illustrated clearly in the trading relationship which developed between the European Community (EC) and the member states of the GCC. In the wake of the oil price hikes after 1973, the balance of trade was initially to the advantage of the GCC, with Europe the net importer. In 1973, exports from the GCC to the EC were valued at $5.8 billion and its imports from the EC at $1.2 billion. By 1982, the GCC states were exporting $28.6 billion-worth of goods to the EC, the vast majority petroleum products, and importing $23 billion-worth of goods in return. In 1983, the trade balance reversed. The value of goods exported from the GCC to Europe dropped to $17.2 billion, while the GCC bill for imports from the EC totalled $21.2 billion.[2] Since this time, the net trade balance has remained in Europe's favor, as Europe has economized on oil consumption, oil prices have declined, and the GCC demand for European imports has remained relatively buoyant.

In 1990, GCC exports to Europe were valued at $13.2 billion and its imports from the EC at $18.1 billion.[3] In November 1995, an official EU communiqué stated:

> Despite a small total population of just over 21 million inhabitants, the GCC is the fifth largest market for EC exports, larger than China and the CIS [Commonwealth of Independent States] and the only one of the five with which the EC has, consistently, an export surplus. Total EC–GCC bilateral trade reached over 30 billion ECU in 1994. EC exports amounted to 19.3 billion ECU and the EC trade surplus was 7.9 billion ECU.[4]

Not surprisingly, the GCC states have sought ways to close this trade gap and the introduction of offset programs, in particular in connection with defense contracts, represents one of the mechanisms for retrieving a proportion of the profits made by the GCC's trading partners.

It is in the defense sector that some of the biggest gains still stand to be made in the Gulf, notwithstanding the ban on selling weapons to either Iraq or Iran which the major Western companies have observed since Iraq's invasion of Kuwait. The value of arms sales deliveries to the GCC states between 1987 and 1990 exceeded $31 billion, while Iraq and Iran between them imported around $24 billion-worth over the same period. Between 1991 and 1994, Iraq bought no arms, Iran managed to acquire

$4 billion-worth, while the GCC took delivery of $32 billion-worth. Orders still in the pipeline take the figures higher by a few billion dollars.

Arms sales across the world have declined since the end of the Cold War, which has made the competition hotter for manufacturers keen to protect their production lines. In the Gulf, the United States has won the lion's share of new orders since the 1991 Gulf War, though 1995 saw France outstrip the USA in sales to the developing world, including the Gulf, with orders worth $11.4 billion compared to $6.1 billion for the USA.[5] The previous year, however, the USA was in the lead with $15.4 billion-worth of contracts while France gained orders worth only $3.8 billion. Since the beginning of the 1990s, the USA, Britain and France have vied for position at the top of the league table of arms exporters, with the USA predominant.

Investment is another facet of Europe's relationship with the Gulf. Collectively, the EU member states constitute the second largest foreign investor in the GCC, ahead of Japan and second only to the USA. By contrast to the USA, whose investments are concentrated in the petro-chemical sector, European holdings in the GCC are spread more evenly across various industrial sectors.[6] Western Europe, in turn, ranks as the second most important destination of GCC external investment, the bulk of which is in the form of portfolio investments in deposits, bonds and equities.

To summarize, Europe's principal interests in the Gulf region are as follows: assured access to oil at reasonable prices; favorable conditions for trade and investment; and the safety of European expatriates living and working there. Pursuit and protection of these interests all demand a level of relative stability and predictability and, as far as possible, the existence of governments well-disposed towards Europe in particular and the West in general. These are the factors which underlie Europe's stake in Gulf security.

As will be apparent, European interests in the Gulf overlap with those of the USA, but are not totally commensurate. Europe and the US are at one in wanting assured access to oil supplies at sustainable prices, yet European oil companies are competitors with their US counterparts for contracts in the Gulf and the Europeans would not wish to find themselves overly dependent on the USA for their access to Gulf oil. Equally, European manufacturers are in competition not only with each other but perhaps more so with the USA in the Gulf consumer and defense markets. In fact, competition with their Western partners is a significant factor in the conduct of individual European powers in the Gulf.

European Bilateral Relations in the Gulf

Of all the European powers, Britain and France stand out as the two with the most weight in matters of Gulf security. Both have a legacy of imperial involvement in the Middle East. Britain in particular was the self-appointed policeman of the Gulf sea-lanes for much of the nineteenth and the better part of the twentieth century, in the process forging protective treaty relations with the Arab Gulf littoral states of Kuwait, Bahrain, Qatar, the Trucial States (from which the United Arab Emirates were formed) and Oman. Britain was also in at the beginning of oil exploitation in Iraq and Iran and, to a lesser extent, on the Arabian peninsula. The French gained a stake in Iraqi oil early on and subsequently a foothold in Iran, though they could not breach the American position in Saudi Arabia in the days before energy nationalization in the Gulf.

Today, in the international competition for service contracts and in some cases in equity stakes in Gulf oil and gas development, the French approach is one of establishing a foothold in multiple locations. In contrast to the French, British oil companies operate less as an arm of national policy and are more clearly commercially driven, though they are bound by the constraints of British government policy. Unlike the French, British companies have been deterred from conducting exploratory discussions with embargoed Iraq, because the British government has adopted a stricter interpretation of UN sanctions legislation. Meanwhile, British Petroleum (BP) and the Anglo-Dutch company Shell are contracted to handle the oil set aside by Saudi Arabia in payment for Britain's Al-Yamamah defense contract with the Kingdom.

Aside from the legacy of their imperial past and continuing stake in the international energy sector, Britain and France retain a position of prominence in international security concerns by virtue of their status, alongside the USA, Russia and China, as permanent members of the UN Security Council. This has special significance in the Gulf context given the role of the UNSC in defining and enforcing the sanctions on Iraq. While now outdistanced by Germany and Japan in terms of their global economic weight, Britain and France have managed to retain and justify their 'P-5' status in part because of the size of their military establishments and relative capability in force projection. In the war to liberate Kuwait, the British and French military commitments ranked second and third to the USA among the non-Arab participants in the coalition. Britain's commitment represented its largest overseas deployment since the Second World War.

As of the end of 1995, Britain's naval and military presence in the Gulf included the three-vessel Armillah Patrol, by then in its fifteenth year of patrolling Gulf waters; six Tornado aircraft and a VC-10 detachment assigned to Operation Southern Watch over southern Iraq; fifteen observers with the UN force on the Iraq–Kuwait border (UNIKOM); and loan-service personnel assigned to GCC states in training roles.[7] In addition, Britain was contributing six Tornado aircraft and ground support, plus a VC-10, to Operation Provide Comfort in northern Iraq. British involvement in joint training exercises with GCC states in 1994 included combined naval and air exercises and one company-level (Royal Marines) exercise with Kuwait and another with Oman.[8]

French deployments to the Gulf in 1994–95 included six Mirage 2000C aircraft and a C-135 assigned to Southern Watch; five Jaguars with Provide Comfort and fifteen observers with UNIKOM. In addition, the French have a naval flotilla, air and amphibious forces assigned to the Indian Ocean, and a base presence at Djibouti.[9] France has also mounted training exercises with GCC forces which complement its defense sales programs. In this connection, France has been more forthcoming than Britain in signing bilateral defense agreements with GCC member states.

Both Britain and France signed ten-year undertakings to Kuwait in 1992, though the wording of Britain's memorandum of understanding is reportedly more circumspect than France's agreement. The latter provides for joint training, exchange of expertise and weapons sales, along with a French commitment to assist Kuwait in the event of an external threat.[10] Britain, meanwhile, has undertaken simply to cooperate with the Kuwaiti Defense Ministry and armed forces in their efforts to defend the territory and sovereignty of the Emirate.[11] Britain's relations with Bahrain, Qatar and the UAE are formalized in Treaties of Friendship dating from the British withdrawal in 1971. Negotiations between Britain and the UAE over a memorandum of understanding on defense were concluded by the end of 1996.[12] France, though, has moved more quickly to establish a defense agreement with the Emirates, which has helped smooth the path for defense sales. The two European players differ in their approaches to such agreements, with the British apparently more cautious about exact undertakings.

British and French competitiveness in the defense sector is another distinguishing characteristic of these two European powers in the Gulf. Britain's largest trading partner in the Middle East is Saudi Arabia. Defense-related exports account for about half of British sales to the Kingdom, which totalled $2.3 billion in 1994.[13] Al-Yamamah, the largest single defense contract won by the UK, directly sustains an estimated 30,000 jobs in Britain and a few thousand more in Saudi Arabia. Initiated in 1985, the deal has included the supply of 120 Tornado aircraft, with 48 still to be delivered, Hawk and PC-9 trainer aircraft, naval equipment and some construction work as well as related service, supply and training contracts. Britain's imports from Saudi Arabia, mostly petroleum products, are running at about half the value of its exports to the Kingdom. Under the UK offset program with Saudi Arabia, five joint companies have been set up and more are planned. Britain has also sold defense equipment to the other GCC member states.

France, as a principal supplier of military equipment to Iraq before the Gulf War, must look to the future to try to recoup some of the debts incurred in the process. Meanwhile, the French have raised their profile in the GCC arms market. In November 1994, France won a contract with Saudi Arabia worth $3.7 billion for two air-defense frigates and provision of shore facilities.[14] This came in the wake of an interim deal, worth $693 million, to overhaul four frigates and two supply vessels sold previously to the Saudis. The same year, Qatar ordered Mirage 2000-5 fighter aircraft from the French, valued at $1.4 billion. In 1995, Kuwait ordered fast patrol boats from France worth $455 million, and the UAE signed a deal worth $235 million for seven Panthère helicopters equipped with S15TT missiles and five Cougar helicopters fitted with Exocet AM39 anti-tank missiles.[15]

While trade outside the defense sector may not constitute a direct contribution to Gulf security, the patterns of European bilateral trade relations in the region play a role in determining the regional balance of power. The commercial connections of individual European countries in the Gulf indicate differing relative interests. The overall trade figures, meanwhile, disguise the importance which Gulf ties hold for certain European industries as well as the significance of particular relationships for the domestic economies of the Gulf trading partners. Germany, for example, is the leading Western trade partner of Iran, while the Saudi defense market is crucial to the fortunes of Britain's defense industrial base.

Britain, France and Germany each export around $5–6 billion-worth of goods to the GCC.[16] Italy's exports to the GCC are somewhat less, but it is in keeping with these other European countries in enjoying a trade surplus with the Arabian peninsula states. Of the four, Britain makes the largest net gain, because, for now, it is less dependent than its fellow Europeans on energy imports.

France and Italy both showed a negative trade balance with Iran in 1994, albeit not substantial. Both suffered significant losses when they had to suspend trade with Iraq. Britain, meanwhile, made a net gain on trade with Iran in 1994, though the amount of trade was also not substantial. Britain's imports from Iran were worth $203 million, as compared to exports to the Islamic Republic valued at $440 million.[17] Clearly, this amount of business pales into insignificance when compared to British sales to Saudi Arabia. Germany is in the forefront of European countries doing business with Iran, with Germany the net beneficiary by a 2:1 ratio in 1994.

To elaborate, in 1994 Germany imported $14 billion-worth of oil, of which 26 per cent came from North Africa and the Middle East, including 7 per cent from Saudi Arabia and 2 per cent from Iran.[18] (Upwards of 17 per cent of German oil imports come from Libya and Algeria.) Overall, German trade with the Gulf reveals a sizeable overall balance in Germany's favor. Imports from the GCC states totalled $1.3 billion in 1994, whereas exports were valued at $5.3 billion. The figures for German–Iranian trade reveal a less substantial imbalance in Germany's favor. German imports from Iran totalled $828 million in 1994, while exports to the Islamic Republic were valued at approximately twice this sum, or $1.6 billion.[19] In isolation, these figures appear favorable, but the trend since the beginning of the decade shows declining German sales figures. Germany's exports to Saudi Arabia have decreased in recent years. Iran used to be much more lucrative for Germany, but recent economic woes in the Islamic Republic have caused a cutback in foreign orders and this has hit Germany most critically, as the leading supplier to the Iranian market.

Italy, more so than Germany, relies heavily on Libya and Algeria for energy supplies, though it too imports some Gulf oil. Before the Gulf War, Italy used to have a valuable export market in Iraq and trade with Iran was more lucrative in the early 1990s than has been the case in 1994–95. Italian exports to Iran, worth $715 million in 1994, were outstripped by its imports from the Islamic Republic, which topped $1 billion. Trade between Italy and the GCC totalled $5.2 billion in 1994, with a surplus in Italy's favour of $2 billion.[20] Italian business in the UAE showed growth in 1994–95, but otherwise the trend has been for diminishing returns from, and interest in, Middle East markets in Italy. For one reason or another, Italian trade with the Middle East and North Africa has taken a toll across the board, given the conflict in Algeria, sanctions on Libya and on Iraq, budgetary restraints plus fierce competition in the GCC states, and financial troubles in Iran, aggravated latterly by US sanctions.

Not including defense sales, in 1994 French exports to the GCC states totalled $3.8 billion, of which $1.4 billion-worth went to Saudi Arabia. French imports from the GCC states, principally petroleum products, were worth $3.2 billion.[21] French sales to Iran, which did not include military equipment, were worth $813 million and imports from the Islamic Republic totalled just over $1 billion.[22] As is apparent, France has to import oil from the Gulf to an extent that Britain – with its North Sea resources – does not. This situation helps to reinforce the French policy of seeking a stake in the oil sector where possible in the region, and the French oil company Total has recently picked up the contract with Iran that the US company Conoco was obliged to drop in response to a US presidential executive order in 1995.

Cooperation and Competition with the USA

An important distinction exists between the strategic interests of the USA and those of Europe in the Gulf region. For the USA, the Gulf represents an important, but also distant, source of oil. To meet its own import requirements, the USA can and increasingly does look to reserves closer to home, as in Latin America and West Africa. For Europe, by contrast, the Gulf is comparatively close-by and can be brought even closer with pipelines to the Mediterranean. Both the USA and Europe share an interest in the free flow of oil world-wide at what they term 'reasonable' prices, but the magnitude of their direct interest in Gulf oil varies in accordance with geographical proximity. Meanwhile, as of mid-1995, when the US government banned its oil companies from buying Iranian oil, US oil imports from the Gulf have come only from the GCC, principally Saudi Arabia, and the actual quantity imported from the Kingdom has dropped somewhat in recent years. By contrast, European companies have continued to buy oil from Iran as well as the GCC, and many have shown an interest in an early resumption of dealings with Iraq in the energy sector.

As viewed from Europe, the US posture in the Gulf as the principal guarantor of GCC external defense, leading enforcer of sanctions on Iraq, and initiator of the embargo on Iran, portends significant consequences for the accessibility of Gulf oil. If the GCC states are favored, in terms of their ability to realize returns on oil exports, at the expense of Iraq and Iran, these two disadvantaged states may seek ways to have their revenge in the long run. Meanwhile, there is some concern in European circles that stability in the Gulf is coming to depend too heavily on US military capability and will. In light of the mood apparent in the US Congress in the mid-1990s, which appears to shun almost any overseas military involvement, the readiness of the USA to sustain casualties in the course of upholding Gulf security, should this prove necessary, cannot be taken for granted.

In the near term, there is also some irritation in Europe at US tactics to curtail the activities of allies in the Gulf. Not only has Congress pursued legislation to penalize foreign companies for doing business with Iran, but pressure has been exercised by the USA on allied governments to the same end. The effect has been to compound lack of confidence in the Iranian economy, thereby making a precarious situation worse. For some European countries, notably Germany, which has too much invested in Iran to turn its back on that country, this is a serious issue.

With regard to Iran, the members of the EU have adopted a unified posture termed 'critical dialogue'. This dates from the EU summit in Edinburgh in 1992. In terms of implementation, Germany has been the most concerned to further dialogue with Tehran in the interests of encouraging moderate or pragmatic elements within the Iranian government. Britain has been more critical, but nevertheless values the overall EU approach to the US boycott for fear of driving the Iranians into a position where they have nothing to lose by being more hostile towards the West. While the German court decision in the so-called 'Hykonos' trial has caused a strain in European– (especially German–) Iranian relations, the set-back is likely to be of a temporary nature, and Europeans and Iranians will continue their dialogue at one level or another.

On Iraq, the European line-up also indicates differences with the USA. On maintenance of the UN sanctions regime, the positions of France and Britain hold special importance because of their membership of the UNSC. Britain adheres to a policy very close to that of the American administration. Fearful that Saddam Hussein and his government can never be trusted, the British regard the sanctions as the best means of containing his power and ambitions. In the months preceding the defection of Hussein Kamal, the sense in Britain was that the sanctions regime represented a policy of diminishing returns, given that pressure to do business with Iraq was bound to increase, in Turkey and Jordan, as well as further afield. Consequently, London showed some interest in devising an orderly way to ease the embargo in due course. With the revelations of Iraq's continuing deceit and secret weapons programs that followed the defection, however, the prognosis in Britain has been that the sanctions must remain in place and in full for the duration of renewed UN inspections in the country. Meanwhile, the limited arrangement for Iraq to sell oil under UN supervision, as outlined in UN Resolution 986 of 1995, to enable the purchase of humanitarian supplies, is considered an acceptable alternative in the interests of relieving suffering among the Iraqi people.

France has taken a somewhat different line over the past two years. Prior to Hussein Kamal's defection and the ensuing revelations of covert Iraqi weapons programs, France was outspoken in demanding an end to sanctions as soon as the UN weapons inspectors pronounced Iraq clear of weapons of mass destruction and long-range missiles. With the concurrence of fellow UNSC members Russia and China, France has held to a strict legal interpretation of UN Resolution 687 of 1991 in this regard. In response to US accusations that Paris was merely acting in the interests of renewing business in Iraq to recoup some of its outstanding debts there, the French have complained that US motives include protection of the GCC oil-producers at Iraq's expense.

More recently, however, France has acquiesced in the view that the discoveries following Hussein Kamal's defection indicate the need for much more work to be done by the UN weapons inspectors before sanctions can be lifted. According to French Foreign Minister Herve de Charette, speaking in Amman in September 1995: 'France considers it up to the Iraqi government to comply with the Security Council Resolutions asking it to take every possible step to make known and where appropriate destroy the means of mass destruction which this country has built up. When these resolutions have been implemented, Iraq will of course regain her place in the international community.'[23] Other Europeans have voiced varying opinions on the situation in Iraq, but basically await developments there and within the Security Council to determine events. Commenting on Italy's position with regard to sanctions, the president of the Italian–Arab Chamber of Commerce, Sergio Marini, told the *Middle East Economic Digest* in July 1995: 'In our opinion the policy of Italy and European countries should be a bit different from what it is. Being too close to the US is not always helpful.'[24]

As will be apparent, the Europeans do aim to maintain a common posture in so far as they can over policy issues affecting the Gulf. However, differences of interest still surface to an extent that is less apparent, for example, in the combined EU approach to the Arab–Israeli peace process. In this context, the EU has been more assertive, in part because it has been expected to provide the largest single share of financial aid to underwrite the peace, while not being granted a direct role, in contrast to the USA, in the political negotiations. In the Gulf, meanwhile, the EU has even less leverage.

The EU–GCC Dialogue

The mechanism of an EU–GCC dialogue was established shortly after the formation of the GCC in 1981 and could represent a vehicle for developing a more innovative approach to Gulf security than the essentially militaristic formula associated with the US presence and 'Dual Containment'. That said, divisions within the EU on the one hand and the GCC on the other have held both back from adopting any really promising initiatives hitherto.

The dialogue was initiated by the GCC in the interests of establishing a free trade agreement with the EC. In 1988, the two arrived at a Cooperation Agreement, which set the scene for trade negotiations to commence in 1990. Since then, however, there has been no progress. Two issues have dominated discussions: first, the inability of the GCC members to establish a full customs union and, second, proposals within the EU to levy a carbon tax. The latter has caused consternation in the GCC, while the former has generated impatience at the EU. However, EU members now claim that a carbon tax is not in the offering, for reasons internal to the EU, while GCC members are pledged to move towards a customs union.

A desire to make headway emerged in July 1995 at the meeting in Granada between the European Troika and GCC ministers. Proposals were made on this occasion for moving the EU–GCC relationship forwards on the political, economic and cultural fronts. At the political level, the intention is to strengthen the bilateral political dialogue. At the economic level, the idea is to increase economic cooperation and find a solution for unblocking the ongoing free trade negotiations. At the cultural level, meanwhile, the goal is to develop instruments of cooperation which will promote increased reciprocal knowledge and understanding, especially in the cultural and scientific fields. A follow-up meeting to Granada was held in Luxembourg in April 1996 but the discussions continue regarding the specific proposals for implementing such recommendations.

Judging by the work in progress at the EU Commission,[25] the hope is to apply to the EU–GCC relationship some of the principles developed in the context of EU relations with Eastern and Central Europe on the one hand and with Mediterranean partner states on the other. In fact, the vision of the 'new Middle East' embodied in the Euro-Mediterranean partnership program, launched at Barcelona in November 1995, and in EU contributions to the Arab–Israeli peace process, requires making links between the Mediterranean and the Gulf. In this regard, Europe is looking to the Gulf states to help underwrite the Middle East peace process.

Regardless of good intentions, however, it remains the case that fundamental differences within both the GCC and the EU still stand in the way of unity on both sides. Meanwhile, the Euro-Mediterranean partnership program has yet to prove its worth and the Arab–Israeli peace process is far from secure. One way or another, therefore, the prospects of the EU–GCC dialogue generating a new and workable formula for Gulf security seem remote.

Conclusions

To conclude, it has to be said that, for the time being, Gulf security is essentially defined by the USA. It is the USA which is providing the military presence to counter-balance the combined strength of Iraq and Iran, in defense of the GCC states. The GCC members, Britain and France are all cooperating in this arrangement, however critical they may be of some of the underlying logic of 'Dual Containment'. Within this context, though, the European role in the Gulf is essentially one of injecting a measure of flexibility and thereby softening what would otherwise be a very uncompromising line by the USA. In this way, the Europeans may be helping to prevent the total alienation of both Iraq and Iran and, in company with various members of the GCC, keeping the lines open for future accommodations to emerge.

CHAPTER 6

The Collapse of the Soviet Union and Gulf Security

Robert V. Barylski

This chapter examines continuity and change in Russian foreign policy towards the Gulf; how the collapse of the Soviet Union altered the larger context in which Gulf states must conduct their diplomacy. It begins with an analysis of the Cold War system in the Middle East, the competitive international system in which the Gulf nations developed into major, independent, oil-exporting states. It demonstrates that the Cold War was neither a tightly disciplined bipolar alliance system nor complete anarchy. It argues that the Soviet Union's fragmentation into 15 sovereign states added to the anarchic quality of the Middle East's state system and discusses post-Soviet Russia's foreign policy priorities and problems. It explains why Moscow evaluates its relations with the Gulf states within a larger framework, a structure in which Russia competes with Turkey, Iran, Pakistan and China for influence in the Caucasus and Central Asia. It also discusses some of Russia's post-Soviet, domestic and near-abroad, Islamic problems.

The Gulf states need to build and sustain an effective alliance that protects their sovereignty, territorial integrity and access to world markets. Knowledge of post-Soviet Russia's priorities and national interests will enhance their ability to understand and to anticipate Russian behavior. Knowledge of the strengths and weaknesses of different types of alliances will help them to avoid a repetition of Kuwait's 1990 tragedy.

Historical Background: Old and New Patterns

The long view of political history provides at least three important insights into the patterns of state competition and alliance formation relevant to Russia's relationships with the Gulf region. First, during most of the twentieth century, Western states in cooperation with various indigenous states organized alliances to prevent Russia from expanding its economic, political and military influence into the Middle East. They argued that the great Eurasian power centered in Moscow was driven by imperial ambition towards warm-water ports on the Gulf and the Indian Ocean. Second, the Western powers usually accepted the Muscovite state's domination of the Caucasus and Central Asia. Their main goal was containment, preventing the Czarist empire and its primary successor, the Soviet Union, from undermining their positions in the Middle East. Third, Russian positions in the Caucasus and Central Asia were challenged during periods of Muscovite state weakness. This happened when the Czarist state collapsed in 1917, when Nazi armies penetrated into south Russia in 1941–42, and when the Soviet state disintegrated in 1991. After these periods of weakness, the Muscovite state revived and re-formed its positions in the Caucasus and Central Asia. Russia is attempting to do that now.

The Cold War System

In the 1950s, when the USA, Great Britain and their Middle Eastern allies built the Central Treaty Organization (CENTO) and supported it with additional confidential alliances and agreements, their primary goal was the 'construction of northern tier defense against Soviet imperialism'. However, from the very outset it was clear that the Middle Eastern alliance system could never be as cohesive as NATO due to the Arab–Israeli problem, traditional competition and rivalry within the region, and mixed attitudes towards the Soviet Union and the Western powers.[1] US policy could not build overt military alliances with the key Arab states unless and until Arab–Israeli tensions were resolved.[2] As a result, CENTO was shaped by ethno-political fault-lines. The alliance system began as the Baghdad Pact; but following the overthrow of the Iraqi monarchy in 1958, Iraq's new, anti-Western republican regime withdrew. As a result, CENTO's anti-Soviet, front-line states were non-Arab: Turkey, Iran and Pakistan.

During the Cold War's second and third decades, 1965–85, the Soviet Union's Middle East policy became a money-making machine for the Kremlin treasury. The machine was driven by managed tensions that eventually resulted in major wars in the Gulf region rather than in the former Palestine. The Soviet state earned billions by selling oil at exceptionally high world prices, a temporary situation caused by OPEC, the Arab–Israeli War of 1973, and events related to the Iranian revolution of

1979. The Kremlin netted additional billions in hard currency by selling arms to anti-Western states. Moscow's preferred military customers were anti-Western states that could afford to pay, namely Iraq and Libya, whose income depended upon energy exports.

Western states also earned billions on arms sales to the Middle East, far more than the Soviet Union. Therefore, there was a certain convergence of Soviet and Western interests in this regard. Both were competing to sell arms and had a stake in keeping their clients politically, economically and militarily viable. Both also used regional wars to test weapons systems. Further, the Soviet Union probably netted less from foreign arms sales than Western estimates. In July 1995, Boris Kuzyk, the head of President Yeltsin's special committee on military cooperation, said the real yield averaged about $2 billion per year in actual hard currency from arms sales rather than the $10 to $15 billion reported in some Western sources.[3]

The money-making machine depended upon a particular architecture of interstate relations and oil market factors. One of its most important political features was the stable southern border of the Soviet Union which stretched from Turkey to China. The Soviet dictatorship kept the territory to the north of the border stable, and CENTO, plus a neutral Afghanistan, maintained stability along the southern side. Further, the West's rather conservative foreign policy habits made it possible for the Soviet Union to take risks. Thus, although Moscow periodically lambasted Turkey, Iran and Pakistan for serving as front-line anti-Soviet states, these states did not meddle or intrigue in either the Soviet Caucasus or Soviet Central Asia as long as the Cold War system remained intact. Further, Afghanistan survived as a stable, neutral zone, friendly towards the Soviet Union but without foreign troops or military alliances. The front line was secure and relatively benign for the Soviet Union.[4]

In 1955–56, the Soviet Union successfully challenged the West's ability to exclude it from the Middle East. Soviet support to Egypt during the Suez crisis confirmed that the Soviet Union could exert influence and make the Western powers do things they otherwise would not have done. In 1955, American intelligence analysts concluded: 'For many years the Western Powers have been able to pursue their interests in the Middle East virtually unhindered by direct Soviet interference. This period is now almost certainly at an end.'[5] From then on, Moscow cultivated relationships which by the 1970s resulted in the money-making machine described earlier, but its actions followed a pattern that went beyond common mercantilism.

The Soviet Union was planting its flag in a pattern that slowly encircled the Gulf states. By the late 1970s, its primary client was Iraq but it also had a foothold in Ethiopia and South Yemen and was working certain elements in Somalia and Sudan. It was also constantly complaining about American naval activity in the Indian Ocean, beating the drums to keep the USA from developing strategic facilities at Diego Garcia, promoting anti-Western nationalism and radical modernization destructive to traditional religious, social and political values. Thus, instead of driving through Turkey or Iran directly towards the Gulf and the Arabian Sea, the Soviet Union was slowly surrounding the Gulf, cultivating relationships and building influence. As early as 1956, American intelligence analysts described this Soviet strategy well when they said Moscow 'was hopping over the Northern Tier line'.[6]

Seven Key Events that Destroyed the Cold War System

Seven key events destroyed the Cold War system and replaced it with a loose American-led alliance aimed primarily at preventing indigenous states from making war upon one another: the April 1978 revolution in Afghanistan; the Iranian revolution of 1979; the Soviet military intervention in Afghanistan; the American proclamation of the Carter Doctrine in January 1980; the Iran–Iraq War of 1980–88; the Gulf War of 1990–91; and the collapse of the Soviet Union in 1991.

At first, the Soviet Union appeared to be headed for a major victory: the collapse of the American-led, anti-Soviet alliance system in the Middle East and south-west Asia. In 1979–80, Moscow was looking at a huge breach in the Western alliance system, a chance to expand its influence in a southerly direction. However, a little over a decade later, the Soviet Union had collapsed and its primary successor, Russia, was trying to recover its losses. By 1991 and 1992, it was the south that was marching towards Moscow. The tables had turned and Russia was scrambling to restore the old Soviet defense perimeter along the former southern borders of the defunct Soviet Union.

The Soviet Union's Disintegration

The Soviet political system disintegrated rapidly after January 1991. The Union dissolved itself in December 1991 in three meetings. The first attempted to establish a Slavic, triple alliance of Russia, Ukraine and

Belarus.[7] The second drew the Central Asian states together as a natural grouping of Islamic heritage republics. During the meeting, charges were swapped, one of which found the Islamic state representatives soundly condemning their 'Slavic brothers' for promoting interethnic discord. The third meeting took place in Alma Ata, the capital of Kazakhstan, and proclaimed the Commonwealth of Independent States (CIS) on 21 December 1991. Six new sovereign states of Islamic heritage – Azerbaijan, Kazakhstan, Kyrgyzstan, Tajikistan, Turkmenistan and Uzbekistan – entered the world community and began searching for ways to increase relations with the greater Islamic community to the south. Three – Azerbaijan, Kazakhstan and Turkmenistan – hoped to become major energy exporters. Two – Azerbaijan and Tajikistan – became the object of intensive political competition and experienced civil war and interethnic conflict.

Post-Soviet Russia had two primary foreign policy goals of direct interest to the Gulf states. First, Moscow gave highest priority to the restoration of economic and defense relations with the 14 former Soviet republics which it called its near-abroad. Moscow focused on building a sphere of influence in the near-abroad and on restoring and stabilizing its military position along the southern borders of the former Soviet Union.[8] Moscow was struggling to prevent the USA, Turkey, Iran, Pakistan, China and others from planting flags in the Caucasus and Central Asia. The six newly independent states of Islamic heritage entered the international system and began developing relationships with the greater Islamic world. However, all remained within Russia's sphere of influence to some extent, and Russia implemented a 'dual containment' policy of its own. Second, Russia, as the main legal successor to the Soviet Union, tried to collect debts owed to the Soviet Union by former clients, to rebuild and diversify its client base for weapons sales, and to expand commercial relationships in the greater Middle East.

Russia's 'Dual Containment' Policy

The first time the multinational Russian state broke down was 1917–21. At that time, Moscow took effective action to prevent Turkey from expanding into the Caucasus and Central Asia. It was relatively simple to contain Turkey as Kemal Ataturk had no Western allies. Moscow moved its armies into the Caucasus and overthrew the independent governments of Georgia, Armenia and Azerbaijan, and converted them into Soviet republics under communist rule. Turkey's window of opportunity closed rapidly as the Bolsheviks strengthened their position in the former Czarist empire and built a massive army which peaked at some 5.5 million personnel under arms in the mid-1920s.

Moscow overthrew the fledgling Democratic Republic of Azerbaijan (DRA) which had been formed with Turkish support in 1918.[9] The DRA's leaders were sitting in Bolshevik gaols precisely at the time that the communists held their famous Baku revolutionary congress which called upon the 'peoples of the East' to overthrow colonialism. But Stalin was toying with pan-Turkism and hoped to use it as a shield against Great Britain. Stalin saw Anglo–Soviet competition in the South as the successor to traditional Anglo–Russian competition for empire.[10] He assumed that the British would attempt to take control over Russian Turkestan (Central Asia). The Soviet tool in this adventure was supposed to be Enver Pasha, the former Turkish Minister of War. In 1920, the Bolsheviks invited him to Baku but refused to let him address the great Baku congress. The public, the bazaar and street crowds cheered him in spite of Stalin's efforts to keep him under tight control. Enver Pasha decided to strike out on his own and led an anti-communist, pan-Turkic rebellion in Central Asia. Enver Pasha was killed by Red detachments in what is now Tajikistan on 4 August 1922. His rebel armies peaked at some 20,000 before dwindling into scattered detachments. Other, small-scale, anti-Soviet rebellions operated sporadically across the Soviet–Iranian and Soviet–Afghan borders until the early 1930s. Tajik and Uzbek anti-communist refugees, including traditional leaders such as the deposed Emir of Bukhara, settled in Afghanistan.[11]

Moscow decided to seek an accommodation with Ankara. Lenin's Russia and Kemal Ataturk's Turkey agreed upon a new border in the Caucasus. The two powers pledged cooperation and, in order to cement the deal, the Soviet government gave Turkey military and financial assistance which Soviet sources place at 40,000 rifles, 60 million cartridges, 327 machine guns, 10 million gold roubles, and 200.6 kg of gold in bars.[12] Therefore, Ankara did not support Enver Pasha's anti-Soviet rebellion.

Moscow also decided to support stability in Iran after initially giving aid to national liberation movements in the Czar's traditional sphere of influence in north-western Iran, especially in Azeri-inhabited regions.[13] Bolshevik strategists decided to withdraw from Iran in order to consolidate a *modus vivendi* with Great Britain that was designed to stabilize the southern borders of the Soviet Union. The agreements included a Bolshevik pledge to leave Afghanistan neutral and to refrain from pushing overtly against British interests in Iran and India. Thus, by 1922, Moscow had stabilized its southern frontiers and Soviet supremacy in the Caucasus and Central Asia was not challenged by the Turkish, Iranian or British authorities. The Communist International continued to condemn colonialism but the Soviet state's official policy was quite respectful of Great Britain's sphere of influence. Soviet state interests benefited from stability in the south, and Britain helped to provide that stability.

At the time of the Czarist empire's collapse, the young Turkish state was isolated and needed Russia. When the Soviet Union collapsed, the Republic of Turkey was a NATO member and an American ally. In the 1920s, Great Britain was the primary Western power in the Middle East. In the 1990s, the USA played that role and Moscow expected American military power to help keep the Middle East stable. However, it was unhappy with the lack of American support for the Russian desire to exercise historical claims to a definite sphere of influence in the Caucasus and Central Asia. Russians also noticed that the corporations making the biggest investments in Caspian basin oil (Azerbaijan and Kazakhstan) were primarily from Britain and the US, their traditional rivals in the Middle East.

In the twenty-first century, Russia will probably continue to adopt a defensive, containment strategy aimed at Turkey primarily and Iran secondly.[14] Currently that policy is to block Turkish aspirations in the greater Caspian region while being far more cooperative with Iran. This stems from three sources. First, Russia seeks to block Turkey from the Caucasus and the Caspian. Its natural allies in this strategic game are Armenia and Iran.[15] From 1991 to 1993, Armenians captured territory from Turkic Azerbaijan and thickened the Armenian buffer that stands between Turkey and Azerbaijan. Neither Iran nor Russia took any effective action to reverse Armenia's gains. But since neither Moscow nor Iran wished to endorse the practice of using military force to revise internationally recognized boundaries, the Armenians in Azerbaijan found it expedient to call themselves the independent Republic of Nagorno Karabagh rather than an integral part of Armenia. Turkey criticized Russian policy but was careful not to cross the line between open competition with Russia and direct conflict. For its part, Moscow was resigned to a competitive relationship with Ankara but also wanted to keep it within bounds.[16]

Iran is concerned about its political integrity because there are twice as many Azeris living in Iran as in the Republic of Azerbaijan. This situation is geographically referred to as Northern and Southern Azerbaijan in Azeri circles. The first post-communist government in Azerbaijan

(1992–93) was led by Abulfaz Elchibey, a nationalist who advocated a closer association between Northern Azerbaijan, Southern Azerbaijan and Turkey. His private comments were very candid on this subject although his public remarks were more circumspect. Elchibey's desire for a Turkic entente between Turkey, Northern Azerbaijan and Southern Azerbaijan quite predictably drew Russia and Iran closer together.[17] Elchibey's successor, Heydar Aliyev, adopted a more balanced approach and sought good relations with Turkey, Iran and Russia. He tried to prevent Russia from achieving a dominant position in Azerbaijan.

Russia and Iran also share a common interest in stability in Central Asia and in the stability of the region's post-Soviet political borders. A continued Russian presence in the region gives Iran comfort in that Russian influence helps prevent Turkey from expanding into those Turkic regions. Given the large Turkic Azeri minority in Iran, any government in Tehran should share Russia's interest in limiting Turkey's ambitions. Similarly, Russia and Iran share an interest in preventing the civil war in Afghanistan from destabilizing Central Asia. Iran certainly does not need trouble in its north-east while it still feels threatened from Iraq and from domestic Turkic nationalism. Therefore, Iran has generally played a constructive role and has encouraged the parties in the civil war in Tajikistan to seek a political settlement.

Moscow has argued that the United States is motivated by 'great power' jealousy and mercantile greed when it objects to Russian military and nuclear reactor technology sales to Iran. It points out that these are very modest when compared to what President Jimmy Carter agreed to in 1978 when America and Iran were allies. The Russian litany of complaints at US policies in the region usually begins with the CIA plot to overthrow the Mossadeq government in 1953 and continues to the present with President Clinton's arm-twisting to prevent Russia from selling Iran arms and nuclear technology. Since Carter was willing in 1978 to support the development of a nuclear industry in Iran, a country rich in oil and which regularly allowed huge amounts of natural gas to burn freely, Russia argues that it should currently be able to sell nuclear reactor technology to Iran.[18] Such chiding gives vent to accumulated resentment towards the world's leading power: 'Washington should realize that Russia is not going to sacrifice its interests and good relations with neighbors to please America, and second, that Russia has no desire whatever to join in the US policy of "containing" this or that country (a policy well familiar to Russia) let alone in attempts to overthrow that country's government.'[19] But Russia has and will continue to play containment and balance of power games of its own. It would be a serious mistake to allow emotion to cause a misunderstanding of the geo-political game in progress. Moscow has concrete interests at stake and is protecting them. In the 1990s, Moscow was actively containing Turkey, preventing Azerbaijan from developing its domestic oil industry freely, and pressuring Azerbaijan to bend its foreign policy to serve Russia's national interests. When containment serves those interests, Russia contains. When non-interference in the internal affairs of countries serves those interests, Russia does not interfere. When regime stability is important, Russia supports the regime. When and if regime change becomes important, Russia can be expected to assist the shift of power.

The Gulf states sit on the underside of the competition between Russia, Turkey and Iran and should expect Moscow to give highest priority to Russian interests in the Caucasus and Caspian region. The tripartite competition should continue into the twenty-first century but the leverage Moscow exerts could change depending upon whether Turkey or Iran appears more threatening to Russian interests at any given time. Iraq is also part of the regional state system and an important element in the balance of power. As a general rule, Russia will want to prevent any anti-Russian coalition from developing along its southern borders and will behave in ways that discourage Turkey, Iraq and Iran from challenging Russia's position in the greater Caspian region. If Russia's 'balancing' activities effectively check the regional aspirations of any state, it can enhance the security of the Gulf's smaller states by preventing that state from becoming a hegemonic power.

Russian–Iranian cooperation demonstrates that Moscow and Tehran can prevent ideological differences from undermining diplomatic strategies when state interests are sufficiently important. However, Moscow did not endorse the late Ayatollah Khomeini's general international political goals. It accepted Iran's right to develop its internal political system in keeping with Khomeini's ideas, but it rejected Iranian efforts to export political revolution into neighboring states.[20] The governments of the former Soviet republics of Islamic heritage adopted similar policies.

Democracy and Russian National Interests

During the Soviet period, Moscow propagated an authoritarian, socialist, modernizing ideology which clashed with the traditional Islamic culture and values of the Middle East. Post-Soviet Russia's attitude towards the domestic politics of other states should be more pragmatic and less ideological. However, the Russian state's movement towards democratic governmental processes does not eliminate the Kremlin's need to be interested in the domestic and foreign policies of the states of Islamic heritage in the Caucasus, Central Asia and the Middle East. In fact, the advent of Russian democracy tends to strengthen nationalist influence in Russian foreign policy. Groups seeking to unseat the ruling party will tend to criticize its foreign policy. For example, in the immediate post-Soviet period, the Yeltsin administration initially followed Gorbachev's pro-Western foreign policy orientation. However, during 1992, the Yeltsin government adjusted this policy somewhat when it noticed that the Russian electorate agreed with nationalist critics who argued that the Kremlin needed to assert Russian national interests more aggressively.

During the December 1993 legislative election campaign, Vladimir Zhirinovsky, the head of the Liberal Democratic Party of Russia, stirred ethno-national passions by urging Russians to reassert control over the Caucasus and Central Asia as part of a grand imperial scheme. Zhirinovsky's campaign revived the idea that it was Russia's destiny to extend its sphere of influence to the Arabian Sea. In a bombastic political booklet published in 1993, *The Final Thrust to the South*, Zhirinovsky argued that the great powers should divide the world into spheres of influence and that Russia's should include Afghanistan, Iran and Turkey.[21] His primary target was Turkey and Pan-Turkic ambitions. But he also called for the weakening of Iran by setting up separate governments for the Kurds, the Belouch and other minorities. Zhirinovsky imagined a future transportation hub centred on Moscow with the following spokes: Moscow–Delhi, Moscow–Kabul, Moscow–Indian Ocean Port, Moscow–Tehran, Moscow–Baghdad and Moscow–Ankara.[22] And he envisioned Russian as the language of interethnic communication in this Russian empire.

Zhirinovsky's party received the largest percentage of the popular vote in the December 1993 elections. However, in the December 1995 parliamentary elections, his chief rivals, the reformed communists, emerged as the most popular party with twice as many votes. They ran on a 'Strong Russia' platform, but their foreign policy goals concentrated on restoring economic and defense relations with the former Soviet republics. Russia Our Home, the political party supporting the Yeltsin administration, came in third. After the December 1995 elections, Yeltsin replaced Foreign Minister Andrei Kozyrev with Yevgeny Primakov. The personnel change had two purposes. First, it was a signal that Yeltsin was responding to popular discontent with Kozyrev who was closely associated with pro-Western policies. Second, it indicated that Russia would focus more diplomatic energy on the former Soviet republics, the greater Caspian region and the Middle East. Primakov is an expert on the Caucasus and Middle Eastern affairs.

Russia's Domestic and International Islamic Problem

Zhirinovsky represented an extreme version of a traditional Russian foreign policy goal, one rooted in the history of the Russian state and its extension into the Islamic world. Czars, general secretaries and presidents have defended and will continue to defend Russia's territorial integrity and Russian economic and security interests in the Caucasus and Central Asia. Dictatorship and the Cold War served these goals by preventing Soviet 'citizens' of Islamic heritage from demanding independence, and by isolating them from the global Islamic community. Russia is continuing to use dictatorship for that purpose. Although the Russian Federation became a democracy of sorts, Yeltsin's government did not insist that the newly independent states in the Caucasus and Central Asia also adopt democratic forms of government for two reasons. First, Russian strategic thinkers associated domestic political competition with anarchy and instability and they wanted stability in the Caucasus and Central Asia. Second, they feared that open political competition for power in that region would give anti-Russian nationalists a chance to take power. Therefore, in the twenty-first century, even a democratic Russia will, for reasons of state, sometimes prefer authoritarian and semi-authoritarian states in the Caucasus, Central Asia and parts of the Middle East, much as the United States did in Mexico, Central America and the Caribbean during much of the nineteenth and twentieth centuries.[23]

The Islamic world reaches into the Russian Federation, and the potential political radicalization of Russian citizens of Islamic heritage is of concern to Moscow. Competition between Slavic Christians and Turkic Muslims for wealth, power and territory is part and parcel of the history of the Russian state. Although the Czars presented themselves as the heads of an Orthodox Christian state, they were also Eurasian despots who ruled a vast, multinational and multiconfessional state. It was in their interest to prevent a general political division between Muslims and Christians, but they also practised a traditional divide-and-conquer policy. At times this set Christians against Muslims, at other times it was Muslim against Muslim or Christian against Christian. In the Caucasus, the Muscovite Czars exploited traditional enmity between Christian Armenians and

Islamic Turks. However, in Central Asia, they worked the traditional rivalries within Islamic Turkic groups and between Turkic and Persian Tajik communities. In fact, the current civil war in Tajikistan is at least partly a battle to determine whether Tajiks will finally break the Turkic Uzbek group's grip on their republic's political life. Further, clan and regional political competition adds to the ethnic struggle's complexity.[24]

Therefore, although it is possible to theorize about a grand, anti-Slavic, Islamic jihad arising in a great wave stretching from Turkey to western China, the real political world is quite fragmented and competitive. Each region has its specific political features and there is no solid foundation for any general unified jihad against Russia in the Caucasus and Central Asia unless the Russians themselves forget the lessons of history. The region's natural ethno-political and clan fault-lines provide ample opportunity for Russian diplomacy to implement a strategy of checks and balances. Similarly, pan-Turkish ideology has limited appeal and several centers are competing for Turkic loyalties. The Central Asian peoples of Turkic extraction have not been involved with the Anatolian Turks for hundreds of years and have their own national and regime interests. The former Soviet republic of Uzbekistan is the most populous state in Central Asia (22 million), has Central Asia's largest city, Tashkent, and can claim a glorious imperial heritage of its own: Timurlane's empire and historic Samarkand. Thus, modern Uzbek nationalists can view themselves as the natural successors to Timur and the natural leaders of Central Asia. Such Uzbek nationalism is a natural antidote to any efforts by Turkey or Iran to draw Central Asia into their spheres of influence.

Nevertheless, Russia has a Muslim problem embedded in the ethnographic composition of the Russian state and the states along its southern borders. Beginning with Gorbachev's January 1990 decision to use troops against the citizens of Baku who had all but overthrown Azerbaijan's communist regime, and extending to Yeltsin's deployment of some 40–50,000 troops and armed police against the Chechen rebellion, most of the deaths caused by politically-motivated, armed conflict in the former Soviet Union have involved peoples of Islamic heritage. The 1990 events, which the Azeris call Black January, cost some 200 lives and constituted the most significant, state-directed violence against civilians of the entire Gorbachev era.[25] The head of the Islamic communities of the Caucasus, Sheikh Ali Pasha-Zade, criticized Gorbachev for using the military against Azeri demonstrators and raised questions about his ability to evaluate events in the Islamic community properly.[26] The sense that Moscow was engaging in violent yet avoidable confrontations with peoples of Islamic heritage was widespread among Communist Party members in Azerbaijan. Their theoretical journal warned Moscow to examine its prejudices and to learn to deal with the region's politics without resorting to extreme measures based upon distorted ideas about Muslims in general.[27]

The fact that the West reacted very mildly to the killings in Azerbaijan, but gave substantial attention to Soviet oppression in the Baltic republics where the loss of life was less than one-tenth as great, suggested that the West operated a double standard in its policies towards the former Soviet Union. Initially, the more European of the former Soviet republics enjoyed greater sympathy from the West in the struggle for national independence than did the more southern, Islamic republics. Some Russian analysts argued that the West should support Moscow because it was holding the line against Islamic extremism. This line of thinking applied to Foreign Minister Kozyrev's appeals for Western support to help pay the cost of Russian peacekeeping efforts along the Tajikistan–Afghanistan border.[28]

Russian policy-makers understood that they needed political allies of Islamic heritage in order to be successful at preventing anti-Russian forces from attempting to reduce Russian dominance in its 'security zone' in the Caucasus and Central Asia. Post-Soviet Russia's first two Foreign Ministers, Andrei Kozyrev and Yevgeny Primakov, rejected simplistic, anti-Islamic thinking, and tried to implement a foreign policy strategy rooted in traditional Russian *realpolitik*.[29] Russia would use military power if necessary to prevent radicals from exploiting ethnic and religious differences that could cut deeply into the Russian Federation's political integrity.[30] And, although Russia preferred to resolve problems peacefully, it understood that tests of strength were inevitable. This conceptual framework was evident in President Yeltsin's November 1992 warning: 'They are trying to drag people into a grand adventure. They are counting on spreading fratricidal conflict into the neighboring republics of the North Caucasus in order to pull all of South Russia into its orbit.'[31] The 'they' in Yeltsin's remarks referred to anti-Russian nationalists of Islamic heritage who were inspired more by Turkey than Iran. During his 1996 election campaign Yeltsin charged Turkey with supporting the Chechen rebellion and quipped that 'the Turks have always threatened us'.[32]

The Russian Foreign Ministry made certain that its diplomatic missions informed Islamic states in the Middle East and south-west Asia that Russia's actions in the north Caucasus and Tajikistan were related to specific security situations and were not a general attack on Islam. Deputy Foreign Minister Viktor Posuvalyuk reaffirmed this point on the eve of an increase in military involvement and fighting in Tajikistan. Posuvalyuk explained that Islam was the religious faith of a significant part of Russia's population, and that it was protected and respected in democratic Russia. He further stated that Russia would develop positive working relations with the full range of Islamic-heritage states in the Middle East. Nevertheless, Russia would take effective action against 'attempts to exploit Islam for political purposes', especially when such activity affects 'the territorial integrity, sovereignty, and security of Russia'.[33]

Not all Russia's domestic Islamic political–administrative issues were being settled by war. The most important Islamic-heritage area, Tatarstan (the historic seat of the Golden Horde which once subjugated the princes of Moscow), has survived as an autonomous republic within the Russian Federation. In February 1994, after three years of political haggling, the federal government in Moscow and the republic's government in Kazan signed treaties and agreements defining the separation of powers between the Russian Federation and Tatarstan.[34] The Russian Federation (pop. 150 million) recognized that one of its 89 *subyekty* or member states, Tatarstan (pop. 3.75 million), was a special case with the right to define its powers in a formal treaty. Tatarstan will not be permitted to act as a sovereign state in the international community, but it will be able to make autonomous economic and cultural agreements with sovereign states. President Mintimer Shaymiyev demonstrated Tatarstan's special status by negotiating significant international economic agreements, including US export-import bank loans.[35] In April 1996, President Yeltsin selected President Shaymiyev to serve as his primary negotiator with the Chechen rebellion's leader, 'President' Djokhar Dudayev.

The case of Tatarstan is a reminder that modern Russia has its roots in the multinational Russian empire which never actually achieved the status of 'nation-state'. For this reason, Russia is different from other world powers and in terms of ethnic/national identities more resembles Turkey, Iran and Iraq than it does the USA, France or Germany. Modern states that are not nation-states understand certain regime interests and state interests rooted in their multinational character. Such states have chronic problems with political and territorial integrity which avoid easy solutions.

Russia put military power behind the defense of its state integrity and made the North Caucasian military district the new home for powerful military forces that had to be withdrawn from Germany and the Baltic republics following the disintegration of the USSR. This North Caucasian military build-up required changes to the Conventional Forces in Europe (CFE) agreements, which were signed in 1991 by NATO and Warsaw

Pact member states. Turkey understandably objected to Russia's military realignments. However, Russian military leaders were adamant, and warned that Russia would break the CFE Treaty if the Western powers refused to accept modifications. Deputy Chief of Staff, Colonel General Vladimir Zhurbenko, gave public interviews on the subject, and Russian diplomats pressed the case privately with the Western powers.[36] After his October 1995 talks with President Clinton, Boris Yeltsin announced that the USA would reinterpret the CFE Treaty in order to accommodate Russia's concerns.

The Chechen war of 1994 to 1996 was a domestic Russian policy failure. It was one thing to place large military inventories and conventional armed forces in the region between the Black and Caspian seas, it was quite another to defeat the drive for independence launched by the Chechen people in 1991. For three years, Yeltsin undertook a variety of covert actions aimed at toppling the secessionists. When he finally decided to use force in December 1994, Yeltsin's military and defense leadership failed to prepare properly and nearly lost the initial campaign. Federal troops were reluctant to use lethal force against fellow Russian Federation citizens. Russia's senior military officers, including Minister of Defense Pavel Grachev, regarded the war as yet another sign that the civilian leaders were incompetent to manage the nation's affairs properly. Significant hostilities took place from December 1994 to May 1995. In December 1995, the Russian Ministry of Defense reported that about 2000 Russian military personnel had been killed in the Chechen war.[37] No reliable numbers for rebel deaths were available. As is often the case, civilians were the main victims of the war with over 20,000 killed, including many ethnic Russians. The war severely damaged Grozny, the regional capital, and did enormous damage to Chechnya's infrastructure, but it did not defeat the rebels. The rebels used the intermittent cease-fires to return to, and strengthen their positions within, the villages, towns and cities.

The war damaged Russia's image in the Middle East, and inhibited Russia's efforts to improve economic, political and military relations with Middle Eastern states whose general populations followed the Chechen struggle for independence with great interest. Formally it was referred to as an internal minority problem, a campaign by federal government forces against regional separatists. The Yeltsin administration presented the war as a conflict between authorities and 'illegal armed formations', rather than a religious war between Christians and Muslims, or an ethnic war between Chechens and Russians. But the rebels invoked Islam and ethnic survival and the world press picked up those themes even though the rebel leader, Djokhar Dudayev, was a former Soviet air force general. Dudayev, who had been indoctrinated in the secular, Soviet system, was certainly not a traditional Islamic leader. Virtually all the parties directly involved in the battle were citizens of the Russian Federation except for a small number of internationalist volunteers and mercenaries. The latter included Chechen returnees from Turkey and the Near East, some anti-Russian nationalists from western Ukraine and Latvia, some veterans of the Afghan jihad, an undetermined number of pan-Turkic Grey Wolves, and some fighters from other Islamic regions of the Caucasus.

How could such a diverse group of fighters make their way into Russian territory? The question points to one of Russia's main security problems, the lack of properly defined and defended state borders. While Russia was safely tucked away in the Soviet Union, it was protected by Soviet borders which were really the external borders of Georgia, Armenia, Azerbaijan, Turkmenistan, Uzbekistan, Tajikistan, Kyrgyzstan and Kazakhstan. Post-Soviet Russia sought military agreements with all eight former Soviet republics that stretch along the southern border of the former Soviet Union from the Black Sea to China. By early 1995, all had accepted but Azerbaijan.[38] Such border agreements give Russia a direct role in the defense of the line which Russian policy-makers see as the southern extent of Russia's sphere of immediate security interest. Further, Russia negotiated military base rights agreements in Georgia and Armenia, and Armenian troops have participated with their Russian counterparts in joint military exercises. This Russian activity was clearly designed to suppress pan-Turkic nationalists. Russia is determined to prevent Turkey from displacing it in the Caucasus, the Caspian and Central Asia. As previously mentioned, Iran shares the same national interest.

The Greater Middle East and Russia's Holding Strategy

The Middle East's alliance system never achieved the level of discipline found in Europe (on both sides) during the Cold War; yet it did provide some order and stability. When Iraq was aligned with the then Soviet Union, and Iran and the Gulf States were aligned with the USA, a loose bipolar alliance system maintained a peace in the greater Gulf region. The USA and the Soviet Union had sufficient influence in the region to prevent serious conflict. As the Cold War wound down, the conflict management effect of bipolar competition in the region was no longer able to dominate the dynamics of interstate disputes, and the two great powers faced an increasingly anarchic regional system.

However, a non-Cold War event, the Iranian revolution, is the most evident and proximate cause of the breakdown of stability in the Gulf. In 1979, Tehran condemned both the USA and the Soviet Union, and actively sought a new regional system based upon an ideological community centered in Iran. The Iran–Iraq War soon followed. The Soviet Union temporized, supporting Western efforts to contain the Iranian revolution while leaving diplomatic bridges standing between Moscow and Tehran. Once the war was over, it became clear that Soviet and American policies were diverging towards Turkey, Iran and Iraq. American 'Dual Containment' was aimed at Iraq and Iran. Russian 'Dual Containment' was primarily aimed at Turkey and secondarily at Iran.[39] Further, Russian policy-makers attempted to expand relations with Gulf states that had been staunchly anti-communist during the Cold War for three reasons. First, Russia wanted to prevent anti-communism from becoming 'anti-Russianism' in the post-Cold War era. Second, Russia wanted to increase economic and commercial relations with the oil-rich Gulf states, including the sale of arms. Third, by supporting the territorial integrity, independence and political stability of the Gulf states, Russia enhanced its own security because the greater Gulf region is immediately south of the greater Caspian region.

The Soviet Union began promoting interdependence and power-balancing as the foundations for 'New Thinking' in foreign policy after Gorbachev took power in 1985. Though the trends had appeared earlier, Gorbachev and Soviet Foreign Minister Edvard Shevardnadze accelerated the rate of change. In 1987, the Soviet Union agreed to put Kuwaiti shipping under Soviet protection when the USA was hesitating to make that commitment. Moscow policy-makers supplied Iraq with weapons but were more positive towards Iran than was the USA, and they positioned the Soviet Union to cultivate the Iranian market as soon as the war ended in 1988. By rejecting Soviet Cold War, two-camp thinking, Gorbachev successfully expanded the Soviet role in the Gulf region and made it possible for the Soviet Union to begin working to mutual advantage with traditional states. Moscow's plan was to expand its markets and to offer itself as an additional security insurance policy, a constructive addition to the regional security system. This core idea survived the collapse of the Soviet Union, the transfer of power from Gorbachev to Yeltsin, and remains the central concept for Russian policy towards the Middle East and the Gulf.

The new Russian strategy has met with some success in the Gulf. In 1994, Kuwait hoped to enhance its security by improving relations with

Russia. Moscow offered to use its diplomatic influence in Baghdad to help resolve outstanding issues between Kuwait and Iraq. At the same time, Kuwait decided to place some $700 million in defense orders with Russia. Russia's Deputy Foreign Minister for Middle Eastern Affairs, Viktor Posuvalyuk, described this cooperation as a typical example of the positive role Russia intended to play in the region, one linked to concrete Russian national interests. He argued that Moscow was working harder than others, meaning the USA, to restore Iraq to a more normal position in the international system of states. Russia's material interest in Iraq is well known and Posuvalyuk's candid mercantilism increased his credibility. Russia argued that the Western powers led by the USA wanted to keep the Middle East's markets for themselves. The Cold War had gone but the competition was still there. The old anti-Western language fitted the new Soviet diplomacy like comfortable old clothing.[40] Russia competed with the West in the Middle East before the communist revolution, during the communist period, and after the fall of communism. Indeed, competition is inherent in the structure of the international state system. Russia and the West will continue to compete in the Middle East for the foreseeable future.

Russia lost world market share from 1990 to 1992 because of domestic political instability, and an overly Western-leaning foreign policy orientation. During 1992, Russian strategic thinkers recovered from their infatuation with Atlanticism and rediscovered traditional national interests. The Yeltsin administration stepped up efforts to rebuild its markets. It attempted to recover lost positions, and to gain entry into markets traditionally dominated by Western firms. Thus, Moscow sought to revive foreign military sales in the Arab world from Algeria to Egypt, and from Syria to Iraq. Russia was determined to enhance its military, political and particularly economic relations with the GCC states. Was Russia provoking a new Middle Eastern arms race? Would Russian sales create new imbalances and insecurities in order to generate more business? Moscow's diplomats denied such charges and insisted that arms would be sold on a 'balanced basis' without injury to the security of third parties.[41]

In January 1993, Russia's Minister of Defense Grachev toured the Gulf in advance of Russia's participation in the upcoming international arms show in Abu Dhabi. Grachev explained Russian policy goals as follows: 'The goal of Russia's military–technical relations with the UAE and other countries of the Gulf is to guarantee the region's peaceful development, to strengthen security and stability. Russia will develop these ties in a measured, balanced way and will not permit their utilization to the detriment of regional security.'[42] At the Abu Dhabi arms show, Grachev candidly explained that Russia was very interested in sales to help finance the Russian defense industry which had suffered a dramatic decrease in state defense orders.[43] Russians returned home with some contacts but had few hard sales to announce. They complained that the new Russian state was still hampered by Soviet bureaucratic incompetence and a government that did not know how to support its military–industrial complex's international marketing efforts. Further, officials with purchasing authority in the Gulf were unwilling to make long-term, substantive commitments to Russian military hardware and technical support because they were convinced that Russia was unstable. It would not be prudent to tie one's national security to an unstable state.[44] However, Grachev's contacts led to some sales and to improved relations with the Gulf states whose leaders became more comfortable with the new Russian military.

Political instability and administrative clumsiness have continued to hamper Russian sales as evidenced at the 1995 Abu Dhabi show.[45] Some analysts complained that Russia's decision to sell several older submarines to Iran had prompted Gulf states to place $1.5 billion-worth of anti-submarine system orders with Western firms, far more than Russia had gained from selling the subs.[46] In theory, Russia could become a major weapons exporter. Its main practical obstacles are domestic, Russia's political instability and ineffective central government. Russia has persisted and continues to cultivate its new contacts. On 8 May 1995, Minister of Defense Grachev and Deputy Minister of Foreign Affairs Posuvalyuk invited the Moscow representatives of the Gulf Cooperation Council to a special meeting. At the meeting, Grachev expressed Russia's support for the work of the GCC to enhance regional security and stability and to improve relations with Russia. Russia was following up on Grachev's diplomatic tour earlier in the year and on Russia's marketing efforts at the Abu Dhabi arms show in hopes of expanding arms sales and building stronger political relations.[47]

Russia's post-Soviet encounter with the Gulf states is not limited to selling arms. Russia has been working on plans for domestic economic development and is attempting to revitalize its once quite large energy export industry. Russia thought it would be prudent to discuss investment opportunities in Russia with Gulf colleagues who understood the energy industry, to include the developing global energy market. To head the discussions, they chose Prime Minister Viktor Chernomyrdin, an ex-perienced Soviet energy executive who had negotiated scores of joint projects with a wide range of foreign private and state partners.

Chernomyrdin toured the Gulf in November 1994. It was natural for Gulf investors to diversify their portfolios through participation in Russian area energy development projects. Oman took a substantial position (50 per cent) in the first major pipeline, the key link between Kazakhstan's largest oil fields and the Russian Black Sea ports.[48] In theory, the Russian state's massive oil and gas monopolies could spin off a number of integrated oil firms that could compete with the major Western multinationals which currently dominate the international oil industry.[49] However, in the energy field as in arms production and sales, Russian domestic political instability has impeded progress.

In thinking about Gulf security over the coming decades, planners should consider a scenario in which the Russian state recovers economically and politically from the initial weakening caused by the collapse of the Soviet Union. If the Russian recovery is linked to the successful development of the greater Caspian region's oil and gas reserves, there will be a major increase in economic activity in the entire region between the Russian heartland and the Arabian peninsula. Arab and Iranian financial and commercial centers should experience a major increase in business contacts within and between Russia, the Caucasus and Central Asia. New air, highway and railway lines will carry more goods from the former Soviet Union to world markets through Arabian and Iranian ports, and through Pakistan as well, if and when the political situation in Afghanistan and Tajikistan stabilizes. This is a natural outcome of the collapse of the Cold War system, which was a barrier to North–South trade.

The challenge will be to design and implement policies which enhance prospects for positive economic development and discourage regional warfare. The region needs a reliable security system to enable further economic development. Although it would be relatively easy to get all the states concerned to adopt some general declaration of peaceful coexistence and commerce, history warns against collective security systems which lack effective, crisp decision-making and -enforcement mechanisms.

Constructive Engagement and Security Confusion

Russia's post-Soviet policy of Constructive Engagement in the Gulf region will tend to confuse the relationship between the GCC and the USA, with the potential for reducing GCC protection against regional instability. When delays and doubts are introduced into security alliances, their effectiveness is reduced. If after a decade or two, all the powers in the region have acquired a non-standard collection of Russian and Western weapons, and have increased their occasional tendency to play Russia off against the USA, the Gulf states will find themselves in a matrix system of interdependencies. Such systems are not effective substitutes for unambiguous security partnerships.

By weaving more and more economic, political and security relationships with Iraq, the Western powers, Russia and the Gulf states thought they had given Saddam Hussein too big a stake in the status quo to risk a military adventure. His invasion of Kuwait proved them wrong. The Gulf states did not attempt to deter Iraq militarily, partly because they were convinced that they were containing the Iraqi regime through a web of financial and business relationships. Further, between August 1990 and January 1991, Moscow's diplomats complicated crisis-management negotiations. Instead of two-party consultations between the American-led coalition and Iraq, the diplomatic game expanded. Gorbachev kept calling for more time even as the coalition forces were poised to strike. Soviet behavior might have persuaded Saddam Hussein that time was on his side. Even after Desert Storm was underway, Moscow continued to try to broker a cease-fire.

After the war, the six GCC states, plus Syria and Egypt, met in Damascus in March 1991. They developed a general plan to move towards an Arab collective security system although neither the USA nor the Gulf states expected the plan to develop into an effective regional defense system. Enthusiasm for the idea decreased as the eight states began to consider the institutional and technical problems of implementation.[50] Collective security has been possible for NATO, primarily because the Soviet Union remained an overriding, strategic military threat from 1949 to 1991. Even the formidable NATO had difficulty responding to the civil wars in former Yugoslavia after the collapse of the Soviet Union. It was ultimately not possible to construct a permanent security relationship between the six GCC states, Egypt and Syria, given their multiple individual interests and the absence of a single, overriding strategic military threat.

The GCC's need for a reliable security alliance with a great power was made manifest in 1994. In spring and summer of that year, the Russians launched a diplomatic campaign to lift the UN sanctions against Iraq in exchange for preferential treatment when Iraq began paying its debts and developing new oil fields. France, offered similar incentives by Baghdad, also began to support a removal of sanctions. Iraq's arrangement with Russia pledged repayment of some $7 billion in debt and promised an additional $8 to $10 billion in new construction and equipment purchases. When these terms were announced in September 1994, they were described as a diplomatic victory for Russia.[51] However, by offering to assist in the premature certification of Iraq's compliance with the post-war agreements, Russia damaged its credibility with the GCC states. Russia had worked hard to sell arms in the Gulf and to present itself as an authentic regional power that could be relied upon to help prevent conflict. GCC diplomats quite naturally asked Moscow to explain its willingness to lift the sanctions against Iraq before Iraq had accepted Kuwait's borders and state integrity, and settled outstanding issues related to prisoners of war and reparations.[52]

Those who believed that Russia and France had acted too hastily were vindicated when Saddam Hussein deliberately increased regional tensions. In October 1994, he began military deployments that appeared to be preparatory to another attempt to annex Kuwait. He knew that Operation Desert Storm had been very costly to Kuwait and Saudi Arabia. How many times could they afford to mobilize against him? Could he use repeated military 'bluffs' to bankrupt the GCC and its Western allies? Could he intimidate them into lifting the UN sanctions on his terms? In any event, Saddam Hussein once again demonstrated the weaknesses inherent in the interdependence theory. After contemplating such issues, the GCC and its Western allies paid the cost and responded with Operation Valiant Cause, a strong show of force, and refused to permit Iraq to win the game. While the American-led coalition was mobilizing its forces in the Gulf region, Russia was still trying to broker a deal for Iraq. Saddam Hussein was insisting upon Western agreement to conditions for his troop withdrawal. Moscow supported the project, and in effect diplomatically rewarded Saddam Hussein for flexing his military muscles and precipitating the October crisis. The West reacted forcefully and the sanctions stayed in place.[53]

After the GCC and the West had convincingly demonstrated that their alliance was viable and that they had the will and the ability to deliver another crushing military blow to Iraq, Saddam Hussein's National Assembly and Revolutionary Command Council passed resolutions which 'recognize the State of Kuwait's sovereignty, territorial integrity, and political independence'. Iraq also pledged to respect the inviolability of the borders defined by the UN Iraq–Kuwait Border Demarcation Committee.[54] However, such promises do not remove the power imbalances inherent in the Gulf region. Small states are vulnerable to pressure from their larger neighbors. Russian efforts to mediate disputes create a complex web of relationships. The GCC needs reliable external guarantees, and only the USA can perform that function in the regional system.

Moscow sent Prime Minister Chernomyrdin to the Gulf region to repair any damage done by Iraq's show of force and to explain Russia's involvement in the crisis. He stressed Russia's efforts to restrain Saddam Hussein and presented Russia as a stabilizing factor in the region. Chernomyrdin's six-day tour took him to Saudi Arabia, Kuwait, the UAE and Oman. He continued to defend Russia's policy towards Iraq as aimed at stabilization and normalization of relations. He attempted to present Moscow as a reliable partner in regional security, and also called upon all states to increase economic relations with Russia. Iran mimicked Moscow's policy and suggested that it too was prepared to make a positive contribution to regional security.[55]

Managing Oil Markets

Russian oil export and investment policies are driven primarily by Russian domestic politics. In order to forecast Russian international energy policy, it will continue to be necessary to follow Russian domestic politics. In 1921, when the Soviet state was struggling to achieve economic and political viability, Lenin was eager to sell foreign capitalists major stakes in the Chechen and Azeri oil fields. Soviet Russia's national interests required Moscow to crush the independence movements in the Caucasus and to find ways to exploit the region's natural resources. In March 1921, Lenin advocated selling 25 per cent of interests in Grozny (Chechen) and Baku (Azeri) oil which he viewed as Soviet assets. He wanted to use foreign capital to restore the economy and to rebuild the Soviet state: 'By leasing out one-fourth of Grozny and one-fourth of Baku, we shall be able – if we succeed – to raise the rest of them to the modern technical level of advanced capitalism. There is no other way for us to do this at present.'[56]

Soviet oil production peaked under Gorbachev in 1987 at around 12 million barrels per day (b/d) as the Soviet energy agencies obeyed the Kremlin's commands to pump and sell as much as possible in order to fill the Kremlin's coffers. Such irresponsible, politically-driven oil policies resulted in waste and damage to oil fields which a more conservative approach could have avoided. As a result, Soviet output began to decline. Gorbachev's frantic pumping and selling also helped to contribute to a decline in international oil prices. The collapse of the Soviet state in 1991 disrupted the Soviet oil system's integrity and production fell. By 1995, output had dropped to some 7 million b/d. Thus, the collapse of the Soviet Union withdrew some 5 million b/d from world production.

Russia wants to increase its hard currency earnings by restoring some of the 5 million b/d of lost production. However, the Russian state lacks the regulatory, legal and financial infrastructure required to move effectively in this area. Further, the competition for international investment capital to develop new oil projects has intensified. As long as the Soviet Union existed, Soviet state agencies planned and directly controlled the development of Soviet energy resources. But from 1990–91, as the Soviet government disintegrated, centralized energy planning and development disappeared. As a result, there were more and more projects seeking capital, and the major investments moved towards those states where deals could be completed most efficiently. Investment in Russia fell behind two other former Soviet republics, Azerbaijan and Kazakhstan. While Moscow sank deeper into a political morass, Azerbaijan and Kazakhstan completed agreements with multinational corporations. Many oil industry analysts believed that the production of approximately 2 million barrels of Caspian basin oil, and the export of this oil to world markets in the first decade of the twenty-first century, was possible, even likely. But Moscow has used the means available to it to delay the Caspian's development. The Russian government continues to prevent the 'near-abroad' region from emerging as an independent oil-exporting system, a third 'Turkic' energy hub, between the Russian Federation's energy system and the Middle East's.[57] Moscow wants Caspian oil to move through the Russian pipeline system. This would enable Russia to collect transit and handling fees from Azerbaijan and Kazakhstan and their foreign partners, and would also permit Russia the leverage available to all states which provide oil pipeline transportation services: the ability to stop the flow should it choose to do so.

Moscow was even more eager to make money from Iraq's oil, so eager that it was willing to risk upsetting the balance of power in the Middle East. In the summer of 1994, Russia, France and Iraq began talking about 'big' projects in Iraq that could add 3 to 6 million b/d to the world oil market above and beyond what pre-UN embargo Iraq had produced. All oil-producing states took notice. Some Russian commentators speculated that Moscow, Baghdad and Tehran had a definite community of interests and might attempt to coordinate their oil policies as part of their general resistance to American hegemony in international affairs.[58] Orderly oil markets enhance the national security of the Gulf states. Russia's Iraqi initiative did not inspire confidence in the Gulf concerning

Russia's intention to support orderly markets. By advocating measures that would have upset markets, Russia once again damaged its credibility as a reliable partner for GCC states.

Nevertheless, President Yeltsin was acting in concert with Russia's interests. In the summer of 1994, Yeltsin gave higher priority to the Russian partnership with Iraq than to his new relationships with the smaller Gulf states. The Russian–Iraqi plan would have given Russia several billion dollars of annual income. In his February 1996 State of the Federation message to the Russian Parliament, President Yeltsin confirmed that the Brezhnev and Gorbachev regimes had kept themselves afloat financially by selling oil and gas abroad and using their 'petro-dollars' to supplement the Kremlin's declining revenue stream from domestic sources.[59] He criticized them for wasting such funds on ill-conceived domestic projects and military adventures. But Yeltsin planned to do the same, by taking the lion's share of the profits from oil for the Soviet treasury, and returning only some $3.40 to $4.00 per metric ton to Russian producers. The Russian armed forces advocated keeping oil, gas and other 'natural' monopolies under state control and using revenues to support national defense. General Anatoly Kulikov, Minister of Internal Affairs, floated this proposal in the spring of 1996. Foreign investors eager to purchase a stake in the Russian oil industry were predictably dismayed.[60]

Conclusion and Recommendations

This chapter has moved back and forth between systemic overviews and details, the evidence which supports the main statements about the overall architecture of international relations in the greater Middle East. It argued that the Cold War alliance system had broken down in the Middle East a decade before the collapse of the Soviet Union. The USSR's fragmentation in 1991 added to the instability and uncertainty created by the Iranian revolution of 1979 and the Iran–Iraq War, 1980–88. However, instead of degenerating into anarchy, the regional system of states demonstrated a degree of resilience as enduring patterns of behavior rooted in the region's history, demography and geography reasserted themselves. The old frameworks were not completely swept away although they began adapting to new trends.

For example, Moscow's diplomats have definite systemic goals rooted in traditional Russian patterns of behavior. They seek tight security alliances with the former Soviet republics in the Caucasus and Central

Asia, and a loose alliance with Iran and Iraq in order to hold Turkey in check. Further, as seen in the war between Iran and Iraq, a strong Iraq is a Russian-desired counter-balance to Iranian expansion into the Middle East. In this regard, it is opportune for Russia to attempt to exploit some of the region's natural political fault-lines. Russia has worked hard to stabilize some areas while destabilizing others. This is how most observers understood Russia's *realpolitik* in the Caucasus during the 1990s. The pattern is likely to endure.

The GCC states cannot demand immediate, effective military support from Russia if regional tensions increase, or if a clear need arises for decisive action, because Russia's primary national interests are tied up in the Caspian region and Central Asia, not the Gulf. Russia will give higher priority to its national interests in Iran and Iraq than to its new relations with the GCC states. Turkey, Iran and Iraq form a sub-system of international relations that has a direct bearing on Russia's primary zone of national interest – the greater Caspian region. By contrast, the Western powers have a primary security interest in the GCC as expressed in the Carter Doctrine and made manifest in Operations Desert Storm and Valiant Cause. There is no similar Russian commitment, nor is Russia likely to give one soon, for three reasons. First, for the next decade or so, its primary interests will be the near-abroad and Russia's own internal political and economic problems. Second, as the Russian state rebuilds its energy industries, it will find itself competing with the Middle East for the European market, and instability in the Gulf can make Russia more attractive to Western Europe as a stable, geographically adjacent source of oil and natural gas. Third, Russia is likely to continue to give its greatest attention to its traditional customers, Iraq and Iran. Preferential Russian attention to Iraq and Iran has somewhat negative implications for smaller states such as Kuwait and the United Arab Emirates. Nevertheless, Russia will cultivate a presence in the Gulf region, participate in regional balancing and resist being marginalized by the West. Moscow will present itself as a modest counter-balance to American influence, an indigenous member of the regional international system, and seek to attract financial participation in Russia's economic reconstruction by Gulf investors. The Gulf states can and should pursue potentially lucrative trade and investment opportunities with Russia and all former Soviet republics.

From 1990 to 1995, the Soviet Union divided into 15 sovereign states. Only one of the 15, Russia, claimed the Soviet Union's position as a great power. The new Russia tried to play on every field. It was simultaneously friends with Iraq, Iran and Kuwait. It presented itself as a non-Western state that could help reduce one-sided dependence upon the United States and the Western powers in regional security affairs. However, Russia was too weak to function as a reliable substitute for Western security guarantees. In the 1990 Gulf crisis, Russia's actions tended to increase confusion about alliance responsibilities, a situation that produced security system immobility. In 1994, Russia's actions in support of a speedy end to the embargo on Iraq were designed more with the Kremlin treasury in mind than Gulf security or international oil market stability. The same is true of Russian arms sales to Iran.

Russian domestic and foreign policy priorities require that the Kremlin demonstrates success at building positive relations with the greater Islamic community. Moscow will want to be friendly with Muslim states even while it keeps the political aspirations of its own citizens of Islamic heritage in check and imposes limitations on the sovereignty of the former Soviet republics of Islamic heritage. The region's basic ethnographic structure simultaneously creates natural enemies and allies for Russia. Democratization tends to increase regional instability and diversity since periodic elections make it difficult for statesmen to maintain a steady course. Political liberalization permits discontented minorities to demand political autonomy and/or independence. Even a democratic Russia is likely to be sympathetic to authoritarian regimes which support its policies.

Five policy recommendations spring from this analysis of continuity and change in the Russian factor in Gulf security. First, Russia and several former Soviet republics will soon become important energy-exporting states. Therefore, the Gulf states should discuss long-term energy export plans with Russia, Azerbaijan, Kazakhstan and Turkmenistan in order to improve prospects for orderly energy market development. Gulf policy-makers will also want to monitor domestic political changes in Russia that can affect energy export policy. Second, since Russia will continue to seek to earn hard currency by selling arms, the Gulf states should support initiatives to limit the arms race in the greater Gulf region. Third, Gulf states should support the integrity of political borders in the former Soviet Union. The unravelling of political borders in the Caucasus, South Russia and Tajikistan would be destabilizing for the greater Middle East. Fourth, Gulf states should actively encourage North/South trade in order to benefit economically from the increased trade flows from Asia through the Gulf region into the former Soviet Union. If increased trade promotes stability and reduces the risk of war, so much the better. Fifth, Gulf states should retain crisp security alliances with a strong military power such as the USA in order to deter regional aggression and to keep the trade routes open. Although the Middle East is the source of ancient civilizations, its political geology is still very active when compared to that of Western Europe, for example. Eruptions and quakes are quite likely due to the unique combinations of domestic and international forces at work in the region. It is vitally important to keep security responsibilities and security decision-making procedures clearly defined.

Radical Russian nationalists such as Vladimir Zhirinovsky threatened to rebuild Russia and to march to the Arabian Sea, while radical anti-Russian nationalists in the Caucasus and Central Asia proposed an Islamic liberation push up the Volga to Tatarstan. Responsible Kremlin policy-makers such as Yevgeny Primakov rejected such political extremism and presented Russia as a moderate power with a definite sphere of influence in the Caucasus and Central Asia and a generally constructive interest in the greater Gulf region. Russia has a definite state interest in maintaining a balance between Turkey, Iran and Iraq, one arranged to prevent either Turkey or Iran from challenging Russia in its historic sphere of influence. Strong, independent Gulf states are compatible with Russia's basic interests. However, the overall balance requires that an outside power such as the USA be their primary military ally. Russia cannot play that role without damaging its delicate relationship with Iran and Iraq.

PART THREE

Gulf Security and Regional Affairs

CHAPTER 7

Revolutionary Islamism and Gulf Security in the Twenty-first Century

David E. Long

The Arabian Peninsula is the Cradle of Islam. The religion's two holiest sites are found there – the Haram Mosque in Mecca and the Prophet's Mosque in al-Madinah. Nearly two million of the faithful visit those sites each year during the annual *hajj* or Great Mecca Pilgrimage, and for most it is a once-in-a-lifetime experience. Citizens from the GCC states may attend the *hajj* without a special *hajj* visa required by Saudi Arabia of pilgrims from other foreign countries. Most Gulf Arabs, however, have been many times, and are now actively discouraged by the Saudi Government from repeatedly attending the *hajj* because the huge numbers that attend are stretching their logistical capabilities to the limit.

As a result of living in the Cradle of Islam, Gulf Arabs have a different mentality toward Islam than most other Muslims. Being a Muslim is not the mystical religious experience of some Muslims from far away, but a familiar, everyday experience that is almost as automatic as breathing. Characterizations of modernized Gulf Arabs, particularly Saudis, as 'secular' because they have accepted many of the ideas and consumerism of Western secular society are simply off the mark. Gulf society is Islamic to the core.

Attitudes toward the application of Islam in both private and public life is another matter. There is a growing number of Westernized Gulf Arabs who, while remaining privately pious, have abandoned many of the social mores associated with the Gulf's traditional Islamic society. This process is more accelerated in some Gulf states than in others, but exists throughout the region. Both modernization and the secularization that inevitably accompanies it have created strains in the traditional Islamic societies of the Gulf and have caused a backlash among those who wish to return to the pre-modernist Islamic social order.

Solving the conundrum of how to bring the benefits of modernization to their people while resisting the secularization that goes with it is a major preoccupation of all Gulf governments. Thus, along with five year economic and social development plans, Gulf governments have also supported Islamic institutions, Islamic religious activities and have been major sponsors of Islamic organizations such as the Office of the Islamic Conference, the Muslim World League and the Muslim Brotherhood.

Despite these efforts, however, they have been increasingly challenged by a radical few for not doing enough and for being in league with secular, atheistic elements in the West to destroy the Islamic way of life. The threat of militant, revolutionary political Islamic organizations looms as potentially one of the greatest threats to political stability in the Gulf in the twenty-first century.

The Emergence of Revolutionary Islamism In the Gulf

In assessing the medium- and long-term impact on Gulf security of radical political Islam – revolutionary Islamism – we should begin by looking at its reemergence in the latter part of the twentieth century. To help clarify this phenomenon, let us first make a distinction between religious Islamic fundamentalism, or puritanism to be more precise, and Islamism. The former refers to the personal and corporate belief in a narrow construction of Islamic law – the 'fundamentals' of the faith – and the rejection of what are seen as innovations (bid'a) that have crept into the religion since the time of the Prophet Mohammad and his Companions.[1] Implicit in that belief, the purification of Muslim society is in strict conformity with the holy law.

Islamism, as the term has come to mean, is a contemporary political ideology aimed at creating, maintaining and governing such a society. The Islamist political message calls for a rejection of all Western social and political influences as secularist and for a return to a romanticized historic past in which strict Islamic moral and social norms governed society. (Islamists in Saudi Arabia call themselves Salafiyya, 'followers of the pious ancestors.')[2]

Most Islamists seek to establish their political order through peaceful means by reforming existing political systems to make them conform more closely with their understanding of Islamic law. There is a small but growing number of radical, revolutionary Islamists, however, who believe that the goal of creating a puritan Islamic political system is so imperative and that the enemies of true Islam are so strong as to justify any means of achieving it, including violence and terrorism if need be. The vehicle for enforcing their concept of purity upon Muslim society is *jihad*, the personal and corporate obligation to propagate virtue and suppress evil.

Both religious puritanism and political Islamism have been extant in the Gulf since the earliest days of Islam. Over 250 years ago, a renewal of the religious puritanism occurred in central Arabia with the Wahhabi revival movement and its strict monotheistic doctrine of Tawhid. The revival spurred an outpouring of political Islamism as the House of Saud, which embraced the Wahhabi revival, endeavored to spread its teachings throughout the Arabian Peninsula.

By the mid-twentieth century, varying degrees of Islamic puritanism continued to exist throughout the Gulf, particularly in Saudi Arabia; but revolutionary Islamism as a rallying cry for radical political change was insignificant. On the contrary, during the Cold War years, the call for radical political change came not from the right but from the left – Communism and associated radical Arab socialism. In the 1950s, 1960s and 1970s, the vocabulary of socialism and secular Arab nationalism was the primary idiom for expressing social and political discontent throughout the Arab world.

By the 1990s, these Western, secular ideologies had lost much of their popular appeal and their slogans had largely been replaced by the language of Islam as the idiom of protest. As a result, states throughout the Arab world again began to perceive a new threat from the right – revolutionary Islamism.

Iran and the Rise of Revolutionary Islamism

The Iranian revolution of 1979 has been seen by many observers as a bell-weather of this shift. The Islamic scholar John Esposito asserted, 'In the Gulf, as elsewhere in the Muslim world, Iran served as a catalyst for an opposition whose primary causes were indigenous factors.'[3] Iran's role as catalyst for Islamist revolution, however, was noticeably less applicable in the Gulf than it was elsewhere. Among the largely Sunni populations of the Gulf states, there was little love lost for either the imperial Persian ambitions of the new Iranian regime nor its Shi'a religious leadership and their revolutionary Islamist doctrines. Shi'a communities in the GCC states (minorities except in Bahrain) may have initially identified to a degree with the Iranian revolution, but as time ultimately proved, their skepticism toward Iran's theocratic regime far out-weighed their grievances with their own Sunni-dominated regimes in terms of where their loyalties lay. Initial concerns both in the Gulf and in the West of large-scale Shi'a political unrest manipulated from Tehran was heightened by Shi'a riots in Saudi Arabia in 1980 and by an Iranian-inspired coup attempt in Bahrain by the Shi'a Front for the Liberation of Bahrain in 1981. Iran has continued to support dissident Shi'a groups in Saudi Arabia, Bahrain and elsewhere, but it has never been able effectively to export its revolutionary Islamist doctrines to the Arab side of the Gulf.[4]

Indeed, Iran's attempts to disrupt the annual Mecca Pilgrimage in order to spread its revolutionary message and portray the Saudi hosts as unfit to administer the *hajj* were on balance counter-productive. Iran rejected the Saudi claim to be the Custodians of the Two Holy Places (Khatim al-Haramayn) as well as its policy of disallowing political demonstrations at the *hajj*. Beginning in 1982, Iranians attempted to disrupt the *hajj*, waving posters of Khomeini and chanting slogans against the United States, the Soviet Union, and Israel. Events culminated in 1987 when more than four hundred people were killed as Saudi security forces attempted to quell Iranian-instigated riots. Instead of disgracing the Saudis, however, Iran was itself discredited as most of the Muslim world condemned its actions as desecrating the *hajj*.

Revolutionary Islamism in the Gulf in the 1990s

The Iraqi invasion of Kuwait was the final death knell of secular Arab nationalism as a revolutionary political force in the Middle East. It will certainly remain an important political factor and may even stage a comeback, but it is no longer the unrivaled voice of political radicalism and militancy that it once was. Revolutionary Islamism has assumed that role.

Prior to the Kuwait invasion, most Arab Islamists had castigated Saddam Hussein and his secular Ba'athist political ideology. Saddam himself, realizing the rising appeal of revolutionary Islamism, quickly adjusted and called for a Jihad against the non-Muslim Western opponents and their Gulf Arab allies. He skillfully manipulated regional economic and political grievances and ethnic, national and confessional prejudices to portray the US-led coalition's military response to his invasion as a conflict between Dar al-Islam and Dar al-Harb – the Abode of Islamic Law and the Abode of War, of unbelievers. As a result, demonstrations broke out in a number of Arab countries where revolutionary Islamism and/or anti-Gulf Arab feeling was high.

Gulf Arabs rallied behind their governments during the Kuwait crisis and were stunned and bitter at what they saw as a perfidious abandonment by fellow Arabs in their hour of need. The conservative Gulf regimes who had generously supported Islamic political organizations for years, reacted angrily when so many of the latter expressed sympathy for Saddam. Sudan's Islamist leader, Hassan al-Turabi, once a recipient of Gulf financial support, became viewed as an enemy who turned his country into a conduit for Iranian financial aid and training for Islamist terrorist groups. At the same time, Gulf governments and citizens alike also expressed gratitude to the Arab and Western members of the military coalition who come to their aid.

Five years later, on November 13, 1995, Islamist terrorists launched a bomb attack on the offices of US training mission to the Saudi Arabian National Guard that killed seven, including five Americans, and wounded 60 others.[5] Several obscure revolutionary Islamist groups claimed responsibility for the attack. One group, calling itself the Movement for Islamic Change in the Arabian Peninsula demanded the expulsion of all US military 'Crusaders' and an end to Saudi rule. Another, the Tigers of the Gulf, warned: 'If the Americans don't leave the kingdom as soon as possible, we will continue our actions.'[6]

Seven months after that, on June 25, 1996, Islamic terrorists exploded another bomb at a housing complex for US military personnel in the Saudi port of al-Khobar on the Gulf coast, killing 19 Americans and wounding over 100 more.[7] Subsequent Saudi investigations indicate that one of the possible origins of the perpetrators was an Iranian-supported conspiracy involving Saudi Shi'as calling themselves Saudi Hizbollah.[8] The act shows that therefore revolutionary Islamism has found listeners among the Shi'a as well as the Sunnis in the Gulf. Shi'a terrorism and particularly an Iranian connection to it are highly disturbing to government authorities, although in most GCC states, Shi'a dissidence is still more of a sectarian minority problem than a nation-wide problem. While it has the potential to weaken the fabric of Gulf societies, it has not as yet posed an immediate threat to the Gulf regimes. In any case, what happened in the intervening five years since Desert Storm to provoke such attacks is instructive in assessing the long-term threat of revolutionary Islamism to Gulf stability.

For years, the revolutionary Islamist message had been preached by zealous Islamic preachers throughout the Peninsula, but outside a few younger members of the professional religious class, few had listened. Aside from its jingoistic attraction to local young nationalists frustrated by the subordinate geopolitical status of their countries, it had not been widely appealing to a great majority of the people in the Gulf who would not relish abandoning the creature comforts acquired through oil wealth that the dour, ascetic fanatics of Islamism would have them do.

As the explosions graphically demonstrated, however, the appeal of revolutionary Islamism in the Peninsula has been growing among the general public. The causes of its popularity are not so much government corruption and resistance by Gulf rulers to sharing power, despite the emphasis placed on these factors by Islamist activists seeking a more sympathetic Western reception of their agenda, or even antipathy toward all things Western, which the Islamists preach at home with the latest communications technology. To a great extent, frustration over corruption and the lack of participation in the political process at home are more symptoms than causes.

Instead, the root causes stem more from the clash of traditional Islamic values and western secular values caused by rapid economic and social development programs as the Peninsula states seek to modernize their countries, and by increasingly unmet economic expectations as flat oil revenues do not keep pace with soaring population growth. Gulf regimes have long sought to reduce the inherent friction between tradition and modernization, but the very success of their development programs has made this task increasingly difficult. Economic expectations are increasingly unrealized, despite the fact that with large oil revenues there is very little real poverty in the Gulf. Part of the problem is the reduction in welfare programs by most Gulf states due to current account problems resulting from declining oil revenues and overspending over the past 15 years. For all these reasons, there has arisen in virtually every Gulf country since the Kuwait crisis small groups of Islamic political activists who are increasingly militant. It is from among these revolutionary Islamists and their followers that the perpetrators of the bomb explosions in Saudi Arabia came.

Three factors stand out as catalysts of this trend. The first was a campaign sponsored by Iran and aimed at veterans of the Afghan war of 1979–1988 to create a sense of being a part of a greater Islamist community dedicated to its sacred mission of Islamic political revival. Iran has had far greater success in exporting revolutionary Islamism in the Gulf through peaceful means than through tactics of violence, terrorism and subversion,[9] and the Islamic fervor of opponents of the Soviet-dominated Afghan regime provided it with an unparalleled opportunity. During the course of the war, thousands of Muslim volunteers from all over the Muslim world including the Gulf joined the fight – an outpouring of idealism not unlike the international volunteers in the Spanish Civil War.

After the war, the veterans from the Gulf returned quietly to their homes and most might have remained so had not Iran included them it its campaign to encourage Islamist revolutionaries world-wide to network with each other, perpetuating a common sense of mission. Although these revolutionary Islamists ostensibly eschewed all forms of modernity, their networking with Islamists far away was and continues to be carried out by fax, audio tapes and more recently by the internet. Thus it came to pass that formerly isolated individuals in the Gulf who had shared a common experience coalesced into a loose community of Islamist radicals eager to seek new causes to espouse. They were not then nor have they become a monolithic dissident organization as they are sometimes portrayed, but they do form a nucleus around which dissident organizations can coalesce.

The second catalyst is more demographic than ideological and involves a growing generation gap in the Gulf. With a median age of roughly 15 years old and one of the highest population growth rates in the world, the Gulf states are undergoing an unprecedented population explosion.[10] Historically high birth rates have become out of line with rapidly falling death rates due to the introduction of modern health care. The result has been the slow but steady creation of an underclass of young people that cannot be absorbed into the economies of the Gulf states and who are increasingly alienated from society. The combination of the lack of a strong work ethic and the unrealistically high economic expectations generated by the petrodollars of the 1970s and 1980s have created mounting frustrations for this group as the kind of jobs which they would find acceptable are no longer available. Few are destitute, as they can apply to their families for funds to live on, but their lives have become meaningless and hollow. In short, the Gulf is creating a whole underclass of young people who are marginalized economically, socially and, ultimately, politically. It is from this group that most of the new followers of revolutionary Islamism have been drawn. By contrast, the political activists of older generations still seek for the most part to work within the existing political systems, such as in Kuwait where Islamists have been elected to the National Assembly and in Saudi Arabia where the older generations of religious leaders, no less puritanical than their militant juniors, see the established order as a better vehicle for religious reform than a religious dictatorship on the Iranian model.

The third catalyst of the rise of revolutionary Islamism in the Gulf is the high profile of US military forces that remained in the Gulf following the Kuwait crisis to defend the Gulf states from the continued hostile intentions of their larger northern neighbors, Iran and Iraq.[11] US forces were asked to remain not out of any desire by the GCC states to abdicate their own defense responsibilities, nor out of any political designs by the United States, but out of recognition that Iraq under Saddam and Iran historically continued to harbor hegemonic ambitions in the Gulf.

The United States took great pains to keep as low a profile as possible, but as the number of US military personnel expanded greatly over the past six years, American sensitivity in seeking to avoid the perception (or portrayal) of a permanent military presence relaxed. Activities such as ship and aircraft visits and overflights that were once undertaken only after careful consideration and consultation became routine and justified as a virtual right based on the protection US troops provided.

Following the Kuwait war, outspoken religious leaders, always sensitive to any foreign and particularly non-Muslim presence, became magnets for xenophobic young people who read into the military presence a loss of national honor and American imperial designs.[12] For example, Shaikh Safar al-Hawali, Dean of Islamic Studies at Umm al-Qura University in Mecca, charged, 'If Iraq has occupied Kuwait, America has occupied Saudi Arabia. The real enemy is not Iraq. It is the West.'[13]

Between 1991 and 1995, Islamists in several Gulf states became increasingly bold in pressing demands for more strict enforcement of Islamic law and more participation in the political process. In 1993, an Islamist opposition group calling itself the Committee for the Defense of Legitimate Rights (CDLR) called for an elected representative government, strict application of Islamic law and the removal of the Saudi government. It was made up of disaffected modernists, a few of the more reactionary members of the religious establishment, and younger, militant Islamists or Salafis. CDLR claimed to be an independent 'human rights' commission, probably in part to gain sympathy in the West. In reality, its focus was on enforcing Islamic law, not on human rights which as a Western secular humanist concept would be considered anathema to Islamists. Most of its members were arrested or lost their professional licenses, and in 1994, the Committee relocated to London. The same year, Shaikh Safar al-Hawali and another prominent Islamists, Shaikh al-Audah, were arrested in Saudi Arabia, leading to demonstrations in al-Audah's home town of Burayda. The government at first sought to persuade the Islamists, many of whom wee in the religious establishment, to mute their criticisms, but this only encouraged them to speak out more intemperately. In 1992, both the government and senior religious leaders spoke out publicly against the agitators and when this proved ineffective, the government intensified its efforts to counter Islamist demands. For a while, quiet returned.

Then, in November 1995, the first of the two bomb attacks occurred in the Kingdom. The act was unprecedented and sent shockwaves not only throughout Saudi Arabia, but up and down the Gulf as well. In the spring of 1996, the Saudi government announced it had executed those responsible for the first bombing which could have been part of the motive for the second attack. At any rate, the entire Saudi population has had to face the ramifications of a breakdown in internal security in the face of a small group of fanatics.

Political agitation also escalated to civil disruptions in Bahrain, although there, a broader cross-section of the population was involved. In 1992, 300 prominent people, including Sunni and Shi'a clerics, businessmen and intellectuals, petitioned the Amir to reopen the elective National Assembly, closed since 1975. The Amir instead created a non-elective Consultative Assembly with equal Sunni and Shi'a representation (Shi'as make up about 70 percent of the population), excluding members of the royal family and Sunni and Shi'a Islamists.[14] In October 1994, a second petition was submitted, this time bearing some 25,000 signatures of which about one fifth were women's.[15] It called for the restoration of the 1973 constitution (originally proposed by the National Assembly and approved by the Amir) and denounced restrictions on freedom of speech and the press, the unemployment situation, deportation and political exile.[16] In December 1994, three Shi'as who had signed the petition were arrested, including a popular young cleric, Shaikh Ali Salman. The arrests ignited widespread demonstrations in Shi'a villages and prompted an immediate reaction by the government.[17] The violence lasted for six months, and has sporadically re-erupted ever since.

The agenda of the protesters is not really Islamist in the strict sense of the term since all the leading dissident organizations claim to support democratization, pluralism and human rights, none of which are compatible with a narrow Islamist view of legitimate government under the Sharia. Nevertheless, the leadership of the protest movement is dominated by Islamist political activists; and while they are still relatively moderate in their political demands, if the protest movement becomes more radicalized as its frustrations mount, there is good likelihood that the Islamist leadership will become doctrinally more radical also.

Islamism and Gulf Security in the Twenty-first Century

There is little doubt that revolutionary Islamism will continue to be the greatest potential internal threat to Gulf security well into the twenty-first century. Appealing to Islamic symbols and doctrines, no matter how selectively, still affords the comfort of a familiar, universally acceptable rallying cry for the politically disaffected.

It would be a mistake, however, to assume that a revolutionary Islamic security threat in the Gulf would take the same form as revolutionary Islamist threats elsewhere in the Muslim world. In Egypt and Algeria, for example, violent Islamist opposition has focused on the secular political systems as the root of all the social and economic ills that are at the heart of popular disaffection. The GCC states, meanwhile, are traditional Islamic monarchies; and all of them use to varying degrees the symbols and doctrines of Islam to legitimize their political institutions. As a result, revolutionary Islamists in the Arabian Peninsula cannot condemn the current regimes for denying the validity of Islam in politics, but must persuade the public that the regimes have not lived up to their own Islamic principles. This is a far more difficult task.

It is ironic that in seeking a rallying cry for their political agendas, the revolutionary Islamists have seized on Western-style grievances – government corruption, a lack of public participation in the political process, and a denial of human rights – rather than more Islamist grievances such as failing to enforce stricter public conformity with Islamic law. This could be in part to win sympathy from human and civil rights activists in the West, but is probably aimed more at wining a broader popular constituency among a general public more concerned with those issues than with conformance to Islamic law.

The most 'Islamic' issue on their agenda is that of foreign troops remaining on their soil after Desert Storm, and even that issue has been distorted both in the Gulf and beyond. For example, a poll taken during the Kuwait crisis by a Pakistani magazine, *Herald*, asked, 'Should US troops be defending the Muslim holy places in Saudi Arabia?' Ignoring the fact that the nearest American combat unit was hundreds of miles from the holy places, what is surprising about the poll was that, with the question posed the way it was, 86 percent of the respondents said no.[18]

The fact remains that no matter how distorted or self-serving revolutionary Islamist charges, accusations and claims are, there is a modicum of truth behind them, else their message would not appeal to so many young people. The best way to defend against a long-term threat such as revolutionary Islamism is for the Gulf states themselves to take remedial steps before there is a crisis. This does not mean merely seeking to co-opt Islamists with financial aid to Islamic institutions (or individuals!) or increased power sharing with the religious establishment. The senior religious leaders (*'ulama*) are already a part of the political process; it is the junior clergy and the angry young men who surround them from whence comes the threat of revolutionary Islamism. Instead, Gulf governments must seek to deprive the revolutionary Islamists of the public grievances that they can use as rallying cries. Raising the level of public participation in the political process, increasing accountability by public servants, and seeking to address the runaway population explosion are vitally necessary in all the GCC states to avoid a continued build-up of public disaffection.

Runaway population growth is addressed in Chapter 12. The other two areas are discussed briefly here. The first is increasing public participation in the political process. The traditional means of participation in the Gulf was through an informal system of consultation (*shura*) between the rulers and ruled, and the national consensus (*ijma'*) which resulted from it. The concentration of oil money in the hands of the government, and the increasing complexity of government has made this informal system inadequate. The problems to be addressed by public policy are too complex and too time-sensitive for ad hoc consultations.

This does not mean that each Gulf state should rush to create Western models of representative government. For participation to be effective, it must conform to the constraints of local political cultures. In some instances, for example, a representative assembly where elected members can openly criticize government policies and call for more accountability can serve as a safety valve to relieve dangerous pent-up frustrations among the general population. That has been the case in Kuwait and could most likely relieve current high political tensions in Bahrain.

Other Gulf states are not yet socially or culturally prepared for representative democratic institutions. As the recent experience in Yemen bore out, 'democratization' through elected assemblies does not necessarily lead to more public political participation and could prove counter-productive. This does not obviate the need for real participation, however. The important thing is for institutions of public participation, whether consultative assemblies or representative assemblies, to encourage real participation and not merely to stand as cosmetic palliatives to ward off public pressures.

A second imperative to avoid the threat of revolutionary Islamism is to increase public accountability – holding public servants accountable for how they disburse public funds. One should begin by looking at the current acceptable standards of public morality in the Gulf. Western critics, for example, inevitably make the mistake of measuring government 'corruption' in the Gulf by Western standards – standards so high that even Western governments do not live up to them. In a region where personal integrity has been traditionally far more binding than the fine print on a contract, and where *caveat emptor* reigns supreme, a technical, bureaucratic, legalistic approach to accountability of public funds is not likely to be effective. As governmental operations increase in technical efficiency, technical standards of public accountability will inevitably improve. They already have. But regardless of what standards currently exist, no one in the Gulf condones breaching local standards, and such instances occur daily. Excessive displays of greed and avarice rather than the system itself should be the focus. The problem of accountability in the Gulf is the official tolerance of, or at best, indifference to, excessive avarice and greed, not the violation of a Western definition of corruption. With rapid population growth and increasing maldistribution of wealth, public opposition for such behavior will continue to increase in the twenty-first century and its contrast to the puritanical, ascetic behavior of the Islamists will stand out all the more clearly.

Despite the two terrorist attacks in Saudi Arabia in 1995 and 1996, revolutionary Islamism is at present not a major threat to Gulf security. Failure to disarm public disaffection through governmental reform, however, could in the long-run become a self-fulfilling prophecy – a serious threat could easily materialize by the twenty-first century. No state can tolerate open defiance of the established political order; but doing nothing until the threat becomes a crisis, and then indiscriminately using force to crush any and all Islamist domestic political opposition is bound to be counter-productive. Violence begets violence, and once the cycle has begun, it is extremely difficult to end it. Moreover, in such an atmosphere, the legitimate threat of revolutionary Islamism can all to easily become an excuse for not addressing legitimate grievances of government in-adequacies and failures, including the failure of the rulers to consult with the ruled. The challenge for the Gulf states is to work with their critics in creating evolutionary change or face the alternative of revolutionary change.

CHAPTER 8

Boundaries, Territorial Disputes and the GCC States

Richard Schofield

It is, of course, impossible to be absolutely sure about what, precisely, will comprise the political map of the Arabian peninsula and Gulf region at the midway point of the twenty-first century. Having said that, a reasonably educated guess can be made on the basis of recent trends, current processes and historical patterns. Whether or not the current framework of territory will endure – and one should be aware that it has not yet completely evolved – will probably depend on the following factors: the degree to which the modern, largely Eurocentric precepts of territory and sovereignty have been accepted in this politically youthful region; the degree to which the current political map has evolved; the degree to which the expansionist designs of the major regional powers can be confined to history; the degree to which the region will remain a strategic economic asset to the Western powers;[1] and, lastly, the degree to which the current framework of state territory is being regulated and institutionalized at the regional level. This chapter examines all of these factors in great detail. To argue, as it ultimately does, that the current framework of state territory is likely to endure, is not, however, to say that those disputes which remain will be easily settled.

The chapter consists of four sections. The first examines the degree to which the current regional territorial framework should be regarded as final and permanent. The second reviews the manner in which the Gulf Cooperation Council (GCC) has recently preoccupied itself with the regulation, institutionalization and, where appropriate, finalization of this framework. A third section then looks at recent trends and developments in the region on a case-to-case basis, concentrating on the two disputes which have dominated the agenda of successive annual summit meetings of the GCC in recent years: the Bahrain–Qatar dispute over the Hawar islands and the Dibal and Jarada shoals, and the Iran–UAE dispute over the sovereignty of the islands of Abu Musa and the Tunbs in the Lower Gulf. A fourth and last section will conclude that the disputes of the region are being increasingly polarized into those which have recently been settled and those which remain to constitute threats to regional stability.

Permanent and Final? The Contemporary Territorial Framework

It has often been remarked that the system of modern state territories established by the European colonial powers in the Arab Middle East and North Africa was demonstrably at odds with indigenous concepts of spatial and social organization. Put very crudely, the inheritance of the European precept of linear state boundaries presented the governments of these newly independent states with awkward challenges of national integration, most notably to reverse the traditional allegiances of a significant proportion of their respective populations. In modern international law, sovereignty is explicitly linked to territory, but in Islamic constitutional law the picture is quite different: '[t]he basis of the Islamic state was ideological, not political, territorial or ethnical'.[2] Sovereignty (*siyada*) was regarded as a divine attribute. The whole of the Islamic world would ideally form a single political unit, the *umma*, under the control of the *khalifa*. For practical purposes alone, the *umma* was sub-divided into more or less discrete political units, controlled by sultans or emirs, whose authority and power (*sultah*) was generally secular.[3] Other than this general feeling of belonging to the wider *umma*, a tribesman – of Eastern Arabia for instance – might conceive of a territorial loyalty 'to his domestic abode, his wells, his gardens, his palm trees, or, in the case of a nomad, his dirah, or tribal grazing grounds'.[4]

It is not proposed to delve any further into such questions here. Suffice it to say that, whatever the problems posed by national integration, there are strong grounds for believing that the present framework of Middle Eastern state territory will endure. Even in those parts of the Middle East and North Africa in which the physical environment and social tradition conspire to render a territorially-defined system of states particularly inappropriate from an ecological point of view, national interest would appear to have triumphed. As O'Brien commented: '[T]he states of the Sahara may have been "artificial" creations of colonial cartography, ecologically absurd in relation to the nomadic way of life, but one should not underestimate the appeal of a nationalism to the educated youth of the desert.'[5] For the region as a whole and despite all of its shortcomings, the present framework of territory should, almost certainly, be regarded as permanent. In the words of Drysdale and Blake: '[T]he political spheres they [international boundaries] define have acquired a seeming permanence, and the state constitutes as basic, legitimate and universal a unit of political geographic organization in the Middle East and North Africa as elsewhere.'[6]

INCREASINGLY FINALIZED AND PERMANENT – BOUNDARIES IN THE GULF REGION: The same can be said, increasingly, for the predominantly youthful states of the Arabian peninsula; only, however, because of considerable strides taken in recent years. Linear international boundaries are an increasingly accepted and permanent feature of the Arabian political landscape. They are not mere lines on maps but tangible features on the ground, from the 'Berlin Wall'-like fortifications Kuwait has placed along its border with Iraq, through the pillars and fences that mark political boundaries in the south-eastern Arabian desert, to the stone cairns that will soon be renovated to demarcate the Saudi–Yemeni boundary in the high mountains of Asir.[7] After much progress in finalizing territorial limits in recent years, the Saudi–Yemeni boundary east of Asir remains the only Arabian land border to be delimited and negotiations have been progressing intermittently since July 1992 towards this end. What is more, in another recent development, Arabian boundary agreements have now been concluded and registered in a manner which has finally convinced the international legal community that the geographic facts they introduce are intended to be permanent.

Of course, one still hears the argument that the contemporary system of linear boundaries is a European concept imposed upon a cultural landscape for which it holds no relevance. In a passive phase of the Iraq–Kuwait dispute during the early 1980s, Iraqi President Saddam Hussein was heard to say: 'Why do we need to solve the border issue. Kuwait's borders extend as far as Baghdad and ours reach as far as Kuwait [city].'[8] Here he was clearly borrowing from Ibn Saud's terminology from the 1920s.[9] Naturally, Iraq's attempted annexation of Kuwait in 1990 posed a grave challenge to the very heart of the system of territorially-defined states established during Britain's stay as colonial power in the Gulf up until 1971. Immediately questions were raised about the origins of the emirates of the western Gulf littoral. How had this territorial framework evolved and how capable was it of withstanding serious internal and external challenges such as the Iraqi invasion of 2 August 1990? The move on Kuwait also served as a potent reminder of the vulnerability of the smaller Gulf states to the territorial acquisitiveness of their larger, more powerful neighbors.

HISTORICAL FOOTNOTES? THE REGIONAL TERRITORIAL AMBI-TIONS OF SAUDI ARABIA, IRAN AND IRAQ: Before Ibn Saud effectively agreed during the course of the very same Anglo–Saudi frontier negotiations to adopt the European method of framing territorial claims in ways which could be depicted upon a map, he had always displayed a marked preference for coming to private territorial arrangements with Najd's neighbors in Arabia. The earliest example of this predilection came in 1921. During the previous autumn, at the height of the Jahrah crisis, Ibn Saud had stated that he recognized Kuwait as extending only as far as the walls of the port of that name. When Sheikh Ahmad succeeded his uncle Salim to become ruler of Kuwait in March 1921, however, the Najdi emir would emerge from bilateral talks to announce that there were no longer any problems with the al Sabah and that, as such, there was no need to fix a boundary between the two states.[10] In Article 6 of the 1927 Anglo–Najdi Treaty of Jeddah, Ibn Saud had agreed, following the 1922 Uqair Protocol (which had initially delimited the Kuwait–Najd boundary), to respect the territorial integrity of Kuwait but only to maintain friendly and peaceful relations with the ruler of Qatar. Hence, as mentioned above, Saudi Arabia prefaced the Anglo–Saudi frontier negotiations during June 1934 with a maximum territorial claim which – while incapable of being plotted cartographically – recognized the al Thani state.

A brief mention needs also to be made of the territorial ambitions that Iran and Iraq have harbored historically along the western littoral of the Gulf. Shah Muhammad Reza Pahlavi's announcement that the in-habitants of Bahrain were free to decide their own fate in 1969 effectively disposed of a claim that had been maintained with varying degrees of conviction and intensity since the mid-1840s, when the Persian Minister Hajji Mirza Aghassi claimed that the whole of the Gulf and its islands belonged to the Qajar state. The finding of United Nations representative Vittorio Guicciardi that the vast majority of Bahrainis wished to retain independence from Iran was unanimously endorsed by the Security Council. When this endorsement was ratified by the Iranian majlis, the territorial claim, which had been maintained for decades in only a nominal sense, was officially dropped.[11] Iranian claims to a share of the waters of the Shatt al-Arab and the sovereignty of the islands of Abu Musa and the Tunbs in the Lower Gulf are long-standing. Both the Shatt and the islands dispute are serious cyclical affairs, however, with the latter having temporarily displaced the former – because of Iraq's current isolation within the Arab fold – as the current focus of Arab–Iranian rivalry in Gulf waters.

Iraq's historical restlessness at its lack of frontage on the Gulf has manifested itself in the continual expectancy of successive Baghdad governments for Kuwait to compensate Iraq territorially for its geostrategic misfortune. For over half a century, Iraqi claims to Kuwait have essentially been prosecuted on two levels which are themselves contradictory. First, Iraq has periodically laid claim to the whole of Kuwait. The arguments for the amalgamation of Kuwait within Iraq – based upon that state's inclusion within the Ottoman province of Basra in the period before the First World War – have been extended most notably on three occasions: during 1938 by Iraqi Foreign Minister Tawfiq al-Suwaidi at a time of significant instability within Kuwait; during 1961 by Iraqi leader Abdel Karim Qasim on the announcement of Kuwaiti independence (the first Kuwait crisis); and, most recently, in 1990–91 to justify Iraq's invasion and occupation of the emirate. Close legal scrutiny does not support the Iraqi historical claim. Nevertheless, because of its generally latent characteristics, it is extremely difficult to predict precisely when the claim to Kuwait will next be resuscitated by a government in Baghdad.[12]

The second, essentially pragmatic, Iraqi territorial claim, made much more consistently – if less dramatically – over sixty years or so, has sought generally but unavailingly to change the existing boundary delimitation between the two states, so as to improve Iraq's limited access to Gulf waters. It has been fuelled by the persistent belief that Iraq has somehow been deliberately shut out of the Gulf. Certainly, Iraq is acutely aware of its position as a geographically disadvantaged state.[13] Though Iraq's charges of conspiracy are overplayed, there is a strong case for maintaining that Britain deliberately and successfully 'squeezed out' the Ottomans from the Gulf during the first decade or so of this century.[14] Notwithstanding the United Nations' supposedly final settlement of the Kuwait–Iraq boundary in May 1993 and Iraq's eventual if unequivocal acceptance of its findings eighteen months later, it would be a brave commentator who would confidently predict that the last has been heard of Iraqi territorial claims on Kuwait. Having pre-dated by some three and a half decades Saddam Hussein's accession to the Iraqi presidency, they must stand a good chance of surviving him.[15]

FILLING THE GLASS OF SETTLED ARABIAN LAND BOUNDARY DE-
LIMITATIONS: With the aid of the accompanying maps (see Maps 8.1a,
8.1b, 8.2 and 8.3), it is possible to review briefly the way in which the
Arabian territorial framework has evolved in the last quarter-century.[16] It
will be noted that only in the present decade has there been a discernible
momentum towards finalizing the Arabian political map.

On departing the Gulf as protecting power in 1971, Britain left a
rather untidy territorial legacy for the newly independent states of the
south-western Gulf littoral. Some boundaries existed: the first sea-bed
boundary agreement in the Gulf was concluded between Bahrain and
Saudi Arabia in 1958, while Qatar and the Riyadh government agreed
upon a land boundary delimitation in 1965.[17] These were the result of
direct negotiations with Saudi Arabia.

Britain's territorial legacy in the north of the peninsula had already
been modified considerably by this stage (see Map 8.2). Here, rather vague
northern boundaries for the Saudi kingdom had existed since the mid-
1920s with the awards by Britain's colonial boundary-makers in this region,
Sir Percy Cox and Sir Gilbert Clayton. Saudi Arabia and its northern
neighbors – of which Kuwait had been the last to be granted independence in 1961 – would modify the old colonial lines for convenience and
expediency. Saudi Arabia and Jordan arrived at a comprehensive territorial
settlement in 1965. Disposing of residual discontent over the status of
Aqaba and Ma'an, the agreement basically constituted a land swap. Jordan's
minuscule coastline on the eastern shores of the Gulf of Aqaba was
lengthened in return for Saudi Arabia being granted inland desert territory
to which it had long laid claim. It was a model which, with a little more
luck and determination, might have been successfully transferred to settle
the Iraq–Kuwait dispute over the islands of Warbah and Bubayan before
the disastrous events of August 1990.[18]

By agreements of 1965 and 1969, Kuwait and Saudi Arabia partitioned
the Neutral Zone introduced to separate their territories by Cox at the
1922 Uqair conference. Doing so was relatively painless, since the coffers
of both states would continue to be augmented massively by the oil
reserves underlying the territory. Saudi Arabia and Kuwait are now trying
to negotiate a similar arrangement for the offshore component of the
old Neutral Zone.

Saudi Arabia and Iraq had partitioned Cox's other Neutral Zone – also
introduced at Uqair – in boundary agreements of 1975 and 1981. These
also smoothed out what had previously been a jagged boundary delimitation (see Map 8.2). Even a full decade later, in the early 1990s, not everyone

in the international community was aware of this modification to the alignment of the boundary or, at least, of its implications. This would give rise to an unusual situation as allied Desert Shield forces lined up late in 1990 against Iraq. American field commanders apparently had maps in their hands showing the old Saudi–Iraqi boundary delimitation, and the Europeans' maps showed the new boundary line. Frantic transatlantic consultations ensued to put the matter straight.[19] Although the modified 1981 Saudi–Iraq delimitation was soon shown on contemporary Iraqi and Saudi maps and the exchange of ratifications of 26 December 1981 took place as early as February 1982, its precise details were released only during the 1991 Gulf War.[20] In the summer of 1991, Saudi Arabia registered the text of the treaty (with its boundary coordinates) with the United Nations in New York.

To the south of the peninsula, the 1970s and 1980s had been notable only for the lack of progress in finalizing the political map. The only development of note saw Saudi Arabia move to secure the long-standing strategic objective of a sovereign access corridor south of the Qatar peninsula through the Khor al-Udaid to the waters of the Gulf. Formal recognition of Saudi control of the territory in question – long a reality – was given only under sufferance by Abu Dhabi in a border agreement of July 1974. In return, Saudi Arabia officially dropped any lingering claims to territory further east in the Buraimi/al-Ain region. UAE sensitivities were at least partially ameliorated by an agreed modification of the boundary in 1993, whereby the UAE's westernmost territorial limits were extended into the Khor al-Udaid.

It was not until the 1990s that states in the southern peninsula made concerted efforts to finalize the political map. Having maintained Ibn Saud's territorial claim in the south consistently for more than fifty years, Saudi Arabia surprised some observers by agreeing with Oman in March 1990 to withdraw its own claims to the frontier line (see Map 8.3). In fact, the shape of the settlement had been apparent years earlier, as evidenced by a Saudi Military Survey map of 1986, which showed the very same line for the Oman boundary. As the agreement of 1990 was being concluded, there had been speculation that Saudi Arabia would be granted non-sovereign access facilities through Dhofar in the western sultanate, to provide a strategic pipeline outlet on the Arabian Sea. There is no evidence to show that Saudi Arabia gained any such rights, though the March 1990 agreement did suggest that if the circumstances were right, long-standing Arabian boundary disputes could be solved politically.

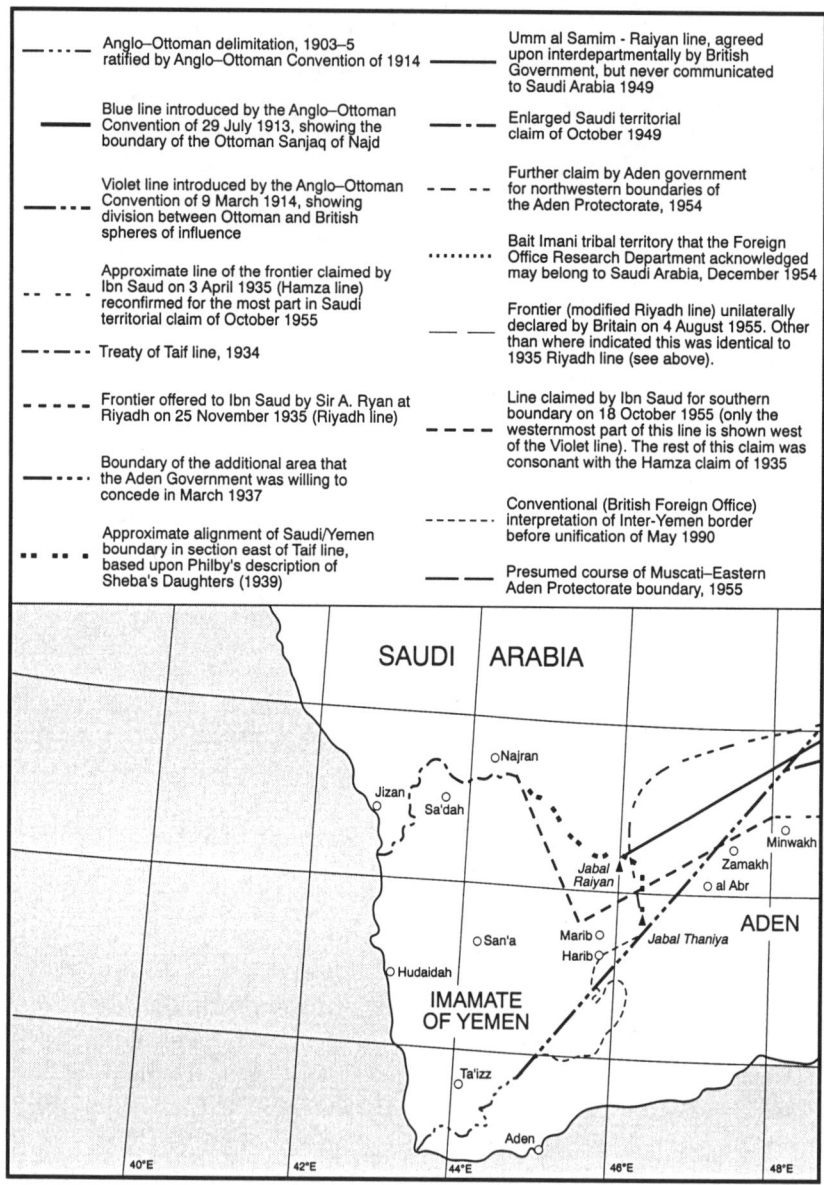

Map 8.1a Evolution of territorial limits and claims in southern and south-eastern Arabia, 1903–1955

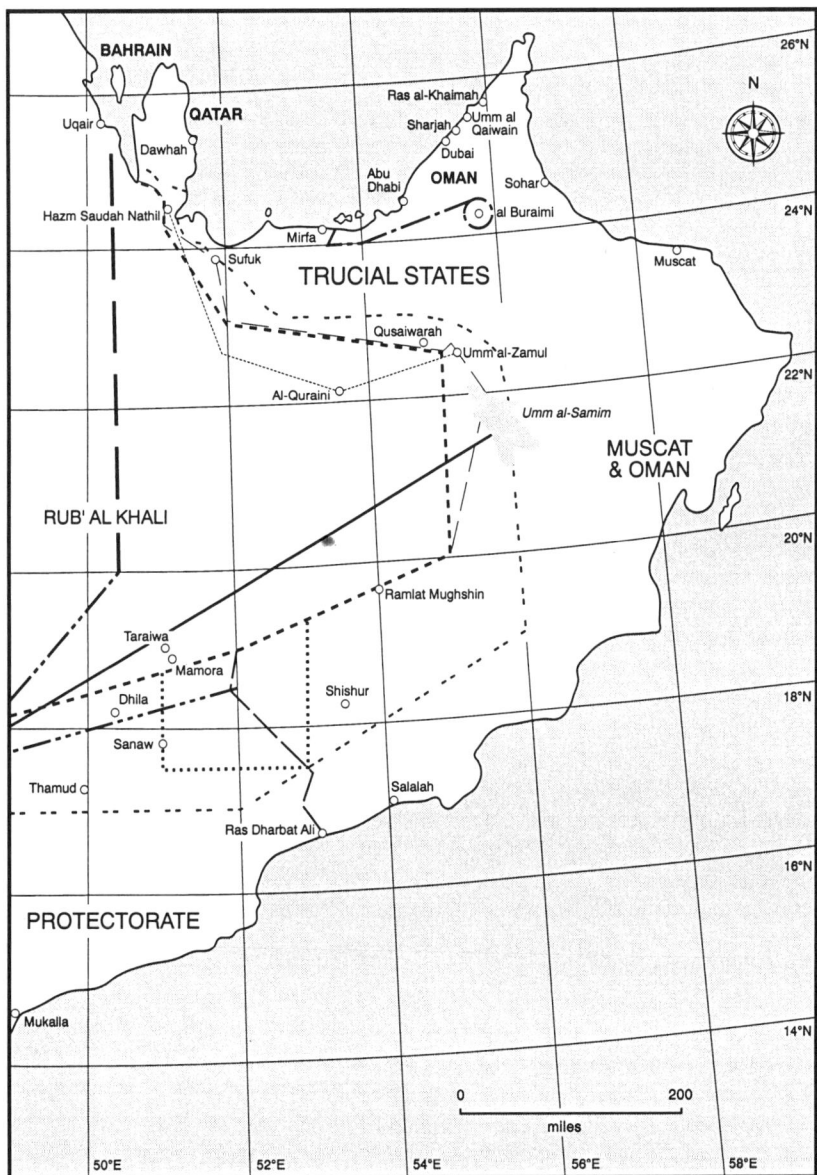

Map 8.1b Evolution of territorial limits and claims in southern and
south-eastern Arabia, 1903–1955 (cont)

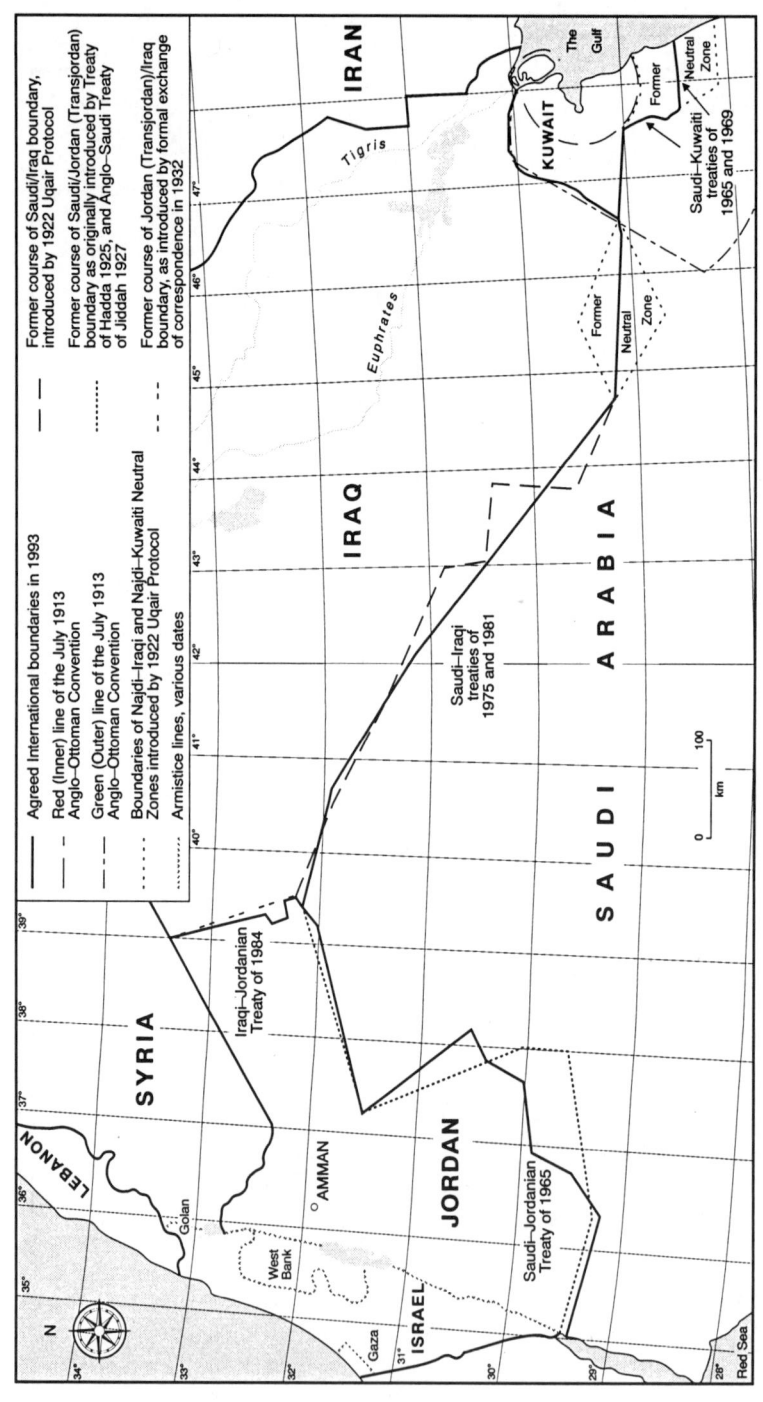

Map 8.2 Evolution of delimited state territory in northern Arabia, 1913 to the present day

Former course of Saudi/Iraq boundary, introduced by 1922 Uqair Protocol

Former course of Saudi/Jordan (Transjordan) boundary as originally introduced by Treaty of Hadda 1925, and Anglo–Saudi Treaty of Jiddah 1927

Former course of Jordan (Transjordan)/Iraq boundary, as introduced by formal exchange of correspondence in 1932

Agreed International boundaries in 1993

Red (Inner) line of the July 1913 Anglo–Ottoman Convention

Green (Outer) line of the July 1913 Anglo–Ottoman Convention

Boundaries of Najdi–Iraqi and Najdi–Kuwaiti Neutral Zones introduced by 1922 Uqair Protocol

Armistice lines, various dates

SYRIA

LEBANON

Golan

West Bank

Gaza

ISRAEL

AMMAN

JORDAN

Iraqi–Jordanian Treaty of 1984

Saudi–Jordanian Treaty of 1965

SAUDI   ARABIA

IRAQ

IRAN

Tigris

Euphrates

Saudi–Iraqi treaties of 1975 and 1981

KUWAIT

The Gulf

Former

Former Neutral Zone

Neutral Zone

Saudi–Kuwaiti treaties of 1965 and 1969

Red Sea

N

0   100
km

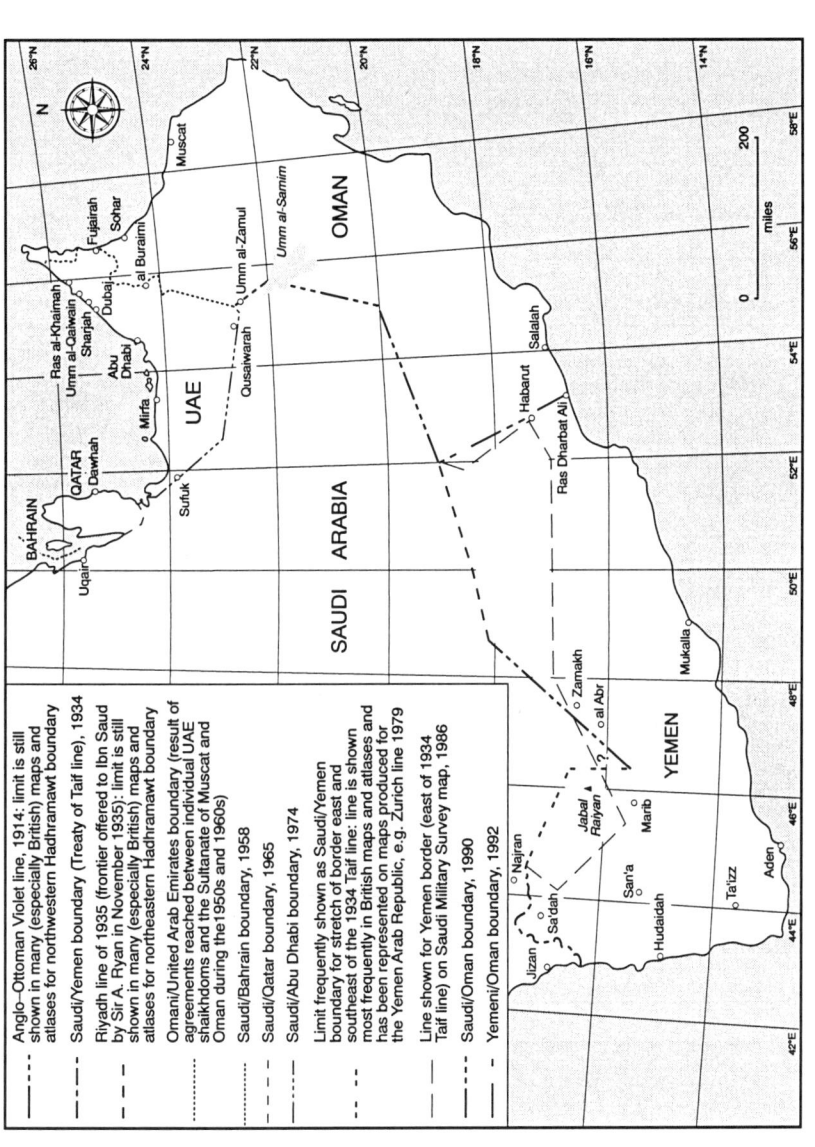

Anglo–Ottoman Violet line, 1914: limit is still shown in many (especially British) maps and atlases for northwestern Hadhramawt boundary

Saudi/Yemen boundary (Treaty of Taif line), 1934

Riyadh line of 1935 (frontier offered to Ibn Saud by Sir A. Ryan in November 1935): limit is still shown in many (especially British) maps and atlases for northeastern Hadhramawt boundary

Omani/United Arab Emirates boundary (result of agreements reached between individual UAE shaikhdoms and the Sultanate of Muscat and Oman during the 1950s and 1960s)

Saudi/Bahrain boundary, 1958

Saudi/Qatar boundary, 1965

Saudi/Abu Dhabi boundary, 1974

Limit frequently shown as Saudi/Yemen boundary for stretch of border east and southeast of the 1934 Taif line: line is shown most frequently in British maps and atlases and has been represented on maps produced for the Yemen Arab Republic, e.g. Zurich line 1979

Line shown for Yemen border (east of 1934 Taif line) on Saudi Military Survey map, 1986

Saudi/Oman boundary, 1990

Yemeni/Oman boundary, 1992

Map 8.3 The contemporary framework in southern Arabia

The Sultanate of Oman's boundaries can now be fairly characterized as fully evolved in international law. The move to finally settle the Oman–Saudi boundary seemed to give fresh impetus to efforts to finalize the Oman/United Arab Emirates boundary delimitation. In May 1991, at the same time as the Muscat and Riyadh governments were exchanging instruments of ratification of their March 1990 border treaty, Oman and the UAE set up a joint committee to discuss bilateral issues including the border. Their efforts culminated, almost two years later, in the statement on 9 April 1993 by Omani Foreign Minister Yusuf bin Alawi bin Abdullah that 'the frontier dispute is completely settled', following the signature of a 'lasting agreement' between the two states.[21] At around the same time, the architect of the UAE's patchwork quilt of internal boundaries, Julian Walker, returned to complete the process he had begun as a British government official in the late 1950s, now advising on the final drawing of indeterminate stretches of the boundaries of the emirates of Sharjah and Ras al-Khaimah. Meanwhile, during October 1992, Oman and Yemen had agreed on a land boundary delimitation, a procedure for its de-marcation and the manner by which the territorial limit would be extended offshore into the Arabian Sea. The text of the agreement and the bound-ary coordinates it introduced were immediately made available to the public. Oman took the same opportunity to make public the text of its March 1990 border agreement with Saudi Arabia.[22] As already mentioned, a slight, westward shift of Abu Dhabi's (UAE's) boundary with Saudi Arabia along the Khor al-Udaid was agreed in 1993.

A SURPRISING REVERSE AT KHAFUS: Such apparently unchecked momentum towards finalizing the Arabian territorial framework would receive a jolt from an unexpected quarter in the autumn of 1992 with the flare-up at Khafus on the undemarcated Saudi–Qatari border.[23] For a full quarter of a century, most observers had assumed that the border delimita-tion introduced by a Saudi–Qatari agreement of 1965 was acceptable to central government in both Riyadh and Doha. Reportedly, the territorial limit established by the 1965 agreement approximated closely to long-standing Qatari claims which had previously been articulated through Britain, then responsible for Qatar's foreign affairs in dealings with the Saudi government. Though the text of the 1965 agreement was not made public until the autumn of 1992,[24] it was known that the line was basically that claimed by Britain on behalf of the ruler of Qatar at the Anglo–Saudi Dammam conference of February 1952. Atlases and maps produced recently in both states show this same line, which has never been demarcated.[25] So, too, do contemporary British and American operational and tactical pilotage charts.

Despite Saudi Arabia's acceptance of the border introduced by the 1965 agreement in the years that followed, some problems began to surface in the early 1990s. In late 1991 and early 1992, these tensions coincided with consultations between Qatar and Iran as to the possible ways in which their huge, shared North Dome offshore gas field (referred to as the North field in Qatar and the South Pars field in Iran) might be exploited.

Though one should not underplay the serious strains in Saudi–Qatari relations occasioned by the incident, it was always a fair presumption that the difficulties over the border would be transitory, since there was no real difficulty with the boundary delimitation itself. Of course, it was not yet demarcated, though this had caused no apparent problems until the early 1990s. Tensions in 1992 were and remain to this day political. It had always seemed likely that Saudi Arabia and Qatar, once they had begun to address the immediate fall-out from the Khafus incident, would take the fairly obvious step of agreeing to demarcate the 1965 delimitation so as to ensure against any future dispute over its precise alignment. This is exactly what happened in late December 1992 following the shuttle diplomacy between Doha and Riyadh of Egyptian President Hosni Mubarak.[26]

There is no evidence that the Saudi–Qatari land border has been demarcated, even though it is now four years since President Mubarak's seemingly successful intervention. The land border was closed in June 1995 as the heir apparent, Sheikh Hamad, deposed his father to become Emir.[27] It was soon reopened but the change of guard in Qatar seemed to have no effect on the apparent stalemate of efforts to demarcate the land boundary delimitation introduced by the 1965 treaty between the two states. In April 1996, the governments of Saudi Arabia and Qatar announced that they had finally reached agreement on a procedure to demarcate their common land boundary.[28] Though it seems that markers have yet to be put in place to demarcate the boundary, much less has been heard since of its disputed status, a state of affairs helped by the recent (December 1996–January 1997) rapprochement between Hamad and Khalifa. Qatar's recent maritime disputes with Bahrain have also deflected attention from the emirate's sole land boundary, as we shall see.

The Khafus incident and Saudi–Qatari relations over the undemarcated border neatly illustrate the assertion of the French social scientist, Jacques Ancel, that there are no problems of boundaries, only problems of nations. Unlike many of the other territorial disputes reviewed in this chapter, its roots are clearly political. A basic consideration of geographical scale is involved here too. Qatar has only one land boundary – with Saudi Arabia. Saudi Arabia has six other land boundary delimitations to concern itself with. The issue would seem to matter most to Qatar. The land border may well continue to be used as the barometer of relations between Riyadh and Doha in the future.

The GCC and Territorial Disputes

It is as well to consider what has been the motivation behind the recent rush to delimit Arabian state territory and to ask how, if at all, it is being promoted and regulated by the Gulf Cooperation Council (GCC), surely the only regional organization capable of doing so. The increasing pre-occupation of the GCC during the last four years or so with the further entrenchment, institutionalization and (where appropriate) finalization of the territorial framework of Arabia has been primarily a response to Iraq's catastrophic move on Kuwait but also an acknowledgement of the pressing territorial concerns of member states hosting GCC annual summits at the close of each calendar year.

REGULATION OF BORDERS AND TERRITORIAL DISPUTES BEFORE 1990: Prior to the Iraqi invasion of Kuwait in August 1990, the GCC had not been particularly active in either promoting the resolution of territorial disputes, or in developing a policy to institutionalize the pre-vailing framework of state territory. Article 10 of the GCC Charter, signed on 25 May 1981, defined the responsibilities of that organization's 'Commission for the settlement of disputes', yet there is no evidence to suggest that the commission has ever met to treat territorial disputes between member states. The Bahrain–Qatar dispute over Hawar and the shoals – the one dispute to have figured regularly on the agenda of the GCC during the last decade and a half – has been addressed at the ministerial level instead. Member states of the GCC have chosen generally not to refer territorial problems for formal treatment by the council.

Perhaps the greatest single achievement of the GCC in its dealings with the territorial disputes of the region before 1990 was to prevent Bahrain and Qatar from going to war over the disputed ownership of a low-tide elevation in the waters which separate the two states. Until the Khafus border post incident of late September 1992, the Bahraini–Qatari clash on the Dibal shoal during the spring of 1986 perhaps constituted the greatest internal challenge to have confronted the GCC. Its settlement was certainly one of the institution's notable successes. Conflict was averted only after the decisive intervention of Saudi Arabia, which brokered a settlement whereby the two states would return the situation on the shoals to the status quo ante. After the GCC had set up a monitoring group to ensure that the two sides implemented the agreement, Qatar evacuated Dibal early in June 1986.[29]

The GCC has never been slow to condemn Iranian territorial advances or actions taken by the Tehran government which appear to threaten the territorial stability of the Gulf. Throughout the course of the 1980–88 Iran–Iraq War, the GCC protested Iranian advances into Iraqi territory proper, consistently demanding an immediate withdrawal to recognized international boundaries.[30] The stance was never expressed more strongly than following the Iranian capture of the Fao peninsula in 1986. Generally, however, the GCC stopped short of extending unequivocal support to Iraq's claim to full sovereignty over the Shatt al-Arab river. However, the leaders of the GCC states were all present at the Extraordinary (Arab League) Baghdad Summit of late May 1990, which resulted in the issue of a more forthcoming closing statement. In this, the Arab League called for UN-sponsored Iran–Iraq negotiations which would 'guarantee Iraq's rights and sovereignty over its territory, particularly its historical right to sovereignty over the Shatt al-Arab'.[31] Despite such solid support for its claim to the Shatt al-Arab, Iraq was relaxing, or contemplating relaxing, its own stance on the issue just before it made its disastrous move on Kuwait on 2 August 1990.[32]

THE DAMASCUS DECLARATION AND THE REGULATION OF STATE TERRITORY: Throughout the 1980–88 Iran–Iraq War, one of the GCC's most frequently articulated principles had been that the territorial integrity of the eight states of the Gulf was inviolable. The principle was, of course, shattered completely by the Iraqi invasion of Kuwait on 2 August 1990. Security was, naturally enough, the priority of the GCC states in the immediate aftermath of the successful allied campaign to oust Iraq from Kuwait in early 1991. The expressed purpose of the 6 March 1991 Damascus Declaration was to define a workable collective security structure involving the GCC states, Syria and Egypt. Greater regulation of existing borders was deemed an important component of regional security. This principle was explicitly articulated in the declaration, along with others which worked for the maintenance of the regional territorial framework: the peaceful resolution of disputes; respect for international law; mutual non-interference; and good neighborliness.[33] The plans envisaged in the declaration for a collective security structure (in conventional military terms) may never see the light of day, but this fully ratified document remains an important statement of policy, principle and intent – certainly as far as the regulation of state territory is concerned.

FURTHER ELABORATION AT ABU DHABI, DECEMBER 1992: It is not at all unusual for regional groupings such as the GCC to give a high priority to the immediate foreign policy concerns of the member state hosting their annual summit meeting. This has been the tendency where annual GCC summit meetings and the pressing territorial issues of its member states are concerned. The precedent had been set well before the Abu Dhabi summit of December 1992. Two years earlier, in Doha, most observers had expected the GCC summit to result in a considered response being drawn up to the dire situation in the northern Gulf. Instead, perhaps more time was taken up by consideration of the Bahraini–Qatari dispute over the Hawar islands and the Dibal and Jarada shoals.[34]

The issue of the Abu Dhabi 'declaration' by the thirteenth GCC summit on 23 December 1992 would reinforce and extend those principles enunciated in the Damascus Declaration that worked for the entrenchment and regulation of the regional territorial framework. The sections of the declaration bearing on territorial issues were explicitly directed towards Iranian culpability earlier in the year for the resurrection of the long-established – though previously (since 1971) suppressed – cyclical dispute over the sovereignty of Abu Musa island. The second clause of the Abu Dhabi declaration read:

> The GCC member states' regional and international dealings are based upon respect for the principle of good neighbourliness as a basic and legal rule, for the states' independence and sovereignty over their territories, and respect for the principle of non-interference in the internal affairs and for each state's sovereignty over its resources.[35]

The third clause – a direct consequence of Iranian actions on Abu Musa and within the text of which Iran was explicitly castigated – laid great stress on the 'inadmissibility of the acquisition of land by force':

> Their adoption of the principle of dialogue and negotiation as a basic means to settle conflicts between states, in accordance with the UN Charter and international law and norms; rejection of the principle of threatening to use force in relations among states; and their abidance by the principle of the inadmissibility of the acquisition of land by force.[36]

It was the first occasion upon which the principle had been articulated in such terms or in such detail by the GCC.

GCC CALLS FOR FINALIZATION OF THE ARABIAN POLITICAL MAP, MANAMA, DECEMBER 1994: The fifteenth annual GCC summit in Bahrain during December 1994 was notable not so such for the enunciation of any new principles regulating limits to state territory, as for its apparent urgency to see territorial disputes between member (and neighboring) states settled and the political map of the Arabian peninsula finalized. Once again, territorial problems were high on the agenda. The parting message from the GCC Supreme Council was that member states should make every effort to resolve their (inter-GCC) territorial disputes through bilateral negotiations before the next annual summit, scheduled for Muscat in December 1995. In its final communiqué of 21 December 1994, the Supreme Council implored member states to: 'redouble efforts to sort out outstanding bilateral problems ... before the Supreme Council reconvenes in its 16th session'.[37] Some six weeks later the Bahraini Foreign Ministry would expand upon what had apparently been decided at the summit with regard to the conduct of territorial disputes between member states. According to this source, if no progress had been made in bilateral consultations before the end of 1995, then the disputes in question could be returned for the consideration of the Supreme Council at the Muscat summit. It was further suggested that the GCC's 'Commission for the settlement of disputes' might finally be activated at Muscat to treat territorial disputes.[38]

Once again, however, statements of the GCC on territorial policy had much to do with the immediate interests of the host state. Ever since the summer of 1991, Bahrain had disputed the manner in which Qatar had referred the Hawar dispute to the International Court of Justice (ICJ) in The Hague. The ICJ's verdict of July 1994 that it did, after all, possess jurisdiction to try the territorial dispute on the basis of Qatar's earlier and unilateral application, was ostensibly a defeat for Bahrain. It was, therefore, in Bahrain's interest for the GCC to announce a strong preference for 'in-house' dispute resolution by bilateral means. The soft 12-months timetable also reflected Bahrain's urgency to reach an out-of-court settlement before formal proceedings began in The Hague.

Yet the Supreme Council's directives of December 1994 also reflected what has been a discernible urgency of component states in recent years to see the Arabian political map finalized. There have been pragmatic considerations at work here. Beginning in the early 1990s, several Arabian states accelerated efforts to develop hydrocarbon reserves in border regions. Because of their politically sensitive locations and general remoteness, these fields had often been ignored prior to this point but the economic imperatives of maximizing production in a flat oil market were now to outweigh such reservations.[39] Perhaps this development helps to explain the considerable progress made in finalizing border delimitations in southeast Arabia in recent years, for there has been a need to consolidate state authority right up to the absolute limits of the territory of the state. The need for precisely delimited boundaries is clear in this respect if exploration and development is to proceed without disputed claims and border incidents. By this stage, there was only one serious 'in-house' territorial problem for the GCC to consider, the Bahrain–Qatar dispute over the sovereignty of the Hawar islands and the Dibal and Jarada shoals. The rest of the GCC political map had essentially evolved. This reality was acknowledged in another part of the closing statement at Manama, which somewhat contradicted the directive to 'go settle, soon and bilaterally'. This said that territorial disputes should not be treated by the council 'in a way which might give them a false significance', adding that 'they must be contained within their normal magnitude, which is small'.[40]

FOLLOWING UP ON THE MANAMA DIRECTIVE OF 1994: It would soon become clear that the directive issued at Manama for GCC states to settle disputes bilaterally within 12 months reflected Bahrain's wish that the Hawar dispute might somehow be withdrawn from the ICJ agenda in The Hague and be solved at the bilateral level instead. As has already been commented, it has been the norm for pronouncements of GCC policy to promote the agenda of the member state hosting the annual summit meeting. By the time of the Muscat summit early in December 1995, it was evident that the Hawar case would not be withdrawn from the ICJ. This, coupled with the fact that Oman, the host state, possessed finalized land boundaries with all of its Arabian neighbors and also an agreed maritime delimitation with Iran, suggested that boundaries and territorial disputes would not be prominent on the summit agenda. This proved to be the case.

In short, GCC policy towards the resolution of Arabian disputes and the finalization of the political map of the region has not been proactive but reactive. It has been and is likely to continue to be a response to regional instability; an effective acknowledgement of the need for the tidy expropriation of natural resources, especially where the drawing of seabed boundaries in the Gulf is concerned (a task, incidentally, which is far from complete); and, finally, it is forged out of sensitivity to the territorial concerns of member states hosting the platform upon which policy statements are made.

The Conduct of Regional Disputes Since the Issue of the December 1994 Manama Directive

The issue of the Manama Directive has not proved quite as significant as it might have done. Yet the principle of settling 'in-house' disputes bilaterally appears now to be an accepted one. As such, it is instructive to review the recent conduct of the major disputes of the region. First, a review will be made of those instances in which the Manama Directive appears to have had an influence in promoting the finalization of the territorial map. Second, a summary will be provided of what could be termed the coincidental progress of the last two years. Then more detailed case-studies will document developments in the two disputes that have dominated the agenda of recent GCC summit meetings: the Bahrain–Qatar dispute over sovereignty of the Hawar islands, the ownership of the Dibal and Jarada shoals and the status of the Qatari coastal settlement of Zubara; and the Iran–UAE dispute over the sovereignty of the islands of Abu Musa and the Tunbs.

ICING ON THE CAKE OF PRE-EXISTING BOUNDARY DELIMITA-TIONS IN SOUTH-EAST ARABIA: Progress towards the finalization of the political map in south-eastern Arabia was much heralded within the GCC states during 1995. Yet the nature of the progress was, in truth, more akin to the 'tidying-up' of issues which had basically been settled at an earlier, if recent, point in time.

Nineteen ninety-five witnessed the tying-up of loose ends and little more. On 3 June, lavish celebrations greeted the completion of the demarcation of the international boundary between Oman and Yemen.[41] Official documentation associated with the completion of the demarcation process was deposited at the Arab League Secretariat in Cairo. Just over a month later, a series of detailed maps of the Saudi–Oman border was signed by senior officials of the two states at a ceremony in Riyadh.[42] These gave more substance to the coordinates specified in the delimitation introduced by the March 1990 border agreement, which was short on detail.

Finally and moving slightly to the north, Saudi Arabia confirmed its border treaty of July 1974 with Abu Dhabi (United Arab Emirates) by registering the full text of the document with the United Nations in the late spring of 1995.[43] The alignment introduced by this boundary had not been in doubt and has been clearly shown for a good decade or so on official maps produced in Saudi Arabia, UAE, Britain and the USA.

Controversy during the early 1990s had instead revolved around the treaty's provisions for the exploitation of natural resources straddling the territorial limit.

In general, developments in the south-eastern peninsula during 1995 equated well with the directive given at the 1994 GCC summit for member states to solve remaining territorial disputes quickly and with minimum fuss. While the arguments themselves did not comprehensively address the several problematic territorial issues of the region, the sum effect of these refinements has been to render less appropriate the criticisms typically made of Arabian boundaries and, more specifically, the agreements which have introduced them. Saudi Arabia can now point to the fact that it has renegotiated or modified all of the territorial understandings concluded between Ibn Saud and the British − or frequently imposed by the latter − during the early part of the century. This is doubtless of importance politically to the Kingdom. Saudi Arabia's smaller but historically mindful Arab neighbors along the western/southern Gulf littoral will also be reassured by the growing evidence that the territorial framework has evolved to a point of no return.

COINCIDENTAL PROGRESS TOWARDS THE COMPLETION OF THE POLITICAL MAP: In one of the cases mentioned here (Saudi Arabia–Yemen), the nature of progress made in the last two years has been more in the way of a promise of eventual settlement. In the other (Iraq–Kuwait), a definitive legal settlement of the boundary has been accepted by all parties, but the geo-strategic determinants which have made this territorial limit such a live wire historically remain to threaten the future stability of the north-western Gulf. The GCC's Manama Directive influenced many of these developments.

On 10 November 1994, the Iraqi Revolutionary Command Council passed a decree which extended unconditional recognition to the United Nations Iraq–Kuwait border delimitation/demarcation. Its first two clauses read as follows:

> 1. The Republic of Iraq recognizes the State of Kuwait's sovereignty, territorial integrity and political independence;
>
> 2. In compliance with UN Security Council Resolution 833 of 1993, the Republic of Iraq recognizes the international borders between the Republic of Iraq and the State of Kuwait, as demarcated by the UN Iraq–Kuwait Boundary Demarcation Commission, formed under paragraph 3 of Resolution 687 of 1991, and respects the inviolability of the above borders.[44]

For much of the previous two and a half years, Iraq's attitude had bordered on outright rejection of the UN demarcation team's decisions on the precise course of the boundary. From the late summer of 1994, however, there had been mounting speculation that Iraq would give its blessing to the UN boundary line that Kuwait (strongly supported by the USA and Britain) had demanded of it. Iraq's unconditional acceptance of the boundary was warmly welcomed by the Supreme Council of the GCC in the closing statement to the Manama summit in December 1994.[45]

In a Memorandum of Understanding concluded in February 1995, Saudi Arabia and Yemen recommitted themselves to the short, existing stretch of their boundary bordering the Red Sea and further agreed to brick up this line. They also agreed upon a procedural framework for negotiating Arabia's last indeterminate territorial limit in the desert wastes further east. Tangible progress in the rounds of negotiations held up until now – these have been running intermittently since July 1992 – has been slow, though it is not necessarily in the interests of either state to reach a speedy settlement. Despite the inexorable progress of recent years towards finalizing its land boundaries, Saudi Arabia may consider that there is more benefit to be gained in its dealings with Sana'a from an indeterminate border. The Yemen government itself may consider that the territorial compromises it would need to make to facilitate agreement would be too difficult to defend before its own domestic constituency.[46]

Oil prospecting in the disputed borderlands has yielded disappointing results to date. This has made the negotiations easier since the stakes have been lowered, but has also lessened the urgency to arrive at an agreed delimitation of state territory. As shown in Map 8.3, there is a considerable overlap of contemporary territorial claims in the southern peninsula. This degree of overlap has been significantly increased as a result of Yemen forwarding its first ever claim along the disputed border-lands during the summer of 1996.[47] For the indeterminate stretch east of the existing 1934 boundary (Treaty of Taif line), Yemen would now claim a boundary running along the 20th parallel – considerably further north of the territorial claims Britain had entered for the Aden Protectorate in the period up until 1967.[48]

Despite the present incongruence of Saudi and Yemeni claims, one should never rule out the prospect of this dispute being solved by a quick political fix should conditions appear especially conducive in the future.[49]

ICJ SET TO DELIVER VERDICT ON BAHRAIN–QATAR MARITIME DISPUTES: As a result of an ICJ decision of February 1995, the prospects for a resolution of open issues between Bahrain and Qatar appear good. The dispute is now in court and a decision of some sort will be reached by the ICJ. When the ICJ finally delivers its award (which is unlikely to occur before 1998) it will be making a ruling on the ownership of three features – the Hawar island group and the Dibal and Jarada shoals.

Since this is the one inter-GCC dispute which has periodically dominated the agenda of successive summit meetings for the last fifteen years, it is as well to go back just over six years and look at the origins of the disagreement over whether the ICJ had the right to try the territorial dispute, as it concluded in July 1994 that it had, confirming this decision seven months later.

After years in which the Manama and Doha governments had kept themselves busy preparing defenses of their claims to Hawar and the shoals in anticipation of the dispute being referred to the ICJ for a ruling, a watershed appeared to have been reached at the 1990 GCC annual summit in Doha. Here, Bahrain and Qatar apparently concluded an agreement which stipulated that, should no out-of-court settlement be attainable within six months, then the case should be forwarded to the ICJ for a ruling.[50]

Nevertheless, on 8 July 1991, with Qatar evidently believing that the six-month deadline had passed without the requisite progress having been made, the Doha government referred the dispute to the ICJ. The reference was to remain unilateral, however, for Bahrain contested the basis of jurisdiction invoked by Qatar in letters addressed to the ICJ in July and August 1991. It was now for the ICJ to rule on whether it possessed jurisdiction itself to try the dispute following the Qatari referral of July 1991. Qatar maintained that its action was the culmination of a procedure agreed to at the December 1990 Doha summit. This had been 'concluded in the context of mediation of King Fahd of Saudi Arabia'.[51]

Because of a backlog of cases at The Hague, the ICJ could not rule upon whether it possessed jurisdiction to try Bahrain–Qatar territorial disputes until July 1994, having heard pleadings from both states four months earlier. Had the court ruled that it did not possess jurisdiction, it might have been expected that Bahrain–Qatar maritime disputes would have been returned to Saudi mediation.[52] However, on 1 July 1994, the ICJ ruled that it did, after all, possess jurisdiction to rule on the disputes.[53] The ICJ announced that both parties were now to be given the opportunity to submit the whole agenda of dispute, including Zubara. Bahrain and Qatar were reminded that previous agreements (that is, those concluded under the aegis of Saudi/GCC mediation in 1987 and 1990) had obliged them to submit the dispute to the ICJ for a binding settlement. The end of November 1994 was set as the date by which the two states were to submit their respective cases, either separately or jointly. Bahrain and Qatar subsequently held three meetings to try and agree upon a joint submission.

In its ruling of 15 February 1995, the ICJ confirmed its ruling of the previous summer that it possessed jurisdiction to treat Bahrain–Qatar disputes over the sovereignty of the Hawar islands and the shoals and the status of the Qatari coastal settlement of Zubara. Essentially following the December 1994 directive of the GCC Supreme Council to solve 'in-house' disputes bilaterally (see section above), for which, as summit host, it was probably largely responsible, Bahrain meanwhile urged the following, alternative course of action upon Qatar for treatment by the ICJ:

1. continue treating the dispute on a bilateral basis;
2. forward it for consideration by the Supreme Council at the December 1995 Muscat summit should no progress have been made in consultations;
3. press for the activation of the GCC's 'Committee for the settlement of disputes' to deal with this and other (inter-GCC) territorial disputes.

Perhaps apprehensive about Bahrain's lack of enthusiasm for treatment of Hawar etcetera by the ICJ, Sheikh Hamad of Qatar (then Crown Prince, now Ruler) immediately invited Saudi Arabia to resume its mediating role in the maritime disputes.[54] This had effectively (though not officially) ceased following the signature of the Bahrain–Qatar accord of December 1990, which had specified a timetable for reference of the dispute to the international courts. The gesture was soon welcomed by Bahrain and Saudi Arabia agreed in principle to resume its mediating role.

It soon became clear, however, that Bahrain and Qatar maintained differing expectations of Saudi Arabia's reactivated role. Bahrain might have hoped and may still genuinely hope that some sort of bilateral understanding can be reached that will occasion Qatar to withdraw the Hawar case from treatment by the ICJ. This seems unrealistic on two counts, however. First, Saudi mediating successes in the 1971–90 period were generally to ensure that the dispute never escalated into open hostilities. Second, Saudi mediation through the aegis of the GCC during the late 1980s was specifically geared to paving the way for a reference of the dispute to the courts. For its part, Qatar saw nothing incongruous about Saudi mediation running concurrently with treatment of the dispute by the ICJ. After all, the Bahraini–Qatari agreements of both 1987 and 1990 specified clearly that the mediating efforts of the Riyadh government would continue during ICJ hearings.

Meanwhile, the Qatari government prepared its memorial for submission to the ICJ to meet the court-imposed deadline of February 1996. Come February 1996, as Qatar was about to submit its memorial, Bahrain requested that the ICJ provide it with an extension in which to produce a memorial of its own. It was granted. The Manama government submitted the document in question to The Hague in the late summer of 1996. Each side has until the end of 1997 to write its own counter-memorial, after which court hearings will begin in earnest in The Hague.

The ICJ's current treatment of the Hawar dispute, after years of procedural wranglings, guarantees a decision on the sovereignty of the islands and shoals. This will be arrived at, probably at some point during 1998. Implementation of the award may prove to be the real acid test of Bahrain–Qatar relations and the GCC's ability to diffuse unrest in its own house. Ironically, Saudi Arabia's traditional mediating role in this dispute may become most critical at the very moment that the case has been settled in international law. A cursory glance at recent territorial awards made in The Hague, especially those introducing maritime delimitations, would suggest that the ICJ will endeavour to arrive at an arrangement with which both states will not be entirely dissatisfied.

The GCC is adopting a wait-and-see attitude towards the ICJ's current treatment of Bahrain–Qatar maritime disputes. Though it has expressed no enthusiasm whatsoever for the court's current treatment of an Arabian territorial dispute, its silence on the matter since the ICJ announcement of February 1995 suggests that it is resigned to its possible consequences.

THE STALEMATED DISPUTE OVER ABU MUSA AND THE TUNBS: The fourth week of November 1995 witnessed the first bout of bilateral contacts for three years between officials of the Iranian and UAE governments on the Abu Musa and Tunbs dispute. Even though expectations were not particularly high, the fact that the two sides were talking in Doha (at the invitation of the Qatari Foreign Ministry) was seen as a positive sign. The aim of the meeting was to agree upon an agenda for treatment of the dispute in future bilateral negotiations. Unfortunately, the talks broke down quickly as had those convened during the autumn of 1992 in Abu Dhabi to redress the damage done by the much-publicized incidents on Abu Musa during that year. It seems that a preparedness to talk did not signal any relaxation of the differing and opposing stances that Iran and the UAE maintain towards the islands question.

The UAE delegation went into the meeting with their Iranian counterparts in Doha at the same time as the agenda they would articulate and defend was published by the UAE government. The agenda was thoroughly consistent with officially stated positions of the GCC throughout 1995 and that articulated during July 1995 by the Foreign Ministers of states signatory to the 1991 Damascus Declaration. As had been the case back in the short-lived and unsuccessful negotiations of autumn 1992, the first item on the UAE agenda was a demand that Iran end its military occupation of the Tunb islands. Almost certainly, as in autumn 1992, the talks broke down here. According to various Reuters reports, the UAE agenda for proposed talks was as follows:

1. Iran terminates its military occupation of the Tunb islands;
2. Iran guarantees to abide by the express provisions of the 1971 Iran–Sharjah Memorandum of Understanding on Abu Musa and to cancel any measures which have or are violating this agreement;
3. the issue of sovereignty of Abu Musa should be settled;
4. the disputes should be referred to external arbitration should bilateral negotiations not produce a settlement within a specified time period.

Time and space do not afford the opportunity to delve deeply into the origins and historical conduct of the Abu Musa/Tunbs dispute,[55] save to say here that Britain, as protecting power, actively defended the claims to and occupation of the islands by the Qawasim of the southern Gulf littoral until it vacated the Gulf politically in 1971. Following Britain's departure of Gulf waters, Iran immediately and forcibly occupied the Tunb islands and positioned its military in the northern half of Abu Musa island following the conclusion of a prior agreement with the Ruler of Sharjah. Sharjah had entered into this arrangement voluntarily but reluctantly.

The arrangement in question was the Iran–Sharjah Memorandum of Understanding (MOU) on Abu Musa, concluded on 23 November 1971 and first announced by the Ruler of Sharjah himself six days later. The essentially pragmatic MOU was most notable for the way in which it accommodated the full sovereign claims of both Iran and Sharjah to the island. Its first clause read as follows: 'Neither Iran nor Sharjah will give up its claims to Abu Musa nor recognize the other's claim.'[56] In other words, the question of sovereignty was finessed – hence the desire of the UAE in November 1995 to finally settle the issue. The MOU provided for the positioning of Iranian forces in key strategic areas – basically the hilly terrain in the north of the island – as defined on a map attached to its text (see Map 8.4). Within this designated area, Iran possessed full jurisdiction, but outside, it fell to Sharjah as before. Iran and Sharjah each recognized a territorial sea for the island with a breadth of 12 nautical miles in which nationals of both parties would enjoy equal fishing rights. The Buttes Oil Company would continue to exploit hydrocarbon reserves (from the nearby Mubarak oil field, now operated by Crescent of Sharjah) under the conditions specified in its existing concession agreement with the Ruler of Sharjah, for as long as these conditions were acceptable to Iran. Lastly, Iran was to give Sharjah $1.5 million annually in aid until such time as its annual oil revenue reached twice this amount; this would take three years in point of fact.

Given the previous impasse in this dispute, an arrangement that allowed for the flying of each party's flag on the island seemed, on the face of it, a fairly logical and sustainable compromise. The arrangement for the divided administration contained within the MOU was highly imaginative and pragmatic given the apparent insolubility of the dispute and the regional political realities of the time. The 1971 MOU withstood several challenges in the following two decades. In declaring war on Iran during September 1980, Iraqi President Saddam Hussein announced his intention of restoring Abu Musa and the Tunbs to the Arab homeland. During 1987, the regime for Abu Musa set up by the 1971 MOU was seriously infringed with an Iranian move into the southern, Sharjah-administered part of the island. By the time Iran realized that the attempt had been aborted, the Iranian military on the island had already lowered the Sharjah flag. They then hurriedly rehoisted it and returned to their allotted positions. Iranian patrols into the south of the island had become an increasingly regular feature since 1983.

Perhaps the visit during February 1992 of Iranian State President Hashemi Rafsanjani to Abu Musa and other islands in the Lower Gulf had signalled a change in Iranian policy towards territorial issues in the Lower Gulf. Yet, well before this time and increasingly during the course of the 1980–88 Iran–Iraq War, Iran had expressed misgivings about what it termed the 'security situation' on Abu Musa. It privately justified its own encroachments from 1983 onwards into the Sharjah-administered part of the island by pointing to the increasing number of visits made by non-Sharjah nationals to the feature. Iran's seizure and arrest of a Dutch sailor, 'armed' with a flaregun, during the third quarter of 1991, led to the intensification of protests that too many unknown third-party

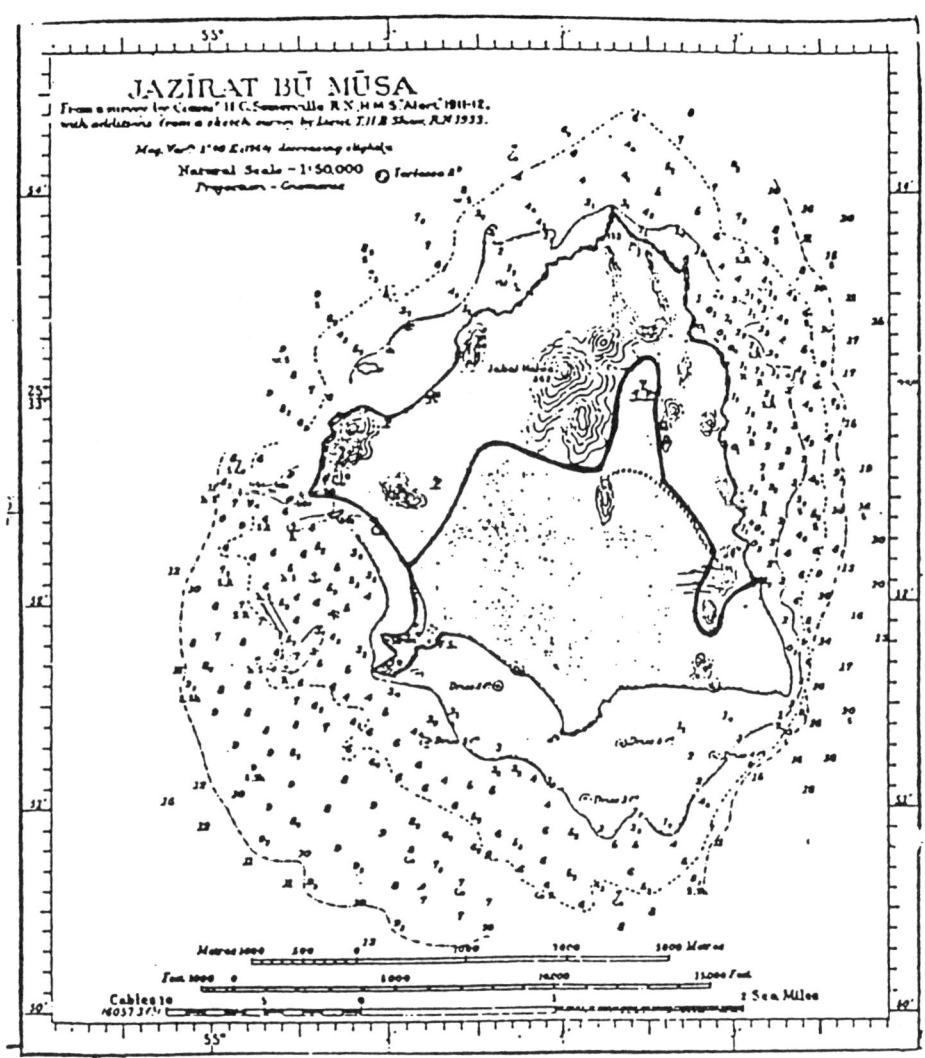

Map 8.4 Territorial jurisdiction in Abu Musa island folowing the conclusion of the November 1971 Iran–Sharjah Memorandum of Understanding.

Source: P. L. Toye (ed) *Arabian Geopolitics 2: The Lower Gulf Islands* (Farnham: Archive Editions, 1993), vol 6, p 491.

nationals were going back and forth between Sharjah and Abu Musa. In January 1992, Iran requested that Sharjah agree to the Tehran government issuing security passes to non-nationals visiting the island from the southern Gulf littoral.[57]

Then came the well-publicized incidents of April and August 1992, which temporarily seemed to suggest that the 1971 MOU was no longer workable or that, at best, it needed renegotiating. In April 1992, the Iranian authorities prevented a group of non-national employees of the Emirate of Sharjah (comprising Pakistani, Indian and Filipino laborers and technicians, and also non-UAE Arab, mainly Egyptian teachers) from entering the Sharjah-administered part of the island. The dispute intensified with reports on 24 August 1992 that Iran had refused entry to a large group of over one hundred third-party nationals. These were mainly Egyptian teachers and their families, many of whom had originally been denied entry to Abu Musa in April. Iran had backed down on the first occasion following strong representations from the UAE Federal Foreign Ministry, ostensibly so that pupils resident on the island could complete their exams during May/June 1992. It had apparently hinted, however, that the UAE and Iran would need to make strides in addressing the 'security problem' before the beginning of the next academic year in September 1992. With no progress made and not wholly unexpectedly (at least as far as Sharjah was concerned), the teachers were turned back in late August 1992 as they returned to prepare for the commencement of the new school year.

Following the August 1992 incident, Iran faced a barrage of criticism from Arab and Western media. It reacted on two levels. Perhaps defensively, the Iranian government admitted some responsibility for the incidents on Abu Musa. Foreign Minister Ali Akbar Velayati ascribed them to the misjudgement of 'junior Iranian officials'.[58] These comments followed the dispatch during September of an investigating team from the Iranian Foreign Ministry to the island. As a result of their recommendations, Iran's local naval commander was apparently sacked.

On another level, Iran tended to adopt a 'crisis, what crisis?' line on the whole affair.[59] Especially following the breakdown of negotiations in Abu Dhabi, the Iranian government was keen to make clear that it still felt fully committed to the 1971 MOU it had signed with Sharjah on the administration of Abu Musa. In early October, both Velayati and the Iranian Supreme Security Council delivered clear statements to this effect and the Iranian government has continued to do so ever since.

Following the flare-up of the Khafus incident and Iran's admission of at least some responsibility for the resurrected dispute, tensions between Tehran and the Arab states of the Lower Gulf appeared to ease a little during the last two months of 1992. They were certainly rekindled, at least in a verbal sense, with the issuing in late December 1992 in Abu Dhabi of the final communiqué of the thirteenth GCC summit. Here the Supreme Council called upon the Islamic Republic of Iran to cancel and abolish measures taken on Abu Musa island and to terminate its occupation of the Greater and Lesser Tunb islands, which belong to the UAE.[60] The Supreme Council also affirmed 'its complete solidarity and absolute support for the UAE's position and [supported] all the peaceful measures and means it [the UAE] deems appropriate to regain its sovereignty over the three islands in accordance with international legitimacy and the principle of collective security'.[61] The Supreme Council's statement provoked graphic defiance from Tehran, with Rafsanjani underlining in no uncertain terms that Iran's presence on Abu Musa and the Tunbs was permanent and non-negotiable: 'Iran is surely stronger than the likes of you … to reach these islands one has to cross a sea of blood … we consider this claim as totally invalid.'[62]

The war of words that continues to the present had been set in motion. Yet, at the local level, life on Abu Musa had returned to something approaching normal relatively quickly. Quite soon after the incidents of 1992, the ferry from Sharjah was running to the island as usual. The oil-sharing arrangements for Abu Musa introduced by the 1971 Iran–Sharjah MOU had never even been interrupted by the incidents of April and August. Similarly, the Egyptian teachers at the heart of the August 1992 incident experienced no difficulties in returning for the start of the school year in 1993 and have not experienced many since. It would be a clear overstatement, however, to say that the 1971 MOU is fully operational at the local level. Sharqawis and their employees have experienced far more agitation from Iranian officials than they did before 1992; spot-checks of documents are far more stringent and frequent than they were previously. There are reports that the Iranian military has been far more bullish in patrolling the divide through the island and that encroachments into the Sharjah-administered south continue unabated. The question of the issue of security passes – the catalyst of the 1992 incidents – has still to be resolved. There is still the occasional utterance from Iran that third-party nationals are free to visit the Arab half of Abu Musa, so long as they apply first to the Iranian authorities on the island for security passes. Though not all is as bleak as it is sometimes painted, the potential for problems at the local level still exists.

For the four-year period since the Abu Dhabi GCC summit, the dispute has basically remained locked in the same war of words. Repeat pledges made by the GCC to employ all peaceful means to restore UAE sovereignty have been met with Iran's overdramatic and defiant words about crossing a sea of blood. There seems little reason to believe that the islands dispute will not continue to be the focus of Arab–Iranian rivalry in the Gulf for some time to come. As mentioned at an earlier stage, territorial disputes are often used as the physical expression of wider interstate rivalries or interregional mistrust. Perhaps the Abu Musa and Tunbs dispute is a further case in point. Because of the geography of the dispute, with the waters of the Lower Gulf separating the disputing parties, there may also be an element of safety in channelling rivalries in this manner. Assuming that there is no likelihood of the UAE attempting to regain control of the islands by force and presuming that Iran does not violate the terms of the 1971 MOU in an outlandishly foolish manner, the dispute is still likely to remain.

Most developments of note during the last three years have tended to feed or rejuvenate the war of words rather than concern wholesale changes on the ground on Abu Musa. Following his accession to the post of Secretary-General of the GCC in 1993, Sultan Fahim bin Sultan al-Qasimi increasingly promoted the idea that the dispute over the islands should be settled by a reference to the International Court of Justice in The Hague or else by impartial third-party arbitration. There were reports during 1993, particularly in the Gulf media, that the UAE was considering the possibility of referring the dispute unilaterally to the ICJ. Legally this was not possible because a reference cannot be made without the express agreement of the two parties to the dispute. However, publicizing such an intention might at least have had the effect of placing Iran on the defensive, especially given the strong and consistent support lent to the UAE's position on the islands by the states of the Arab world and prominent members of the international community.

This support crystallized throughout 1994 and 1995. During the early summer of 1994, King Fahd of Saudi Arabia appeared to take a personal interest in promoting proposals for peaceably returning the islands to UAE sovereignty. Iran took notice, repeating its warning of December 1992. Then, during March 1995, the USA took the unusual step of departing from its position of neutrality in the territorial disputes of the region. Former Secretary of State Warren Christopher added his name to a joint communiqué issued by the Foreign Ministers of the GCC countries after a meeting in Jeddah on 12 March 1995. This read as follows:

The ministers expressed their deep appreciation of the UAE's efforts to peacefully resolve the issue of the Iranian occupation of the three islands – the Greater Tunb, the Lesser Tunb and Abu Musa, which belong to the UAE. The ministers urged the Islamic Republic of Iran to respond positively to the initiative of the UAE and to agree to refer this dispute to the ICJ.[63]

The United States' overt support for the position of the UAE in the islands dispute was consistent with condemnation of Iran a month earlier for having significantly remilitarized the northern half of Abu Musa island and the Lower Gulf more generally. Chief among American concerns were the periodically large number of Iranian ground forces stationed on the island and the movement by the Iranian military of air defense capabilities to Abu Musa and other Lower Gulf islands.[64] There can be little doubt that Iran strengthened its military presence on Abu Musa considerably during 1995. The northern half of the island was used as the base for many Iranian military exercises in Gulf waters; there were 33 such exercises in 1995, though these varied considerably in scale while the majority were not centered around Abu Musa and the Tunbs. Iran's mobilization has, of course, altered the status quo on Abu Musa. Iran's expansion of its unconventional arms, mine warfare and submarine capabilities in recent years, its development of long-range missiles and air defense systems are, understandably, viewed nervously in the emirates of the southern Gulf littoral.[65] An escalation of war games in the Lower Gulf as a control link to Tehran is worrisome. Similarly of concern is the permanent assignment of the United States' Fifth Fleet to Bahrain. There always remains the danger that Abu Musa might become the scene of a (Iranian–US) naval clash, over which the UAE would exert very little control.

Yet, following the directive given at the December 1994 GCC annual summit meeting in Manama for member states to settle their disputes bilaterally within the year, GCC policy towards the islands question has shifted. Previous calls from the council for Iran to agree to the islands case being submitted immediately to the ICJ for a ruling contrasted starkly with the council's reluctance to make the same recommendations for the Bahrain–Qatar maritime disputes. In 1995, the GCC eliminated this contradiction in policy with its newly announced view of settling 'in-house' disputes by bilateral means. This new policy would be articulated formally at the close of a meeting of Foreign Ministers signatory to the 1991 Damascus Declaration in July 1995:

The ministers renewed their support and backing to the UAE's sovereignty over its three islands, and urged Iran to hold direct talks with the UAE on the status of these islands at the earliest opportunity. Meanwhile, they backed the UAE's call for referring the issue to the International Court of Justice if no agreement is reached through dialogue.[66]

Officially, at least, there was now no reason why Iran and the UAE should not recommence bilateral negotiations for the first time since the unsuccessful efforts of the autumn of 1992. For Iran's consistently professed position since the incidents of that year had been that it was always willing to enter into bilateral talks with the UAE over Abu Musa with no pre-conditions. And so, as mentioned earlier, the talks of November 1995 ultimately ensued in Doha.

Immediately following their breakdown, both sides indicated a willingness to talk in the future. It was not long, however, before the GCC pointed out that the UAE had entered into negotiations in good faith – and had thereby complied with the directives given in Manama a year previously – only to be rebuffed once again by Iranian intransigence. Familiar sections of the closing statement issued in Muscat would meet with equally familiar rhetoric from Tehran.

As a way of concluding this lengthy section, it might be as well to consider briefly just why the dispute was resurrected so dramatically in 1992. As with other critical phases of the dispute in history, actual or perceived change in the regional balance of power was the catalyst. Whether or not Iran's objectionable behavior on Abu Musa during 1992 was a local administrative blunder, a knee-jerk reaction to its exclusion from collective security arrangements being formulated for the Gulf, or a calculated move designed ultimately to enhance its strategic position in the Lower Gulf, remains an unanswered question.[67]

The Polarization of Settled and Unsettled Disputes

The glass of settled Arabian territorial limits has been filled from half to nine-tenths in the last quarter-century. The degree of this progress has accelerated rapidly during the 1990s, as we have witnessed. Importantly, however, no great political obstacles have laid in its way and it has been a relatively painless process. Yet the glass of settled boundaries has probably been filled as high as is currently possible and practicable – in a sense nine-tenths is the foreseeable limit.[68] For the territorial problems which now confront the Arabian peninsula and the Gulf and that will continue to do so in the medium-term are the same, serious challenges which have long threatened regional stability: the historically entrenched Irano–Arab territorial disputes over the Shatt al-Arab and Abu Musa and the Tunbs, the explosive Iraq–Kuwait question and the not quite so explosive Hawar and shoals dispute.

If one puts the Hawar dispute to one side and accepts that it is never likely to be a major threat to the stability of the region, it will be noticed that these disputes (with the exception of the Shatt al-Arab) all involve GCC states and their non-GCC neighbors. To this collection might be added the Saudi–Yemen dispute, though since formal negotiations have been under way only since the summer of 1992 to settle this, it is perhaps stretching it a little too far to categorize it as historically entrenched. What makes the Irano–Arab and Iraq–Kuwait disputes so resistant to final and permanent settlement is their cyclical nature. However, they have been regulated in international law at various points in history and whether or not the territorial limits concerned have been delimited and/or demarcated, these disputes have tended to move from long periods of dormancy to much shorter and intense periods of dispute or even conflict. Perhaps the most useful research that could be undertaken would be to identify the triggers that determine the lifespan of these cycles.

The rather obvious though important point has already been made that changes, intrinsic or perceived, in the regional balance of power in the Gulf region have dictated the cycle of dormancy and activity for the Iranian–UAE dispute over the sovereignty of Abu Musa and the Tunbs. It is probably more beneficial, however, to try and identify less general and more case-specific determinants of dispute. If one looked, for example, at the demarcated Iraq–Kuwait boundary from a strict legal viewpoint, it would surely be concluded that this territorial limit had evolved to a point where it could be described as final and permanent. If one reflects, however, upon the convoluted history of Iraq–Kuwait boundary and sovereignty disputes, it is possible to identify a number of critical factors or constants that may well determine whether or not territorial stability or instability will characterize the borderlands of the north-western Gulf in future years. These are as follows:

1. the practicalities and politics of Iraqi access to the Gulf;
2. the interrelationship of Iraq–Kuwait territorial disputes with the Shatt al-Arab question;
3. the proven readiness of recent Iraqi governments to renounce supposedly final international boundary settlements when it has been expedient to do so;

4. the historical restlessness of the Iraqi state and the developing territorial consciousness of its population;

5. the (in)ability of Iraq, Kuwait and Iran to cooperate in the management of the borderlands of the north-western Gulf.

The acid test for the newly demarcated territorial limit will surely come at some point in the future, when a United Nations force no longer polices the border zone, when Iraq has been reintegrated into the Arab fold and, perhaps, when Iran–Iraq relations next sour seriously over the status of the Shatt al-Arab boundary. In the medium- to long-term, cooperation in the management of stretches of the Iraq–Kuwait border may prove the most secure route to territorial stability. This may seem politically unpalatable to Kuwait at the present time, given its recent disastrous experience at Iraqi hands, but ultimately this small state cannot change its geography.

After recent periods of conflict in the region, cooperation and compromise are unlikely to characterize near-term relations in the Gulf. The regional and international isolation of Iraq and Iran and, until recent times at least, Yemen, means that filling the glass of settled boundaries in the region completely may long prove elusive. The GCC itself would seem to judge that disputes existing between members and non-GCC neighbors are themselves subject to a different set of rules from those conducted within. This has only further polarized the treatment of disputes and their prospects for resolution.

In recent times, two territorial disputes have dominated the agenda of all levels of successive GCC meetings. Both are maritime, one 'in-house' (Hawar and the shoals) and one involving Iran (Abu Musa and the Tunbs). From a reading of its own policy statements, there is enough evidence to suggest that the GCC considers each dispute to be subject to different rules where the question of territorial settlement is concerned.

A clear enthusiasm for a reference of the Abu Musa and Tunbs disputes to the International Court of Justice for a judgment contrasts with the very marked reticence of the GCC to condone the ICJ's current treatment of the Hawar and shoals dispute. As alluded to earlier in the chapter, there have at least been some efforts made during the last year to bridge the gap in this position. A reference of the Abu Musa and Tunbs dispute to the ICJ is advocated now only after bilateral efforts to solve it have been exhausted, which fits in more neatly with the directives given by the GCC Supreme Council for states to solve outstanding territorial disputes as a matter of urgency on a bilateral basis.

It should also be stated that much of the enthusiasm for a reference of the Lower Gulf islands dispute to the ICJ stems from a genuine belief that, certainly as far as Abu Musa is concerned, the UAE would stand an excellent chance of having its title confirmed by the courts. Recent reticence to condone the ICJ's treatment of the Hawar dispute has also, as we have seen, had much to do with the tendency for annual summit meetings to project the foreign policy (and territorial) concerns of the host state. This is a position that could easily be modified from one year to another.

As far as third-party arbitration is concerned, the GCC and its component states will probably adopt a quiet, wait-and-see attitude until the ICJ delivers its verdict on Hawar and the award has been physically implemented – potentially the most troublesome stage of the whole dispute. By the time this stage has been reached – which will not be until 1998 at the earliest – there may be no serious 'in-house' GCC territorial problems left to grapple with. Such has been the progress towards the finalization of the Arabian political map in the last half-decade or so.

Concluding Remarks

On balance, there is reason to believe that the contemporary territorial framework in the Arabian peninsula and Gulf region will survive the ravages of time and be with us throughout the next century. The oft-envisaged scenario whereby, ultimately, the coastline of the Gulf will be shared three ways between the dominant regional powers of Saudi Arabia, Iraq and Iran becomes less and less convincing by the year. Iraq's enduring restlessness is likely to be kept in check – in the short term at least – by the international community, certainly for as long as Kuwait retains its strategic economic importance for the West. In the medium-term, Iraq may well chip away successfully into the northern margins of Kuwait so as to improve its own access to Gulf waters, but that should probably be regarded as the limit of any sustainable territorial expansion. Iran, Iraq's geo-strategic counter-weight to the east, would tolerate nothing more on a permanent basis. Though those classic Iranian–Arab cyclical disputes over the Shatt al-Arab and the Lower Gulf islands will continue to fester and periodically explode, there is little reason to believe that Iran harbors any territorial designs on its Arab neighbors.

For the foreseeable future, only the GCC seems capable of regulating the Arabian territorial framework on a region-wide basis. The continuing absence of Iraq and Iran from any Gulf-wide grouping in which territorial (and other) grievances can be aired effectively means that the region's most serious and historically entrenched disputes will be increasingly difficult to settle. For the considerable aid lent by the GCC in publicizing and thereby internationalizing its member states' disputes with Iraq and Iran has correspondingly accelerated the adoption of these territorial disputes as national questions in the Iraqi and Iranian public consciousness. Room for compromise is not growing but lessening.

The GCC has evolved a policy and body of legislation which work for the maintenance of the current territorial framework and which encourage bilateral means as the way of settling any residual disputes. Great progress has been made during the 1990s towards finalizing the political map of Arabia. Importantly, however, such progress has been relatively painless since no insuperable political obstacles have lain in its path. It has been underscored above all by the universal and pragmatic realization that precise and clear boundary delimitations are needed in order for hydrocarbons development to proceed smoothly and securely in border areas. Naturally, there remain difficulties within the GCC house. The strides made towards a finalized political map have been varied in type and level; some remain merely promises of eventual territorial settlement. Despite recent efforts to bring into line policy towards inter-GCC territorial disputes and those existing between members and their non-GCC neighbors, the GCC basically remains undecided about its preferred mode of dispute resolution and, especially, the wisdom of referring Arabian disputes to the international courts.

GCC policy towards territorial questions has to date been rather fragmented but, above all, reactive. As was the case following Iraq's recent wars in the northern Gulf, it has been and will continue to be a response to regional instability. As has been the case since Arabian states embarked upon frontier oil exploration programs at the turn of the 1990s, it will continue to acknowledge the need for the expropriation of natural resources, especially where the drawing of sea-bed boundaries in the Gulf is concerned. Finally, GCC policy will doubtless be driven by sensitivity to the territorial concerns of member states hosting the platform upon which policy statements are made, typically GCC summits at the year end.

CHAPTER 9

The Greater Middle East Co-prosperity Sphere: The Arab–Israeli Problem and Gulf Security

Glenn E. Robinson

Reminiscent of the earlier Zionist imperative to 'normalize' Jewish life, the post-Oslo Arab–Israeli peace process is supposed to make the Middle East once again a 'normal' region of the world. That is, by ending this bitter conflict, the Middle East can rid itself of the issue most responsible for its political and economic disrepair, and can get on with the normal and sufficiently challenging business of development. To the degree that the Middle East has been left behind much of the rest of the world because of all the resources wasted fighting and preparing to fight Arab–Israeli wars, it can now use those resources towards productive ends. In fact, not only will the end of the Arab–Israeli conflict free up resources for development, it will also lead to greater regional economic integration and to societal pressures for further political openings. Peace begets prosperity and possibly democracy – or so the argument goes.

The ultimate impact of the end of the Arab–Israeli conflict on the larger Middle East, including the Gulf states, is still anybody's guess. The return to power of the Likud party even casts doubt on whether the conflict really has ended. Assuming that no rollback occurs, the purpose of this chapter is to outline competing visions of what the end of the Arab–Israeli conflict means to the Middle East. The chapter is divided into three sections. First, I highlight three versions of this future: the 'official' line briefly sketched above; an Islamist counter-vision; and a pan-Arabist response. In the second part, I challenge a number of assumptions implicit or explicit in these competing versions of the future, with particular attention paid to questionable assumptions in the official line. Finally, using a variation of the global economic system approach,

I outline an alternative view of where the Middle East may be heading as a result of the containment (if not cessation) of the Arab–Israeli conflict.

Contrary to the usual predictions, I argue that the containment of the Arab–Israeli conflict will not diminish the importance of that issue in the larger region, particularly the Gulf. Rather, the diminution of the conflict will likely transform (and is transforming) the nature of the engagement from one of arm's-length rhetoric to direct entanglement. In short, the regional system of domination that Israel has established militarily in the Levant will likely give way to a geographically larger and more complex pattern of economic and political interaction and hegemony in the Middle East as a whole.

Competing Visions of a Transformed Middle East

A consensus exists that the end of the Arab–Israeli conflict will change the face of the Middle East in the years to come. There is little agreement, however, as to what that new face will look like in the twenty-first century. The current edition of the 'peace process' – a term much abused over the past three decades – is by far the most serious. Beginning in October 1991 in Madrid, when much of the Arab world, as participants or observers, sat with Israel, the USA and the soon-to-be-deceased Soviet Union to discuss ending the Arab–Israeli conflict, and continuing through the 1993 and 1995 Oslo accords between the PLO and Israel and the 1994 Jordan–Israel peace treaty, this process has had many successes.

Perhaps the greatest symbolic indicator of the changed nature of the issue came in November 1995 at the funeral of the assassinated Prime Minister of Israel, Yitzak Rabin. Included at Rabin's funeral in Jerusalem were representatives from Oman and Qatar as well as Egypt, Jordan and the PLO. In his first visit to Jerusalem in 28 years, King Hussein personally gave a moving eulogy for Rabin. Shortly thereafter, Oman, Qatar and Bahrain all invited Rabin's successor, Shimon Peres, to make state visits to their countries. Thus, out of the tragedy of assassination came strong symbolic evidence that the Middle East was indeed changing.

The funeral and its aftermath provided support for the dominant vision of a new Middle East. The most comprehensive statement of this vision is found in Shimon Peres' book, *The New Middle East*, which has been translated into Arabic and can be found in a number of Arab countries.[1] This vision, which I call the official line, is by far the most optimistic scenario advanced by any party. Pushed strongly by the governments of the USA and Israel, and to a lesser degree by Jordan, Egypt, the Palestinian Authority and most of Europe, the official line goes something like this: a comprehensive resolution of the Arab—Israeli conflict as envisioned in the Madrid process will greatly enhance the economic well-being of the region in at least two ways. First, it will free up resources used by states for security purposes so that they may be used for development instead. Second, reducing the instability and uncertainty that always accompany conflictual states will make the region much more attractive to investors both from within the region and outside it. Significantly, increased investment both by states and the private sector will spur economic growth, which in turn will make the region even more attractive to investors. The increasing regional economic integration that would naturally accompany this dynamism would reinforce the peace, as the parties would have strong vested interests in maintaining regional stability. In short, peace will bring prosperity, and prosperity will further strengthen the peace.

An implicit extension of this argument rarely made directly by the governments involved (for obvious reasons) is that regional stability and economic growth will naturally lead to pressures for more accountable and democratic governance in the Arab world. The relationship between sustained economic growth and political liberalization is widely accepted. After all, one cannot operate a modern market economy for long while enforcing strict controls on information flows and decision-making. Thus, peace not only leads to economic well-being, but it further leads to more democratic polities.

In the official version, the security of all states in the region is enhanced as a result of this process. In the Gulf, for example, Arab states no longer have to let Arab—Israeli political criteria interfere with economic decisions, nor will they need to worry about conflict and instability overflowing from their west. Security concerns need only be limited to more 'normal' phenomena, such as balancing regional powers in the Gulf, namely Iran and Iraq. In current Washington parlance, it is a 'win—win' scenario for all parties, both Arab and Israeli.

This is not the only scenario envisioned for the end of the Arab—Israeli conflict, but it is the most optimistic, and it has a hegemonic status in the US discourse on this issue. Two regionally-based opposition lines are also heard. The first is usually expressed by Islamists, particularly social Islamists.[2] A number of Islamists, of course, completely reject the presence of Israel in the Middle East on any grounds. They argue that Palestine is part and parcel of the broader Islamic homeland; that it is

Islamic *waqf*, or endowment, to be held by Muslims in perpetuity. As it is *waqf*, no Arab political leader has the right to relinquish any part of Palestine.

While such a rejectionist line is heard widely among Islamists, a more prevalent objection among Islamists is to the terms of the deal. Two arguments are prominent. First, the whole Madrid process is seen to be just a consolidation of Israeli/Jewish power at a time of Arab/Muslim weakness. This is not a fair, negotiated, just deal which could be justified on Islamic principles, as the Camp David Accords were by Egypt's most prominent Islamic scholars. Rather, the Madrid–Oslo process is little more than the imposition of Israeli demands, backed by American power and sanctioned by Muslim debility. Second, and as a logical continuation of the first argument which sees Israel on the offensive, Islamists argue that Israel will seek to corrupt the Muslim world with its Western-inspired moral depravity. It is one thing to have a *modus vivendi* in which Israel is powerful but isolated. It is quite another to have a peace which allows Israeli tourists and businessmen to have free rein in Muslim societies, further corrupting Muslim youth.

A second vision in opposition to the official line comes from Arab nationalists and some political Islamists. For them, the current peace process will likely consolidate Arab ruin for somewhat different reasons. Like its Islamist counterpart, the nationalist opposition also sees the Madrid–Oslo process in terms of a triumphant Israel and a defeated Arab world. However, instead of spreading Israel's moral bankruptcy, the current peace process seeks to translate Israel's regional military supremacy into economic and political domination, in complicity with US-backed Arab regimes. As with the Islamists, the nationalists see this as an unjust, one-sided 'peace' from which little good can come. Such nationalists argue that no deal should be struck at a time of Arab weakness. Given the collapse of their international patron, the Soviet Union, and the disunity and despair which beset the Arab world as part of the second Gulf War, the Arabs were at the nadir of their political power. Conversely, Israel was riding on the coat-tails of the world's last superpower and was in a position virtually to dictate the terms of settlement. For the nationalists, this was exactly the wrong moment to sue for peace. Furthermore, as Israel consolidates its regional domination through economic penetration of the Arab world, it will be nearly impossible ever to roll back its position of power. Peace, for the nationalists, means the extension of Israel's war aims through other, primarily economic, means.[3] Economic integration is another way of saying political domination. As Michael

Barnett aptly put it: 'While Shimon Peres imagines transplanting the Benelux model to the Middle East, in fact the relevant model is right at home – that of the current economic relationship between Israel and the occupied territory. The view from many Arabs is that Israel stands primed to conquer the Middle East by market power rather than by military power.'[4]

On the table, as it were, are three visions of what the end of the Arab–Israeli conflict will mean to the future of the Middle East. One dominant vision, the official line, is unremittingly optimistic, while two oppositional visions, Islamist and Arab nationalist, are far more parsimonious. Of course, for most people in the region it is a matter of wait and see. However, all of these scenarios are replete with questionable assumptions which need to be examined.

Dubious Assumptions in the Post-peace Scenarios

Each of these three visions of the post-peace Middle East is based on correlations and assumptions which may not be tenable. A number of these questionable relationships are examined below, with particular attention paid to those found in the official line. I may be criticized for not including what is perhaps the most debatable assumption: that the present process is leading towards a comprehensive peace. If the question of Palestine is at the heart of the conflict, then the present situation does not bode well for a truly comprehensive peace. At the end of the day, it appears likely that Palestinians will be left with a series of unconnected cantons in the West Bank and Gaza of limited sovereignty, and that their large diaspora and refugee communities in the Middle East will be ignored. If such a scenario transpires, then the very notion of a 'comprehensive' peace is ludicrous. However, for the sake of this chapter, I will assume that a comprehensive settlement is in the works.

Assumption 1: there is a positive correlation between external peace and internal democracy and stability. This assumption is the 'democratic peace' thesis turned on its head. The democratic peace thesis has been a major issue in the study of international relations over the past decade. It holds, briefly, that democracies are far less likely to go to war against other democracies; the vast majority of wars in history, including recent history, have been fought either between non-democracies or between a democracy and a non-democracy.[5] The line of causation, then, is that internally democratic polities are the linchpins of external or regional peace.

The official line reverses this line of causation, implying that a regional peace is likely to lead to internal political liberalization and greater stability. By removing the external enemy – Israel, for example – which had justified vast military build-ups and internal repression, the *raison d'être* for repression is removed, leading to pressures for internal political reform and liberalization. Reformed polities at peace with their neighbors is a recipe for enhanced stability region-wide. Even Israel, already democratic, would be in a position to liberalize further with regional peace, especially with regards to its still-repressed Palestinian minority.[6]

This assumption has so far not panned out. In fact, the available empirical evidence suggests just the opposite: that peace has led to further internal repression and instability. Stated another way, there has been an inverse correlation between peace and democracy. In each of the three polities in the Middle East that have recently signed a peace agreement – Jordan, the Palestinian Authority and Israel – peace has led to a reversal of democratic policies and an upsurge in instability.

One by-product of Jordan's October 1994 peace treaty with Israel was the reversal of much of its democratization program. Begun in 1989 as a response to rioting in Jordan among some of the Hashemites' most ardent supporters, Jordan's democratization program had had many successes. Jordan had held democratic parliamentary elections in 1989 and 1993, greatly liberalized press restrictions, ended the state of emergency which had been in effect for years, legalized political parties, and expanded the civil and political rights of its citizens. While Jordan was still a long way from becoming fully democratic, it certainly was taking appropriate steps in that direction.

Since its peace treaty with Israel, a number of these steps have been reversed. Two areas stand out. First, for all intents and purposes, press censorship has been reimposed. While Jordan's press was never fully free, the threshold for activating official scrutiny by critical reporting of, especially, the peace process and its aftermath, is much lower in 1996 than it was in 1993. Second, following its treaty with Israel, Jordan's regime cracked down hard on the non-violent opposition it had long tolerated, particularly its Islamist opposition. The regime's new-found intolerance of such opposition was demonstrated on a number of occasions, most notably in the autumn of 1995 when a number of vocal Islamists were imprisoned, including the popular Layth Shubaylat. (Shubaylat, the head of the Engineers Syndicate in Jordan, received more votes than any other candidate in the 1989 parliamentary elections.) Opposition activities are often tried in military courts, where the accused is less likely to get a fair hearing. The next parliamentary elections, scheduled for 1997, will be a test of the democratic rollback seen since Jordan signed its peace treaty with Israel.

Palestinian political life has likewise suffered as a result of the peace process. Widely viewed as the most democratic of all Arab societies, Palestinians have long practised pluralistic politics both internally in the West Bank and Gaza, and externally in the PLO institutions abroad. The Cairo Agreement of May 1994, which implemented limited autonomy in Gaza and Jericho, established the Palestinian Authority and began the rollback of pluralistic life among Palestinians. The Palestinian Authority is today one of the most arbitrary and corrupt regimes in the world – no mean feat for such a young polity. Recently when one of the most prominent Palestinian human rights activists, Iyad Sarraj, complained to a *New York Times* reporter about the 'corrupt, dictatorial, and oppressive' nature of the Palestinian Authority, he was immediately arrested and imprisoned without charge, ironically supplying evidence for the veracity of his comments. While the sins of the Palestinian Authority need not be recounted here, it is enough to suggest that the Palestinian political process, widely defined, is far less liberal and pluralistic now than it was prior to the Oslo peace process.[7]

Even Israel, the biggest single 'winner' in the peace process, is likely to be a more volatile and unstable place as a result of the political dynamics unleashed by Oslo. Writing before the assassination of Rabin, Israeli scholar Ilan Peleg argued that Israel is fundamentally divided between two cultural camps, one universalist, emphasizing democratic inclusion; and the other particularist, emphasizing an exclusive, corporatist vision of the Jewish state. Peleg notes that this contradiction – what he calls the *Dilemma of Essence* – existed even during the days of the pre-state Yishuv, but it has never been fully resolved, nor even fully addressed. Revisionist and Labor Zionism are still battling for the soul of Israel, albeit with different labels today. The conflict with the Arab world meant that this division did not have to be confronted; ending the conflict may have profoundly destabilizing consequences for domestic Israeli politics:

> From the very beginning Israel has lived a logical contradiction. While it declared itself a democracy, it has been, in reality, a genuine democracy for Jews alone. An evolving peace made, for the first time, the possibility of widening Israeli democracy a reality. In an even more fundamental way, the peace process allowed Israelis to start dealing with the Dilemma of Essence: who are we? what do we want to be? As long as the Arab–Israeli conflict existed, it was natural to maintain a tribal democracy, belligerent and self-

absorbed, mobilized to a man. Not only the religious, but even the secular could have organically maintained this posture. Above all, the ongoing conflict allowed and enabled Israel to avoid making big decisions about its own essence. The peace process is for Israel a blessing and a curse. It could potentially end the conflict with the Arabs, but it will almost surely force Israel to deal with the Dilemma of Essence, thereby leading inevitably to a deep domestic conflict, a *Kulturkampf*.[8]

While the assassination of Rabin by a right-wing Israeli was a single act, it could be a harbinger of future unrest and instability as parallel Israeli societies with two very different visions of what it means to be Israeli compete for political and social dominance. The 1996 elections gave further evidence as to just how deeply divided Israel has become. Rather than ushering in a period of liberalism and stability in Israel, the peace process may well have unleashed its antithesis.

Assumption 2: peace will lead to regional economic development. A second dominant assumption in the official line, found prominently in Peres' work, is that the peace process will begin a period of real economic development in the Middle East as precious resources are transferred from military to civilian uses and investment expands significantly due to enhanced regional stability. In fact, the promise of prosperity, more than any change of heart about the justice of one's cause, has been perhaps the greatest driving force for supporters of the peace process.

There is no debate that the Middle East is in desperate need of economic growth, as it is among the worst performing economic regions in the world.[9] From 1985 to 1995, the Middle East and North Africa had the most rapid economic *contraction* in the world, worse even than sub-Saharan Africa. In spite of its handful of oil-driven economies, the Middle East by almost any measure is being left behind economically, especially when compared with East Asian countries. Its rates of savings and investment are comparable to other areas of the Third World, but only half that of East Asian countries. In the 1980s, while world trade expanded by 5 per cent per annum, it contracted 1.5 per cent per year in the Middle East and North Africa.

Reflecting a lack of integration into the global trading regime, prices in the region are more removed from international prices than any region in the world, save sub-Saharan Africa. While per capita exports of manufactured products are unchanged in the Middle East over the past two decades, they have risen seven-fold in East Asia. Average productivity from 1960 to 1990 was not only a fraction of its East Asian counterpart, but was well behind Latin America and the Caribbean area as well. Not surprisingly, investor confidence in the region is low. Most disturbing, of all foreign direct investment in the developing world, the Middle East attracts the least percentage, tied with Africa. In 1993, for example, the Middle East received a paltry 3 per cent of all foreign investments, a figure virtually unchanged in over a decade. By contrast, Latin America received 26 per cent, while East and South Asia received the lion's share at 58 per cent. Even Central Asia and Eastern Europe, still in turmoil from their recent transitions from communist rule, received three times more foreign investment than the Middle East.

Perhaps the starkest indicator of the Middle East's poor economic performance in recent decades is seen through a longitudinal comparison with East Asia. In 1960, the seven major economies of the Middle East had a per capita income slightly better — $1500 per person per year compared to $1450 — than the seven best performers in East Asia: Hong Kong, Korea, Singapore, Taiwan, Malaysia, Indonesia and Thailand. Today the situation is reversed, with those Asian countries being nearly three times richer per capita than their Middle East counterparts. Worse still, the gap between rich and poor states in the Middle East is huge, so that if one subtracts the handful of very wealthy states in the Middle East from these figures, the remaining states are far poorer than these aggregate figures suggest.

The end of the Arab—Israeli conflict is supposed to reverse this downward economic spiral. In theory, the stability and even liberalization of the area (assumption 1) will invite far more investment both from within the region and by foreign investors. Billions of dollars in private and public monies, currently held abroad because of the economic and political uncertainty of the Middle East, will likely return to the region as a result of peace, the argument goes. Greatly enhanced regional trade will further spur the economic boom. After all, the Middle East has many of the requisites for growth: areas of technical know-how (Israel, for example), areas which are capital-rich (the oil states), and areas of abundant and reasonably cheap labor (Egypt, for example). The conflict has prevented these areas from merging in a productive way. The end of the conflict should release these factors to combine in productive and profitable ways.

Advocates of this position point to Israeli trade missions already active in the Middle East, government-to-government business arrangements, such as the 1995 Qatar—Israel natural gas deal, and meetings of business and government officials designed to enhance trade in the region as evidence for the coming economic boom. As Crown Prince Hassan of

Jordan famously announced at the autumn 1995 economic summit held in Amman: 'The Middle East is now open for business.'

While the assumption of a causal relationship between peace and economic growth certainly has more empirical evidence to substantiate it than the first assumption, it is far from a proven relationship. Even assuming that the regional actors could come to terms on large-scale economic cooperation and integration – no easy task considering the baggage of historical conflict they carry – there are a number of phenomena beyond the control of the regional actors which may impede development. Two are worthy of mention here. First, there is a real possibility that international trade and investment will increasingly be concentrated in blocs. The three most important blocs will centre on Europe (the European Union and its satellites), North America (NAFTA and its partners) and East Asia (a Japan, China and 'Tigers' bloc). It is likely that the Middle East as a whole will be left out of these blocs. While individual countries may be able to find a niche in one of these blocs, the region as a whole will not be included. Constructing a parallel bloc is certainly commendable, but it would in no way be able to compete with the highly industrialized blocs mentioned above. Preferential trade relations, not to mention investment, would be concentrated within blocs, leading to significant economic activity and growth within each bloc, far less outside. Restrictive trade blocs are not inevitable, but they certainly are possible. Relatively open blocs are likely – but will still work primarily to the benefit of the included states.

Second, investment capital may not be available to promote economic growth in the coming years. As noted above, the Middle East attracts only 3 per cent of international investment capital. This situation is not likely to change dramatically in the near future. Others have noted that the Gulf oil states could step into the breach and provide the necessary capital to promote regional economic growth. Again, given the soft oil market and the budget deficits many of these states are running, capital in sufficient quantity to spur economic growth in the region is not likely to be forthcoming from this quarter.[10]

Assumption 3: economic development leads to political liberalization. There is a large literature in political science positing the positive correlation between economic development and democracy.[11] In the official line, if the presence of regional peace does not lead to political openings in the largely authoritarian regimes in the area, then certainly the economic development which will follow peace will. Either way, it is the dawn of a new liberal political era in the Middle East.

While the general proposition that there is a relationship between economic prosperity and political democracy is undoubtedly true, the important details of specific cases vary widely. For example, in a number of Latin American cases in the 1980s, a key intervening variable for a democratic outcome was a severe economic recession, which forced regimes to seek to expand ruling coalitions in order to spread the blame for poor performance. In other words, economic development was not a sufficient explanation for democratic outcomes. Prosperity followed by crisis leading to a democratic opening was the most common causal path.[12]

Moreover, there is no reason to believe a priori that economic growth will *necessarily* lead to political openings. In a number of cases the opposite has happened. For example, Steven Heydemann has shown how the authoritarian Ba'athist regime in Syria was strengthened by the economic growth resulting from its *infiraj* economic liberalization program. The logic is straightforward: economic prosperity makes available more resources for a state to extract, and such enhanced patronage resources can be used to consolidate authoritarian power.[13] The People's Republic of China may be following a similar path whereby tremendous economic growth over recent years has rejuvenated authoritarian power, not undermined it.

Thus, even if the peace process does deliver its promised prosperity – which cannot be assumed – it is a further leap of faith to hold that such prosperity will open up the largely authoritarian states of the Middle East. In fact, if such prosperity transpires, it may well further entrench such regimes and herald a new era of authoritarianism, not democracy.

Assumption 4: the peace process will enhance regional security. Like the other assumptions of the official line, the notion that regional security will *ipso facto* result from this peace process is not so apparent when scrutinized. If one accepts the late Yitzak Rabin's distinction between personal security, or the security of the individual, and state security, then security is likely to be undermined by this process. The security of states in the region is neither obviously enhanced nor lessened by this process. The prevailing power structure in the Levant remains unchanged. If anything, the *im*balance of power in the region is heightened as a result of the peace process, as Israeli military hegemony is consolidated and legitimized by the international community. Such an imbalance of power is more dangerous than a balance of power, no matter how well-meaning dominant states may be.

More problematic is the notion of individual security in the peace process. Individual citizens are almost certainly more at risk as a result of peace than they were prior to Madrid. The biggest losers in the peace process are Palestinian refugees living in surrounding Arab countries. For them, the risks have multiplied recently. An implicit cornerstone of the peace process is the cleaving off of the diaspora Palestinian community from that in the West Bank and Gaza. Put bluntly, diaspora Palestinians – mostly refugees and their descendants – are excluded from the peace process. Their fate lies in the hands of individual countries in the region. Lebanon has made clear its desire to rid the country physically of its entire Palestinian community; in the meantime, it has denied work permits to resident Palestinians, and has greatly restricted areas of residence for Palestinians. The future of Palestinians in Jordan is also problematic, although Jordan has done more for Palestinians than any other Arab country. While a small ultranationalist bloc calls for the expulsion from Jordan of all Palestinians, a more likely result will be their exclusion from political life in Jordan (with political rights in Palestine instead). The future of Palestinians in Syria is equally uncertain.

More than individual Palestinians may be at risk. The peace process has brought with it an upsurge in violent acts against individual Israelis as well. Far more Israeli civilians have been killed in Israel by terrorist acts after Oslo than were killed during the entire Palestinian intifada. It is likely that such violence will continue, although not at the pace of the February–March 1996 bombings. Moreover, if Ilan Peleg is right, then many more Israelis may be imperilled by fellow Israelis in the years to come.

In sum, many of the most important explicit and implicit assumptions of the peace process are, at the least, problematic. At the same time, assumptions found in competing visions are equally dubious. For example, can a country as small in population as Israel really completely dominate economically much larger countries, not to mention the region? Egypt has been at peace with Israel for two decades and has not been subjugated economically by Israel. The social depravity feared by Islamists would require Muslims to be overwhelmingly impressionable and Israelis to be utterly morally bankrupt – hardly a likely scenario.

The likely result of the peace process for the Middle East as a whole will almost certainly be more complex and subtle than the proponents of the official line or their competitors imagine. In the following section, I outline one plausible scenario, seeking to integrate relevant economic and political dynamics. While I make no claim to prophesy, the kind of scenario outlined below strikes me as a more likely outcome of the process. At the very least, it should spark some debate as to the direction that the 'new' Middle East is headed.

The Greater Middle East Co-prosperity Sphere

The prevailing wisdom holds that the Arab–Israeli question will become decreasingly important in the Gulf and in the region more generally as political reconciliation continues. That is, were the peace process to march on – assuming that a new working formula is agreed upon with the Netanyahu government in Israel – states in the Gulf and elsewhere will be less encumbered by the Arab–Israeli question and will be freer to act in their own interests. The ideological noose of reaching an Arab consensus on the issue will loosen to the point of disappearance.

Contrary to this scenario, I argue below that it is likely that peace will lead to more direct and greater entanglement between Israel and its partners on the one hand, and the Gulf states on the other. Put simply, peace is likely to create a regional economic *system* for the first time which directly connects the Gulf to the Levant, albeit not exactly in the way Shimon Peres envisions. Such a system would replace the economically disconnected set of Middle East states with a far higher level of economic interaction – as the official line proponents hold – but will have different characteristics than the harmless 'integration' model suggests. I argue that such a system will be hegemonic, in that it will have an unequal hierarchy of power and benefit; that it will consist of core, comprador and peripheral states; and that it will be based on national self-interest. In short, given the vastly different strengths of the region's economies, the dynamics of the future economic system in the Middle East may well parallel the dynamics of the earlier expansion of the global capitalist system.[14] In this case, the regional core countries would consist of Israel and the Gulf oil states, while the comprador states are likely to include either Jordan or Egypt and Palestine.

THE RISE OF AN ISRAELI BOURGEOISIE: Three dynamics are central to understanding why such a hierarchical system may develop in the Middle East. First, a powerful bourgeoisie has come of age in Israel which seeks to translate Israeli military dominance in the Levant into economic benefit. Israel is no longer a socialist edifice which stays afloat economically through the largesse of the USA. Rather, Israel is now a fast growing, dynamic economy which is producing high-end capital goods.

In fact, since 1992 Israel has had one of the fastest growing economies in the world.

It was Israel's business community that largely pushed the Labor Party into making peace with its Arab neighbors at a time of unsurpassed Israeli power. For them, permanent Israeli control of a few miles of territory in the West Bank was not nearly as important for Israel's security and well-being (and their own profit) as access to untapped Arab markets. Giving up parts of the West Bank was a small price to pay for a peace which could bring real prosperity to Israel. It is not self-evident that the Israeli bourgeoisie will complete its project. The 1996 Israeli elections demonstrated that the orthodox community in Israel is a potent challenger to the interests of the bourgeoisie. In fact, Israel's stock market lost 5 per cent of its value immediately upon hearing of Netanyahu's victory for fear that business, like the peace process itself, was in jeopardy. While the business community would certainly welcome Likud's free market policies, it benefits far more from trade with the Arab world and the investments which flow from peace.

Assuming that Likud's victory does not ultimately derail the ongoing process, Israel has two comparative advantages that will make it part of the regional economic core. First, Israel is well supplied with capital-intensive, high-tech industries – the sort of industries which will be crucial to the future of the Middle East. Its highly educated workforce, its advanced research infrastructure, and its proven ability to attract investment in this sector (Intel, a giant in the computer chip world, is currently building the largest foreign investment industrial plant in Israeli history) means that it will be the regional center for capital-intensive, high-end products. Second, Israel has a unique ability to penetrate markets in the West which other states in the region do not. That is, Israel has special trade relations with the United States and Europe normally reserved for only the closest trading partners. Israel's ability to gain access to such markets may prove particularly attractive to other states in the region. Utilization of Israel's marketing abilities world-wide would become more attractive for Arab states if international trading blocs become more restrictive generally.

Thus, the rise of a powerful Israeli bourgeoisie after decades of socialist economic stagnation presaged Israel's willingness to make peace with its Arab neighbors. The combination of a dynamic economy, a strong state with an established extractive capacity, and a powerful military able to protect key Israeli interests in the region means that Israel may well be able to translate its military hegemony in the Levant into economic prosperity. The British empire showed well that economic hegemony brings more power and wealth than military might alone ever could. There is no reason why Israel should not seek to do the same regionally.

THE SUBCONTRACTOR STATE: A second regional dynamic which is currently unfolding and which will push along a regional economic system is the rise of the 'subcontractor' Arab state. Dependency theory identifies comprador classes as key players in the emerging relations of dependency between rich and poor states. Compradors are the self-interested intermediaries between powerful foreign economic interests and local markets. Citizens or residents of the less-developed state, compradors are well situated to further economic penetration by the business interests of core states into peripheral societies.[15] Rather than comprador *classes*, per se, the regional economic system taking shape in the Middle East consists of comprador *states*. I call these states subcontractor states largely because that is the term many analysts in the region employ to describe them. Simply put, the role of the subcontractor state is to be the self-interested intermediary between Israel and the Arab periphery and between Israel and the other core states of the Gulf. While subcontracting states will not gain the advantage out of the Middle East economic system that the core areas will, they will be much better off than the Arab periphery (which will consist of most Arab states).

The competition to be Israel's principal Arab subcontractor is already well under way. The main contenders are Jordan, Egypt and the Palestinians. Israel's economy is ten times larger than either Jordan's or that of the West Bank/Gaza, and is far larger than those of Egypt, Jordan and Palestine combined. Palestinians will likely play a subcontracting role in any event given the nature of the peace process. That is, joint Israeli–Palestinian ventures in the region are likely to be more palatable to fellow Arabs than a straight Israeli presence. Such arrangements were consummated symbolically when one of the most important intifada activists from the PFLP signed on to distribute Israeli pharmaceuticals in the West Bank, with an eye to exporting Israeli pharmaceuticals to Jordan and beyond.

The major competition is between Egypt and Jordan. Egypt has a domestic market 15 times the size of Jordan's and has a large and well-established business class. The state's infrastructure, however, is largely collapsing, with no real turnaround in sight. Jordan, on the other hand, is closer to Israel and the markets which Israel most wants to enter – those in the Gulf. Jordan is also seen as being on the rise economically, with an improving infrastructure and a less intrusive regime, friendly to the business community. The competition to be Israel's principal sub-contractor was seen openly in the economic summit in Amman in the autumn of 1995 when Jordan and Egypt had a public squabble over whose peace with Israel was better (Jordan's because it was warmer or Egypt's because it was longer) and therefore who was a better economic partner for Israel. This public squabble was widely viewed as embarrassing in the Arab world.

Seeking subcontractor status makes sense for these states for at least two reasons. First, like comprador classes, subcontractor states will benefit economically. Not only will there be greater profits and investments flowing through the state from Israel with such increased trade, but reverse flow from the Gulf to Israel and beyond may also occur, giving such a state greater access to international markets. Enhanced resource flows will also provide the subcontractor state easy access to more revenues for state activities.

This leads to the second major benefit for subcontractor states: in-creased revenue flows from trade will lessen the need for the state to resort to direct personal taxation to raise revenues. Compelling a state to extract resources through direct taxation may improve the prospects for eventual democratization, but it is also a recipe for political instability and unrest in the short term. Conversely, relieving a state of the need for personal taxation gives that state a freer hand in choosing what it will do with revenues. Thus, subcontracting states will have a strong impulse to remain authoritarian in their politics because there will be little leverage for democratization efforts. This is particularly true if the business community is enjoying the benefits of subcontracting, and does not view democratization as in its interest.

FUTURE THINKING IN THE GULF: The third dynamic which may well lead to the economic system described here is Gulf economic planning for its post-oil future. In many ways, the Gulf oil states are already part of the core within the global economic system. They will certainly be part of a regional core, along with Israel. The Gulf will remain economically important as long as it sells oil on the international market and as long as it remains a relatively rich source of capital for investment. In spite of recent budgetary problems, the Gulf oil states will likely fulfil this role into the future. The question, then, is not whether these states will remain important – they will – but why and how they would be integrated into a regional economic system. Put another way, why would these states seek to become economic partners with Israel? Again, there are at least two reasons – both based on economic self-interest – to believe these states and Israel will seek closer cooperation in the future. First, as these regimes continue to think about life after oil – or, more precisely, further complementing their petro-chemical industries – it should become apparent that future industries should conform to the comparative advantages of the Gulf states: they ought to be capital- not labor-intensive in these sparsely populated areas, and they should concentrate, therefore, on more technologically sophisticated products. In short, the economic future of the Gulf is much the same as the economic present of Israel. Thus, for assistance in developing such a sector, it is reasonable for the Gulf states to turn to Israel and other high-tech niche states such as Taiwan or South Korea. As a bonus, concentrating on capital-intensive industries will allow these states to lessen their dependence on imported labor, a long-held policy objective.

This begs the question of why Israel? The Gulf states could just as easily turn to East Asian NICs for sectoral development. This is where Israel's second advantage is seen: its proven record of being able to penetrate the American and European markets even as trading blocs become more restrictive. Israel may well be seen as a key partner for getting Gulf products (other than oil) marketed in the West. In addition, of course, one can anticipate political payoffs from the USA if the Gulf states utilize Israel as an economic partner.

THE NEW MIDDLE EAST: The New Middle East, then, may have as its cornerstone a regional economic system for the first time in its history. But such a system, if it approximates what has been outlined above, will be of unequal advantage to the states involved. There will be a hierarchy of power and benefit. The principal winners – the regional core states – will be Israel and the Arab Gulf oil states. These states would benefit disproportionately compared to the other regional states. Their relative (although not absolute) advantage would increase if international trading blocs become more restrictive in the twenty-first century. There would be a second tier of subcontractor states that would probably consist of Palestine and either Jordan or Egypt. The primary task of these states, for which they will benefit handsomely, is to act as a partner to Israeli economic interests in the Arab world. Such a partnership would not be a sign of complete Israeli economic domination of the Levant, as some Arab nationalists fear. Rather, it would indicate a hegemonic system where

Israel would be able to translate its military prowess into economic gain as the region's pre-eminent, but not omnipotent, player.

The periphery of this regional system – the periphery of the periphery, as it were – would include everyone else: the rest of the Levant, Yemen, Sudan, much of North Africa and parts of the Asian subcontinent. These areas will be the biggest relative losers in this new system, as they have been in the extant non-integrated Middle East. This is not to say that they would be absolute losers, as a pure Wallersteinian approach would maintain. Their situations may improve modestly in an absolute sense, but these are countries that will be shut out of general economic prosperity, if such transpires in the Middle East.

If such an economic integration does occur, the concomitant political ramifications would be enormous. Again, unlike the rosy scenario found in the official line, the political consequences of such a change are likely to increase upheaval and turbulence, at least in the near term. While teasing out these political changes is beyond the scope of this chapter, doubtless they will not lead to political harmony and stability, at least not for a long time. There is no reason to believe, a priori, that such upheaval would enhance the security of the Gulf states.

PART FOUR

Internal Determinants of Gulf Security

CHAPTER 10

Economics and Security in the Gulf

Charles F. Doran

Roughly calculated, the Gulf states are, in temporal terms, perhaps one-third to one-half of the way through their cycles of revenue generation from oil. Have these policies accomplished what they wanted in this first phase of their development? What are the strategies they have so far adopted to achieve eventual revenue independence from oil? Is there a better alternative? These, and the related matter of how economics contributes to political security in the Gulf, are the questions this chapter tries to answer.

Three Models of Oil-led Development

Three broad strategies of economic development compete for consideration by the Gulf oil-exporting countries. While each strategy is grounded in reasoned argument, each strategy also contains flaws; flaws in the end that are so deep as to encourage a further search for an alternative. But each strategy also warrants careful examination, since each has strong proponents, and to varying degrees is reflected in the actual developmental programs of Arab Gulf governments. Only by examining each of these broad economic development strategies in detail are the assumptions shown to be disappointing. By elimination, an alternative strategy therefore becomes a more serious candidate for consideration.

SPECULATIVE DEVELOPMENT: Between the years 1970 and 1980, total annual OPEC revenue increased by a factor of 37.[1] Saudi Arabian revenue increased by an even more impressive factor of 85. Figures for the UAE in comparable years amounted to a phenomenal 98. This means that in 1980 the UAE was earning 98 times more oil income, less inflation, than

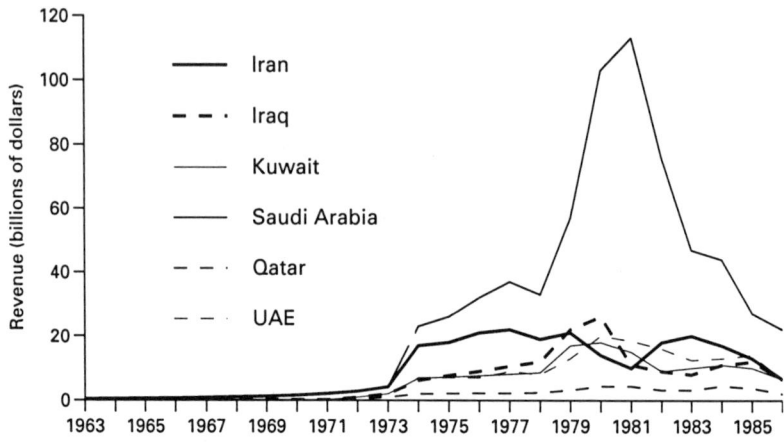

Source: OPEC statistical bulletins, 1983–86

Figure 10.1 Annual oil revenue 1963–86 (billions of dollars)

it had a decade earlier. Despite the subsequent decline in annual revenues for all of the members of OPEC as the world price for oil dropped thereafter, the heady revenue increases in the decade of the 1970s encouraged, and still encourage, a speculative attitude towards development.

Summarized informally, the strategy can be expressed as 'Wait for the next oil price rise!' The strategy suggests that another oil price increase of the magnitude of the rise of the 1970s can be expected to fill the treasuries again, particularly of Arab Gulf oil-exporting countries. The size of the potential increase in oil revenues is so large that revenue gains from all other strategies seem inconsequential. Because of this possibility, the temptation to wait for such an increase is also great. Even if the probability of another oil price hike is not as high as a government and its respective society might prefer, the potential pay-off in terms of future revenue streams is so enormous that, 'other things being equal', the government can be persuaded to wait.

The argument for waiting is also compelling to the average citizen. If the possibility exists that oil revenues could again increase exponentially, the citizen can be persuaded to abandon other, often more painful development strategies, and to play the oil lottery against time. Thus an entire national consciousness can emerge that supports the notion of waiting for another oil price bonanza. Such a bonanza can make all other strategies trivial. A speculative approach to economic development for the oil-exporting countries becomes seemingly plausible and widely accepted.

How plausible is such a strategy of speculative development for the Gulf countries? Although the course of action may make less sense for other OPEC members, or for OPEC as a whole, the strategy could still make sense for individual Gulf countries. In particular, if the so-called reserve-to-production ratio is large enough, sufficient time may exist for the world price of oil to increase greatly. The larger this ratio, the longer the time horizon of production capability, and the more attractive the speculative strategy to development. Strictly in terms of reserve-to-production statistics, time may be on the side of individual Arab Gulf countries.

For OPEC as a whole, using the figure for 'proven' reserves for 1986 and the average production levels between 1976 and 1986, the reserve-to-production ratio is 26.[2] According to these data, assuming the same annual production levels, and no new additions to reserves, OPEC has at least 26 years of production ahead. Now these are heroic assumptions. They cut in very different directions as well. The notion that all of the reserves would be used up to the last barrel is hardly realistic. Conversely, the idea that production levels will not increase as world demand increases, and that 'proven' reserves are either accurately estimated or constant in the face of drilling activity, is historically unlikely. Nevertheless, the production horizon of a quarter of a century for OPEC as a whole does not look overstated. Most important is the awareness that OPEC reserves represent about three-quarters of the world's proven reserves. This means that, at current consumption levels and with other factors unchanged, the price of petroleum may well sky-rocket near the end of the production period.[3] This is precisely the price hike that the proponents of speculative development project with confidence.

What do the figures in the reserve-to-production ratio look like for individual Gulf countries? For Saudi Arabia, using the same 1976–86 period, and OPEC figures for its proven reserves as of 1986, the time horizon for production is slightly less than the OPEC average, or 22 years. For the UAE using comparable years, the reserve-to-production ratio yields a time horizon of 61 years. Theoretically, Saudi Arabia could run out of oil before the upward price hike occurred. The UAE would certainly not. Experienced analysts, however, will remain very sceptical of the proven reserve figure for Saudi Arabia, as it may be too conservative by a factor of four-to-five. By most estimates, it is virtually certain that OPEC as a whole will meet the upper limit of its production capability long before the producers of the Arabian peninsula will.

In theory, then, both Saudi Arabia and the UAE have a sufficient production horizon to suggest the possibility that one or more major price hikes will occur in the global price of oil, thus rendering non-oil development strategies seemingly irrelevant. For these countries, the strategy of speculative development might appear quite appropriate. Just wait for the right interval of history and the coffers will once again fill.

What is wrong with this scenario for development? First, when price begins to rise as demand for oil exceeds supply, a great deal of new production comes on line that was previously unprofitable. This includes production resulting from deep drilling, tertiary recovery, reconditioning of old stripper wells and new, high-cost exploration.[4] This rise in supply is the effect that dampened prices following the 1981 recession.

Second, substitution will take place.[5] Oil, though the preferred form of energy, is not the only form. Everything from coal to natural gas to nuclear energy – even solar-produced energy – becomes more attractive when the price of oil increases sufficiently. Over time, the elasticity of supply for alternative energy sources is quite high. Technological innovation can bring on stream entirely new energy forms such as nuclear fusion. This process could conceivably replace oil altogether in many now reliable markets. Moreover, once innovated, such new energy sources will not easily be displaced.

Third, a sustained oil price increase will cause reductions in energy demand, some of them irreversible.[6] Again, over time, the elasticity of demand for energy is surprisingly high. Gas mileage for vehicles has been improved by a factor of two in the last two decades. Similarly, reductions in usage rates have occurred with regard to heating fuels, because of better insulation; and also in electrical generation and usage, because of more efficient production and transmission methods, and improved motors. Even patterns of energy consumption change as people learn to 'turn down the thermostat' and dress a bit more warmly.

The upshot of this analysis is that what initially looks promising – that is, that an oil price hike will occur and provide a greatly increased revenue stream to Gulf economies – begins to look like a very long shot upon which only the high-risk gambler is prepared to bet.[7] Development strategies ought not to be formulated on such a roll-of-the-dice mentality. Perhaps the oil price hike will come. Perhaps it will not. Development strategies for the Gulf countries ought to find a firmer foundation in concept and method.

RENTIER DEVELOPMENT: According to this strategy, a per cent of oil-based revenue is invested in the economies of the advanced industrial countries. Interest and dividends which accrue from this investment are reinvested or used as a source of income, or both. This investment can take the form of either direct or portfolio investment. Kuwait has used this approach to development, and by some reports is now earning as much from this source as from oil revenue itself.

The advantage of this approach is that, in contrast to the former strategy, it seems like a 'sure thing'. Advanced industrial economies may suffer recessions and they may have weak sectors but over time they are likely to continue providing solid returns. By investing in the developed economies, the oil-exporting economy ties its own future income stream to the dynamism of the strongest economies in the world.[8] There is a sense of permanence and security about such investments that is perhaps hard to equal anywhere in the developing world today, although at the micro-level all investments carry some risk.

Likewise, this investment strategy has the advantage that it can be practised by individuals as easily as by governments. Capital markets in London, Paris, Tokyo and New York are very sophisticated and very accessible. Not only can investments by oil-exporting countries be made in a highly 'liquid fashion', that is, for a somewhat lower interest premium in high-grade short-term securities, but they can be managed and monitored anywhere in the world with the benefits of electronic communications.

Where then is the downside to such an investment strategy? First, the problem of 'border risk' can never be removed entirely, although it can be minimized through the use of intermediaries and through low visibility accounts. Individuals and governments can never completely escape from the threat that they are 'held hostage' to the decisions of a foreign government. The level of border risk is very low for investors and governments of the moderate Arab states. Because the interests of these states and of the major industrial powers are very close in terms of the global energy market – both wish to maintain steady supply and demand – the danger of controls being imposed by the industrial states is not great. As the value of the financial holdings by the oil-exporting countries increase, assuming they can actually be traced, the industrial economies themselves become somewhat vulnerable to the short-term decisions of the Gulf investor. Thus a tacit *modus vivendi* arises between the interests of that investor and the interests of the world economy in maintaining stable, reliable working relations. Over time, both the Gulf economy and the advanced industrial economy acquire a sense of interdependence that encourages cooperation and the absence of unpleasant surprises. Still, the issue of border risk will remain in the minds of the Gulf investor, a spectre larger perhaps than the size of the actual risk.

Second, depending upon the specifics of investment methodology – automatic or by periodic decision, bureaucratic or by judgement of a small group of decision-makers – the transparency of the investment may not be as great as desired. Insufficient information may exist upon which to make decisions about accounting, type of investment and rate of return. Thus the matter of who benefits and by how much, a problem regardless of the nature of savings and investments, becomes even a greater problem when the actual investments are off-shore. There is no intrinsic reason why reporting should be more difficult or less complete from abroad than from at home, and in fact the opposite under certain circumstances could be the case. Nevertheless, the necessity of producing a return from foreign investments to those who will benefit throughout the society is a matter too serious to disregard.

Third, and this is potentially the most damaging aspect of rentier development, is that it is in reality a substitute for development. That is, rentier development by its nature is a kind of proxy for a genuine investment in the home economy. Regardless of the attractiveness of the economic return, and regardless of how splendid the stability of the income flow, the investment is still in a foreign economy. It does nothing directly to establish, improve or, importantly, to diversify the local industrial base. The domestic economy of the oil-exporting country, when viewed as an engine, may remain as poor as it ever was. Domestic employment is not directly created by the rentier development strategy. After a century of rentier economic development, the local economy may be composed of many wealthy citizens, but the economy itself will be no more self-sustaining or robust than it was at the time oil was first discovered.

A further dilemma with the rentier development strategy is that if income distribution is highly unequal, the lower classes are unlikely to realize much of the return even as a secondary or tertiary effect of the original investment. If a corresponding investment were made at home, jobs would be created, and workers would receive some income directly in the form of salaries and wages. Thus the employment side of rentier development is troubling in concept and practice. Some jobs of course will be created as a result of rentier development, but they will largely be in very localized service industries, in governmental positions and in jobs related to the maintenance of homes, retail sales and professional employment.

INDIGENOUS DEVELOPMENT: Given the shortcomings of the prior two strategies for economic development in an oil-based economy, indigenous development ought to hold much appeal. Indigenous development involves expansion of the industrial and service base of the economy. It is 'home-grown' development. The advantages of this brand of development to an oil-based economy are quite apparent. Savings that are locally generated can be more compellingly channelled into business that is locally owned and managed. Returns on investment in stable, newly industrializing economies can be very high, as countries as diverse as South Korea, Brazil and Taiwan have recently demonstrated. An expanding local GDP will in turn attract outside investment, further accelerating growth.

Politically, the home-grown variety of economic development is also attractive. Loyalty to a regime is bolstered by a property-owning middle class that looks to government to protect those interests that these citizens have aggravated at some risk. Infrastructure in transportation, communications and education all have more social and political meaning for an individual in a society where that individual has something at stake commercially. Thus, in the long-run, a society that has a growing market economy is likely to be more stable and more contented than a society in which everyone is dependent solely upon receipts from an ever-declining oil base.

Indigenous development is also important as a training ground for the members of society. By learning tasks of entrepreneurship and industrial management, many new roles are created where responsibility and integrity become equated with preferred social values. Education takes on a purpose and has a consequence in a growing market economy that is less evident in other forms of oil-led development. Perhaps the most important consequence of indigenous development is that the country as a territorial entity is defined and built. Resources are used to create income-generating business in local towns and cities. A sense of community and pride emerges. The next generation of citizens will inherit both the rewards and the responsibilities associated with commercial enterprise that is both local and dynamic.

However, if the advantages of indigenous development are evident to oil-exporting countries, so are the problems.[9] First, the indigenous economy is often too small to enjoy the proper economies of scale. The only way these economies of scale can be realized in the local economy is to become export-oriented. The problem there is that in order to become export-oriented the local firm in the small economy must obtain economies of scale. The bottom line is that an indigenous economy will require substantial nurturing and support from the state until such economies of scale are achieved.

Second, foreign technology that is state-of-the-art can be purchased abroad, but the small economy confronts a difficult and technical challenge in adapting this technology to the indigenous environment, or even adequately applying it in a way that enables the firm to compete in the increasingly global export market.

Third, non-tariff barriers often exist that interfere with both investment and trade flows. These barriers often require that permits be obtained from the government. Such a system breeds corruption. Individuals control 'local monopolies', whose only purpose can be to enrich these individuals at the larger cost of the society as a whole. The permit system drains off capital for bribes to get around the restrictions, thus undermining the integrity of the civil service, bureaucracy and political structure. The inefficiency that results helps to ensure that the economy remains small, poor and unproductive.

Fourth, oil-exporting countries everywhere are subject to a malady that has been dubbed the 'Dutch disease' because of the problems associated with oil and gas revenues earned in the North Sea and added to the thriving industrial base of the economy.[10] Afflicting the economy by causing inflation, and by appreciating the currency, the so-called Dutch disease results from the size of the very large oil and gas revenues that flow into the economy. They induce excessive imports, especially for consumer goods, thus subverting the indigenous import-competing industries. The buying power of the currency is so large that people buy abroad instead of locally, because foreign goods are relatively inexpensive.

In addition, the highly appreciated currency discourages exports. Exports are after all now very expensive for foreigners to buy. Thus the indigenous industrial base is frustrated. It is flooded with cheap imports and finds that its exports, even with reasonable levels of productive efficiency at home, remain very expensive by the standards of pricing on the world market.

All of these problems intensify if economies are small, protected and overly dependent upon a single commodity. 'Nationalism' becomes a recipe for economic isolation and inefficiency. Furthermore, the bargaining power of the small, oil-led economy is diminished and marginalized on the world market because it increasingly must confront large trading blocs like the EU, NAFTA and ASEAN. These blocs often bargain as a group and can set terms that will not assist the isolated actor – a tactic OPEC members well understand. OPEC can also bargain on some matters as a bloc, but once outside the realm of oil-related issues its political unity and communality of interest are often lacking. Over time, the isolated Gulf states will find that the international marketplace is less friendly to its attempt to gain admittance to the ranks of the industrial countries if any (or all) of the three foregoing developmental strategies is the guide to planning and economic evolution.

Regional Economic Integration

By elimination, then, the optimum economic strategy for the Gulf economies may be that of regional integration. Regional integration automatically provides for the oil-exporting country that which those strategies previously discussed cannot. Unlike the strategy that banks on another oil price hike and its resulting revenue windfall, regional integration is an incremental strategy that lacks the high risk associated with mortgaging the economic future of Gulf countries to the global oil market. In contrast to the rentier strategy, regional integration builds on the territorial foundation of the state, leaving a legacy of income-producing firms and capital to the next generation of Gulf citizens. And, as opposed to individual nation-state modernization, the regional integration option emphasizes the potential for economies of scale and specialization, such that genuine economic growth becomes feasible in a self-sustaining fashion.

Regional integration is of course not untried.[11] Nor has it been a conspicuous success elsewhere in the Middle East.[12] But there are many lessons now available regarding both the failure and the potential success of regional integration in the developing world context.

Why have integration efforts failed elsewhere in the Middle East, for example, in Egypt, Syria and Jordan? A review of the failures may help the analyst to find the formula for success.

First, integration schemes have failed because they have been long on institutional imagination and short on economic basics. By this I mean they have tried to set up political 'superstructures' without paying the proper attention to the economic essentials of an enlarged market. In particular, they have neglected the reality that businessmen prefer to undertake transactions as effortlessly and as cheaply as possible. For example, currencies in which businesses conduct transactions inside the trading area or common market should be freely convertible. Without this provision, the cost of exchange becomes several per cent of the cost of doing business, with the majority of economic benefit accruing to the exchange bureau.

Second, customs services should be open to trade and commerce and not permitted to impede or discourage the movement of goods. If non-tariff barriers are used as devices to create artificial local monopolies, the cost of doing business will inflate and integration between countries deflate. If governments regulate the issuance of permits for the entry of goods, or do so on the basis of quotas, the flow of commerce will be stifled, and the incentive to private enterprise reduced.

Third, tariffs themselves must be minimized and, more importantly, they must be equalized among the members of the market. Otherwise an expensive system of trans-shipping and smuggling can arise that functions as a substitute for the free market.

Fourth, members of the market must refrain from providing counter-productive subsidies to domestic industries. Such subsidies often distort market dynamics, and as a result domestic commercial enterprises cannot compete within world markets. The so-called 'infant industry' argument must be judged prudently, and recognized as a market aberration. In many cases, subsidies result in the diversion of investment, especially foreign investment, from one of the market members to another.

Fifth, barriers to investment must be eliminated. Sometimes there is fear among the smaller members that the investors in one larger member may simply 'buy up' everything and 'push out' the local capitalist. This concern is frequently exaggerated. For example, if a foreign investor buys a local firm, the price paid is a function of international competition. The local firm is not forced to sell, and if it does sell, its owners receive the proceeds from the sale. Since the marketplace is dynamic in nature, the proceeds from the sale of the local firm can be reinvested elsewhere with a potentially greater return to the investment. Barriers to investment make no economic sense.

Sixth, discriminatory taxation schemes are illogical if they discourage investors from other member states from operating within one's own market. Like the non-tariff barriers, they reduce the incentive to do business and that in turn will undermine the productivity and growth of the trade area.

Seventh, if possible, the members of the trade area or common market ought to pursue complementary industrial bases. In other words, if all of the members produce the same thing, the potential benefits of trade will not be as great as if there is some diversity of production. On the other hand, a most basic explication of comparative advantage articulated in the eighteenth century by David Ricardo shows that relative differences in prices of traded goods are sufficient for gains to trade to be realized.

So even with identical industrial bases, for example, oil and agriculture for each of the members, trade will eventually result in specialization and a more productive set of economies. Total productivity for the market is best achieved through complementarity, however.

Eighth, politically, the regimes must be compatible. This does not mean that all of the political regimes must be identical in character. But if there is a symmetry to political composition among members, it is helpful. When change occurs politically, this symmetry will ensure that members will react to the change in the same general way, and often in consultation between the member states.

Ninth, ideally, the perspectives of the member states on (1) internal security, and (2) external security would be reinforcing. That is, if the member states look at threats to their own political regimes either internally or externally in a similar way, this communality of perspective reinforces the desire for a common economic union. More will be said about the complexities of economics and security within a regional economic entity, but when politics reinforces economics integration proceeds more readily. Let us now turn to the Gulf Cooperation Council to determine how well it measures up to these criteria of economic integration.

The Future of the Gulf Cooperation Council

According to criteria eight and nine, the GCC is very well designed. Not only is the GCC an agreement among monarchies, but the nature of the external threat is well understood by the membership.[13] The menace of communism stemming largely from the then-Soviet Union represented the principal out-of-region threat, while the machinations of revolutionary Iran and the rising power of Iraq combined with the emerging phenomenon of Islamic radicalism provided the other principal sources of anxiety. Internal threat reinforced by external threat corresponded to the common sense of membership and economic architecture of the GCC.

Early plans for large common commercial projects seemed at first very promising. Some of the projects mentioned were integrating Qatar, Kuwait and Saudi Arabia into a single gas grid; building a GCC refinery in Oman; constructing a 1700 km oil pipeline to link Oman and the other GCC states, thus bypassing the Straits of Hormuz; creating a GCC joint stockpile of oil in case of emergency; establishing a Gulf Investment Authority and a Gulf Investment Corporation with an initial capitalization of $2.1 billion; integrating GCC members' electric power grids; unifying members' fees for telex, telephone and post; establishing a peninsular

Table 10.1 GCC scorecard on integration achievements

Exploitation of economies of scale	C
Indigenous generation of technology	D
Reduction of tariff and non-tariff barriers	C
Currency appreciation and inflation (the 'Dutch disease')	B-
Currency convertibility	A
Customs coordination	B
Elimination of distortive subsidies*	D
Elimination of barriers to foreign investment**	C
Ending discriminatory taxation	C
Complementarity of industrial bases	C
Political compatibility	A
Common perspective on external threats	A

Key: * At least four of the GCC countries do not offer privatization programs. Kuwait and Oman are attempting such programs along with Iran. ** Four GCC countries do not allow foreign investment. Saudi Arabia, for example, allows GCC investors to buy stakes in new issues and in some existing stocks, including Saudi Basic Industries Corporation.

railroad network; constructing the Saudi Arabian–Bahrain causeway; and efforts to represent the GCC in petro-chemical negotiations.[14]

It is apparent that most of the early thinking centered on petroleum-related projects, and that most of these projects involve government money. It is also apparent that many of these projects remain in the planning stage, no doubt in part due to the downturn in oil prices. Yet the projects outlined also reveal much of the thinking about economic cooperation in the Gulf. Economic planning is dependent upon government initiative, or at least governmental funding, and is driven by the desire to establish huge projects in oil-related industry or in infrastructure. Missing is a lower level of projects, funded by the private sector in non-oil-related industries that benefits from an openness of trade and commercial ties across the member states.

Unfortunately, the tactic of 'import substitution' was exercised. Relying on high external tariffs and non-tariff barriers, the concept was to encourage the creation of local (infant) industries. But this 'hot-house' form of project cultivation achieved no better result in the Gulf region than previous projects of similar design achieved in Latin America or elsewhere in the developing world. And while this concept has been abandoned as a failed experiment in most other places in the face of privatization and freer trade, vestiges of import substitution live on within the GCC.[15]

What made import substitution at first seem reasonable in the Gulf was the vast amount of money apparently available for joint projects. The availability of money was sometimes and unwisely regarded as an alternative to marketplace fundamentals. Hence many of the projects, such as some of those in agriculture, gave no thought whatsoever to comparative advantage or other market dynamics.

Although tariffs were reduced, they were not equalized among member countries. In the absence of equalization (creation of a common external tariff), rules of origin and content are required so that trans-shipping within the market is not encouraged. The difficulty with the operation within the GCC states is that the GCC has formed neither a common market nor a free trade area. As a result, the GCC possesses neither the common external tariff that would solve the problem of trans-shipping, nor the elaborate rules of origin and content such as are found in the NAFTA and other trade areas.

Subsidies continue to flourish both internally to the member states of the GCC, and hence externally within the GCC structure as well. Market signals cannot operate properly in such an atmosphere and enormous amounts of capital are wasted. In an era of austerity, the cost of subsidized projects is felt more directly. Investment also is still restricted. The principle of 'national treatment' is not observed inside the GCC. While restrictions on the purchase, of say, residential beach properties might not be so damaging to the economy, restrictions on the purchase and sale of commercial property, industry and service enterprises guarantees that the GCC as a regional trade area will not function optimally.

Basic to this economic evaluation of the Gulf countries is that the GCC must go back to 'first principles'. It must build economically upon what was (and remains) a very wise and politically feasible foundation. The GCC ought to abandon the import substitution mode of operation, not just because funds are no longer so readily available for large and expensive projects, but because the approach is unconstructive and distortive of the aims of regional integration. Individuals and firms should be enabled and encouraged to fund attractive projects. The Gulf has both sufficient managerial and entrepreneurial talent to administer such projects and enough private capital to undertake the financing. Government should not be the principal source of risk capital, not because there is anything wrong with government financing per se, but because all too often government projects ignore market signals and remain dependent upon government subsidy.[16]

An enduring problem for the GCC is that many of the member economies are not managed in accordance with the principles of free market economics. Therefore the task of creating a regional economic unit following those principles is made doubly hard. 'Deepening', to use the jargon of economics on regional integration, is less evident in the GCC than is the case within other regional trade areas.

One last set of recommendations is calculated to strengthen the degree of economic integration within the Gulf area and therefore the economic viability of each of the states in the long term. This is the matter of the complementarity of industrial structures.

Increasing Size and Industrial Complementarity

Data are always a good economic anchor. Reliable data reveal that the GCC countries in combination, including expatriate labour, possess a population of no more than 20 million. Data also reveal that the entire land area of the GCC countries is 2.26 million square km, 90 per cent of which is located in Saudi Arabia. In order to obtain adequate economies of scale and of industrial complementarity, the GCC must increase its market size.

While setting aside for the moment the daunting problems of political feasibility, the inclusion of Iraq and Iran into an eventual regional trade area makes great economic sense.[17] With at least 20 and 65 million people respectively, these two countries would also double the land area encompassed by the grouping. Present GCC countries are far richer in per capita terms than Iraq or Iran, which to some extent offsets the larger economic base of the latter countries.

One of the large benefits of regional economic grouping to Kuwait, the UAE, Qatar, Bahrain and Oman in this arrangement is that these countries would very likely become the trading centers for the larger regional grouping. The initial and successful efforts of Bahrain and Dubai would be extended to other coastal locations as the foci of financial and commercial activity region-wide. Gulf shipping would become the major axis of transportation in a way that is just becoming visible.

Given the size of the Iraqi and Iranian population bases, the potential for specialization within the region as a whole is much enlarged. By exploiting economies of scale, industry within the region would enjoy opportunities to gain competitive advantage on a world scale. The vision for the grouping should not be to supplant imports into the region but to become more export-oriented. Similarly, the objective is not only to provide goods and services related to the oil industry and its offshoots, but to begin to find niches and specialities in commercial areas not associated with the oil industry. In so far as the offsets currently obtained in oil or defense-related production are competitive only because of subsidies and artificial protection, they will provide only limited strengthening and diversification of the regional industrial base.

Only by achieving real industrial diversification will the Gulf region prepare for a future in which its oil and gas reserves are in substantial decline. Only through regional integration will the GCC countries obtain enough economic reach to achieve the requisite efficiencies. It is by no means too early to plan for this reality in the final decade of the twentieth century. Once the GCC has deepened its own market, regional integration should seek to encompass Iraq and Iran within the framework of a regional Gulf trading area as well. Once the principle of national treatment is solidly established, the GCC can provide much of the needed capital required to develop the Gulf economies as a group.

The Complex Relationship Between Integration and Security

How can the GCC countries in the present political climate possibly consider joining economic forces with Iran or Iraq or both? The very suggestion is politically problematic. But political circumstances do change. Strategically, it is important to have the optimum regional configuration in mind, bending political conditions and requirements to that strategy when the eventual opportunity arises. Regional economic integration and regional security can be mutually reinforcing objectives. Lasting political security for the individual Gulf countries, in the age of spreading nuclear weapons and accurate missiles, is likely to be increasingly difficult to assure by military means alone.[18]

In theoretical terms, the relationship between integration and security seems to be as follows. At low levels of conflict, low levels of integration are insufficient either to counter the effects of that conflict or to build a base for increased integration. At high levels of conflict, integration is likely to falter, as is evident for example in the Central American Common Market. But at low levels of conflict and high degrees of integration, integration is in fact able to mute additional tendencies towards the kind of nationalism that breeds intense conflict. Here the example is the

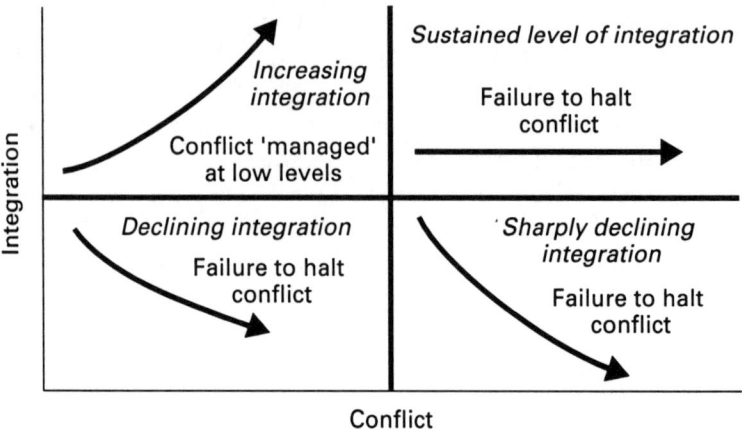

Fig 10.2 The relationship between integration and conflict

European Economic Community (EEC) or Common Market that grew up in an atmosphere of relatively benign conflict. It has become strong enough to deter the type of nationalism that tore Europe apart during the first half of the twentieth century.

As Figure 10.2 reveals, the relationship between integration and conflict is such that two thresholds exist, a conflict threshold and an integration threshold. The fundamental principle is that in order to keep the conflict below a threshold that would lead to war in a region, integration must already have been achieved at a level above the integration threshold. This means that integration must occur in a fashion that is deep enough and sophisticated enough to ensure that further integration is self-sustaining. The resulting reduced probability of serious conflict helps facilitate integration that is self-sustaining.

For developing countries in a region where conflict has been as prevalent as in the Gulf, however, this integration threshold is difficult to cross even during a period of comparatively uninterrupted peace. Yet the road to security for the region must take into account the location of the integration threshold, and the GCC governments must be prepared to cross it, if the region as a whole is finally to enter an interval of assured security.

Even assured security must be backed up by adequate military and defence capability. But if the threat of conflict were reduced through the achievement of a proper level of Gulf economic integration, the task of preserving that peace would be a lot easier. A resulting 'peace dividend' could further reinforce economic integration if some of the money now spent on arms could be invested instead in more productive plant and equipment, thus fostering greater economic growth for the region as a whole.

However fanciful these ideas may now seem, they are well worth examining because of the size of the benefit they hold downstream for a more stable future in the Gulf region. Economic integration is thus not just good developmental strategy. Economic integration is also, under proper conditions of political nurture, a very plausible route to enhanced regional security.

Integration, Security and Economic Development in the Gulf

A spate of articles has appeared recently expressing anxiety about the economic health, and consequently the political health, of the GCC countries. Some have extrapolated this from the declining trajectory of revenue measured in real dollars since the heady days of 1980–81.[19] Others worry openly about the 'slow but sure decay of the economic and political structures of the United States' key regional allies'.[20] Adjacent to a two-page advertising spread in *The Economist* on the attractions of Bahrain's economy, was an article which asserted that the Bahraini government 'plays down the opposition (which ranges from Shi'a Islamist radicals to secular technocrats), portraying its leaders as "mad mullahs" backed by Iran'.[21]

Given the podia from which these authors speak, and the traditional interest they have expressed in the Gulf region, they cannot be dismissed as casual or analytically irrelevant. On the other hand, interpretation can often be selective and forecasts wrong. Missing, for example, is an awareness of the courage with which Saudi Arabia has attacked its deficits, leading it towards a possible current account surplus, the first in more than a decade.[22] The deficits are large expressed as a per cent of GDP – as large as 75 per cent – although the implicit collateral is not GDP per se but reserves of oil. The reduction of water and electricity subsidies for industrial users was a forward-looking decision that will move the economy towards more effective reliance on market signals. In the same interval that critics were challenging the capacity of the Gulf governments to govern, the New York *International Investor* was increasing the 1994 credit ratings for the UAE, Qatar, Kuwait, Bahrain and Oman, although not for Iran.[23] Yet Iran was able to reschedule its short-term debt into medium-term instruments outside the International Monetary Fund through a 12-nation consortium led by Germany.[24]

Similarly, the tumult through which the executive branch of government in Kuwait and the Kuwaiti Parliament have gone concerning the specifics of Kuwait's debt resettlement program can be regarded as the Gulf equivalent of the process by which the US President and Congress have approached the similarly problematic US budget, albeit with power shared a little more broadly in the latter case. In short, for many countries in the world, including both France and Japan, the financial restructuring that is occurring is neither easy nor without enduring political consequence.

Not to approach and consider seriously the social and political dynamics of financial adjustments, in terms of the long-term question of developmental strategies, is probably very unwise. That is why this chapter explores three familiar developmental strategies for the GCC countries and rejects them all. A fourth strategy, though more challenging to design and to orchestrate, contains the potential for achieving a number of objectives simultaneously. Regional economic development, if pursued as a genuine market-based program, not dependent solely on government-sponsored industrial and infrastructure projects, can lift the Gulf region into a more sustainably prosperous and more militarily secure twenty-first century.

More pointedly, not only is regional development the key to long-term economic prosperity for the Gulf, even after oil revenues enter absolute decline, but regional economic development is also the pathway, perhaps the best pathway, to assured security for the member states. Regional economic development requires more than a plan, it requires commitment politically from the governments that will stand most to benefit on both commercial and structural grounds.

If European economic unity after 1945 could end strife that had been so violent as to produce hostilities on a global scale twice, why cannot that same sense of unity occur in the Gulf? Historical analogies are never perfect, but the application of the European experience to the Gulf looks something like this. Europe spent the first half of the twentieth century fighting war; the Gulf devoted a chunk of the second half of the twentieth century to the Iran–Iraq War and to the war to liberate Kuwait. Europe applied itself in the second half of the twentieth century to creating an integrated community that would preserve the peace. Can the Gulf region do the same in the first half of the twenty-first century? Can the Gulf region replicate not just the destructive interval of Europe's history, but also its constructive phase?

To complete the analogy is to build a metaphor with respect to the European community in the Gulf, which is perhaps not so institution-alized, but has some of the same trade and commercial linkages. For this to happen, the GCC countries will need to work very hard indeed during the next 50 years. They have two reasons for doing so: prosperity and security.

CHAPTER II

Social Transformation, Changing Expectations and Gulf Security

Jill Crystal

This chapter analyses the impact of social transformation on Gulf security in the twenty-first century. Radical and rapid transformations of the Gulf states' social structure have occurred steadily over the last several decades, as the population has become younger, more urbanized, ethnically and religiously more diverse (owing to the influx of expatriates), more educated, wealthier and politically more engaged. These and related transformations will affect Gulf security in the coming decades in two distinct ways. First, social transformation can affect Gulf security when social groups attempt to make foreign policy themselves: either directly, by pressuring the government for a policy change, or indirectly, by initiating and sustaining contacts with other governments or other foreign actors. Second, Gulf security is affected whenever social groups put pressure of any kind on the state, or on other social groups, so great that it disrupts ordinary political life and thus attracts or threatens to attract the attention of other states, which may then be tempted to reshape their own foreign policy accordingly or even to intervene directly.

Social Stratification in Historical Perspective

Historically, scholars have devoted relatively little attention to social stratification in the Gulf, rarely going beyond a few often simplistic observations about the enduringly traditional nature of society. The conventional wisdom in the West on the Gulf until recently was that although some demographic changes had occurred, significant social transformation had not, and certainly no important social transformation had occurred independently of the state.[1] While this view was particularly true of some of the older orientalist scholarship, both the modernization and dependency literatures, as well as the more recent rentier state literature, argue that independent social groups are essentially unimportant in the Gulf, that associational life is weak, and that the public space between the family and the state is narrow.[2] Although a few writers have paid attention to some aspects of social transformation – for example, generational change, or the appearance of a technocratic new middle class – discussion of social stratification has been limited.[3]

Recent scholarship has contested this view, drawing a far more nuanced and diverse picture of Gulf society.[4] Studies of Kuwait, in particular, offer empirical refutation of these standing assumptions about social structure. There one finds rich and diverse social groups: merchants, Islamic associations, cooperatives, diwaniyyas, virtual political parties, cultural societies and alumni, sports, professional and other associations, all exhibiting both social coherence and political ambition.[5] The Iraqi occupation of Kuwait offered a peculiar window on this phenomenon, providing the opportunity to watch associations, from mosque groups to cooperatives and diwaniyyas, transform themselves in order to deal with the occupation and form the social basis for political organization. The new body of research demonstrates that civil society in the Gulf is different, and potentially quite different, from what it first appeared. This diverse social stratification, although newly studied, is not itself a particularly new phenomenon. Some important political groups – tribes, leading families – are rooted in a social structure that pre-dates the state. Others are rooted in part in the Gulf's recent economic and political history.

Many of the social groups that exist today can be understood only in the context of the societal transformations catalysed by oil revenues. In the Gulf as elsewhere, the sources of capital and the mechanisms through which revenues enter the economy are the key to understanding the emergence of new social groups (such as expatriates and oil sector workers), the transformation of old groups (such as the merchants), and the emergence of new coalitions between the two.[6] To give one important example, oil revenues initially caused many merchants, historically one of the most politically mobilized social groups in the Gulf, to leave formal political life in Kuwait and Qatar.[7] As profits from oil accrued directly to the rulers and from outside the traditional economy, these revenues allowed rulers to establish unprecedented independence from historical social groups, such as merchants, and enabled the rulers to encourage the merchants willingly to opt out of the political process. But this arrangement was only part of an ongoing dynamic. Because oil revenues also allowed the state to co-opt social groups politically rather than destroy them, it paved the way for their eventual return to politics.

Although oil also transformed the state into an institution itself capable of reshaping society in important ways, the process of expanding state power *vis-à-vis* society is not inexorable, even in states where oil revenues allow rulers tremendous flexibility. Under some circumstances social groups are able to retain both autonomy and some negotiating strength and re-enter politics when circumstances propel them. The factors that have allowed the economic elite to retain particular cohesion and strength and to retain their identity even in the face of an expanding state include: the size of the economic elite; the division of labor between the political and economic realms in the period before oil; the historical autonomy from the state and institutionalization in peak associations such as a chamber of commerce; the degree of pre-oil political mobilization; and the extent of mechanisms for maintaining group culture and identity (such as intermarriages to sustain alliances, diwaniyyas, and the degree of articulation of related political traditions and historical memory). These factors enabled some groups, most notably the merchants, to bridge a crisis, particularly the transition to oil, and reconstitute themselves when the crisis passed, in turn allowing them to re-enter politics at a later point. Kuwaiti merchant groups assumed such an important role in the pro-democracy movement of the late 1980s, continuing into and after the Iraqi occupation. A similar process has occurred in all the Gulf states.

At the same time, oil revenues gave rulers not only the freedom to divest themselves of historic economic elites, but also the capacity to use the new oil-induced bureaucracies to develop and in some cases create new allies among state employees and the recipients of new/improved state services. For the smaller GCC states, this process often involved the British who became deeply involved not only in the new state but in reorganizing the relationships between the rulers and the tribal leaders. By providing money and arms to the tribal leaders, the British were able directly to shift the balance between them and the sheikhs. British legal and administrative changes similarly took power away from the various tribal and religious councils. In time, regimes began to use oil revenues and state institutions to restructure society, whether through the establishment of social service agencies, state employment or other policies. This expansion of state functions in turn had further consequences, as it created many of the rising expectations, the sense of entitlement that became increasingly difficult to contain after the fall in oil revenues in the 1980s placed new constraints on the state's ability to deflect social protest by providing state subsidies and government employment.

Whether old or new, a variety of social groups exist in the Gulf today and can be characterized in three general ways. First, many of the most important groups are organized round economic interests. Some of these interests have their historical origin in the dominant groups of the pre-oil period, most notably the business interests organized today through the chambers of commerce and other associations which support commercial interests. Labor, where it is national and organized, as in Bahrain, is also a historically important group, although not as important as it once was, owing to the arrival of expatriate labor.[8] Other economic interests are organized round sectors, particularly where nationals dominate, for example the oil industry.[9]

Second, other groups are organized around old familial-based communal identities refashioned in new ways. Various communal affiliations, whether tribal, religious or regional, continue to form the basis of voluntary organizations, even when nominally organized around other concerns.[10] Still others are organized around demographic similarities, gender or age, that cut across communal and class lines. One of the best examples of the former is the various Shi'a institutions which historically formed the basis for strikes and demonstrations in Saudi Arabia and Bahrain in the 1930s and the 1950s, and again in the 1980s and mid-1990s. In Kuwait, similar institutions have formed the basis for electoral blocs.

Third and last, other social groups are organized around their relationship to the state. Some are united by their relationships to the state, either as political advisers with special access to the palace, or as bureaucrats identified with a particular sector. Others share their opposition to the existing state or their vision of an alternate regime. In this regard, the dominant opposition voices in the Gulf, as throughout the Arab world today, are Islamists, encompassing a range of groups who consciously organize political opposition by invoking Islamic vocabulary and principles. Historically, Arab nationalists are another, albeit weaker, example of this sort of grouping. Since the Gulf War, both Islamists and modernists have increasingly expanded vocalized dissent throughout the Gulf; in the case of the former, preaching fiery sermons and distributing them by fax and audio-tape. They have been particularly active in Saudi Arabia and Bahrain. Although there is some overlap between these two groups, they essentially exist in politically contested space, seeking to occupy the same niche vis-à-vis the state.

To sum up, then, the social groups that exist today are powerful and real. Some are rooted in the pre-oil economy and society; others have been created by the state. But all have been affected by the presence of oil revenues. Changes in the economy created new groups, changed old groups and transformed the relationship between those groups and the state. Policies introduced by the state amplified some of these changes and tempered others.

Social Stratification and Gulf Security Today and in the Twenty-first Century

A combination of traditional and more contemporary groups thus forms the basis for organized social activity and associational life in the Gulf today and is likely to continue to do so in the coming decades. These social groups in turn affect Gulf security in at least three important ways.

The first is when social groups attempt to impose their own priorities on their country's foreign policy, either directly, by pressuring the government for a policy change, or indirectly, by initiating and sustaining contacts with other governments or foreign actors. Direct pressure, when applied through conventional channels, is the stuff of politics, so common that one does not often think about the degree to which it affects security. Because foreign policy is concentrated in the executive branch, pressure to change it is seldom publicly visible. Even legislative and consultative assemblies, where they exist, rarely discuss foreign policy in the same depth as domestic policy, owing both to the preference of the executive branch and to the ordinarily primary domestic concerns of local constituencies (for example, with housing, education, health care). In the Kuwaiti case, where the National Assembly makes the process more visible, two factors make this reluctance especially pronounced. All elected officials must be sensitive to constituent concerns and, now that the Iraqi invasion is in the past, those Kuwaiti concerns are overwhelmingly domestic: concern for better services such as health care, education and state subsidies, all in an effort to re-establish normality after the trauma of occupation. The second reason for the Assembly's ambivalence regarding foreign policy is that dabbling with foreign policy has played a role in getting the assembly suspended in the past.[11]

Just because public pressure on foreign policy has not manifested itself through the legislative branch does not mean it does not exist; it is just harder to see. Economic policy is a good example. A range of social groups pressure the government for foreign economic policy that may be at odds with security concerns, narrowly conceived. The most obvious of these is immigration policy. State security services naturally would prefer to make entry requirements as stringent as possible. Other groups, however, have an interest in much more liberal requirements: for example, business elites (an economic group) want relatively open labor migration, mothers running households (a gender-based social group) want visas for household staff, and in-country foreign laborers want expanded work options for themselves and relatives at home. These three groups all pressure the state through very different means. Business interests lobby the state directly through formal organizations such as chambers of commerce and Ministries of Trade, as well as indirectly through personal ties; women lobby the state indirectly, through family connections with state actors; and expatriates will lobby the state indirectly through their own governments, and to a lesser extent by working directly through other expatriates from their country who are employed in the bureaucracy. In all cases, these efforts have implications for state security. Ultimately, foreign policy can come about as a result of the relative strengths of the competing interest groups. The more institutionalized the process, as in Kuwait, the more successful they are likely to be; the less institutionalized, as in Saudi Arabia and Qatar, the less success is likely. The security threat itself posed by more open immigration can be direct, as when expatriates explicitly associated with opposition groups slip through immigration barriers in the guise of labor. Depending upon the relative openness of the society, there is probably an even greater indirect security threat of expatriates spreading ideologies and concepts that regimes find threatening: for example, Nasserist Egyptian schoolteachers yesterday or Islamists today. Both of these can have an impact on security by increasing domestic instability or creating tensions, or at least a new dynamic between the host state and the states where these expatriates originate. In any event, a threat to state security is not the objective of those social groups pressuring domestically for increased immigration, but it might be an unintended consequence.[12]

Groups can also try to affect foreign policy more directly, as has occurred increasingly throughout the Gulf by Islamist groups since the Gulf War. One specific example is Oman, where in 1994 the state was unexpectedly faced with protests from Islamist groups regarding the country's apparent normalization of relations with Israel. As a result, several hundred militant Islamist members were arrested on charges of sedition, undermining social unity, and exploiting Islam for destructive purposes. Many were convicted and subsequently imprisoned.[13] A particularly interesting aspect of this incident was the large membership of the protesters in politically important tribes from the south of Oman. Subsequently, the Sultan announced the following year that he would amnesty those arrested and sentenced, apparently in an effort to appease the southern tribes. While these tribes may not have been overly concerned with connections to Israel, they were apparently very concerned with what by Omani standards were unusual arrests and criminal prosecutions. Thus while the Islamists themselves may well have offered no real threat to the regime, their imprisonment prompted some concern on the part of the larger groups to which they belonged and whose support the government did value.

There are also examples of more localized groups attempting to shape foreign policy. In Kuwait, relations between Iran and Iraq are both underpinned by domestic constituencies. In the autumn of 1995, government actions against local Iranian Shi'as (many Shi'a business owners retain ties with co-religionists in Iran) were interpreted by some Shi'as as a government reaction to US pressure to boycott trade with Iran. The Shi'as complained that the Kuwaiti government had arrested and deported many Iranian businessmen without sufficient grounds, some of whom had resided in Kuwait for decades. Even assuming that the conclusion of US pressure was invalid, the Shi'a interpretation and subsequent objection make it a foreign policy issue.

Another Kuwaiti example is domestic attitudes towards future foreign policy with Iraq. Here public opinion, while certainly likely to remain strongly anti-Iraqi into the twenty-first century, may nonetheless be tempered by the existence of many old, strong family ties between Kuwaitis and Iraqis, ties that cut across sectarian lines – that is, include both Sunni and Shi'a families in Kuwait with family ties to Iraq.[14] This is not to say that Kuwaitis are willing to forgive and forget. Indeed, their reluctance is tied to another domestic issue that bleeds into foreign policy: the fate of the Kuwaiti prisoners in Iraq. So volatile is this issue that the Kuwaiti government, although publicly in favor of pressing for the prisoners' return, closed down the private organization working for their release, since their increasing popularity was perceived as threatening. Although Kuwaitis are not willing to forgive and forget Iraq's actions, the tempering ties of family and clan may eventually make them more amenable than the government itself to coming to terms with some new Iraqi government. (Bear in mind that it was not so long ago that Iran was the bogeyman, during which time Kuwaitis of Iranian descent were suspect.) Indeed, Kuwaitis may prove more willing to forgive the Iraqi people than to forgive the Jordanians or Palestinians, with whom no tempering ties exist, just the memory of the public positions of their leaders during the Gulf War.[15] And while relations with these communities will eventually be restored, the policy will require much public preparation on the part of the government if it is not to evoke a hostile response from a range of social groups.

The case of Kuwaiti–Iraqi relations also raises the issue of the 'bedouin' – nomadics who exhibit only a weak identity with either state. Most of the bedouin in Kuwait are of Iraqi tribal origin (for example, Anaizi) who came to Kuwait in the 1960s and 1970s when the economy was stronger and state sovereignty was not as robust as it has become in more recent years.[16] Because so many are, or are believed to be, tribes of Iraqi origin, some of whom cooperated with the Iraqis during the invasion, they are suspect. Because certain Shi'a bedouin were overtly associated with pro-Iranian operations in the 1980s, they are doubly suspect. These bedouin supported a troublesome foreign policy position twice, as it were, and there are few tempering ties (bedouin tribal members with strong Kuwaiti family ties have often chosen to leave that group and become Kuwaitis). Recent efforts to regularize the status of the bedouin have not so much resolved the problem as formalized it.

As these examples illustrate, groups of diverse purpose and character can have a direct and significant impact upon Gulf security. An indirect way groups influence foreign policy, and thus affect state security, is by initiating and sustaining contacts with other foreign actors or governments. In this regard, three political groups continue to be regionally important. The first is comprised of Arab nationalists and their liberal descendants today; the second is that of the Islamists. The third group, largely specific to the Gulf, is that of the tribes. When regional governments whose agenda resonates with one or more of these groups comes to office, that government, especially in its early stages, will encourage a linkage with these external groups both logistically and ideologically. The conduct of the government particularly during the early months of both Nasser's Egypt and Khomeini's Iran supports this argument. The foreign policy positions of Islamist groups, to include Islamist groups who focus primarily on a domestic agenda, have also attracted the concern of other countries, notably of France with respect to North Africa and of the USA generally. The regional dimension of Islamist politics also affects domestic politics, when local Arab nationalist groups who fear the rising Islamist strength become less likely to challenge the sitting government on any issue.

Foreign nationals also exhibit transnational political concerns and loyalties, but they are rarely powerful enough in the host country directly to affect policy. A partial exception to this general condition occurred in the case of the Palestinians in Kuwait before and during the Gulf War. While their support for the Iraqi invasion was far more muted than that of Palestinians elsewhere, the Iraqi belief that these Palestinians would support an invasion contained security implications. Even before 1990, their presence had a subtle impact. The Palestinian role in the civil wars in Jordan and Lebanon prompted Kuwaiti fears concerning the potential for Palestinians to accept a similar role in Kuwait. In the 1980s, new attention to security was directed at Palestinians as well as at other non-nationals. As the intifada began to affect Kuwaiti politics, serving as one more spur to the pro-democracy movement, the government reassessed its position. In February 1988, demonstrators marching in support of the intifada clashed with the police, prompting several arrests. At the same time, Palestinian resentment gradually began to grow. Although years of residence and work had given many Palestinians a vague – and largely unrealized – sense of entitlement to the benefits of Kuwait's wealth, the time in Kuwait had done little to erase the social, economic and political disparities between Kuwaitis and resident non-nationals, Palestinians included. The other nationals, however, could look forward to going home (as, indeed, most did after a few years); most Palestinians could not. The intifada began to politicize this Palestinian resentment. These factors turned the Palestinian population into a security issue, albeit a somewhat unusual one.

The rapid transformation of communications technologies in recent years has facilitated the ease of cross-border contact. As satellite dishes expand, faxes become ubiquitous, computers become more widespread, and servers, and with them e-mail and Internet access, appear throughout the Gulf and the region, it has become far harder for local governments to control or even monitor these new forms of communication. Before the arrival of the PC, computer technology (when mainframes dominated) allowed governments to improve their ability to monitor and control the population. But once access to this new generation of technology, particularly to the ungovernable Internet, became widespread, it moved from public to private control, evading rather than facilitating state control. These technologies make it easier for groups outside the state's borders to work with those within to shape foreign policy. Interest in and access to this technology has flourished since the Gulf War, which generated a thirst for instant news. The Saudis have been quick to recognize the importance of satellite service. In 1991, Walid al-Ibrahim, a brother-in-law of King Fahd, led a group of investors to start MBC, the Middle Eastern Broadcasting Center, using Arabsat satellites operated by a consortium of Arab state television companies, and broadcasting from London. Reminiscent of Al-Sharq al-Awsat, MBC takes a more neutral and open tone when appealing to a broader audience than broadcast media inside the Kingdom. But the Saudis have been unable to monopolize this technology. Satellite service has grown remarkably quickly. MBC competes with Egyptian government-supported ESC (Egyptian Satellite Channel) and with two private satellite services: in 1993 Arab Radio and Television (ART) began broadcasting in English and Arabic; in 1994 Orbit satellite, with Saudi owners, followed. In 1994, Orbit's features included interviews with Saudi dissidents.[17]

Gulf security is also indirectly affected by social transformation. This occurs whenever social groups exert political pressure on the state or on other social groups sufficient to disrupt ordinary political life. This disruption attracts or threatens to attract the attention of other states, which in turn may then be tempted to reshape their own foreign policy, or even on rare occasions to intervene directly. In the Gulf, there have been a few recent instances where social opposition has produced destabilizing pressure on the government so great that it has affected Gulf security.

The first case is Kuwait. In the months before the Iraqi invasion in 1990, Kuwait was wracked by internal dissent, by a pro-democracy movement that had begun in the diwaniyyas in 1989 and that had as its underlying force the discontent of key social groups. Both Islamists and modernists, including former Assembly members and merchants, alienated by the government's inability to provide the expected level of economic support owing to the fall in oil prices, became openly politically active. These groups formed a political coalition and began pressuring the government to reinstate the National Assembly. This coalition built upon the pro-democracy Constitutionalist Movement which emerged following the closure of the Assembly in 1986 and began calling for its reinstatement as well as reinstatement of the suspended articles of the 1962 Constitution. The movement gained further momentum in 1989 when former National Assembly members began organizing more publicly round these issues.

Misreading and overestimating this organized opposition to the status quo, Saddam Hussein apparently believed that if he invaded Kuwait, opposition forces would join him, or at least acquiesce in his presence, thus enabling him to set up a compliant government. At the outset of the invasion, Iraq actually asserted it had entered Kuwait in support of a local rebellion. As was soon made clear, however, the domestic opposition had no intention of overthrowing the government, let alone supporting the Iraqi invasion. Indeed, the Kuwaiti opposition was, if anything, more anti-Iraqi than the government in the period just before the invasion. For example, the pro-democracy movement included several former parliamentarians, who had strongly opposed Kuwait's wartime aid to Iraq during the Iran–Iraq War.

The National Council, the partially appointed, partially elected, quasi-legislative body set up by the Kuwaiti government in June 1990 to appease pro-democracy elements, had been still more vocal in its opposition to Iraq. The same can be said for Shi'a-dominated underground opposition sympathetic to Iran, or at least sympathetic to Iranian Shi'as, who were equally non-supportive of Iraq's invasion. When Iraq nevertheless named Kuwaitis to a new government, they refused to serve. Their supporters issued a communiqué opposing the invasion, calling for the restoration of the legitimate Kuwaiti government, and even affirming their commitment, albeit with qualifications, to al-Sabah rule. Finally, and in frustration, Iraq rounded up Kuwaiti naval officers captured during the invasion, and forced them to serve in the brief Kuwaiti cabinet.

In sum, the Iraqis misread the domestic opposition groups in pre-invasion Kuwait. Believing they had at least some local support, they first attempted to set up a quisling government of Kuwaitis. This effort was a complete failure, as dissidents from the pre-invasion period joined forces with regime loyalists to oppose the Iraqi forces. The Iraqis could not even attract the few Kuwaiti Ba'athists – there were a few – to join them. In retrospect, Saddam Hussein apparently thought that the Kuwaiti opposition was much more anti-government than it in fact was, and that he could take advantage of it.

This discussion illustrates the way in which political turmoil can attract the involvement of other states in very important ways. Ironically, had Kuwait's national identity been more fragile, its society less civil, less diverse, had it in fact been the contrived historical creation Iraq asserted it was, Iraq would probably have succeeded in putting in place a nominally Kuwaiti government that might have granted to Iraq the financial and strategic concessions it sought. Then perhaps Iraq would have found annexation unnecessary. However, unable to set up even the semblance of a Kuwaiti government, Iraq had no choice but either to leave, or to put in place an occupation administration. This series of calculations turned in part on a particular reading (a misreading, as it turned out) on the part of the Iraqi government of social unrest in Kuwait.

Bahrain is another case where social groups have put enough pressure on the state that the ensuing turmoil has attracted the attention of other states. Following the Iranian revolution, the mere presence of a comparatively large Shi'a community in Bahrain (and the comparatively smaller ones in Kuwait and Saudi Arabia) provoked the interest of the Iranians. The indigenous grievances of that community helped to produce a receptivity to Iranian attentions. The coup attempt of 1981 in Bahrain, and other incidents of Iranian involvement, or suspected involvement, ensued. But with the end of the Iran–Iraq War and the fading of some of the revolution's promise, this involvement was thought to have declined. Then in December 1994 hundreds of people were arrested in connection with a petition calling for the reinstatement of parliament, dissolved in 1975.[18] Again, the government raised the issue of Iranian involvement. Opponents to the status quo clearly and disproportionately included sectarian-based (Shi'a) opposition groups.

Another interesting case is the change of power in Qatar in 1995. Sheikh Hamad's assumption of rule from his father Sheikh Khalifa was a transformation that, to all appearances, occurred with some real social support for a change (albeit with rather mixed feelings about the method) which, as a result, dissuaded Gulf neighbors from a stronger reaction. Had there been more domestic (Qatari) opposition to the move, which in a different social environment there might have been, an ensuing protest might well have precipitated a stronger reaction from neighboring states, notably Saudi Arabia.

The implication of this reading of events is that when opposition is open and public, it can attract the interest and even the direct involvement of neighboring states in domestic politics, and thus, at minimum, engender security concerns or questions. By and large however, regional security is rarely threatened by political opposition groups within Gulf states. If anything, the greater danger to Gulf security may well lie in the overreaction of Gulf governments to predictable, limited and essentially unthreatening pressure for public participation. When is it likely that Gulf political opposition will endanger regional security? In order for social protest to become a significant security concern, a few conditions must exist. First, there must be real domestic grievances and there must be significant inadequacy in the government's response to these grievances. Second, there must be an outside power which perceives that their interests are significantly affected by the political activity within the affected state. Some expansion of this argument is necessary.

First, for regional security to be placed at risk, a potentially volatile domestic opposition to state policy must exist. The case of Bahrain is a good example. Whatever the level of Iranian involvement historically, active Iranian involvement in Bahrain's internal government affairs would probably not have occurred had not the indigenous Shi'a community of Bahrain believed that it had genuine and independent domestic grounds for complaint. In general, either new demands arise, or old ones are suddenly unmet, but something must make previously depoliticized or demobilized groups want to enter or re-enter politics. Sometimes new demands seem to arise spontaneously whenever sufficient wealth exists to generate an educated population with the necessary leisure time and financial wherewithal for political activity. As the early modernization literature suggested, there is an apparent historical relationship between economic development and an increase in political demands.[19] These new demands often take the form of a political participation agenda. What is striking in the Gulf is the diverse social origins of groups pursuing an agenda of greater political participation today: members of extended families, business elites, tribes (adapting tribal institutions such as primaries to electoral politics in Kuwait), the Islamists, and so on. Even nominally apolitical groups such as cooperatives are organized through electoral processes. To a certain extent, economic growth and the social changes associated with growth (education, urbanization, and so on) produce these kinds of pressures, a rise in active but essentially non-confrontational political behavior. This is particularly the case with the younger generation, educated and raised on expectations of rising wealth; expectations that in some cases have not been met in the last decade.

Throughout the Gulf, the new schools built with oil revenues have created natural cohorts of graduates. Their collective identity is heightened by political crises such as the recent Gulf wars; perhaps a watershed in socializing political events for a generation of Gulf citizens and residents. Links established in youth, crystallized by shared political experience, often endure a lifetime. This change is doubly noticeable in the Gulf where rapid improvements in public health in recent decades have produced an unusually large younger generation, deepening the division between that small portion of the population which remembers the period before oil and the current generation which does not. This generational divide has become apparent in Oman in recent years.[20] Elsewhere, the divide is real, but often weakened by cross-cutting identifications to family and sect.

For this to become a regional security concern, however, it must escalate further. To understand when that occurs, we must understand something about governments' response to these pressures. Social groups with interests must not only exist, they also need to be politicized. This is actually fairly unusual in the Gulf. Several key social groups have historically eschewed politics. Economic development may produce a pro-democratic movement; it may also create groups who simply push for more economic or other publicly non-participatory concessions. This is partly because oil revenue has allowed rulers to buy off opposition. It is also partly because nominally apolitical mechanisms for tempering, recognizing and responding to complaints exist, including diwaniyyas or family ties.

For social opposition to develop disruptive potential, groups must feel that historical forms of less overt political participation are closed or ineffective. The presence of democratic institutions is likely to minimize this feeling of political inefficiency. Kuwait, for example, has had historically fewer instances of violent confrontations when dissent grew than its neighbors, notably Bahrain (where the brief Assembly was closed), and these have been the fewest during periods of political approachability. But even in less approachable systems, whenever historical access is closed or ineffective for meeting concerns, groups will likely seek other avenues of access. These include the bureaucracy, the palace and ultimately the street. When social groups have significant unresolved grievances, and the means available for redress are inadequate, they will engage the state more disruptively. Recognizing this, especially since the Gulf War, regimes throughout the Gulf have all experimented with limited political openings: the new and elected consultative council in Oman, the appointed consultative council in Saudi Arabia, and the proposed municipality elections in Qatar.

Once mobilized, groups can increase their political effectiveness through additional organizational development. They often choose to identify and build upon core social constituencies in civil society, in the space between the family and the state. They are then able to recast their concerns in more universal terms, and resultingly expand their support base. Yet they need to do this carefully enough in order not to prompt a crackdown by the state. In fact, to prevent this, they must also create centers of support within the state. Their ability to survive as opposition groups thus depends on the nature of their underlying unifying power base and the extent to which they can expand that base. Expansion of their political base necessarily includes the developing of strategies which permit them to organize within the limited public space the government allows, and the ability to articulate their interests in terms that appeal to those beyond their core constituency, without pushing the bounds of political permissibility.

Even where disaffection runs deep, political mobilization is rare in the Gulf, precisely because building political organizations is such a long, difficult process. This is particularly true in the Gulf where informal avenues of political expression, based largely on family ties, are effective, widespread and enduring. Family gatherings are both an effective means for pressuring the government indirectly, and a way for people to vent discontent harmlessly. For this reason, political mobilization has been attenuated throughout the Gulf, notably in Saudi Arabia and the UAE. It has risen to the surface repeatedly only in Bahrain and Kuwait, and for different reasons. In Bahrain, the discontent is so great (economic grievances, sectarian differences, class differences, the US naval base) that the government has periodically been unable to contain it. In Kuwait, the discontent is rather minimal, and while the opposition has at times become quite vocal, their ultimate loyalty to the system has assured a working relationship. Bahrain alone among the Gulf states has a long history of labor organizing (which the government fears) while Kuwait is the only one with a long history of formal political participation (dating back to the elected councils of the interwar period). In Saudi Arabia, Oman and the UAE, the shorter history of political protest (violent or non-violent), coupled with the tempering ties of extended family, have contained dissent, thus far. However, should these ties weaken in the twenty-first century, whether because of economic pressure, population growth, sharpened generation gaps or other factors, then active dissent in these states might also grow.

How the state responds to opposition, whether with concessions or coercion, varies and matters. My present research grapples with this issue, but a few points are worth making.[21] First, there have been tremendous variations in the use of concessions and force in roughly comparable civil disturbances among states as well as within states over time. For example, the Bahraini government's response to opposition in the mid-1990s was quite sharp – some reports indicate as many as 5000 people detained in the 1994 incidents.[22] The Kuwaiti government's response to similar opposition has been more muted.

Second, the nature and severity of the response seem to be a function of several factors. There is no immediately obvious reason why coercion should be the more likely response in the Gulf. Historically, institutionalized coercion has not been the pillar of rule in the Gulf that it has in other Arab states. Kuwait, for example, built its first prison only in 1938 to house a handful of prisoners generated by the Majlis movement that year. States have at their disposal a range of responses to opposition, many of which are accommodational. They can intimidate groups, co-opt them, compromise with them, regulate them or even allow for their representation. In the Gulf, all rulers have at times attempted some sort of popular appeal. Developmentalism is the most common – the belief that the state must play a central role in promoting economic growth and that, to that end, individuals and social organizations must relinquish power to the state, allowing it the routine if temporary use of force against enemies. In exchange, the state promises to maintain a certain standard of living. A second idea is neo-traditionalism.[23] This involves invoking tradition in a particularly selective manner, using a construction that privileges the status quo, regardless of how strong a resemblance it bears to actual historical experience. These ideas can be drawn from any part of history: from religion, from tribal identity, from anti-colonialism. Both sets of ideas – developmentalism and neo-traditionalism – aim simultaneously to legitimize and to demobilize.

Governmental responses to opposition groups are affected by a number of factors. One is these is the nature of the respective economy. Both the level of development (the amount of wealth) and the development strategy pursued (for example, public/private) can affect how states will respond to the rising social expectations of citizens.[24] In general and perhaps obvious terms, states which possess great wealth are more able, and thus more likely to expend significant sums to meet rising expectations. Another factor shaping governmental response is the nature of social stratification. Where classes are clearly defined and class conflict comparatively sharp, the state response in turn seems also to be more extreme. The sharper class consciousness and history of labor organizing in Bahrain, for example, might explain in part the unusually strong state response there. Similarly, the sharper communal differences in the population are, the stronger the state response appears to be. This seems to be the case especially when (as in Saudi Arabia and Bahrain) the government and the opposition are rooted in different societal sects or tribes. Where communal or tribal differences are present and politically activated, the more likely rulers are to move away from the bargaining strategies of parliamentary institutions and towards less participative methodologies. Strong or especially forceful state responses can themselves increase identification with sub-national groupings (for example, tribe) and decrease identification with nation – ultimately a troublesome outcome for the state.

An increasingly important component of social policy within the Gulf, a component which has prompted states to re-evaluate their relationship with many organized social groups, has been the need to garner domestic support for a new or controversial foreign policy position. Although domestic factors are always important, the most powerful need often seems to be one of securing domestic support, or at the very least domestic acceptance, for controversial foreign policy. In all the GCC states, notably Saudi Arabia, the Gulf War crisis prompted a return to public life. In Kuwait, the occupation prompted the government to agree at Taif to allow a reopening of public dissent. Dissent reached the point where opposition groups openly argued that if the pre-invasion government had permitted greater individual freedom of expression, that is if the Assembly had been open, the invasion itself might not have occurred. In Oman, foreign policy concerns prompted Sultan Qaboos to institute a Consultative Council in 1991 and to release hundreds of militants from the south in 1995, as previously noted.

In Qatar, the Emir lifted public censorship restrictions in October 1995 in order to legitimize his accession to power. A month later he announced that Qatar was considering electing members to municipal councils, which would be the first vote in the country. The Emir told the opening session of the 30-member advisory council that his government wanted to increase citizen involvement in government and economic development, and that it was considering amending laws relating to municipalities to allow their membership by elections. Domestic concerns also clearly play a role in prompting governments to open politics to social groups, but even here foreign policy often also plays a role. The fact that Qatar had recently taken moves towards normalizing relations with Israel was doubtless also a major factor in this decision.

Governments then frequently respond to anticipated or actual opposition to sticky foreign policy issues with some liberalization at home. That oil revenues continue to give the rulers the upper hand in these encounters, however, is clear from the fact that these groups re-enter politics only at the ruler's discretion (as in Qatar and Oman recently). Where they do not have the government's support, as in Bahrain, they are rarely successful. There, opposition protests were dealt with swiftly and harshly. Governments thus retain the upper hand.

In sum, for social transformations significantly to affect Gulf security, there must be organized social groups with clearly articulated grievances, pressuring the government either directly or indirectly. There must be a government whose response is in some ways seen as inadequate, at least in the eyes of those groups. Finally, there must be an external power with an interest in the issue. This combination occurs relatively rarely, but each of these components exists at times in each Gulf state. This combination has prompted pressure on both domestic and foreign policy in the past, and will doubtless continue to do so as the Gulf enters the twenty-first century.

CHAPTER 12

Population Growth, the Labor Market and Gulf Security

Michael E. Bonine

Although national security is most often considered in terms of adequate military forces and defensible boundaries, social and economic stability is just as significant for the future of any country. As the states of the Gulf move into the twenty-first century, the changing economic conditions and the needs and desires of their societies must be understood and reckoned with wisely by each of these governments. Fuelled by abundant oil wealth, the Gulf region certainly has witnessed one of the most rapid developments and momentous economic transformations of the modern world. Iran and Iraq, as major petroleum producers, are part of this socio-economic transformation, but the Arab states of the Arabian peninsula have been affected to an even greater degree. With their smaller and more traditional and conservative populations, the rapid development process has had a greater impact on their societies.

Population growth has been phenomenal in the Gulf, accelerated not only by rapid increases in the national populations but also especially by the influx of large numbers of foreign workers to build, service and maintain the houses, shops, roads, industries and infrastructure. The local, national workforces have been insufficient in numbers and skills to carry out the rapid economic development, and so millions of foreign migrants have provided most of the labor. Representing a large percentage of the population in all these states, foreigners have become an absolute majority in Kuwait, Qatar and the United Arab Emirates. Yet, the dominance of foreigners in the labor force, especially for manual labor, industrial jobs and other specific occupations, is even more striking. As Nasra M. Shah has noted: 'labor migration is a demographic fact that has probably taken on greater significance in the Gulf countries than anywhere else in the world'.[1]

This chapter examines the rapid population increase and the labor markets of the Gulf states, focusing on the six Arab members of the Gulf Corporation Council (GCC). The demographic characteristics and the factors influencing the growth of population and labor are analysed, as well as the consequences of the patterns. Projections are then given for the population growth of the GCC states, stressing how the numbers could be staggering by the mid- and late twenty-first century. Finally, suggestions are presented for dealing with the issues of population and labor for the GCC states in the future.

Problems of Population Data in the Gulf

Accurate and especially detailed demographic statistics for the GCC states are often lacking, and the data that are available are often incomplete. Hence a detailed, thorough analysis of the population and labor of the Gulf states has certain limitations. It is particularly difficult because of the great number of foreigners within each country, some of whom may be working illegally. Census data may not be released in full detail or may be underreported. Oman did not have its first census until November 1993, and the previous population estimates were proven by that census to be considerably too low. The reporting of census data is better for Bahrain and Kuwait, with demographic analyses of Kuwait's population being the most extensive and detailed in the Gulf. However, because of the 1990–91 Iraqi occupation and subsequent Gulf War, there now must be a reliance on estimates for Kuwait's population in the 1990s. Despite the limitations of demographic data, the basic patterns and trends of population and labor of the Gulf can still be examined. Reliable estimates by various organizations and/or individuals can be used in many instances, as well as calculating estimates from existing data, even when incomplete.

The Gulf Population in 1992

In 1992, the consulting firm of Birks Sinclair and Associates Ltd (BSAL) in Durham, England, issued one of the most recent analyses of comparable statistics for all of the GCC states.[2] Although BSAL's estimates tend to be conservative, and do not account for all of the increases in both national and foreign populations in the last decade, its statistics are nevertheless useful because of their extensive comparisons among the GCC states.

BSAL estimated the 1992 population of the six Gulf states at 17.6

million, comprised of 59.8 per cent nationals and 40.2 per cent non-nationals (see Table 12.1, Figure 12.1). Figures 12.2, 12.3 and 12.4 show the national and the non-national populations by age and sex in 1992. What is immediately obvious is the great differences in the two groups. The national population is predominantly young, with almost half (47.8 per cent) being under the age of 15. Fertility rates are extremely high, while infant mortality rates have recently declined because of the excellent medical facilities and better nutrition available to GCC nationals. The non-national population, on the other hand, is more typical of a migrant population with three times as many men as women, and two-thirds between the ages of 20 and 35. Most of the non-nationals are single, unaccompanied migrant workers.

Figure 12.1 shows BSAL's estimates for the distribution of national and non-national populations in the GCC states in 1992. There are vast differences between the individual states. Saudi Arabia dominates the GCC demographically: in total population (69.6 per cent), in number of nationals (76.7 per cent), and in number of non-nationals (59.3 per cent). By contrast, Bahrain's or Qatar's total populations are quite small, comprising only 2.6 and 2.4 per cent of the total GCC population respectively. The most significant relationship, however, is the percentage of the nationals and non-nationals within each state. Here the percentages range from 29.1, 32.5 and 34.1 per cent nationals in UAE, Kuwait and Qatar to 65.8, 71.1 and 73.7 per cent nationals in Saudi Arabia, Bahrain and Oman respectively. Even though the great numbers of non-nationals residing in each country are a concern throughout the GCC, the states in which the nationals represent a minority within their own country present some of the greatest challenges at present and particularly for the future.[3]

The non-national population is comprised of mostly Arabs (37.8 per cent) and Asians (57.4 per cent) (Figure 12.1d; with the nationality or region of the non-nationals indicated in Figure 12.1e). The Arab non-nationals in the GCC in 1992 totalled 2.7 million (Table 12.2), including over one million Egyptians and still roughly 600,000 Jordanians and Palestinians, despite the fact that their presence in Kuwait has been greatly diminished since the Gulf crisis of 1990–91. Prior to 1990, Yemenis comprised one of the largest non-national Arab groups in the GCC, mostly in Saudi Arabia. Problems between the Yemeni and Saudi governments in the 1980s began to diminish their number, and when the Yemeni government did not support the allied coalition in the 1990–91 Iraqi occupation of Kuwait and the subsequent Gulf War, about 700,000 Yemeni workers were forced to leave Saudi Arabia.[4] Saudi Arabia still has

Table 12.1 National and non-national populations in GCC states, 1992

	Nationals (1,000s)	Nationals (%)	Non-nationals (1,000s)	Non-nationals (%)	Total (%)	Nationals of GCC	Non-nationals of GCC	Total of GCC
Saudi Arabia	8,066.4	65.8	4,192.7	34.2	12,259.1	76.7	59.3	69.6
UAE	531.0	29.1	1,294.0	70.9	1,825.0	5.1	18.3	10.4
Oman	1,062.3	73.7	380.0	26.3	1,442.3	10.1	5.4	8.2
Kuwait	387.0	32.5	803.1	67.5	1,190.0	3.7	11.3	6.8
Bahrain	330.4	71.1	134.0	28.9	464.4	3.1	1.9	2.6
Qatar	141.0	34.1	272.1	65.9	413.1	1.3	3.8	2.4
Total	10,518.1	59.8	7,075.9	40.2	17,603.9	100.0	100.0	100.0

Source: Adapted from estimates by BSAL, GCC Market Report, 1992, Table 6.1, p 26

Table 12.2 Non-national population in GCC states by nationality and state, 1992 (numbers)

Nationality	Bahrain	Kuwait	Oman	Qatar	S. Arabia	UAE	Total	%
Egyptian	5,000	240,000	31,600	13,870	733,128	81,800	1,105,398	15.6
Sudanese	930	800	11,700	6,580	191,804	45,900	257,714	3.6
Jordanians and Palestinians	4,150	101,500	5,200	48,180	292,301	151,401	602,732	8.5
Lebanese	110	28,000	0	7,530	133,013	34,700	203,353	2.9
Syrian	110	21,000	0	21,680	48,088	20,800	111,678	1.6
Yemeni	0	700	0	2,500	57,170	27,200	87,570	1.2
Tunisian	0	1,650	0	290	2,398	0	4,338	0.1
Moroccan	0	3,050	0	220	3,663	0	6,933	0.1
Other Arab	2,000	93,750	1,700	8,200	102,893	84,200	292,743	4.1
Arab sub-total	12,300	490,450	50,200	109,050	1,564,458	446,001	2,672,459	37.8
%	0.5	18.4	1.9	4.1	58.5	16.7	100.0	
Pakistani	6,500	62,500	51,001	56,740	419,842	231,601	828,184	11.7
Bangladeshi	8,000	60,000	45,701	10,650	322,483	61,100	507,934	7.2
Indian	69,400	102,500	204,901	83,120	611,016	355,501	1,426,438	20.2
Sri Lankan	12,000	46,000	13,600	4,930	316,134	60,300	452,964	6.4
Filipino	9,000	14,500	2,400	0	367,355	35,600	428,855	6.1
Indonesian	0	0	0	0	58,649	0	58,649	0.8
South Korean	2,500	7,500	0	0	87,195	0	97,195	1.4
Thai	1,500	0	800	0	78,503	0	80,803	1.1
Iranian	1,400	4,400	0	4,200	0	61,200	71,200	1.0
Other	0	0	1,000	0	102,538	10,100	113,638	1.6
Asian sub-total	110,300	297,400	319,403	159,640	2,363,715	815,402	4,065,860	57.5
%	2.7	7.3	7.9	3.9	58.1	20.1	100.0	

Table 12.2 Non-national population in GCC states by nationality and state, 1992 (numbers) (cont)

Nationality	Bahrain	Kuwait	Oman	Qatar	S. Arabia	UAE	Total	%
North American	7,000	4,600	9,000	0	79,502	0	100,102	1.4
African	1,400	0	0	0	108,001	8,000	117,401	1.7
Other OECD	3,000	6,700	0	3,400	0	15,000	28,100	0.4
Other	0	3,925	1,400	0	77,004	9,600	91,929	1.3
Sub-total	11,400	15,225	10,400	3,400	264,507	32,600	337,532	4.8
%	3.4	4.5	3.1	1.0	78.4	9.7	100.0	
Total	134,000	803,075	380,003	272,090	4,192,680	1,294,003	7,075,851	100.0

Source: Estimates by BSAL, *GCC Market Report 1992*, 1992, Table 4.3, p 23.

a. Total population by nationality, 1990 and 1992

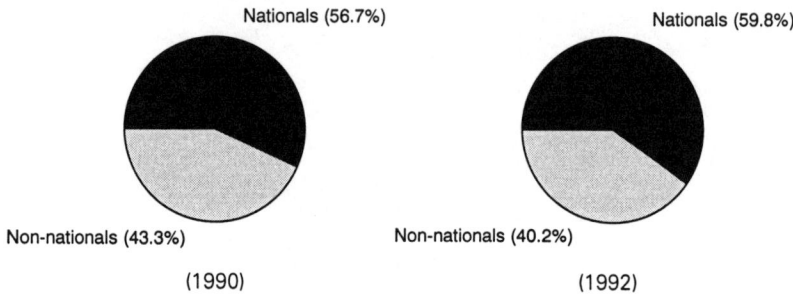

b. National population by state, 1992

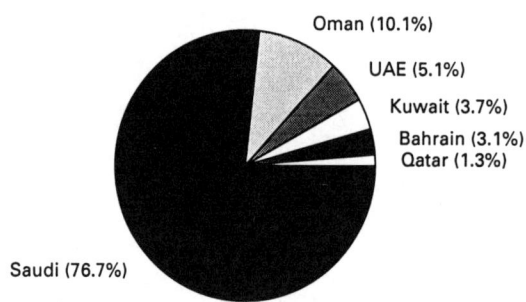

c. Non-national population by state of residence, 1992

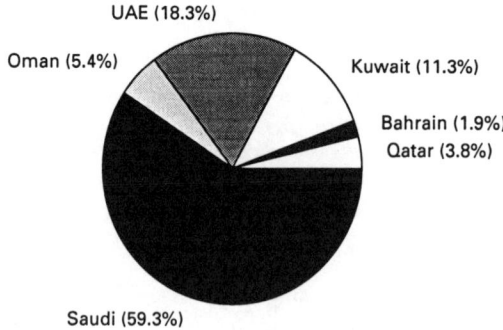

Source: BSAL, 'GCC Market Report 1992'.

Figure 12.1 GCC national and non-national population

d. Total non-national population by ethnic group, 1992

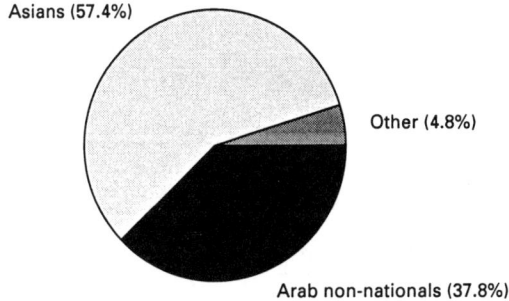

e. Non-national population by nationality, 1992

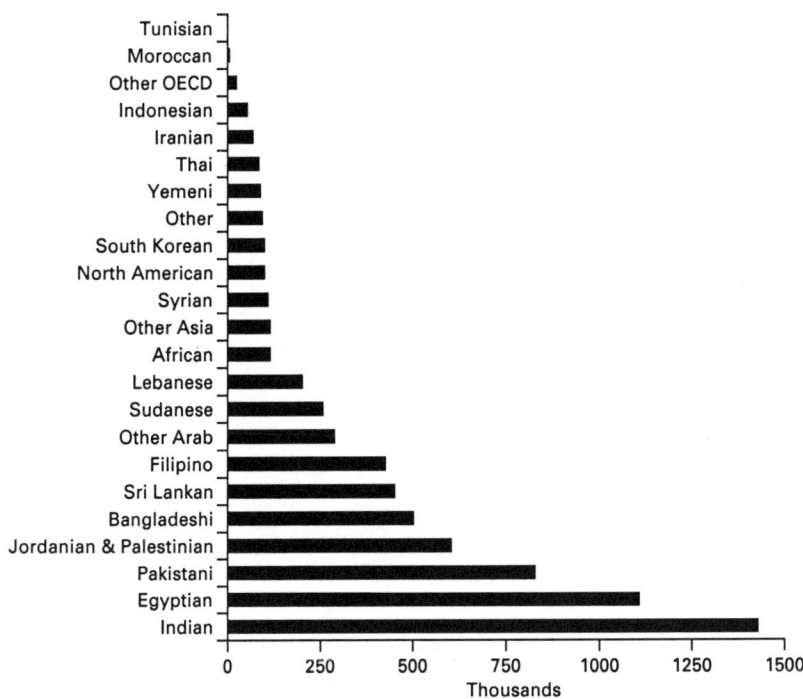

Source: BSAL, 'GCC Market Report 1992' (Durham: Mountjoy Research Centre, 1992).

Figure 12.1 GCC national and non-national population (cont)

a. Total population by age and sex, 1992

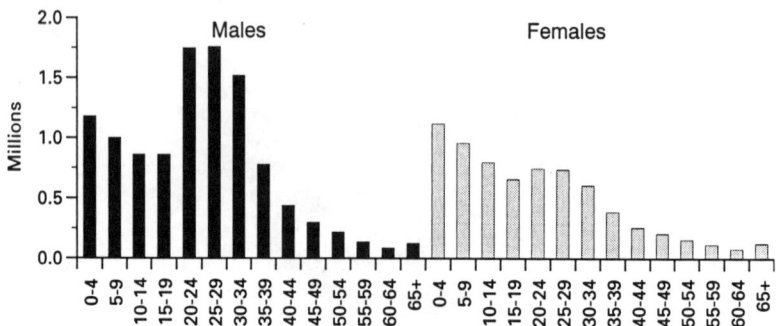

b. National population by age and sex, 1992

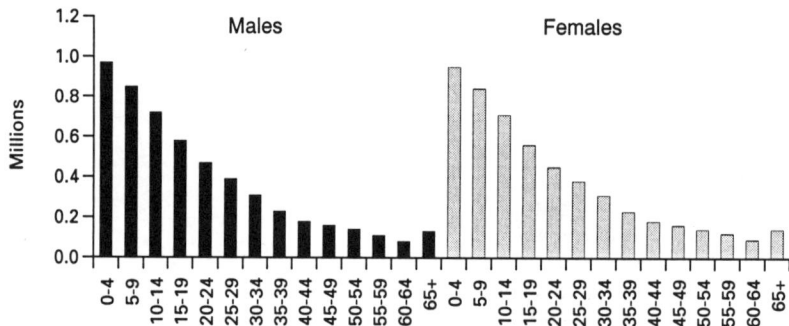

c. Non-national population by age and sex, 1992

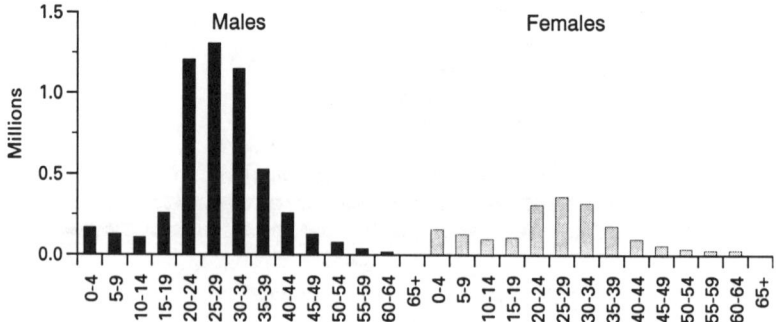

Source: BSAL, 'GCC Market Report 1992'.

Figure 12.2 GCC national and non-national population by age and sex

d. Non-national Arab population by age and sex, 1992

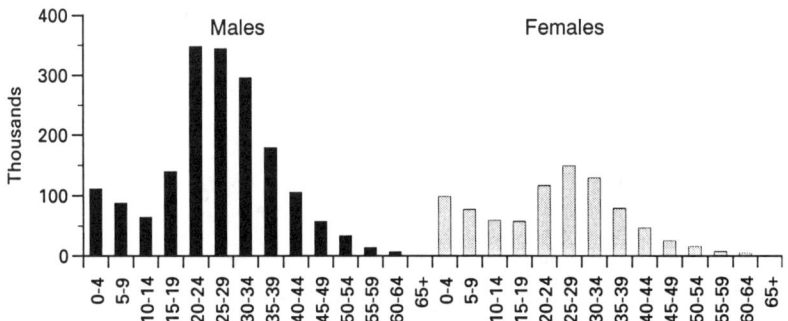

e. Non-national Asian population by age and sex, 1992

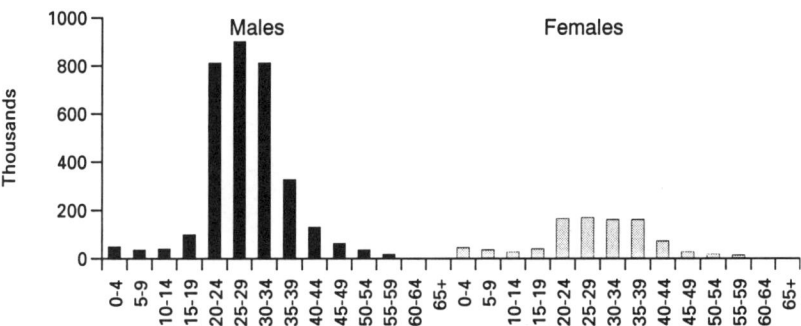

Source: BSAL, 'GCC Market Report 1992'.

Figure 12.2 GCC national and non-national population by age and sex (cont)

a. Saudi Arabia: national population by age and sex, 1992

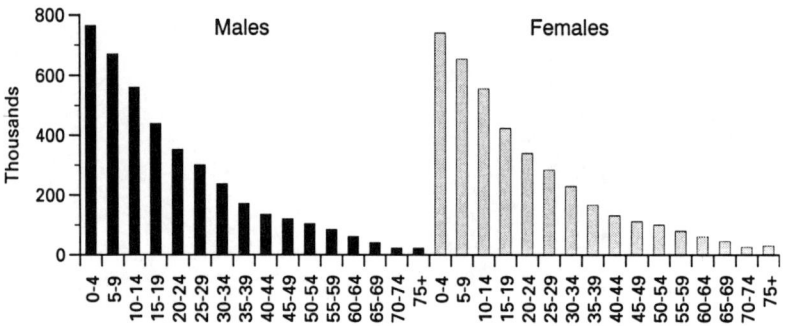

b. UAE: national population by age and sex, 1992

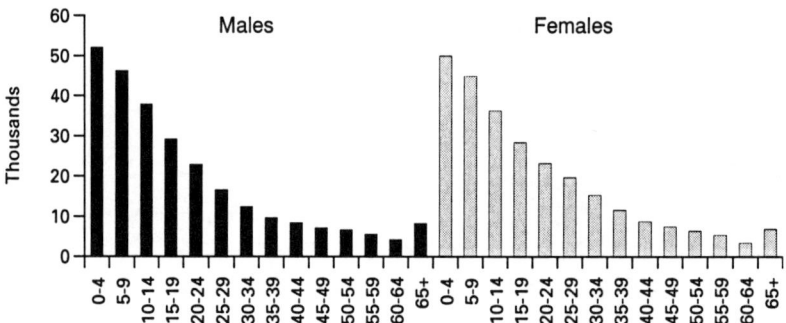

c. Oman: national population by age and sex, 1992

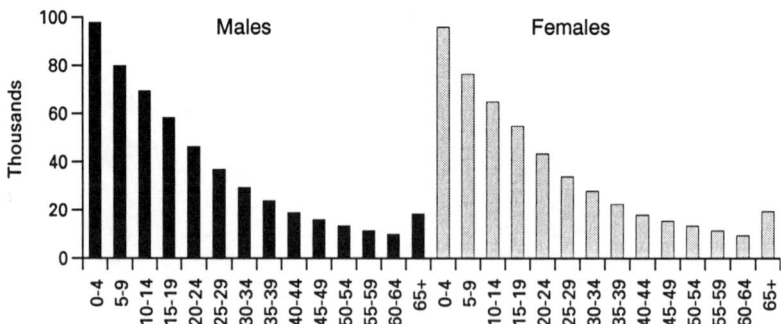

Source: BSAL, 'GCC Market Report 1992'.

Figure 12.3 Individual GCC state national population by age and sex

d. Kuwait: national population by age and sex, 1992

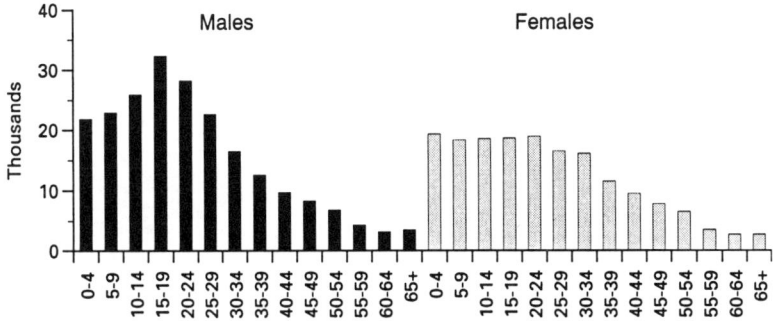

e. Bahrain: national population by age and sex, 1992

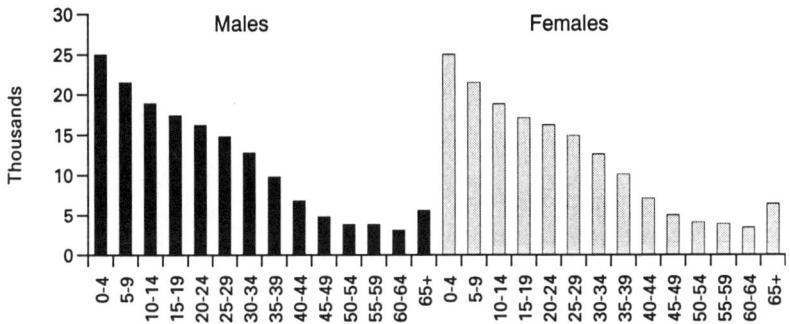

f. Qatar: national population by age and sex, 1992

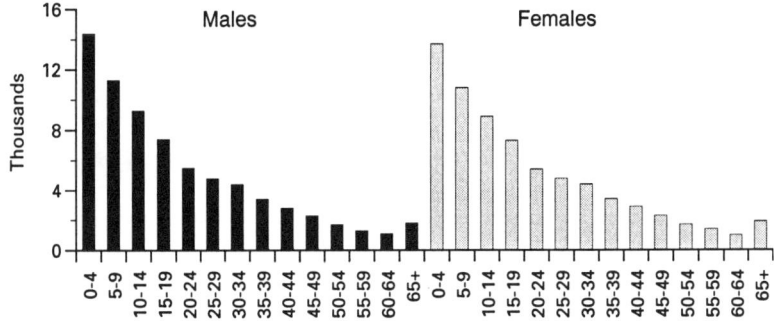

Source: BSAL, 'GCC Market Report 1992'.

Figure 12.3 Individual GCC state national population by age and sex (cont)

a. Saudi Arabia: non-national population by age and sex, 1992

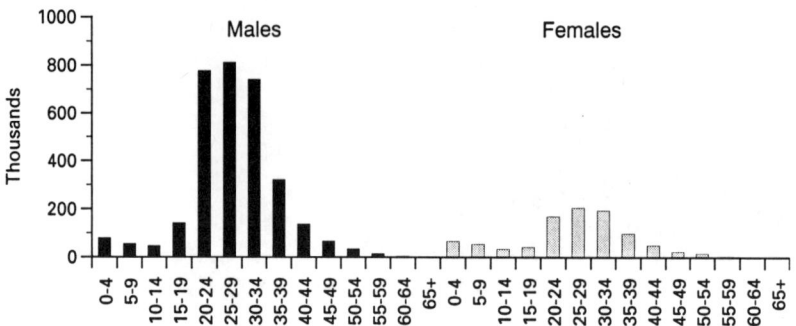

b. UAE: non-national population by age and sex, 1992

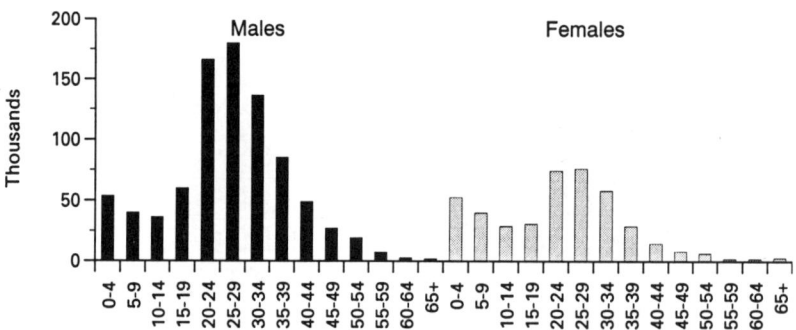

c. Oman: non-national population by age and sex, 1992

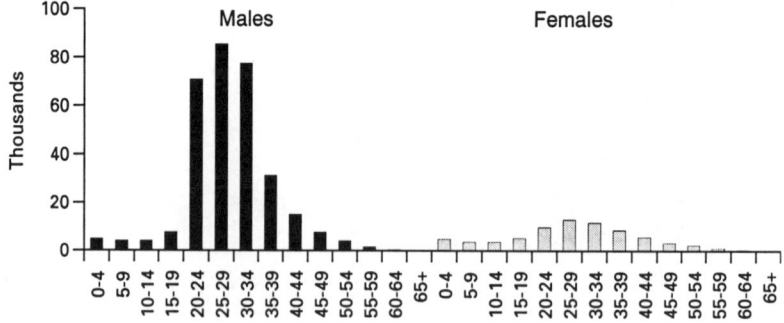

Source: BSAL, 'GCC Market Report 1992'.

Figure 12.4 Individual GCC state non-national population by age and sex

d. Kuwait: non-national population by age and sex, 1992

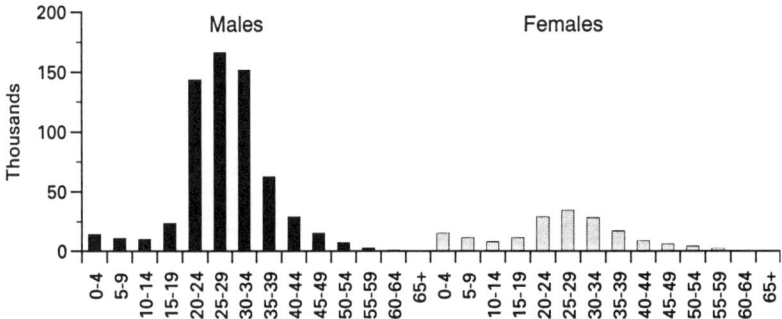

e. Bahrain: non-national population by age and sex, 1992

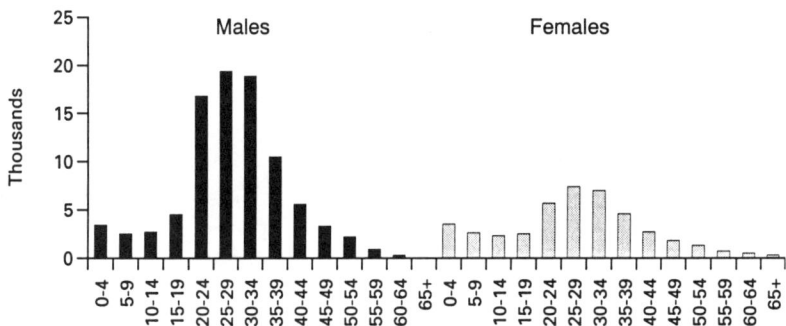

f. Qatar: non-national population by age and sex, 1992

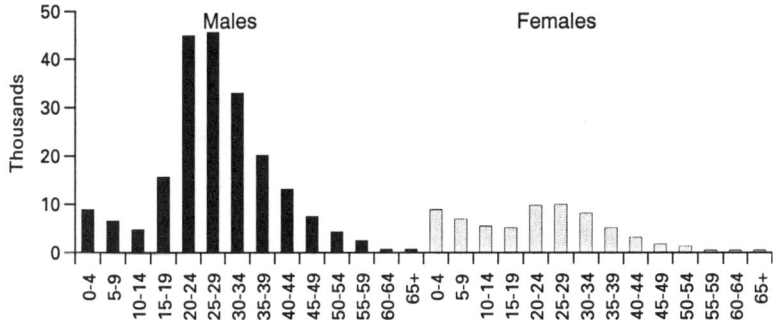

Source: BSAL, 'GCC Market Report 1992'.

Figure 12.4 Individual GCC state non-national population by age and sex (cont)

the most non-national Arabs, 1.6 million, representing 58.5 per cent of all the non-national Arabs in the GCC. Kuwait and UAE each have almost half a million non-national Arabs as well.

The non-national Asians in the GCC totalled 4.1 million in 1992 (Table 12.2). They are predominantly from South Asia, with migrants from India, Pakistan, Bangladesh and Sri Lanka constituting the vast majority (Figure 12.1e). Filipinos are a substantial group as well, as are other East Asian groups such as the South Koreans, Thais and Indonesians. Iranians are also classified as Asians, although they constituted only 1 per cent of the non-national Asians in 1992. As with the non-national Arabs, Saudi Arabia also has the greatest number and highest percentage of non-national Asians (2.4 million and 58.1 per cent respectively; it is significant that since at least 1975 the total number and percentage of Asians in the GCC states have been steadily rising, while the percentage of non-national Arabs has been declining).

The sex and age characteristics of the non-national Arabs and Asian populations are radically different from the national population. But the Asians and Arabs also vary; the non-national Arabs include more females and more younger and older individuals than the non-national Asians (Figures 12.2d and 12.2e). This indicates that the non-national Arabs often are accompanied by their families, while the Asians are mostly single male workers, as well as single females working as maids and nannies and living with their employee families.

The Gulf Labor Force in 1992

Although the population of the non-nationals is certainly substantial in the GCC countries, it is the role of foreigners in the labor force which is even more significant, and potentially troubling for the future. BSAL estimated that in 1992 the total workforce in the GCC states was 7.4 million, with the national workforce totalling 2.1 million and the non-nationals 5.3 million – a ratio of 28.6 per cent nationals to 71.4 per cent non-nationals (see Tables 12.3 and 12.4). Thus, almost three-quarters of the entire workforce in the Arab Gulf states is composed of expatriates. While most of the total non-national population are in the labor force (74 per cent), only 20 per cent of the total national population are in the workforce. This rather low 'labor force participation rate' (percentage of 15- to 64-year-olds employed in the workforce) of the nationals results from: (1) the great percentage of children in the total national population; (2) few female nationals in the workforce; and (3) fewer working-age

Table 12.3 National and non-national workforce in GCC states, 1975

	Nationals (1,000s)	Nationals (%)	Non-nationals (1,000s)	Non-nationals (%)	Total
Saudi Arabia	1,300.0	66.0	668.4	34.0	1,968.4
UAE	44.6	15.3	247.8	84.7	292.4
Oman	88.9	46.3	103.2	53.7	192.1
Kuwait	86.9	29.2	210.6	70.8	297.5
Bahrain	49.6	63.0	29.1	37.0	78.7
Qatar	12.5	16.9	61.3	83.1	73.8
Total	1,582.5	54.5	1,320.4	45.5	2,902.9

Source: Adapted from estimates by Serageldin et al, 1983, Table 4.1, p 26

Table 12.4 National and non-national workforce in GCC states, 1992

	Nationals (1,000s)	Nationals (%)	Non-nationals (1,000s)	Non-nationals (%)	Total
Saudi Arabia	1,590.5	32.7	3,274.4	67.3	4,864.9
UAE	93.0	10.7	776.8	89.3	869.8
Oman	157.9	33.6	312.4	66.4	470.3
Kuwait	101.8	13.6	646.7	86.4	748.5
Bahrain	88.1	48.7	92.7	51.3	180.8
Qatar	35.7	19.1	151.4	80.9	187.1
Total	2,067.0	28.2	5,254.4	71.8	7,321.4

Note: Totals may not be exact due to rounding.
Source: Compiled from estimates by BSAL, *GCC Market Report 1992*, 1992, Table 3.2, p 22; Table 5.2, p 25

males as part of the labor force than are usually found in other countries. This latter pattern is because many nationals are able to meet their economic commitments without employment. Many younger nationals are economically supported by extended family incomes and a generous state-supported, social welfare environment. The labor force participation rates for the national population range from 14.9 in Oman to 26.7 per cent in Bahrain, with Saudi Arabia's 20.1 per cent at (and somewhat determining) the GCC states' average of 20.0 per cent (Table 12.5).

The types of occupations pursued by nationals and non-nationals is revealing (Table 12.6; Figures 12.5d and 12.5e). Of the 2.1 million national workers, one-fifth (20.7 per cent) are in clerical jobs, while about one-third are engaged in professional and technical, administrative and managerial, and sales occupations. Hence, slightly over half (53.4 per cent) of the national workforce is in white-collar (and certainly higher-paying) jobs; 72.9 per cent of the non-nationals are employed in the relatively low-paying occupations of manual labor, blue-collar and service workers (including agriculture).

It is also instructive to examine each of the occupations in terms of the percentage of national and non-national workers (Table 12.6). As indicated above, the nationals are 28.6 per cent and the non-nationals 71.4 per cent of the total workers. Yet, the nationals are 54.9 per cent of the administrative and managerial workers, 62.2 per cent of the clerical workers, and 42 per cent of the sales workers, while comprising only 12.5 per cent of the production workers and laborers and 27.8 per cent of the service workers. These latter two occupation categories represent over half of all workers in the six GCC states, and so the relatively low percentage of nationals in the lower-paying jobs is again indicated.

These employment patterns and statistics indicate that the GCC states are highly dependent upon foreign workers. They not only constitute the vast majority of the total labor force, but also they particularly comprise the workers for the production and service sectors of the economy. In most countries of the world, there are low-status jobs which may be filled by foreign labor, but the situation in the GCC states is unique and extreme. Foreigners are employed in so many occupations and sectors of the economy, and in such great percentages, that a great dependence upon this foreign labor force has been created in the GCC states. Any major economic downturn cannot be solved merely by sending the foreigners home, because there is an insufficient number of nationals prepared to fill the void. Foreigners are indispensable for the functioning of the economies of the GCC.

Table 12.5 Economic activity rate of GCC national and non-national populations, 1992

a. GCC: Economic activity rate of national population and workforce by state, 1992

	Bahrain	Kuwait	Oman	Qatar	S. Arabia	UAE	Total
Population	330,400	386,960	1,062,300	141,000	8,066,400	531,000	10,518,060
Workforce	88,050	101,800	157,930	35,700	1,624,480	93,000	2,100,960
Economic activity rate (%)	26.6	26.3	14.9	25.3	20.1	17.5	20.0

b. GCC: Economic activity rate of non-national population and workforce by state, 1992 (numbers)

	Bahrain	Kuwait	Oman	Qatar	S. Arabia	UAE	Total
Population	134,002	803,075	380,002	272,090	4,192,680	1,294,003	7,075,851
Workforce	92,730	646,660	312,410	151,400	3,274,410	776,800	5,254,410
Economic activity rate (%)	69.2	80.52	82.21	55.64	78.1	60.03	74.26
Total population	17,593,911						
Total workforce	7,355,370						
EAR	41.8%						

Source: Estimates by BSAI, *GCC Market Report 1992*, 1992, Table 3.1, p 21; Table 5.1, p 25; Table 1.3, p 20.

Table 12.6 Occupations of national and non-national workforce in GCC states, 1992

a. GCC: Occupational distribution of national workforce by state, 1992 (numbers)

Occupational group	Bahrain	Kuwait	Oman	Qatar	S. Arabia	UAE	Total	%
Professional and technical	15,790	27,380	7,110	6,390	238,570	6,790	302,030	14.6
Administrative and managerial	2,320	3,310	12,000	9,670	77,930	11,720	116,950	5.7
Clerical and related	22,740	39,300	30,000	5,030	305,370	24,830	427,270	20.7
Sales workers	7,200	3,070	13,900	2,960	225,850	4,000	256,980	12.4
Service workers	12,350	13,930	42,640	680	281,510	34,780	385,890	18.6
Agricultural and related	3,950	80	27,800	5,000	176,540	3,160	216,530	10.4
Production workers and laborers	23,700	8,170	24,480	5,970	284,700	7,720	354,740	17.2
Other	0	6,560	0	0	0	0	6,560	0.3
Total	88,050	101,800	157,930	35,700	1,590,470	93,000	2,066,950	100.0

Note: The total referring to Saudi Arabia is the employment, not workforce, total.

Table 12.6 Occupations of national and non-national workforce in GCC states, 1992 (cont)

b. GCC: Occupational distribution of non-national workforce by state, 1992 (numbers)

Occupational group	Bahrain	Kuwait	Oman	Qatar	S. Arabia	UAE	Total	%
Professional and technical	10,490	67,900	17,180	32,550	471,510	98,650	698,280	13.3
Administrative and managerial	3,520	8,410	9,370	17,710	49,120	7,770	95,900	1.8
Clerical and related	14,460	65,310	6,250	13,020	78,580	82,340	259,960	5.0
Sales workers	6,710	41,390	47,490	7,720	189,920	62,140	355,370	6.8
Service workers	30,720	181,060	81,230	12,870	517,360	177,890	1,001,130	19.1
Agricultural and related	780	13,580	24,990	33,010	203,010	60,590	335,960	6.4
Production workers and laborers	26,050	250,900	125,900	34,520	1,764,910	287,420	2,489,700	47.4
Other	0	18,110	0	0	0	0	18,110	0.3
Total	92,730	646,660	312,410	151,400	3,274,410	776,800	5,254,410	100.0

Source: Estimates by BSAL, *GCC Market Report 1992*, 1992, Table 3.2, p 22 (corrected); Table 5.2, p 25.

a. National and non-national populations, Arabian peninsula, 1992

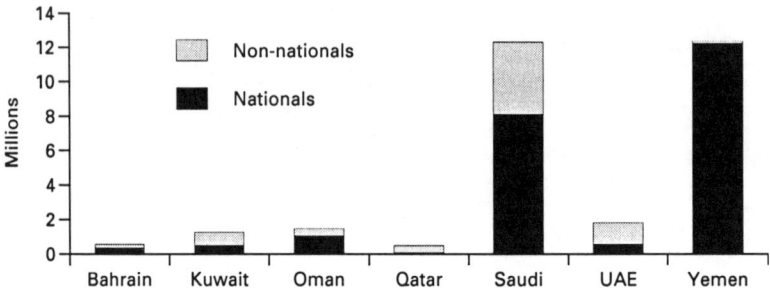

b. National population by state and sex, 1992

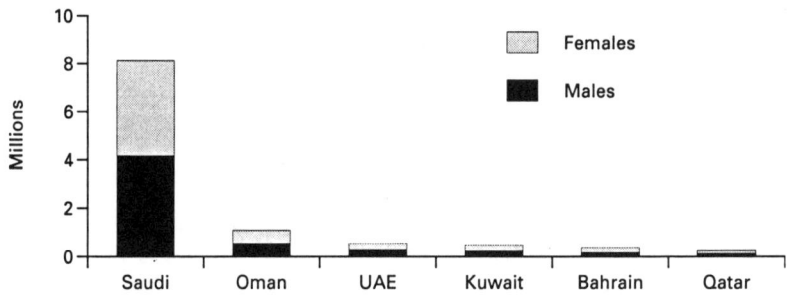

c. Non-national population by sex and state of residence, 1992

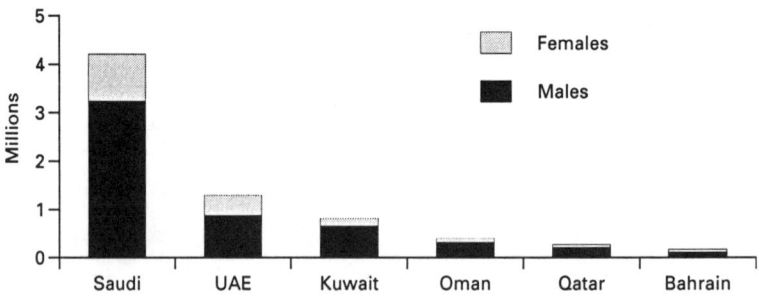

Source: BSAL, 'GCC Market Report 1992'.

Figure 12.5 GCC national and non-national population: various statistics

d. National workforce by occupational group, 1992

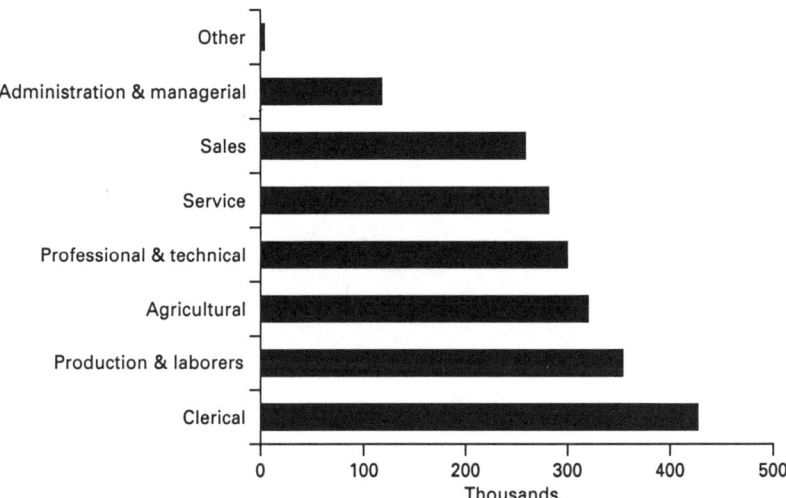

e. Non-national workforce by occupational group, 1992

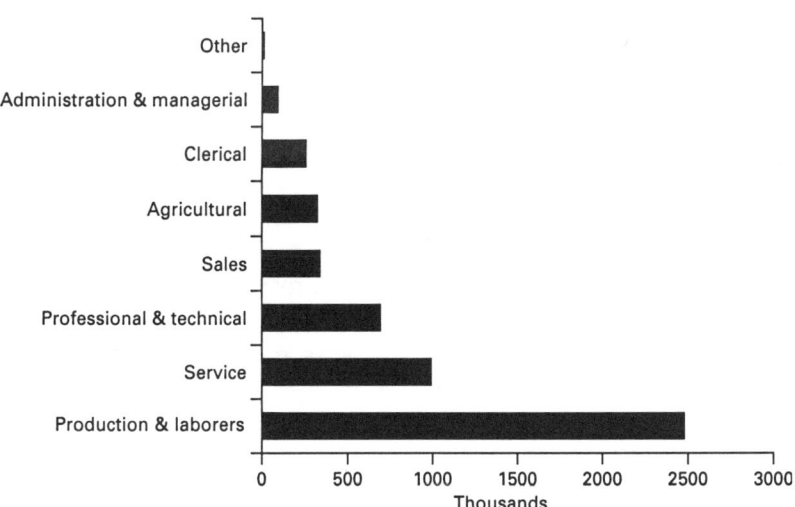

Source: BSAL, 'GCC Market Report 1992'.

Figure 12.5 GCC national and non-national population: various statistics (cont)

Education Levels of the Workforce

Education of the workforce is a concern of all the GCC states, and attempts to raise the educational level and hence the quality of workers have historically been major objectives. Education of the national population has been particularly impressive, although many of these individuals, especially the women, may not become part of the labor force.

Kuwait provides an excellent example of the strides made in education for the national workforce. Over the period 1965–89, illiterate males decreased from 91 to 9 per cent of the population, while the number of males with a secondary or higher level of education increased from 2 to 47 per cent and those with a university or higher education increased to 16.5 per cent. Kuwaiti women who have entered the job market recently are highly educated, with about three-quarters of the female labor force having attained a secondary or higher level of education by 1989.[5] Although the educational level of the non-national workforce was once higher than that of the nationals in the GCC states, with the strides in education for the nationals the foreign workforce is now generally less well educated than the citizens. In addition, the Asian migrants, who have been increasing in numbers and percentages over the last several decades, tend to be less educated than the Arab non-nationals. In Kuwait before the Gulf War, for instance, the educational level of the foreign workers was considerably lower than that of the nationals. After the war, Kuwaiti policies have attempted to limit the less educated and less skilled workers from coming into the country.[6]

Raising the educational level of migrant workers is certainly an admirable goal for the GCC states. It would mean that expatriate workers would be able to accept new and more technologically demanding occupations. On the other hand, a more educated foreign labor force provides more competition for the GCC nationals for many of the better jobs and positions. Thus, the dependency on foreign labor is not lessened by more educated expatriates; it, in fact, exacerbates the dilemma of the small number of nationals in the workforce.

1992 Country Profiles: Population and Labor

Although the general patterns and differences in population and labor for the GCC nations have been discussed, there still needs to be an examination of each specific country in more detail. Generalizations can easily hide significant differences between states which can lead to a significant lack of understanding of the situation in each country. Only by briefly examining each of the GCC states can the individual patterns be discerned and appreciated.

SAUDI ARABIA: The preliminary results of the 1992 *General Census of Housing and Population in the Kingdom of Saudi Arabia* reported a total population of 16.9 million, comprised of 12.3 million nationals and 4.6 million non-nationals. These figures are considerably larger than BSAL's original 1992 estimates of the population. The census indicates about the same number of males and females for the nationals and two and one-half times more males than females for the non-nationals. BSAL has also examined this preliminary census and concluded that the total head count is probably about right, but that the number of Saudis is probably too high.[7] The higher number of Saudis than BSAL's original estimates is attributed to four factors: (1) a larger number of Saudis in the country than previously estimated; (2) a higher rate of natural growth among the nationals; (3) significant naturalization of non-Saudis; and (4) inadvertent over-counting of non-Saudis as Saudis.[8]

For a further detailed analysis of the Saudi population, however, we must turn to BSAL's earlier estimates and analyses.[9] Even in this report, BSAL states: 'the Saudi national population has grown somewhat more quickly over the last few years than past projections had suggested. Improvements in living standards and health care have lowered mortality rates and the total fertility rate has stayed high at 7.7 per cent.'[10] It does note, however, that in late 1990 there were suddenly 90,000 fewer Saudis because of a more stringent application of the definition of a Saudi national.[11]

In BSAL's 1992 estimate, nationals constitute two-thirds (65.8 per cent) of the population, whereas the workforce percentages are substantially different (32.7 per cent nationals). The national labor force participation rate is 20.1 per cent, consisting of a rate of 36.8 per cent for the (working age) males but only 3 per cent for the females. Occupations of Saudi citizens include 19.2 per cent in clerical fields, 17.7 per cent in services, and 15 per cent in professional and technical work (Table 12.6).

The 1992 Saudi non-national population of 4.2 million can be broken down into 3.2 million males and slightly fewer than 1 million (985,480) females. Arabs comprise about one-third of the men and half of the females, with Egyptians, Jordanians/Palestinians and Sudanese being the largest groups. South Asian men constitute the majority of all males, fitting the pattern previously discussed for all the GCC states. Women, on the other hand, show somewhat different patterns, with the largest group being Filipinas, who are mainly domestic servants. Over half (53.9 per cent) of the non-national workers are categorized as production workers and laborers, and another 30 per cent work in either agriculture or professional/technical positions (Table 12.6).

The departure of the Yemenis in 1990 has resulted in a slightly different composition of the non-national population in Saudi Arabia as well as a decline of about 250,000 workers in total. The Yemenis have been replaced principally by Asians, with the single male and single female workers continuing as a pattern.[12]

Literacy has been a major goal of the Saudis, and about half of the adult national population is now literate. There is universal education for children, including women. In fact, there are so many women enrolled in higher education that they are now more educated than the men.[13] BSAL notes: 'this increase in the proportion of highly-educated women is likely to have implications for both the composition of the workforce and the consumption habits of households'.[14] The growing number of educated Saudi women will increase the pressures for easing restrictions and changing cultural attitudes towards women in the public workforce. The educational level among the non-nationals, on the other hand, remains low. Over half (53.8 per cent) of the non-national workforce has not completed primary school.[15] Also, the policy of Saudization, in which educated nationals replace foreigners in technical and other skilled positions, tends to lower statistically the educational levels of the non-nationals.

UNITED ARAB EMIRATES: The United Arab Emirates is the second largest GCC state in total population. BSAL's 1992 estimate was 1.8 million. The UAE also has the largest percentage of non-nationals (70.9) and hence the smallest percentage of nationals (29.1). The workforce is even more one-sided, and includes 89.3 per cent non-nationals. The UAE national workforce of 93,000 represents a 17.5 per cent labor force participation rate, which consists of 31.5 per cent of the males and 3.4 per cent of the females. Surprisingly, the greatest number of the UAE national workforce is in services (37.4 per cent), with clerical workers comprising 26.7 per cent. Similar to the rest of the GCC, the national population is young, with more than half less than 15 years of age (Figure 12.3b).[16]

The UAE non-national population has twice as many men as women, which is a lower percentage of men to women than in any of the other Gulf states. There are about twice as many Asian expatriates as non-national Arabs, although female Asians number only slightly greater than the Arab women non-nationals. This foreign population is concentrated in the 25 to 34 age range, although with a larger percentage of children than other GCC states. Jordanians/Palestinians comprise the largest Arab group, followed by Egyptians and then Sudanese, a pattern true for both men and women.

The Asian nationalities are similar to the GCC pattern, mostly from South Asia and the Philippines, except that very few women are from Bangladesh. Iranians are also a substantial number, the 61,200 comprising 7.5 per cent of the Asians. Finally, most of the non-national workforce are production workers and laborers (37.0 per cent) and service workers (22.9 per cent) with the fewest in administrative and managerial positions (1.0 per cent) (Table 12.6).

OMAN: Oman is the third largest GCC state in population with an estimated 1.4 million residents in 1992. It also has the largest percentage of nationals (73.7).[17] Still, the workforce is comprised of only one-third nationals (33.6 per cent) and two-thirds non-nationals (66.4 per cent). Oman, in fact, has the lowest labor force participation rate for nationals in the GCC, with 14.9 per cent, which is divided between 28.2 per cent of the eligible national males working and only 1.2 per cent of the females. The nationals are in services (27 per cent) and clerical jobs (19 per cent) as well as in agriculture (17.6 per cent). Many Omani nationals are also employed as production workers and laborers (15.5 per cent). Only 4.5 per cent are professionals or in technical fields, with 7.6 per cent in administrative and managerial positions. BSAL notes: 'Omanis in industry tend to be either unskilled workers or top management. Most middle management, skilled, or semi-skilled jobs are filled by non-national workers. There is growing recognition of a failure to provide suitable training for Omanis to fill such positions.'[18]

The non-national workforce in Oman is predominantly production workers and laborers (40.3 per cent), service workers (26 per cent) and sales employees (15.2 per cent). These foreigners are relatively uneducated, with over half (53.6 per cent) not having completed primary school, and another 29.6 per cent completing only primary school. Only 13.2 per cent of the non-nationals are Arabs, with Egyptians and Sudanese being the majority (Table 12.2). The Jordanians/Palestinians are very conspicuous by their absence (5200, comprising 1.4 per cent of the total non-national workforce). Asians from South Asia are the vast majority of non-nationals, with Indians alone being over half of the foreign workforce.

One of the more striking statistics about the 380,000 non-nationals in

Oman is that there are four and one-half times the number of non-national men than there are women. Consequently, there are few families and only a very small percentage of children among the non-nationals. The age graph (Figure 12.4c) indicates an even stronger concentration of males between the ages of 20 and 35, stressing the dominant pattern of single male migrant workers.

KUWAIT: Iraq's 1990 invasion of Kuwait has had far-reaching consequences for the demography of this small state.[19] By October 1990, about 1.3 million people, almost 60 per cent of the total population, had fled the country. The Jordanian and Palestinian populations had decreased from 500,000 to no more than half that number. Then in April and May 1991, considerably more Jordanians and Palestinians left as Kuwaiti accusations and trials singled them out as 'Iraqi collaborators'.[20] There are now fewer total inhabitants in Kuwait than before the occupation and subsequent war; most of the Palestinians and Jordanians have left, being replaced mostly by Asian workers. Not all of the national population chose to return to Kuwait either, while thousands of Kuwaiti males are still missing at the hands of the Iraqis.

The Kuwaiti nationals had become a minority of the total population of the country beginning in about 1965, and this relative proportion of nationals was maintained in part by the mass naturalization of bedouin in the late 1960s, in rough proportion to the realized increase in imported labor during the same period. With the influx of new migrant workers after 1974 the proportion of nationals began to drop, and by 1985 Kuwaitis were only about 40 per cent of the total population. However, the following year the government acknowledged that the 1985 census had somewhat inflated the percentage of nationals by the incorrect identification as nationals of about 211,000 'bedouin' – stateless persons originating from the desert between Kuwait, Iraq and Saudi Arabia. Many of the bedouin were reclassified as non-Kuwaiti Arabs in 1986, and with this stricter definition of citizenship, the Kuwaitis became even fewer in number, comprising 28 per cent of the total population.[21] By 1990, before the Iraqi invasion, there were 572,376 Kuwaitis, representing 26.8 per cent of the population.[22] By 1992, the number of nationals was only 386,960, although this now represented 32.5 per cent of the total population because of the contemporaneous departure of non-nationals during the conflict.

The 1992 Kuwait national population was not heavily dominated by a large youthful population, the only GCC state with such a profile (Figure 12.3d). Whereas in 1990, 46 per cent of the population was under 15 years of age, by 1992 it was only 33 per cent. Also, while Kuwaiti women had outnumbered the men before the Gulf War, in 1992 the women comprised only 44 per cent of the national population.[23]

The 1992 national labor force participation rate was 26.3 per cent, comprised of a rate of 34.9 per cent for males and 15.4 per cent for females, the latter the highest national female participation in the work-force in the GCC (Table 12.7). Of the total labor force, however, nationals, who had totalled 30.1 per cent of the labor force in 1975, comprised only 18.8 per cent of the workers in 1985 and an estimated 15.6 per cent in 1993.[24] Three-fourths of the national male workers in 1992 were in clerical jobs (38.2 per cent), professional and technical positions (19.2 per cent) and services (16.6 per cent). Half (49 per cent) of the national women, on the other hand, were in professional and technical jobs, with most of the rest (39.8 per cent) in clerical positions. The majority of the Kuwaiti women in professional jobs were teachers.[25] The great majority of Kuwaitis work in the public sector, with over 90 per cent in government jobs (and an even higher percentage for the Kuwaiti women). Nationals do not have the incentive to accept work in the private sector because the public sector offers more attractive jobs at higher wages.[26]

In 1992, there were estimates of 803,075 non-nationals in Kuwait, comprised of 490,450 Arabs and 297,400 Asians. Although this com-position was in large part the effect of the Gulf War, it also represented a continuing trend. Prior to 1975, Arabs constituted about 80 per cent of the non-nationals, but during the next decade increasing numbers of workers began to come from South and East Asia. By 1985, the Asians comprised 35 per cent of the non-nationals (or 29 per cent under the revised census).[27] In 1992, there were 240,000 Egyptians and 101,500 Palestinians/Jordanians (Table 12.2), although the latter group had num-bered about 500,000 before the 1990 invasion. Whereas many of the Pales-tinians had families (and the ratio of men to women of the remaining Palestinians indicates this as well), the present non-national Arab ratio is 70.7 per cent males to 29.3 per cent females. The loss of the Palestinian and Jordanian labor as well as Iraqi workers is likely to have a negative impact on Kuwait, because these groups tended to be the best educated and most stable foreign labor force. Even in 1983, for instance, the average duration for participating in the labor force was 15.6 years for Iraqis and 18.5 years for Palestinians and Jordanians.[28]

The Asian workers in Kuwait are almost all men — 91.6 per cent males and 8.4 per cent females — and, similar to most of the GCC Asians, they come principally from South Asia. The even greater predominance of

254

Table 12.7 Female national and non-national population and workforce in GCC states, 1992

	National female population (1,000s)	National females as % of national population	National female workforce (1,000s)	Female econ. activity rate of national female population (%)	Non-national female population (1,000s)	Non-national females as % of non-national population	Female econ. activity rate of non-national female population (%)
Saudi Arabia	3,979.2	49.3	119.2	3.0	985.5	23.5	46.3
UAE	264.2	49.8	9.0	3.4	429.0	33.1	n.d.
Oman	524.6	49.4	6.3	1.2	69.4	18.3	n.d.
Kuwait	170.3	44.0	26.3	15.4	169.6	21.1	43.9 (1993)
Bahrain	165.3	50.0	16.6	10.0	43.2	32.2	40.1
Qatar	70.1	49.7	7.8	11.1	65.3	24.0	n.d.
Total	5,173.7	49.2	185.2	3.6	1,762.0	24.9	n.d.

Note: n.d. – no data.

Source: Compiled from estimates by BSAL, *GCC Market Report 1992*, 1992, from various tables; BSL, *Saudi Arabia in the 90s*, 1989, table 6.2; Public Authority for Civil Information, Population and Labor Profile (Kuwait), April 1993, Tables 2 and 3, in Russell and Al-Ramadhan, 1993, Table 4.

single males among the Asians compared to the rest of the Gulf is because many of these Asians are quite recent immigrants, contracted to fill the jobs of the departed non-national Palestinians and other Arabs. The Asian women are predominantly domestic workers (maids). In 1985, Asian women constituted 13 per cent of the non-national workforce and 61 per cent of the total female non-national workforce.[29] After the Gulf War, domestic servants were one of the first categories of labor to be invited back to Kuwait in large numbers. In August 1993, for instance, the Interior Minister reported that more than 170,000 domestic servants had been imported into Kuwait by mid-1993.[30]

In 1992, the non-national workforce constituted 86.4 of the total workforce. The non-nationals are principally production workers and laborers (38.8 per cent) and service workers (28.0 per cent). About four-fifths of the men and two-thirds of the women are between the ages of 20 and 40, and less than 10 per cent of the foreign population is under 15 years of age, reflecting the predominance of single men and women among the non-nationals.[31]

BAHRAIN: Bahrain's 1992 estimated population of 464,402 is comprised of 71.2 per cent nationals and, unlike the rest of the GCC, the national and non-national workforce are about equal (48.7 and 51.3 per cent respectively) (Table 12.4). The national labor force participation rate is 26.6 per cent, comprised of 43.3 per cent of the eligible men and 10.0 per cent of the women, a significantly higher percentage of national participation in the labor force than found in other GCC states. The national population of Bahrain is also a more mature population than the rest of the GCC, with less than 40 per cent of the population aged less than 15 (Figure 12.3e).

National males are mostly production workers and laborers (32.6 per cent), clerical workers (22.1 per cent) and in services (14.8 per cent). The large percentage in the manual labor positions (the first category) is rather strikingly different than in the rest of the Gulf, reflecting a more successful diversification of the Bahraini economy. The industrialization program also has a much longer history than those of other GCC states. National female workers, on the other hand, are mostly in professional and technical jobs (43.1 per cent) and clerical positions (41.9 per cent).

Non-national males are production workers and laborers (34.2) and clerical workers (26.4 per cent), similar to the percentages found within the entire national workforce. Non-national women, on the other hand, are mostly service workers (62.4 per cent) with another 20.1 per cent professional and technical workers. Asians comprise the majority of the non-nationals (82.4 per cent), most from the Indian subcontinent and India specifically, with twice as many men as women. Arab expatriates represent only 9.2 per cent of the non-national workforce. This segment is comprised of mostly Egyptians and Palestinians/Jordanians.

QATAR: Qatar's 1992 estimated population of 413,091 is about one-third (34.1 per cent) nationals and two-thirds (65.9 per cent) non-nationals, and the total population is the smallest of the GCC states. The national population is quite young, similar to the rest of the GCC, with almost half (48.7 per cent) of the people under 15 years of age. The workforce is one-fifth (19.1 per cent) nationals and four-fifths (80.9 per cent) non-nationals (Table 12.4).

The labor force participation rate of the national population is 25.3 per cent, with 39.4 per cent of the males and 11.1 per cent of the females (15 to 64 years of age) in the workforce. The Qatari national workforce's 27.1 per cent (of the total workforce) in administrative and managerial positions is much higher than any other GCC state, reflecting a focused and energetic Arabization (Qatarization) program. Other occupation categories for the nationals include 17.9 per cent in professional and technical jobs, 16.7 per cent as production workers and laborers, 14.1 per cent in clerical jobs and 14.0 per cent in agricultural jobs.

The non-nationals are 40.1 per cent Arabs, with Palestinians/Jordanians being the largest group, followed by Syrians and then Egyptians (Table 12.2). Males are only slighter greater in number than females (61.1 per cent of the non-nationals being male), reflecting the fact that there are numerous families among this group. Asians are mostly Indians and Pakistanis, and the number of Asian men is about six times that of women (86 to 14 per cent). Approximately one-fifth of the Asian workers is employed in each of the following categories: professional and technical, agriculture, and production workers and laborers.

The GCC States: Current Trends and Projections for the Future

The annual rates of growth of the GCC states for the last two decades (and earlier) indicate continuing, rapid population growth. The total population for all the GCC states increased at an annual rate of 6.17 per cent from 1975–85 and 4.45 per cent from 1985–95. These rates compare, for instance, to the 1995 annual growth rates of 1.5 per cent for the world, 0.2 per cent for the 'more developed' world, and 1.9 per cent for the 'less developed' world.[32] The Middle East is, in fact, one of the fastest growing regions in the world,[33] and the petroleum-rich states in the Gulf are growing even faster than the rest of this region.

In 1975, the six Gulf states had a total of 9 million inhabitants, comprised of 6.2 million nationals (69 per cent) and 2.8 million expatriates (31 per cent).[34] By 1985, the total population had increased to 16.5 million, including 11 million nationals (67 per cent) and 5.5 million foreigners (33 per cent).[35] I estimate the mid-1996 population as 26.8 million, although the percentages and numbers of nationals and non-nationals are more problematic and difficult to determine. Nevertheless, based upon recent censuses and the most recent data on nationals and non-nationals, I estimate that there are 17.5 million nationals (65 per cent) and 9.3 million non-nationals (35 per cent).[36]

Population projections for the GCC states for the future, however, are even more difficult. First, there is the lack of adequate current data. Second, there is the great number of foreign workers, who, at least for the short term, can be decreased or increased in numbers rather quickly in response to changes in national immigration and/or labor policies. Third, there is the dependence of the economy and welfare on the states' continued revenue from the sales of petroleum. Should the demand for petroleum suddenly fall (or increase dramatically), the dynamics of the population would respond, perhaps significantly. Nevertheless, it is still possible – and necessary – to project what the numbers may be in the twenty-first century.

If the populations of the GCC states continue to increase at the present rates, or even with slightly smaller growth rates, the total number of inhabitants soon becomes startling. Figures 12.6 to 12.8 show various scenarios for the growth of the national, non-national, and total population of the GCC states. For each of these groups, the population has been projected to 2150, as well as deriving totals for the end of the twenty-first century, the year 2100. The 1985–95 rate, which is less than the rate of the decade before or the 1975–95 rate, is used for one of the projections (Scenario A), showing the rather astounding, and unrealistic, numbers that would result. There are also projections using the rate of 3 per cent (Scenario B), 2 per cent (Scenario C), and a declining rate over time (Scenario D).

Using the same annual rate of 4.23 per cent increase as 1985–95, the *national* population (Figure 12.6) would increase from 17.1 million in 1995 to 166.8 million by 2050 (Scenario A) and reach 1.3 billion by the year

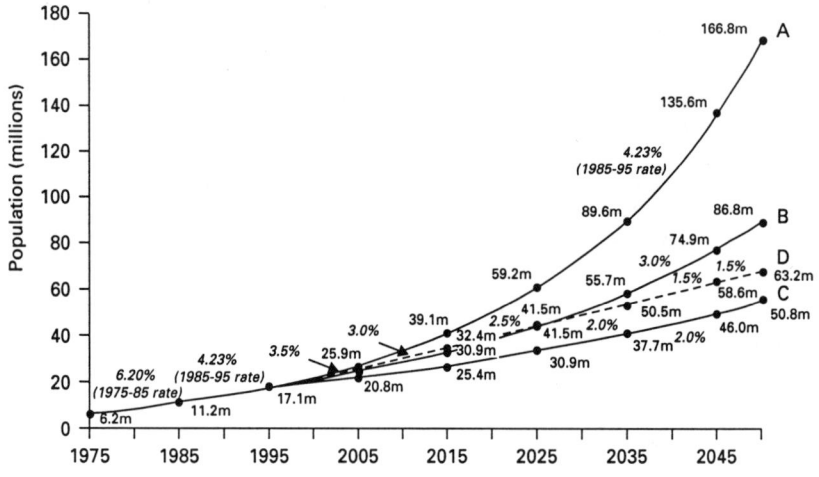

Figure 12.6 GCC national population: projections to the year 2050

2100. Other, more realistic, trends include an average annual increase of 3 per cent (Scenario B), where the total national population becomes 86.8 million in 2050 (but 380.6 million by the year 2100), while a rate of 2 per cent (Scenario C) would reach 50.8 million by the year 2050 and 136.6 million in the year 2100. The rate of 3 per cent may be too high for the entire first half of the twenty-first century, while the rate of 2 per cent is probably too low. Another scenario (D) may be more feasible: a declining rate over the 55 years from 1995 to 2050. If the GCC national population annual growth rate is 3.5 per cent the first decade after 1995, and declines by 0.5 per cent each subsequent decade and is 1.5 per cent for the last 15 years, then the total national population would still be 63.2 million in 2050, almost four times larger than the 1995 total. Projecting to the year 2100, the nationals would total 133.0 million if the rate remained at 1.5 per cent, or 103.9 million if the rate was reduced to 1 per cent for the last half of the twenty-first century.

For the projected growth of the *non-national* population (Figure 12.7), the 1985–95 annual growth rate of 4.86 per cent (Scenario A) results in 123.4 million in 2050 and 1.3 billion in 2100. The more realistic rate of 3 per cent (Scenario B) results in 46 million non-nationals in 2050 and 201.8 million in 2100, while the 2 per cent (Scenario C) rate yields a total of 26.9 million in 2050 and 72.5 million in 2100. The same declining rate of 0.5 per cent per decade that was used for the national population

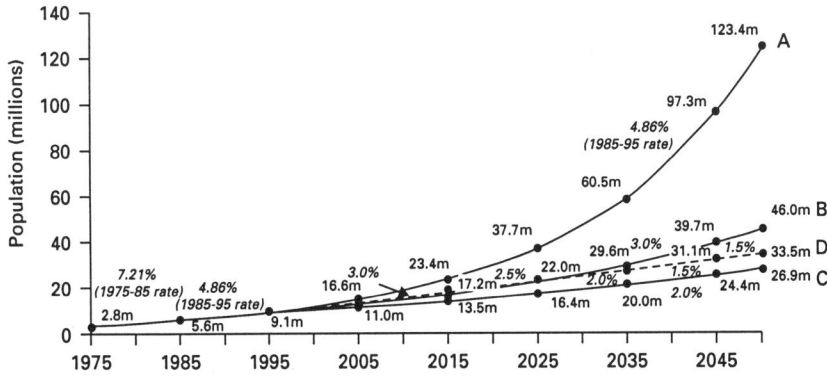

Figure 12.7 GCC non-national population: projections to the year 2050

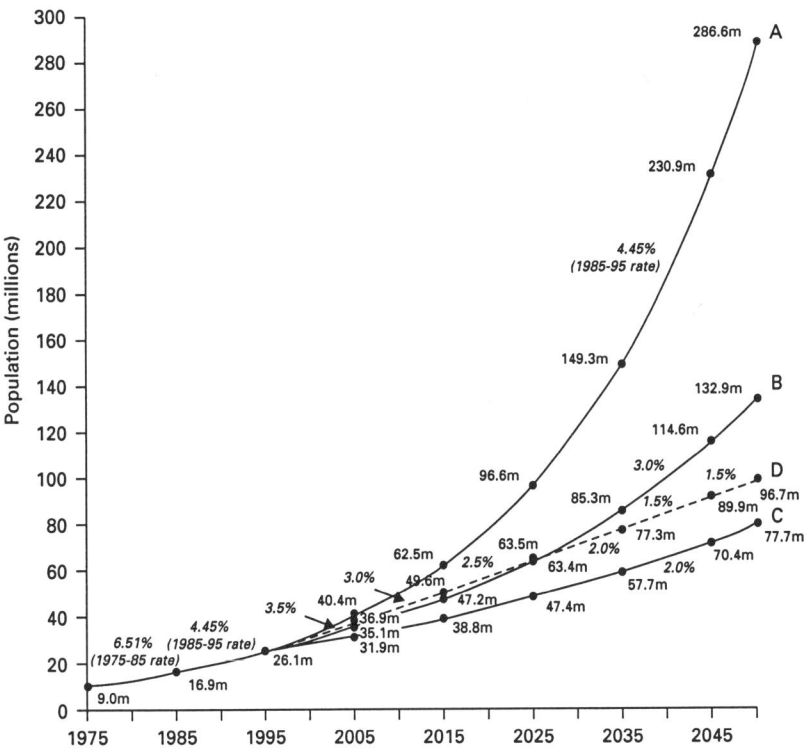

Figure 12.8 GCC total population: projections to the year 2050

increase (Scenario D, declining from 3.5 per cent the first decade) results in a total of 33.5 million non-nationals in 2050 and 70.5 million by 2100; or if the growth slowed to 1 per cent for the last half of the twenty-first century, the total would be 55.1 million foreigners.

Projections for the increase in the *total* population of the GCC states are even more disturbing (Figure 12.8). Using the 1985–95 annual growth rate of 4.45 per cent (Scenario A), the total GCC population would reach 286.6 million in 2050 and an even more unrealistic 2.53 billion in the year 2100. At the annual growth rate of 3 per cent (Scenario B), the total would be 132.9 million in 2050 and 582 million in 2100, while the rate of 2 per cent (Scenario C) reaches 77.7 million in 2050 and 209.1 million in the year 2100. The declining 0.5 per cent per decade annual rate (Scenario D) yields 96.7 million by 2050, and the total would be 203.5 million in 2100 at the 1.5 per cent growth rate or 159.0 million at a growth rate of 1 per cent.

Although it is certainly most unlikely (and even impossible) that the higher rates of increase for the GCC states will occur, these projections, nevertheless, stress the gravity of the demographic trends for the future. Even if the lowest calculated rates of increase occur, and these may be unrealistically too low, the figures are still alarming, and have grave consequences for the future of the economies, peoples and governments of the Gulf. It is probably reasonable to conclude, therefore, that any realistic scenario for the population of the Gulf will result in at least 100 million persons in the GCC states by the mid-twenty-first century – quadrupling the present total population. The great majority of that population will be nationals, not non-nationals whose numbers theoretically can be reduced as needed. The total GCC figure of 100 million may be reached a few years earlier or a few years later than the year 2050, but there is no denying that these are the realistic future totals. The children now being born in the Gulf states will be part of this large population in 2050, coping with the mounting problems resulting from these crushing numbers.

Officials within the GCC states have not acknowledged that the national population increase will become a major challenge in the near future. In fact, national population policies within the GCC states often seem to respond to the misconception that the national population needs to be increased so that the foreign population can be decreased by replacement in the workplace. Pro-natal policies advocate increasing the national populations as quickly as possible. Yet, the projections here emphasize the rapid increase in the number of nationals in the near future. The majority of these citizens will not quickly accept and/or not quickly qualify for the jobs which entail manual labor, blue-collar technical skills, or agricultural production. Further, the increasing rates of literacy and university-level educational opportunities among GCC nationals produce a mismatch between qualifications and jobs available for Arabization. It is poor public policy planning to project that the highly educated Gulf national population will replace the foreigners for most of the less desirable and strenuous jobs.

What will it take to cause a major decline in the rates of population increase? What kind of crisis must occur before there are policies and measures to address these population issues? Unfortunately, because about half of the national population is presently 15 years old or less, the next several decades will see a continued high growth for the nationals, as this group marry and have children. The nations of the Gulf must begin to discuss and advocate family planning, and emphasize that smaller families are a desirable goal in the national interest. Smaller national families also will help ensure the quality of life for the children themselves, because the current lifestyles of the Gulf nationals cannot be sustained in the future with such great numbers. A smaller increasing national population also needs fewer foreign workers for support, diminishing the requirement for foreign labor in the future.

The conclusions to be drawn by this population explosion are inescapable. There is a growing crisis in the Gulf that will not be fully felt until well into the next century. The Gulf region has been largely sheltered from the population problems of poverty and strife which have affected most of the developing world because of the prosperity of oil and the virtually unlimited development of the last several decades. But for the future, the management of population increase within Gulf national societies must be given priority.

Population and Labor in the Gulf: Some Needs and Considerations for the Twenty-first Century

There are many issues regarding population and the labor force which the governments of the GCC states must face in the twenty-first century. This final section brings out some of the principal problems, as well as providing some possible solutions. The first problem is the difficulty of obtaining accurate and comparable demographic data and statistics and the consequences of this. If progress is to be made in understanding and dealing with population and labor issues, accurate data must be obtained,

compiled and released. It is difficult for governmental and non-govern-
mental agencies, consultants and the business community to provide
effective advice and planning if the data are not readily available. So, the
first requirement of dealing with the population and labor problems of
the future is to compile and publish comprehensive and accurate data
with respect to the number and composition of the population, especially
details concerning the foreign population and labor force.

Another point which becomes prominent when dealing with population
and labor in the GCC states is that patterns can vary from state to state,
and differ within regions or provinces of specific countries. Generalizations are often subject to exceptions. This means that policies may not
always be (or should not be) applicable to all of the GCC states. What
might be appropriate when dealing with either the national or non-national
population and workforce in one country may not be relevant in another.

It is certainly true that many major demographic and socio-economic
problems in the Gulf states result from the small national populations
and particularly the meagre national workforce. The fact that almost half
of the national population of the GCC nations are under 15 years of age
means that there will be considerably more nationals entering the workforce in the near future. Yet, instead of providing the labor needed for
the future, these more educated youth will be even more likely to eschew
manual labor and less prestigious, difficult jobs. In fact, unemployment
of educated nationals may begin to be a major problem.

In 1983, Kuwaitis worked on average 39 hours per week, almost entirely
in the public sector, while the non-nationals worked 52 hours per week,
including 64 hours per week on the average by female domestic servants.[37]
This points to one of the major underlying difficulties of the present,
and future, national population of the Gulf: the absence of a strong
work ethic among the general populace. This is a predicament which
must be corrected in the twenty-first century. It means that there must be
continued diversification of the Gulf economies, with less reliance on oil
or oil-based industries. Bahrain has already provided somewhat of a model,
with an almost equal number of national and non-national workers,
and with considerable nationals employed in production and services. If
industrialization and economic diversification take place in the twenty-
first century in the GCC states, but the vast majority of workers continue
to be imported from abroad because the indigenous population does not
compete for the resultant employment opportunities, then the long-term
internal and economic security of the Gulf states may well be challenged.

One difficulty in many of the GCC states is that oil wealth has encouraged lavish lifestyles and increased the expectations of citizens to a degree that can be counter-productive for the long-term future of the societies concerned. A welfare society has been created in which free or subsidized electricity, water, education, health care, housing and even a guaranteed well-paying job in the public sector have in many cases become societal norms. Shah has noted for Kuwait, for instance, that the governmental welfare philosophy has created a 'benevolent patriarch' which provides all of the basic needs and services of the population.[38] Expectations have resulted, in Kuwait, for instance, in competition for status in terms of the number of maids:

> For the Kuwaiti nationals, the presence of a maid (or several maids) is felt to be essential for several reasons including social status, housework, childcare, and perhaps to act as a surrogate while the mother is away at work. The latter is, however, not a necessary condition. Earlier research has shown that Kuwaiti households where the wife was not in the labor force were as likely to have a maid as the ones where the wife was employed. A strong positive association was however present between income and the number of maids employed in the household.[39]

Another major demographic consideration for the twenty-first century is the role of women in the workforce. One of the principal ways in which the national population could become more involved in the workforce is for the women of the Gulf to enter the job market. The Middle East in general and the Gulf states in particular certainly have the lowest participation rates of (national) females in the workforce of any region in the world. J. S. Birks and C. A. Sinclair noted in 1980 that there was in the Gulf a considerable waste of resources because of the bias against women's employment.[40] The labor force participation rates for women, ranging from 1.2 per cent for Oman, 3.0 per cent for Saudi Arabia and 3.4 per cent for UAE to 10.0 per cent for Bahrain, 11.1 per cent for Qatar and 15.4 per cent for Kuwait (Table 12.7), illustrate the conservative traditionalism of Gulf societies, emphasizing that a woman's life should be centered on the home, the family and the husband.

Yet, as the women of the GCC states become more educated, there will be increasing pressures from women themselves to have the right to work in the public sphere. In fact, women who are more educated and who are in the workforce tend to bear fewer children: thus, the problematic growth of the national population could be reduced by public policy which encourages women to join the labor force. Shah notes, for instance, that Kuwaiti women with a university education produce only about half the number of children as their illiterate counterparts.[41] Kuwait has, in fact, provided an example for the Gulf of a much higher partici- pation of national women, with most being in professional and technical or clerical jobs. This pattern could not only be accentuated in Kuwait but it could also be a reasonable way to increase the workforce (and to slow the rapid increase of the national population) in the other Gulf states.

The governments of the Gulf will confront challenging economic and demographic realities within the twenty-first century. Twentieth-century oil wealth has helped to create societies which will not easily be weaned from subsidies and social and government benefits. Policies must be formulated, and implemented, which slowly reduce the dependence on the welfare state, engender a work ethic, educate for skills and trades, and perhaps encourage the increased participation of women in the workforce. Within the framework of the existing and evolving traditions, and the culture and values of Gulf societies, the imperative to craft and implement public policy which addresses the demographic challenges is a very important component of the security calculus of the states of the Gulf in the twenty-first century.

CHAPTER 13

Health, Education, Gender and the Security of the Gulf in the Twenty-first Century

Mai Yamani

No country can be secure unless its citizens are safe and well. Conceptually, the term *security* need not only consist of a political/military dimension but should also include a human one; security can and should address physical protection, material well-being, freedom from dependency, and people's participation in the choices that affect their future and the maintenance of their dignity. While there has long been a global demand for increased economic production and consumption, and improved political relationships between and within countries, there is now also a growing world-wide emphasis on human, social and cultural security, as distinct from the economic and political.

This is a changing concept of security that in the twenty-first century will require the enhancement of social integration, the reduction of poverty and the expansion of productive employment. Secure health and education services are key components of people's welfare, productivity, knowledge and skills. The role of governments in providing social and public services in the areas of health, education, job training and nutrition can enhance social cohesion, prevent social disintegration and create healthier societies. In other words, political security contributes to human security and vice versa.

Although security is a global concern, it remains a relative issue. The security of the members of the Gulf Cooperation Council (GCC) – Bahrain, Kuwait, Oman, Qatar, Saudi Arabia and the UAE – is relative to their social structure, history and geo-political position. Particular criteria for measuring security apply to different societies, and these are never static but change according to economic, political, religious and social circumstances.

This chapter will attempt to examine the long-term effects of social restructuring on traditional values and norms, on existent ethnic diversity and intercommunal relations, on shifting boundaries of gender relations and on the growth of health services and educational programs. The emphasis is on Saudi Arabia because of its central role in the area – its commanding size, geography and demography – and because it has been the focus of my own professional work.

The Islamic Model and Societal Norms

Islam features prominently in the social, political and economic fabric of the region. The legal codes of GCC countries are derived from interpretations of Islamic principles in combination with local tribal traditions. The existence of the holy cities of Mecca and al-Madinah in the region reminds GCC societies of their Islamic identity and obligations. The local religious establishments play significant roles in political legitimacy, although the degree of power the *'ulama* wield varies from state to state according to the ruler's inclination and to internal and external influences. Islam forms the ideological basis of social welfare concepts within GCC societies and thus has an impact on educational and health policy and practices.

The concept of education in Islam has no boundaries and there is a well-known hadith which states: 'Seek knowledge even if from China.' During the Abbasid period,[1] Muslims translated Greek works of philosophy, mathematics and astronomy and the invention of algebra is credited to a Muslim. So-called 'secular' knowledge was encouraged and not seen as separate from other studies. Islam advocated the process of expanding the creativity and capability of its people. This included the search for and the application of medicine for the purposes of healing.[2] A second Islamic concept is that the pursuit of knowledge in Islam is not limited by age. Another popular hadith reminds us to 'seek knowledge from the cradle to the grave'.

Theoretically, the concept of education in Islam does not discriminate between men and women. However, many Islamic legal and social principles can be interpreted negatively as well as positively. For example, according to the Islamic concept of *iltizam* (obligation), a woman is protected in Islamic society by her father, husband(s), brother(s), and cousin(s), who are responsible for her welfare. This could be interpreted as a mandate to restrict her activities to the home, but it also relieves her from financial responsibility and frees her to contribute to the well-being of her community through education, health care and other arenas of social service. Furthermore, a Muslim woman is entitled to maintenance after divorce or separation, *nafaqa*; she has full control over her dowry (*mahr*), her share of inheritance as well as other financial securities. According to the Islamic law, Shari'a, there is no distinction between men and women from the legal age of 16 in terms of ownership, control and use of their wealth. Islam emphasizes the just distribution of wealth by keeping it in dynamic circulation – the underlying principle being that all wealth belongs to God, and the individual is merely an agent entrusted with this wealth and is accountable for the way in which it is used.

A close connection exists between family structure and the system of education and health in the GCC states. Within the extended family structure lies a predominantly patrilinear, patrilocal and patriarchal pattern, Islamic in origin but also stemming from traditional values of honor and shame. These familial and cultural factors have an effect on attitudes concerning the participation of women in certain arenas of public activity. Nevertheless, there are inevitable changes in the patriarchal family system. Due to changing demographic and educational patterns, men are no longer able to dominate women in the way they did in previous generations. Justifications for perpetuating exclusive patriarchy on 'Islamic' grounds are being and will increasingly be challenged by women as they engage more in the Islamic discourse.[3]

The state perpetuates the patriarchal system, particularly in Saudi Arabia where the issue of women's formal participation in public areas is largely ignored. The Majlis al-Shura (Consultative Council), established in 1991 as a step towards participation by the citizenry in the management of their country's affairs, includes no women or any mention of them. The support in Saudi public law for this omission is the still-accepted principle that there is no role for women at any level in public affairs. The total omission with respect to the Majlis al-Shura, however, is interesting because it opens, at least in theory, the possibility for women to have access to these positions if political and cultural attitudes continue to evolve. The intellectual horizons of the current rulers, as well as public opinion, do not as yet approach such a possibility.

Even Islamic opposition movements which have appeared in the GCC states in recent years have not challenged the traditional interpretation of women's roles. On the contrary, many of these movements would like to reverse the momentum of the ongoing evolutionary process. For example, a comparatively well-established Saudi opposition group called the Committee for the Defence of Legitimate Rights (CDLR) was established in 1993 in Saudi Arabia by Abdallah al-Mas'ari and is now run from his exile in London. The CDLR claims to protect human rights in the context of Shari'a and calls upon the Saudi government to uphold civil rights such as freedom of expression and movement. In the whole of its manifesto, however, there is no mention of women's rights or of any public role for women. Essentially the CDLR's critique applies to general areas of alleged maladministration but not to gender issues. Thus, the exclusion of women from public roles is sanctioned not only by the official religious establishment backed by the government, but by prominent segments of the Islamist opposition as well.

Actualization – some would argue romanticization – of Islamic heritage within the oil-rich states of the GCC has inspired a comprehensive provision of free social services by the state, especially in health and education. In addition, oil wealth has permitted the GCC states to provide direct subsidy to its citizens in the form of grants of land and interest-free or subsidized mortgages and business loans. This generous Islamic welfare system is now coming under strain, however; oil revenues have fallen while government expenditures have continued to rise, and rapid population increases have further lowered per capita income. Some GCC member countries have been running considerable budget deficits for most of the past decade and have begun borrowing from pension funds and banks. The economic restructuring necessitated by these developments has resulted in certain tensions emerging between traditional values and economic realities. A disjunction has arisen between people's high economic expectations, formed during the oil-boom years, and the tangible decline in both job opportunities and government services in health and education.

Furthermore, another significant strain derives from pressures exerted by the militant Islamic tendencies. For the first time in recent history, opposition parties have emerged in the GCC and are challenging the existing regimes' efforts to legitimize political rule by claiming adherence to Islamic law. Protest is voiced in Islamic terms, though not in any coherent political movement. Islam is thus potentially as divisive a factor as a unifying one. In the field of education, for example, while Islamic teachings are heavily imposed in national school curricula, these conservative or extremist trends seek to further restrict access to knowledge and professional skills, despite the ideals of Islamic educational exposure.

Ethnic Diversity and Intercommunal Relations

At one level, the GCC countries share religious, economic and political similarities and a sense of social identity. However, ethnic diversity and cultural distinctiveness within each individual state do exist and relate significantly to welfare, economic circumstances and educational issues. In each GCC country, this heterogeneity and internal diversity is often expressed through social boundaries.[4] These take the form of different dialects, specific religious rituals, different food[5] and regional dress, and are especially evident in the absence of interregional marriage. In Saudi Arabia, for example, regional consciousness exists between Najdi tribal members and Hejazi urban settlers, exemplified by how they refer to each other. The more heterogeneous Hejazis, for example, are often called *bagaya hujjaj* (literally 'remnants of pilgrims') or *tarsh al-bahr* ('flotsam of the sea') while Najdis are called *badu* (Bedouin) or *shuruq* (Easterners). Internal diversity in the GCC states has been further accentuated by great influxes of expatriates from all over the world who form a large percentage of the labor population and further affect ethnic boundaries.

Today among the GCC countries, national identity surpasses some of these regional identities. However, interregional tensions, manifested through border disputes when border demarcations conflict with traditional tribal boundaries, are still very much in existence despite historical agreements on political boundaries. While the contemporary system of linear boundaries was basically a European concept imposed upon an alien cultural landscape,[6] international boundaries are now viewed as permanent features on the map. This new phenomenon of state territory in a land marked historically by nomadic migration, makes border disputes an integral part of internal Gulf politics.[7] In turn, the defense of national territory has increasingly become a preoccupation.[8]

In other developing-world countries, interethnic relations have become significantly exacerbated during times of economic crisis. In fact, a majority of ethnic and civil conflicts, for example in Africa and the former Yugoslavia, are associated with economic hardship as ethnic groups strive to maintain the status quo. Recent concern with precise boundaries by the states in the Gulf region is motivated by the concern to secure valuable natural resources geographically and legally. Continuing border disputes highlight areas where some states have continued to take advantage of neighbors. Nevertheless, with several border arbitration processes currently under way (1996) – for example, between Saudi Arabia and Qatar, Qatar and Bahrain and the Yemen and Eritrea – the region may be coming closer to a resolution of these outstanding disputes.[9]

The Welfare System: Expectations

Health and education cannot be addressed in isolation from the critical phenomena of demographic change, unemployment, the challenges of indigenization, the attitudes towards work of GCC citizens, or the expectations of citizens with respect to the welfare system.

The GCC states in combination produce a total annual GDP approaching $200 billion and possess the world's largest oil resources and reserves. Yet they are only now beginning to consider seriously their long-term economic strategies following the boom–bust cycle of the 1970s and 1980s. Economic and social restructuring to reverse the over-generous policies of the 1980s is taking place, but it is proving difficult to reduce the economic expectations of GCC citizens at the same time. The fact that the GCC states' economies are almost totally dependent upon oil, and are experiencing a very slow rate of industrialization, is only part of the structural problems facing economic policy-makers.[10]

Since the 1970s, the generous welfare system in the GCC states made possible by oil revenues has resulted in unrealistically high economic expectations, particularly among younger people. Dependence on state welfare does not have the same stigma in the Gulf that it does in the free market capitalist economies of the West. At the same time, many Gulf governments have also become dependent on welfare programs as a major source of legitimacy. In order to retain constituent support after the critical period of the Gulf War, some GCC governments even promised their citizens improved welfare services. Thus, these governments have found it politically difficult to announce any welfare cuts.

The Saudi government pours tens of billions of riyals into subsidies to ensure that the cost of basics will be brought to a level every Saudi can afford. This applies to subsidies such as those for medicine, bread and, until recently, electric power and gasoline. Free health care is available to all Saudis at government hospitals. The government programs also offer free unlimited education, as well as generous living allowances to Saudis studying abroad.

Despite its generous scope, however, the welfare system has experienced different levels of abuse. Requests for help have not included means-testing and as a result both poor and rich have equal access to the free aid. This practice has encouraged the emergence of a very large number of citizens dependent upon government subsidy. Not only do these citizens lack marketable job skills, more importantly they also lack the inclination to support themselves in a competitive, free market economy. There is little connection between effort and reward. This diminished work ethic exists at all levels, from white-collar to blue-collar, from the maid to the manager. The irony of generous welfare subsidy is that while it has kept people happy, it has also contributed to the unemployment situation of today by reinforcing negative attitudes towards work.

Unhealthy dependence on government welfare is not unique to the Gulf. In the West, welfare programs that entitle people to benefits without work requirements have given rise to a mentality of dependence. Generous welfare provisions by some European societies, notably Sweden, have been cited by political conservatives as antithetical to entrepreneurship.

As a result, reforms in the GCC labor marketplace are necessary for productive and full employment. Job creation has taken place in many different areas, but the public sector still remains the largest employer. In Saudi Arabia, the agricultural industry provides a particularly large number of jobs. However, in agriculture as in most other possible employment avenues, the level of dependency on expatriate labor is alarming. The Jeddah Chamber of Commerce has calculated that about 500,000 members out of the city's 600,000 person work force are expatriates.[11] In a country where there is no minimum wage, it is simply not economically or culturally possible for Saudis to compete with expatriate laborers for unskilled or minimally skilled positions on a wage basis. While migrant labor will frequently accept wages at subsistence levels, Saudi nationals are not prepared to do so. As for Bahrain, the 1991 census indicates that of a population of 500,000, more than one-third consists of foreign workers. In that same year, foreign labor rose by 54,000 while the local national workforce, women included, increased by a mere 20,000.[12] The unemployment of Bahraini nationals combined with an increase in foreign labor has recently created tensions and contributed to the civil disturbances which have occurred in recent years.

GCC nationals, in general, are not filling the new jobs being created by economic growth in the region, despite the pressure of the demographic increase of employment-eligible citizens and the constraints on the region's finances. This can partially be explained by the cultural reality that GCC nationals are reluctant to accept work in an environment where they will be supervised by other nationals. Indeed, even GCC women often refuse to work in each other's homes, resulting in the importation of Asian labor to look after the house and children.[13] Saudi women opening businesses would rather employ Egyptians, Lebanese or other Arab women, in part due to their expertise and work ethic but also because they have fewer constraints related to the Islamic Gulf concepts of honor and shame.

Local unemployment has caused an increase in the number of beggars. It is possible to see veiled women at the doors of the rich and even within shops and malls asking for cash, at times aggressively wielding religious injunctions and sayings. Although not all beggars are locals (some are illegal immigrants from Asia and Africa), they are Muslim and use Islamic concepts of charity and welfare to humiliate the rich into giving. This phenomenon can be seen most clearly during Ramadan, particularly outside the Great Mosques in Mecca and al-Madinah. Actions taken against beggars range from giving them help, to locking them up, to deporting them.

The significant and current problem of unreasonably high levels of unemployment within Gulf Arab economies can be linked to the problem of ethnic tensions. Except for highly technical professions, massive labor migration – mostly from India, Sri Lanka, Pakistan, the Philippines and Africa – represents a source of latent and ethnic hostility. The majority are alienated from the cultural and linguistic milieu and remain poor in relation to a more privileged category of expatriates, that is, the Europeans. Although racial discrimination is illegal, there is substantial societal prejudice based on ethnic and national prejudice, specifically against African and Asian nationals. This can be seen clearly in terms of wage structure, where, for example, four doctors, one English, one American, one Asian and one African, may all be working in the same hospital and doing the same job, yet each is paid at a substantially different rate. Some countries in the GCC make greater allowances for the cultural differences, such as relaxation of the dress code or providing for the leisure needs of their guest workers, while others are stricter in their application of Islamic law.

Women in the Workforce

As detailed in the previous chapter by Michael Bonine, the percentages of working women in the Gulf countries are among the lowest in the world. However, economic necessity may soon create tension with respect to the Gulf societal preference for women to remain in the home. Indeed, from the standpoint of government policy, this has already occurred. Encouraging women to become wage-earners is now a common policy throughout the GCC states. Nevertheless, by educating women in preparation for integration into the workforce, the emphasis remains on jobs that are suited to the 'nature of women', not on broadening women's work options.[14]

Informed sources from state services, *al-khidma al-madiniyya*, claim that women participate in most professions, such as medicine and teaching, and in administrative jobs at airports dealing with other women. Women, however, are excluded from certain professions such as law. Jobs remain strictly segregated according to government orders and social expectations. Commerce and trade remain most prominent in that segregated environment, with women's branches of banks and shops owned, managed and patronised by women only. Women have been increasingly active in the private sector. According to unofficial estimates around 40 per cent of Saudi private wealth is in female hands.[15] This is a result of women's economic capacity under Islamic law, where they have autonomous control and use of their financial resources. Gulf women are aware of this right and the more affluent consider the separation of property in marriage an advantage to be protected. They are aware that money is power, and perhaps the only avenue to empowerment available to them within the Gulf in the near term, with access to other jobs remaining problematical. This economic capacity is legitimized by Islamic law and has important ramifications for women's status in the region.

Voluntary work is increasingly being undertaken by women in Saudi Arabia, especially educated and affluent women desiring to make an impact on their community within an Islamic framework. This has been organized to the extent that information locating and classifying differing needs is compiled using the latest technological developments. Moreover, help is not only thought of in terms of economic transfer from richer to poorer but also in a variety of goods that can be passed on, such as educational skills. For these women, social work via charity is a means of empowering themselves in those Gulf countries that do not encourage their formal participation at the decision-making level. Hence, within these restrictions, status and respectability are achieved in an 'Islamic' context through 'honourable' jobs such as philanthropic schemes including the building of mosques and the setting up of religious endowments, and in actively increasing the knowledge and self-sufficiency of less privileged women.

The problem of joblessness among women should be a priority in the twenty-first century's public policy agenda, one focused on improving the well-being of families. In order to help eradicate the basic problem of unemployment and poverty, those who wish to work but are discouraged from doing so by social factors must be further encouraged by national leadership and given increased opportunities. There is a need to cater to the rising aspirations of women and make full use of their expertise. In Saudi Arabia, the inclusion of trained women in the workforce could help to fill the many gaps in the indigenous workforce now filled by the increased employment of expatriate workers. Although women comprise 55 per cent of university graduates in Saudi Arabia, they form only 5 per cent of the workforce.[16]

Economic restructuring within the Gulf could have a direct effect on women's social development, that is, enhancing their well-being and autonomy as individuals and members of their community within an integrated society. These changes would without question bring about positive economic results, enabling the system to use the skills and aspirations of the thousands of educated women tied to the home by tradition. As seen in Bahrain, where the relatively low level of wages and salaries necessitates more than one breadwinner in the family, more women work, especially in middle management positions.[17] In Kuwait, women participate at senior levels in government and private enterprise, while in Oman women are included in the Consultative Assembly, Majlis al-Shura. There clearly exists, then, a modification of the concepts of honour and shame according to economic circumstances, particularly in situations where more than one breadwinner is needed in a family.

In Saudi Arabia, cultural traditions merge with religious and political dogma, as epitomized in the prevention of physical mobility by not allowing women to drive cars, for example. One wonders whether economic necessity and the need to reduce dependency on foreigners will lead to a change in this law. Concepts of honor and shame directly related to women's work outside the home, especially if in contact with male strangers (non-*mahram*), will eventually be constrained by economic realities. There are countries such as Yemen where driving is legally permitted but socially frowned upon, resulting in women not driving despite there being no legal injunction against it. Other Gulf countries, such as the UAE, address the issue of honor by having women wear traditional veils while at the wheel.

Including women in the workforce is part of the larger issue of indigenization (the replacement of foreigners by local people in the workforce). This has commonly been recognized as a necessary corrective in order to restabilize the economy. 'Saudization' is still in transition. As a Saudi businessman put it: 'If I have the choice between employing and paying a Saudi 4000 riyals while I could pay a Filipino 1000, of course I will employ the Filipino.' Another businessman commented: 'I employ foreigners rather than Saudis because the law does not protect me from the Saudi.' The right economic incentives must be created and the laws must be re-examined. What are needed are substantial cultural shifts regarding women in the workforce and the creation of a new work ethic. These changes can be achieved through educational programs provided there is sufficient political commitment.

Educational Protection

It is generally acknowledged in the Gulf region that the long-term prosperity of a nation ultimately depends upon the ability of its people to manage existing resources and develop new ones. Investment in education is an essential component of any healthy society and an essential pre-condition for positive social development. Governments of the GCC countries have devoted vast resources to programs which fund primary and secondary schools in urban as well as rural areas and university education in the main cities. Primary education is compulsory throughout the region. High and increasing rates of literacy for both sexes are keeping up with the constant growth in population.[18] This widespread access to education in urban areas for both men and women will eventually contribute to the growing equality between the sexes. The association between knowledge and power means that women will gain a greater say in both the domestic and public domains.

The history of education varies from state to state in the GCC countries according to economic and social circumstances as well as current religious influences. For example, Bahrain experienced the development of a more secular educational system from the earlier part of this century, while others continued to rely primarily on religious teachings in the mosques until the 1940s.[19] The tradition of education has also varied in different regions; for example, it was more heterogeneous and established earlier in the urban centres of the Hejaz than in the desert areas of the Najd.

Women's education has been a more recent process, again starting earlier in the century in Bahrain and as recently as the mid-1960s in Saudi Arabia. The first Saudi girls' school was Dar al-Hanan (House of Tenderness), which sought to produce better mothers and home-makers through Islamic-based instructions. The saying, 'The mother can be a school herself if you prepare her well' became a motto for women's education and was reproduced in school books. During the 1960s and 1970s, the trend among the more wealthy Gulf families was to send their children (both sons and daughters) to study abroad, mostly to other Arab countries,

Europe or the USA. This was possible because of the great wealth acquired from oil revenues. Both men and women belonging to the wealthier social strata during that period often pursued degrees from foreign universities. By the 1980s, most Gulf states had established state universities and a trend towards education at home rather than abroad set in. This trend was reinforced by the reduction in government scholarships abroad due to the need to reduce expenditure in the new, less favorable economic climate. Parents also became more reluctant to educate their children in the West when local schools acquired higher standards and broader course offerings, including computing and modern languages.

To prepare for the twenty-first century, educational programs are needed that emphasize not so much 'higher education' but rather provide student graduates with marketable skills for the Gulf economies in the decades ahead. During the oil-boom period, governments offered citizens a high level of material well-being, as well as a free education. However, the beginning of the twenty-first century will highlight the need for creating a social infrastructure to provide equal opportunity for all (including women) in order to meet the requirements of up-to-date technologies. Training programmes designed to create/sustain a skilled manpower base already exist in the petroleum industries.[20] Statistics show that in the area of technical education there are already three institutes for technology, one model agricultural institute, and 44 vocational training centers. In 1988, there was a total of 84 technical institutes in Saudi Arabia. However, given the Gulf's forthcoming demographic challenges, much more can and should be done to align the job skills of Gulf citizens with the economic requirements and opportunities of the new era.

In the light of the common Gulf objectives of economic diversification and indigenization, there is a great need for the continued growth and professionalization of schools which offer occupational education in order to meet the necessary restructuring demands. There must also be more guidance in choosing job specializations that align the region's manpower base with the demands of twenty-first-century Gulf employers. In other words, prospective students must comply with the saying, 'Cut your *thob* according to your requirements and means'.

Under the rising influence of Islam in Gulf politics, educational curricula are increasingly Islamic, particularly in Saudi Arabia, and the number of religious subjects being taught has grown apace. Whatever benefits have resulted, however, this has also placed an added burden on students' capacity to absorb and digest information. The increased amount of time spent mastering religious studies means less time for the study of science and humanities – subject areas of great relevance to the attainment of marketable skills for employment opportunities in the twenty-first-century 'global village'. At the same time, the threat of large-scale public antipathy towards Western secular education suggests that sensitivity to the requirement for Islamic education is very necessary, indeed essential. The challenge for Gulf education policy-makers is to maintain a balance between the aspirations of all their citizens.

Awareness and Participation in Health

The issue of health policies and related statistics in GCC countries is a complex one since health care is provided at various levels by several organizations. In the public sector, there are the ministries of health and education, university hospitals and the various sections of the armed forces. In the private sector, there are professional and voluntary organizations and large companies. Health care in the Gulf states is directly related to the demography of each country, its socio-economic situation, and the structure and finances of the health services. Furthermore, there are cultural norms embedded in Gulf societies related to health, illness and death which need to be addressed in order to improve and maintain health care in the coming millennium.[21] For example, little attention is given to preventive medicine or long-term care. The prevailing attitude to health care can be described as 'the search for a quick fix solution'.[22] More relevant to employment is the ambiguous attitude within the Gulf towards women nurses. The current stigma associated with the nursing profession is something that is proving counter-productive to effective health-care systems.

The expansion of Saudi health-care facilities in recent years is fairly typical of the entire Gulf. In the 1980s, the country remained an active market for health-care imports, and expansion of public health programs remained a priority despite declining oil revenues. Thirty-six hospitals with a capacity of 7550 beds were built between 1980 and 1985. At the same time, private health practice and facilities have continued to expand.[23] Saudi Arabia also continues to rely on the support from the West regarding health issues. For example, the Irish Health Services Development Corporation has been contracted to build all hospitals and clinics in the King Khalid military city. Other joint ventures have also been completed,[24] especially with health companies in the USA.[25]

To increase the quality of health care in the twenty-first century, however, national policies should encourage greater community participation.

Increased community awareness of health issues will help reduce the costs of services by focusing additional attention and resources on preventive rather than curative measures. While in the past the benefits derived from the availability of free health services may have predisposed some individuals to act as recipients, in the future, pro-active community participation and cooperation must become the norm. There are signs that public policy is beginning to recognize the advantages of citizens accepting a greater role. For example, in the Hail and Qasim regions of Saudi Arabia, questionnaires on views and expectations of individuals are being analysed to help craft acceptable public policy solutions for progress towards healthy lifestyles and to increase people's hygiene awareness.[26]

Public health-care management would also benefit from a more efficient and more egalitarian system of determining the ability of claimants to pay for services. While health care in the Gulf states is in theory free for all, in practice, in the Gulf as elsewhere, the rich are sometimes favored at the expense of the poor. Greater attention to standards should give priority to state-supported care to the poor and needy who cannot afford other options, such as private health care.

The role of the media in public health education has already been recognized in GCC countries. In the mid-1980s, a series of 15-minute television programs called *Salamatak* ('Your Safety') was introduced by Pan-Gulf Television, designed to increase awareness of the consequences to health which accrue from smoking, poor sanitation and inadequate nutrition, as well as dental hygiene, and child and maternal health. The same series also noted the value of marriage counselling, vaccination, and breastfeeding of infants.

Looking to the Future

The GCC states have not as yet experienced the economic restructuring that has characterized many 'developing-world' nations. Many of the conditions required for generous welfare provisions are already in place in the economies of the region. Although they are not as affluent as before, people's expectations remain as high as ever. The challenge to Gulf governments in the twenty-first century will include not only certain political and economic changes but equally certain and perhaps more dramatic social and cultural changes as well. The next several years will be a time in which Gulf countries will make important choices with respect to the long-term well-being of their people. In this regard, the basic teachings of Islam provide a solid basis for necessary attention to human and social security issues – issues that will certainly become more demanding as demographic growth provides historic population pressures within the Arab Gulf.

The traditions of public policy formation in the region have always been based upon citizen participation and consensus. These concepts have to be adapted to the present-day circumstances of a complex and large-scale semi-industrial society, yet they must also be retained in their fundamental role of participatory public policy decision-making. New forms and modalities of political participation must be negotiated and implemented between the ruling groups and significant sectors in civil society. People of the region must participate in the societal choices based upon their own requirements, yet education of the citizenry concerning the human and social options available to Gulf societies is also essential to this process. It is clear that these choices will be circumscribed by relatively less per capita wealth. The future and security of the region will depend on how wisely they choose.

Contributors

ROBERT V. BARYLSKI is Associate Professor of Government and International Affairs at the University of South Florida. He analyses the region from China to the Black Sea along both sides of the southern borders of the former Soviet Union, a zone that serves as a buffer and a bridge between Russia and the greater Islamic world. Dr Barylski has published a dozen articles and chapters revolving around three linked sets of interest: the relationship between military power and state viability, the relationship between Russia and states of Islamic heritage, and competition and cooperation in the development of international oil regimes. His articles have appeared in *The Armed Forces & Society, FORUM International, Central Asia Monitor, Europe–Asia Studies, Caspian Crossroads* and *Middle East Journal.* He is currently completing a book entitled *The Soldier in Russian Politics.*

MICHAEL E. BONINE is Professor of Geography and Near Eastern Studies at the University of Arizona, where he has taught for the past 20 years. He received his PhD in Geography in 1975 from the University of Texas at Austin, completing a dissertation on city–hinterland relationships based upon two years of field work in central Iran. He was executive director of the Middle East Studies Association of North America (MESA) from 1982 to 1989. He has served on the board of directors of the American Institute of Maghribi Studies, the American Institute of Yemeni Studies and the Society for Gulf Arab Studies. Dr Bonine's research focuses on urbanism and the urbanization of the Middle East. He has published several books and articles, including *Middle East Cities in Crisis: Population, Poverty and Politics, Middle Eastern Cities and Islamic Urbanism: An Annotated Bibliography in Western Languages* and *Cities of the Middle East and Africa.*

JILL CRYSTAL is an Assistant Professor in the Department of Political Science, Auburn University, Alabama. Dr Crystal did her undergraduate work at Cornell University and received her MA and PhD from Harvard University in 1986. She has published two books: *Oil and Politics in the Gulf: Rulers and Merchants in Kuwait and Qatar* and *Kuwait: The Transformation of an Oil State.* She has also published articles in *Comparative Politics*, *World Politics* and other scholarly journals. Her current research, which she is presently conducting under a grant from the Social Science Research Council, is on political liberalization and its limits.

CHARLES F. DORAN is the Andrew W. Mellon Professor of International Relations at the Paul H. Nitze School of Advanced International Studies (SAIS), Johns Hopkins University, Washington, DC. Dr Doran was educated at Harvard (BA, 1964), Johns Hopkins SAIS (MA, 1966), and the Johns Hopkins University (PhD, 1969). Before joining the SAIS faculty in 1979, he taught as assistant through full professor at Rice University for nine years, establishing and directing an international management program. Dr Doran is the author of more than sixty refereed articles and books and numerous professional papers in international politics and political economy. Representative works include: *The Politics of Assimilation: Hegemony and Its Aftermath* and *Systems in Crisis: New Imperatives of High Politics at Century's End.* Dr Doran's research encompasses security policy, conflict analysis, and commercial, environmental and energy research issues, assessing costs and options facing governments and other actors. He is a regular adviser to business and government officials and has provided congressional briefings and testimony on trade, security and energy policy.

JERROLD D. GREEN is corporate research manager and head of RAND's International Policy Department. He is also affiliated with UCLA as a Visiting Scholar and is Center Associate of the Gustave Von Grunebaum Center for Near Eastern Studies and a Visiting Professor in the Department of Political Science. He has a BA from the University of Massachusetts/Boston as well as an MA and a PhD in Political Science from the University of Chicago where he specialized in the politics of the Middle East. Dr Green has written widely on Middle East themes, focusing on American Middle East policy, the role of religion in the region, inter-Arab relations, Iranian politics and the Arab–Israeli conflict. His work has appeared in such publications as *World Politics*, *Comparative Politics*, *Ethics and International Affairs*, and *The Harvard Journal of World Affairs*.

ROSEMARY HOLLIS is head of the Middle East Programme at the Royal Institute of International Affairs, Chatham House, in London. Prior to her appointment there in 1995, she spent five years as head of the Middle East Programme at the Royal United Services Institute for Defence

Studies, before which she was a lecturer in Political Science and International Affairs at George Washington University in Washington, DC. The focus of Dr Hollis' research and writing generally is on foreign policy and security issues in the Middle East, particularly in the Gulf and Arab–Israeli sectors, and on relations between the Western powers and the region. Her most recent publication is entitled *Iran – Iraq: Dual Containment and the Oil Market.*

CHRISTIAN KOCH is head of the Strategic Studies Department at the Emirates Center for Strategic Studies and Research. He has studied at the University of South Carolina, the American University in Washington, DC and undertook his PhD in the Graduate Fellowship Program for the Study of the Contemporary Orient at the University of Erlangen-Nürnberg on the role of voluntary associations in the political development of the state of Kuwait.

DAVID E. LONG is a specialist on Middle East affairs and counter-terrorist affairs. He is currently a consultant of the King Faisal Foundation in Riyadh, Saudi Arabia, and a Senior Associate of C & O Resources in Washington, DC. A former US Foreign Service Officer, Dr Long has held numerous offices within the State Department including deputy director of the Office of Counter Terrorism for Regional Policy and chief of the Near East Research Division in the Intelligence and Research Bureau. While on leave from the State Department, he was the first executive director of the Georgetown University Center for Contemporary Arab Studies, 1974–75. In 1982–83, Dr Long was a Senior Fellow of the Middle East Research Institute and Adjunct Professor of Political Science at the University of Pennsylvania. Dr Long has been an adjunct professor at several Washington area universities, including Georgetown, George Washington, American University and the Johns Hopkins University School of Advanced International Studies. He has also lectured extensively in the United States and abroad on topics relating to Islam, the Middle East and terrorism. Dr Long is the author of numerous publications including *The Government and Politics of the Middle East and North Africa* and *The Anatomy of Terrorism.*

PHEBE MARR is a Senior Fellow at the Institute for National Strategic Studies (INSS), at the National Defense University in Washington, DC. Before joining INSS in 1985, she was Associate Professor of Middle East History at the University of Tennessee, Knoxville (1975–85) and at California State University, Stanislaus (1970–74). Since joining INSS, Dr

Marr has concentrated on domestic politics in Iran and Iraq, on the implications of the Iran–Iraq War for US strategy, and on the Gulf War and its impact on the region. Dr Marr received her MA in Middle Eastern Studies from Radcliff Graduate School and a PhD in History and Middle Eastern Studies from Harvard University. Her numerous publications include *Riding the Tiger: The Middle East Challenge after the Cold War* and *The Modern History of Iraq*.

JOSEPH MOYNIHAN's most recent appointment was with the Emirates Center for Strategic Studies and Research. Dr Moynihan joined the ECSSR staff following a full military career with the United States Air Force, completing service with the rank of Colonel. He has held a variety of command, staff and academic postings including senior command in the AWACS weapon system, senior staff responsibilities with both the Office of the US Secretary of Defense and the United States Special Operations Command, and a previous research association with the Fletcher School of Law and Diplomacy at Tufts University. His current professional interests include command and control warfare, information warfare, and peace enforcement operations as they relate to the Middle East and Gulf regions. Dr Moynihan received his PhD in International Relations from Saint Louis University, and attended the executive seminar for Senior Officials in National Security (SONS) sponsored by the Harvard University, John F. Kennedy School of Government in the spring of 1992.

GLENN E. ROBINSON received his PhD from the Department of Political Science at the University of California, Berkeley, in 1992. Currently an Assistant Professor at the Naval Postgraduate School, Dr Robinson specializes in Middle East and comparative politics. He has spent considerable time living in the Middle East, having studied at the University of Jordan, Yarmouk University in Irbid, Jordan and the American University in Cairo. The recipient of numerous academic honors and grants from the Fulbright Commission, Social Science Research Council and the United States Institute of Peace, Dr Robinson has published widely on issues related to the Arab–Israeli conflict. His latest book examines the Palestinian intifada and its impact on the post-Oslo Palestinian state-building process.

RICHARD SCHOFIELD is currently Director of Research of the Geopolitics and International Boundaries Research Centre at the London University's School of Oriental and African Studies (SOAS). He is also an associate fellow of the Middle East Programme at the Royal Institute of

International Affairs and currently sits on the council of the British Society of Middle Eastern Studies (BRISMES). Mr Schofield's publications include: *The Evolution of the Shatt Al-Arab Boundary Dispute, Kuwait and Iraq: Historical Claims and Territorial Disputes* and *The Territorial Foundations of the Gulf States*. Mr Schofield is currently undertaking a major research project for the Royal Institute of International Affairs entitled *Unfinished Business: Iran, the UAE, Abu Musa and the Tunbs*. His research into territorial problems has recently taken him to Yemen, the Gulf states, Jordan, Iran, Canada and the United States.

MAI YAMANI obtained her BA in anthropology from Bryn Mawr College, Pennsylvania, before going to Somerville College, Oxford, for her Masters Degree in Social Anthropology. Dr Yamani was awarded a PhD for her thesis on 'Formality and Propriety in the Hejaz', thus becoming the first Saudi Arabian woman to earn a degree from Oxford University. She has taught courses at King Abdul Aziz University and Georgetown University, and is currently lecturing at the Centre for Islamic and Middle Eastern Law at the School of Oriental and African Studies (SOAS), London. Dr Yamani's published works include: 'Birth and Behaviour in a Hospital in Saudi Arabia', 'You are What You Cook: Cuisine and Class in Mecca' and *Saudi Arabia and Central Asia: The Islamic Connection*. She is a contributor to and an active participant in the United Nations Development Programme (UNDP).

Notes

1. Introduction

1. For example, in his remarks at a luncheon at the University of South Florida on 31 October 1995, Ambassador Ekeus developed the thesis that UN inspection of Iraq's capabilities for building weapons of mass destruction provided an excellent indicator of its political–military intentions. Based on his experience, he said, one could conclude that Saddam had not given up any of his ambitions for political hegemony over the Gulf.

2. Iran and Gulf Security

1. For critical views that portray Iran as the premier threat to regional stability see, for example, Patrick Clawson, 'Iran's Challenge to the West: How, When, and Why?', *Washington Institute Policy Papers*, no 33, 1993; Daniel Pipes and Patrick Clawson, 'Ambitious Iran, Troubled Neighbors', *Foreign Affairs*, vol 72, no 1, 1993; and Judith Miller, 'Is Islam a Threat? Yes', *Foreign Affairs*, vol 72, no 2, 1993.

2. For a more positive view of Iran, and of its regional political and strategic role, see the *U.S.–Iran Review* published by the now defunct Forum on American–Iranian Relations based in Washington, DC.

3. Indeed, the degree to which these polarized positions on Iran have been made concrete is illustrated by an event sponsored by the Council on Foreign Relations in New York entitled 'The Carrot or the Stick: A Debate on US Policy Toward Iran' in which Gary Sick (replacing James Bill) debated with Daniel Pipes, with the former advocating a softer US approach to Iran and the latter a much harsher one (4 December 1995).

4. This has become particularly evident in my dealings with specialists on Iran in Europe and Japan. In meetings with such analysts, significant interest in as well as bewilderment about American policy towards Iran has regularly been apparent. This is in marked contrast to the situation in Israel and Egypt where the view of the Islamic Republic is far more critical. Even in the Gulf, attitudes towards Iran are far more diverse than many realize, with different states having diverse views on and relations with Iran depending upon their individual circumstances.

5. For another view of relations among the Gulf states, see Mehdi Mozaffari, 'The "New" Balkanization of the Persian Gulf?', *Cambridge Review of International Affairs*, vol 8, no 2 and vol 9, no 1, 1994/95, pp 136–49.

6. For a particularly thoughtful analysis of recent writings on Iranian politics and society, see Farhad Kazemi, 'Models of Iranian Politics, the Road to the Islamic Revolution, and the Challenge to Civil Society', *World Politics*, vol 47, no 4, 1995, pp 555–74.

7. For an analysis of the socio-political composition of the anti-Pahlavi forces, as well as the patterns of mobilization supporting the upheaval, see Jerrold D. Green, *Revolution in Iran: The Politics of Countermobilization* (New York: Praeger, 1982).

8. See interview with Brigadier General Ja'fari, *Ettela'at*, 28 September 1995, p 8. Reprinted in Foreign Broadcast and Information Service (FBIS), 28 September 1995, p 8.

Eric Hooglund also discusses urban unrest motivated by widespread dissatisfaction with Iran's economic problems in 'The Pulse of Iran Today,' *Middle East Insight*, vol 11, no 5, 1995, p 42.

9. Certainly the best-known opposition is the Baghdad-based Iranian *émigré* group the Mujahedin-e Khalq. Somewhat ironically, this group appears to have been particularly effective in making its case on Capitol Hill in Washington where it has attracted widespread attention from numerous legislators and staffers. Indeed, in a somewhat embarrassing *contretemps*, a serious difference of views emerged between the United States Department of State, which strongly opposes US support for the Mujahedin, and members of Congress who hold the opposite view. If the Mujahedin could attract the same level of support from the Iranian people that they have from Capitol Hill, Iranian politics might look quite different.

10. See 'Tehran Sets Out Austerity Budget', *Financial Times*, 28 November 1995, p 6.

11. For discussion of some of these issues, including Congressman Newt Gingrich's call for financial support to the United States intelligence community to finance the overthrow of the government of Iran and Senator Alfonse D'Amato's sponsorship of a Bill to tighten trade sanctions against Iran and those doing business with the Islamic Republic, see R. Jeffrey Smith, 'U.S. Drive for Tighter Iran Sanctions Gains Speed', *International Herald Tribune*, 11–12 November 1995, p 2. See also Tim Weiner, 'U.S. Plan to Oust Iran's Leaders is an Open Secret Before It Begins', *New York Times*, 26 January 1996, p 1. Finally, it has been reported that the Islamic Republic has responded by allocating $8 million 'to counter U.S. plots against Iran'. See Reuters, 'Iran Allots Money to Counter "Plots"', *Washington Post*, 12 January 1996, p 18.

12. For a clear explication of the US expansion of sanctions against the Islamic Republic see Vahe Petrussian, 'Iran: U.S. Targets Foreign Companies', *MEED*, 5 January 1996, p 24.

13. For reference to the Caspian Research Centre, see FBIS-NES-95–194, 6 October 1995, p 74. A systematic review of FBIS reveals references to literally hundreds of Iranian-sponsored meetings, projects and agreements with its neighbors in every direction except the south-west (the Arab states of the Gulf region).

14. This statement appears in an article entitled 'U.S. Applicants Said Banned from Oil Conference' and was released by Tehran's Islamic Republic News Agency (IRNA) in English. The oil conference referred to was held in Tehran 11–14 November 1995. The statement was reprinted in FBIS-NES-95–200, 17 October 1995, p 86.

15. For discussion of how and why a European view of Iran can differ from that of the USA see Charles Lane, 'Changing Iran: Germany's New Ostpolitik', *Foreign Affairs*, vol 74, no 6, 1995, pp 77–89.

16. See Michael S. Lelyveld, 'Iran Extends Power in Region Via Trade Deals', *Journal of Commerce*, 14 September 1995, p 1.

17. For analysis of this issue by the pre-eminent analyst of Middle East military affairs, see Anthony Cordesman, *Iran and Iraq – The Threat from the Northern Gulf* (Boulder, CO: Westview Press, 1994).

18. This issue is discussed in a review of Cordesman's book, cited in note 17, by Terence Taylor, *Survival*, vol 37, no 4, winter 1995/96, p 177.

19. R. Jeffrey Smith, 'Projected Iranian Buildup Scaled Back Analysts Say: Weak Economy and Western Embargo are Cited', *Washington Post*, 18 November 1995, p 22.

20. For discussion of the problems plaguing Iran's attempt to deploy submarines, see Philip Finnegan and Robert Holzer, 'Iran Steps Up Mine, Missile Threat', *Defense News*, 27 November–3 December 1995, p 1. This article details Iran's attempt to develop an integrated missile and mine capability that will permit it to seal off the Straits of Hormuz.

The problems Iran has encountered with its Russian submarines include effectively operating systems designed for cold war deployment in warm water.

21. Smith: 'Projected Iranian Build-up', p 22.

22. Aaron Karp, 'The Demise of the Middle East Arms Race', *Washington Quarterly*, vol 18, no 4, 1995, pp 38–9. The analysis by Shahram Chubin cited by Karp is *Iran's National Security Policy: Capabilities, Intentions, and Impact* (Washington, DC: Carnegie Endowment for International Peace, 1994), pp 29–38.

23. Thomas McNaugher, 'Iran's Military Posture: Whether "Hegemonic" or "Defensive," Iran's Force Buildup Complicates U.S. Defense Planning', *Middle East Insight*, vol 11 (special edition on Iran), no 5, 1995, pp 30–31.

24. For a detailed analysis of the role political violence and terrorism have played in Iranian domestic and foreign policies both in Pahlavi Iran as well as the Islamic Republic, see Jerrold D. Green, 'Terrorism and Politics in Iran', in Martha Crenshaw (ed), *Terrorism in Context* (University Park, PA: Pennsylvania State University Press, 1995), pp 553–94.

25. Karp: 'Demise of the Middle East Arms Race', p 39. The author provides a brief but balanced overview of the debate about Iran's nuclear weapons capability in his note 30. As the quote provided here indicates, Karp is not persuaded that Iran presents a significant nuclear threat.

26. Ahmed Hashim, *The Crisis of the Iranian State: Domestic, Foreign, and Security Policies in Post-Khomeini Iran*, Adelphi Paper no 296 (London: IISS, 1995).

27. For an unusual and innovative analysis of Iran's ties with China, see Jonathan Pollack, *Should the U.S. Worry About the Chinese–Iranian Security Relationship*, DRR-923-1-A (Santa Monica, CA: Rand Corporation, December 1994).

28. See 'China's Trade with Iran Vexes U.S. Efforts to Halt Arms Spread', *New York Times*, 12 November 1995, p A4.

29. This quote appears, in an emphatic form, in an interview on Iranian Television with Dr Reza Amrollahi, head of Iran's Atomic Energy Organization, who discusses his country's ties with Russia in the realm of developing nuclear technology. This interview was held in conjunction with the opening of the Bushehr Nuclear Power Plant which is due to go into operation some time during the next four years. Dr Amrollahi acknowledges that Iranian scientists are being trained by Russia and that Russian experts are stationed in Iran. He also sounds somewhat defensive when he notes that Iran's interest in nuclear expertise is for peaceful applications and prefaces his statement by noting that 'I have said this repeatedly before and I will say it once again'.

30. For a novel overview of Iraq's WMD programmes from an unusual perspective, see Robin Wright, 'Dr. Germ: One of the World's Most Dangerous Women', *Los Angeles Times*, 7 November 1995, p E6. Wright discusses the husband and wife team where Dr Rihab Rashid Taha heads Iraq's biological weapons program and her husband, General Amer Rashid, directs Iraq's Military Industrialization Corps that is generally assumed to be responsible for all Iraqi weapons acquisition including nuclear, chemical, and biological as well as ballistic missiles.

31. Hashim: *The Crisis of the Iranian State*, p 69.

32. McNaugher: 'Iran's Military Posture', p 32.

33. For an attempt to explore the impossibility of Gulf security without broad agreement among the region's three primary political actors see Jerrold D. Green, 'Gulf Security Without the Gulf States', *Harvard Journal of World Affairs*, vol 4, no 1, 1995, pp 78–89.

34. For a discussion of a possible US–Iranian conflict in Bosnia, see Robin Wright, 'U.S. Worries About Iranian Unit in Bosnia', *Los Angeles Times*, 5 December 1995, p 1.

35. Zalmay Khalilzad, 'The United States and the Persian Gulf: Preventing Regional Hegemony', *Survival*, vol 37, no 2, 1995, pp 95–120. Readers should also see the spirited

exchange of letters after the appearance of the article, with a particularly useful contribution from Shahram Chubin who applauds Khalilzad's analysis but is somewhat more restrained in his view of Iran's regional ambitions. See, Letters to the Editor, *Survival*, vol 37, no 3, 1995.

36. Milton Viorst, 'Changing Iran: The Limits of Revolution', *Foreign Affairs*, vol 74, no 6, 1995, pp 63–76.

3. Iraq Faces the Twenty-first Century

The views expressed in this chapter are those of the author and should not be construed as reflecting the policy of positions of the National Defense University, the Department of Defense or the US government.

1. Phebe Marr, 'Iraq's Future, Plus ça change … or Something Better?' in Ibrahim Ibrahim (ed), *The Gulf Crisis: Background and Consequences* (Washington, DC: Center for Contemporary Arab Studies, Georgetown University, 1992), p 14.

2. Abbas Alnasrawi, *The Economy of Iraq* (London: Greenwood Press, 1994), p 120. Dilip Hiro estimates 82,000. See Dilip Hiro, *Desert Shield to Desert Storm* (London: Routledge, 1992), p 396.

3. John G. Heidenrich, 'The Gulf War: How Many Died?', *Foreign Policy*, no 90, 1993, p 123.

4. Ibid, p 119. Again, Alnasrawi and others give a much higher figure, ranging from 5000 to 15,000. See Alnasrawi: *The Economy of Iraq*, p 120.

5. Alnasrawi estimates the toll in the rebellion at 20,000 to 100,000 – undoubtedly too high. Iran puts the figure for the fighting at Najaf and Karbala at 12,000 which is probably still an exaggeration. Estimates of Kurds who died during the exodus to the mountains are 15,000 to 30,000. The figures used in the text are on the low end of the spectrum.

6. FAO Mission to Iraq, 'Executive Summary and Recommendations', July–August 1995 (unpublished).

7. 'Iraq: Down But Not Out', *The Economist*, 8 April 1995, p 23.

8. Economist Intelligence Unit (EIU), *Iraq: Country Profile 1994–1995* (London: EIU, 1995), p 7. The FAO Mission Report cited in note 6 estimated a growth rate of 2.7 per cent.

9. Anthony Cordesman, 'Iran and Iraq and Strategic Developments in the Gulf: A Graphic Summary' (Washington, DC: Center for Strategic and International Studies, October 1995), p 57 (unpublished).

10. Marr: 'Iraq's Future', pp 146–8. By 1992, electrical capacity had been restored to 90 per cent, telephones had been restored and 104 of 132 bridges had been repaired. See EIU: *Iraq: 1994–1995*, p 13.

11. FAO Mission Report.

12. *Financial Times*, 23 October 1994, cited in Sarah Graham Brown, 'The Iraq Sanctions Dilemma', *Middle East Report*, vol 193, no 24, p 9.

13. EIU, *Iraq: 1994–1995*, p 13.

14. Private conversation with NGO mission in Iraq.

15. 'Medical Aid for Iraq' (MAI) *Report*, September 1994, cited in Graham Brown: 'The Iraq Sanctions Dilemma', p 10.

16. FAO Mission Report. The Report cites an eight-fold increase in infant mortality since 1989 but, again, these figures were obtained from the government of Iraq and could not be independently confirmed.

17. EIU, *Iraq* (London: EIU, 2nd Quarter 1995), p 18.

18. Petroleum Finance Company (PFC), *Country Report: Iraq* (Washington, DC: PFC, December 1994), p 29. Iraq earns oil income from the export of crude to Jordan (50–70,000 b/d), which is allowed for under the sanctions regime; product export to Jordan, Turkey and Iran (20,000–30,000 b/d); and crude transshipped through the Gulf (10,000 b/d). See Cambridge Energy Research Associates, *Report*, February 1995, p 2. Other sources have estimated that oil exports could be as high as 200,000 b/d.

19. EIU: *Iraq*, p 19.

20. EIU: *Iraq, 1994–1995*, p 13.

21. Figures on Iraq's debt vary widely. Those used here are based on EIU reports and Alnasrawi: *The Economy of Iraq*.

22. Michael Eisenstadt, 'Iraq's Military Capabilities: An Assessment' (Washington, DC: Washington Institute for Near East Policy, Policy Watch, October 1994), p 1.

23. Cordesman: 'Iran and Iraq', p 23.

24. Eisenstadt: 'Iraq's Military Capabilities', p 1.

25. This may be worth as much as $1 billion a year, about half of Iraq's foreign exchange earnings. See Rend Rahim Franke, 'Iraq: Race to the Finish Line' (unpublished paper) (Washington, DC: Iraq Foundation, 1994), p 2.

26. The conclusion to the UN Secretary General's report to the UN on UNSCOM's activities in October 1995 following Hussein Kamal's defection asserted that Iraq had been 'concealing proscribed activities', 'misleading the Commission by withholding information', and 'providing incorrect information'. See United Nations, 'Report of the Secretary General on the Status of the Implementation of the Special Commission's Plan for Monitoring and Verification of Iraq's Compliance with Resolution 687', cited in United Nations, *The United Nations and the Iraq–Kuwait Conflict, 1990–1996* (New York: UN Department of Public Information, 1996), pp 789–90.

27. These included Izzat Ibrahim, Sa'dun Ghaidan, Taha Ramadhan, Na'im Haddad, Hasan Ali al-Amri, Sa'dun Shakir, Tariq Aziz and Adnan Khairallah, Saddam's cousin.

28. They included Taha Ramadhan, Tariq Aziz, Sa'dun Ghaidan, Adnan Khairallah, Sa'dun Hamadi, Sa'dun Shakir, Tahir Tawfiq and Tayih Abd al-Karim.

29. They included Taha Ramadhan, Tariq Aziz, Adnan Khairallah and Sa'dun Shakir, with Saddam Hussein as Prime Minister.

30. These ministers were Saddam Hussein (Prime Minister), Tariq Aziz, Taha Ramadhan, Ali Hassan al-Majid, Hussein Kamal, Mohammed al-Sahaf, Mohammed Hamza al-Zubaidi and Safaa Hadi Jamad (a technocrat).

31. Private communication.

32. The term 'anfal' comes from the Qur'an where it means 'spoils of war'. It was apparently used as an attempt to provide religious justification for this act. For a definitive account of this campaign, see Human Rights Watch/Middle East, *Iraq's Crime of Genocide: The Anfal Campaign Against the Kurds* (New Haven, CT: Yale University Press, 1995). See also Michael Gunter, 'A *de facto* Kurdish State in Northern Iraq', *Middle East Journal*, vol 50, no 2, 1996.

33. Phebe Marr, *The Modern History of Iraq* (Boulder, CO: Westview Press, 1985), p 227.

34. Cordesman: 'Iran and Iraq', p 41.

35. *Al-Sharq al-Awsat* (London), 15 May 1996, p 2.

36. Amatzia Baram, 'An Iraqi General Defects', *Middle East Quarterly*, vol 2, no 2 (June 1995) pp 25–32.

37. *Al-Sharq al-Awsat* (London), 15 May 1996, p 2.

4. The Gulf Cooperation Council and the US

1. For a forthright if harsh critique of defense policy planning, see Lawrence J. Korb, 'Our Overstuffed Armed Forces', *Foreign Affairs*, vol 74, no 6, 1995, pp 22–34.

2. This was the conclusion reached during the 1992 edition of the 'Senior Official in National Security Symposium' held at the John F. Kennedy School of Government, Harvard University, 2 March to 29 April 1992. Albert Carnesale, then Dean of the Kennedy School, and Graham Allison, the Symposium co-chair, suggested in a 10 March session, which addressed US national security policy, that the structural post-Cold War security policy environment of the USA could reasonably be compared to 'a shifting of the planet's tectonic plates', a process that often occurs only once a century, and lasts for approximately seven to ten years.

3. A Venn diagram is, of course, too simplistic to represent the cacophony of national security policy voices now present in the debate. Within both parties there is substantial disagreement concerning the very definition of national security, the policy imperatives which spring from these different conceptions, and increasingly 'isolationist' positions are observable on both the political Left and Right, for different reasons. For more on the isolationist impulse in modern-day US foreign policy, see Paul Johnson, 'The Myth of American Isolationism', *Foreign Affairs*, vol 74, no 3, 1995. Johnson takes a fairly centrist position arguing that America's history is an international one, and that America's interests will continue to require international activism.

4. See Carl H. Builder and Theodore W. Karasik, *Organizing, Training, and Equipping the Air Force for Crises and Lesser Conflicts* (Santa Monica, CA: Rand Corporation, 1995), p ix. This study makes several important observations, one of which is that in the pre-Second World War period, the emphasis of the military services was on 'mobilization for war and operations short of war'. No near-term *readiness* of forces to execute immediately a pre-ordained and approved war strategy was maintained.

5. The Cold War did permit the USA to make friends with countries that would have otherwise been politically unacceptable. A particular example is Pol Pot, the national leader of Cambodia who committed attributable acts of genocide on his country's citizens. Readers may note that in the post-Cold War this practice has continued with a similar relationship initially evolving with Saddam Hussein of Iraq. I shall return to the issue of similarities between the Cold War and the current and future relationship between the USA and Iran.

6. Similar bipartisan coalitions also support the security of the state of Israel, the containment of Iran and Iraq and the isolation of Libya. US security policy towards Iran and Iraq will be discussed in greater detail below.

7. For further evidence of the lively debate concerning security policy in Asia, see *Foreign Affairs*, vol 74, no 4, 1995, which includes two views on East Asia, 'The Case for Deep Engagement', by Joseph S. Nye, Jr, and 'The Pentagon's Ossified Strategy', by Chalmers Johnson and E. B. Keehn. Despite the title of the latter piece, the debate is over policy, not strategy. During the Cold War, strategy was frequently debated while the overall policy of 'containment' enjoyed strong bipartisan support. Ironically, it is now policy that is so strongly debated.

8. For example, Representative Robert K. Dornan (R-CA) recently suggested that President Clinton lacks the moral standing to dispatch American military forces to Bosnia because he (Clinton) gave 'aid and comfort to our enemy' during the Vietnam War. As a student, Clinton opposed the war. See Robert Dornan, 'Missed Target', *Armed Forces Journal*, May 1995, p 4. Elected officials of the USA have only rarely accused their presidents of traitorous conduct, and some attribute the present rancor to a general deterioration of

American civil–military relations, caused in part by the anti-Vietnam activities of President Clinton. See Douglas V. Johnson II and Steven Metz, *American Civil–Military Relations: New Issues, Enduring Problems* (Carlisle, PA: US Army War College, Strategic Studies Institute, 1995).

9. Despite charges of insensitivity to local political institutions, the Clinton administration has sought to factor them in. For example, in November 1993, the George Marshall Center for Security Studies held a conference in Garmisch-Partenkirchen, Germany, on 'Democratization as a Component of the US National Security Strategy'. Participants attempted to find a methodology for furthering democratization, one of four areas of the then new Clinton administration's four-component national security policy. The prospect of tasking the US military regional commands of the United States armed forces with the mission of democratization within their respective areas of responsibility was specifically discussed. United States Central Command, the US regional command with responsibility for the Arabian peninsula, was present. Subsequent correspondence between the participants and the Clinton administration was at least in part influential in shaping the democratization component of national security strategy in a way which respected regionally-specific conceptions of the democratic process rather than attempting to export Western conceptions to the non-Western world.

10. From a prospectus for a strategic advisory service entitled, 'The United Arab Emirates: Geo-Strategic Prospects and Risks', undated. The author does not wish to be acknowledged.

11. Gawdat Bahgat is one of the least optimistic analysts with regard to the future stability of the region. Like most regional specialists, however, he fails to address Gulf stability in comparative terms and that, when compared to most of the Third World, the Gulf can claim a high degree of stability. See Gawdat Bahgat, 'Regional Peace and Stability in the Gulf', *Security Dialogue*, 26, no 3 (New York: Sage Publications, 1995), pp 317–30.

12. Stephen C. Pelletiere, during a guest lecture presentation at the Emirates Center for Strategic Studies and Research (ECSSR), Abu Dhabi, UAE, 30 October 1995, was particularly pessimistic about the potential for events in Algeria to reverberate throughout the Arab world, particularly the Mahgrib, but also ultimately the Gulf. An opposing and, in my view, more plausible view is expressed in 'A Radical Islamist Concept of Conflict', by Lew B. Ware in *Terrorism: National Security Policy and the Home Front* (Carlisle, PA: US Army War College, May 1995). Ware notes on page 32: 'Certainly it cannot be denied that radical Islam extends its appeal to the universal Muslim community and in that sense is a transnational phenomenon. But one must be careful to avoid the temptation to perceive in radical Islamism the spearhead of an Islamic civilization crusade with predetermined historical fault lines that pits the Muslim East against the Christian West.'

13. The Clinton administration's nominee for the position of Assistant Secretary of Defense for Democratization and Peacekeeping, Morton Halperin, was never confirmed by the United States Senate, and the plan to reorganize the Office of the Secretary of Defense to enable a democratization portfolio has since been abandoned.

14. On 1 November 1995, immediately following the economic summit in Amman, Jordan, Mr David Lay, the managing editor of *Oxford Analytica*, who attended the summit, presented a guest lecture entitled 'After Amman: The Economic Prospects for the Middle East' at the ECSSR, Abu Dhabi, UAE. The opinions expressed in this section reflect some of the impressions and conclusions Mr Lay shared with me and others at the time.

15. The 1995 summit of GCC leaders in Muscat, Oman produced the requisite condemnation of Saddam Hussein, and firmly stated that the weapons inspection, monitoring and destruction requirements of all relevant UN Security Council Resolutions must be met before any sanctions could be lifted. 'GCC Summit Strengthens Position on Iraq', *Gulf*

News, 7 December 1995, p 1. Since this summit, senior GCC governmental representatives have publicly questioned the utility of continued sanctions.

16. See 'Saudi Prince Seeks End to Iraq Sanctions', *International Herald Tribune*, 14 December 1995, p 2.

17. This view was expressed by Ambassador Rolf Ekeus, Executive Chairman, UN Special Commission, in a speech delivered at the Washington Institute for Near East Policy on 16 November 1995.

18. See Georgie Anne Geyer, 'Gulf War and a Gap of Unfinished Victory', *Washington Times*, 17 January 1996, p 11.

19. For example, of 23 US Air Force generals reassigned in 1995, two were sent to major assignments in the Middle East. Major General Carl Franklin was assigned as Commander of the Joint Task Force–Southwest Asia, Riyadh, Saudi Arabia, with responsibility for the supervision of Operation Southern Watch (OSW), an activity which restricts Iraqi military aircraft and Republican Guard ground units from positions south of the 32nd parallel. OSW has generated more than twice as many air sorties as occurred during Desert Storm in the five years since the war. Major General Charles Henderson was assigned as Commander of the Combined Task Force Provide Comfort, with headquarters at Incirlik AB in Turkey. Provide Comfort protects the Kurdish communities in northern Iraq. See *Air Force Times*, 2 October, 1995 (Springfield, VI: Air Force Times Publishing Co), p 23.

20. Certain GCC states have already begun to question the wisdom of continued sanctions against the Iraqi regime for precisely this reason. See Phebe Marr, 'U.S.–GCC Security Relations 1: Differing Threat Perceptions', *Strategic Forum*, no 39, August 1995 (Washington, DC: National Defense University). Even Marr's analysis, which acknowledges strong dissent from a tough containment policy towards Iraq by Gulf 'educated elites', asserts that support for strong sanctions and tough containment remains 'strong at top leadership levels'.

21. On 4 November 1995, former US Assistant Secretary of State for Near Eastern Affairs Richard Murphy spoke at the ECSSR on 'US Policy towards the Gulf Region'. He acknowledged the ideological component of the hostile relationship between Washington and Tehran but argued that Washington's chief complaints with Tehran were objective: (1) Iran is seeking a nuclear weapons capability; (2) it seeks to undermine moderate Arab governments as part of its policy in support of international terrorism; and (3) it is working to destroy the Arab–Israeli peace process. Even so gifted an apologist of US Middle East policy was not entirely convincing in making the case for objectivity, however.

22. Samuel P. Huntington's 'The Clash of Civilizations?' *Foreign Affairs*, vol 72, no 3, 1993, pp 23–51 was deemed a serious article and widely discussed; *Foreign Affairs* devoted an entire issue (vol 74, no 3, 1995) to 'The Islamic Cauldron' which was alarmist in nature, as was Bernard Lewis, 'Muslim Rage', in the June 1992 issue of *Atlantic Monthly*. On the other hand, Anthony Parsons, 'Prospects for Peace and Stability in the Middle East', *Conflict Studies*, 262 (London: Research Institute for the Study of Conflict and Terrorism, 1993) specifically uses the term 'domino effect' in an otherwise fair discussion of Islamic radicalism. John Esposito has been the most effective voice suggesting a more moderate view. See, for example, his work *The Islamic Threat: Myth or Reality?* (New York: Oxford University Press, 1992). Esposito as a non-Arab, non-Muslim is particularly effective and credible in explaining the diversity within Islam, and the reality that the great majority of Muslims not only reject Islamic radicalism, but they take active measures to ensure that order within their communities is the norm.

23. See Anthony Lake, 'Debate: Confronting Backlash States', *Foreign Affairs*, vol 73, no 2, 1994, p 54.

24. The United States has received international cooperation in seeking to limit arms technology transfers to Iran, particularly from Russia. It has received substantially less

cooperation in the enforcement of a non-weapons-related embargo. Germany, France and Japan all pursue policies of 'constructive engagement' with Iran, ironically similar to US trade policy towards China. The trade and arms embargo issues were the subject of a symposium at the Washington Institute for Near East Policy sponsored by the American Jewish Committee in September 1995 entitled 'Business as Usual? Western Policy Toward Iran'.

25. See Vahan Zanoyan, 'A Relevant Framework for Understanding the Global Crude Oil Market' in *Gulf Energy and the World: Challenges and Threats* (Abu Dhabi: ECSSR, 1996). See also Vahan Zanoyan's contribution 'After the Oil Boom', *Foreign Affairs*, vol 74, no 6, 1995, pp 2–7. The specific numbers and percentages cited here are drawn from the Economist Intelligence Unit (EIU), *Iran* (London: EIU, 2nd quarter, 1995).

26. One Gulf economic analyst concluded that GCC governments 'will have to continue economizing, spending less on services and subsidies than what the population has come to expect'. See Patrick Clawson, 'U.S.–GCC Security Relations II: Growing Domestic Economic and Political Problems', *Strategic Forum*, no 40, August 1995 (Washington, DC: National Defense University), p 2.

27. For example, Ford, Chrysler and General Motors in partnership with the US government are trying to develop a 'next generation vehicle' that will achieve fuel economy of 80 miles per gallon of gasoline, or its equivalent in other fuels. See 'Electric Car Passes Crucial Federal Collision Test', *Times FAX* (a service of the *New York Times*), 22 November 1995.

28. For an insightful discussion of this dilemma, see Robert E. Looney, *Manpower Policies and Development in the Persian Gulf Region* (Westport, CN: Praeger, 1994), p 201.

29. More recently the Commander-in-Chief of United States Central Command, General J. H. Binford Peay, articulated the military measures he thought necessary to defend the Arabian peninsula and the Gulf. Peay articulated 'five pillars': Power Projection, Combined Exercises, Readiness, Forward Presence, and Security Assistance ('Special Bulletin', C & O Resources, Washington, DC, 20 September 1995). Four of these five 'pillars' directly support the policies of 'forward presence' and 'crisis response'. The 'pillar' of Security Assistance supports the economic recovery component of US national security policy as well as the crisis response policy. See Richard F. Grimmett, *Conventional Arms Transfers to the Third World*, (Washington, DC: Congressional Research Sevice, 1995).

30. The US Navy has designated Gulf naval assets as the 5th Fleet and expanded its regional headquarters in Bahrain. The US Air Force has assigned A-10 fighter aircraft in Kuwait, and has recently temporarily assigned fighter assets in Bahrain. The decision to pre-position military equipment for a third US Army Brigade is still pending, while the pre-positioned equipment for the first two brigades already in place is openly discussed. See Kenneth Katzman, *Persian Gulf Armed Forces*, Congressional Research Service Report 95-380F (Washington, DC: Library of Congress, March 1995).

31. The 'lesser included threat' assumption is in fact very questionable. See Builder and Karasik: *Organizing, Training, and Equipping the Air Force*, which provides compelling arguments that, 'qualitatively', much of the non-hostilities-tasking for the present-day United States Air Force is not included within the tasks the USAF must accomplish for successful prosecution of an MRC. The United States Special Operations Command, an organization created by the Nunn–Cohen Amendment to the Defense Authorization Act of 1989, exists largely because the military services have consistently refused to pay sufficient attention to lesser crises.

32. See Gary Sick, 'Iran: The Adolescent Revolution', *Journal of International Affairs*, vol 49, no 1, summer 1995, pp 145–66.

5. Europe and Gulf Security

1. *BP Annual Statistical Review* (London: British Petroleum, 1995).

2. EC Parliament Working Documents, no A 2-199/86, 12 January 1987, Annex II, p 18.

3. Julie Till, 'The GCC–EU Dialogue', *Gulf Report*, no 36, December 1993, p 12.

4. EC Communications Report, November 1995.

5. Eric Schmitt, 'French Pass US in Sales of Arms to 3rd World', *International Herald Tribune*, 9 August 1995.

6. COM(95) 541, Brussels, 22 November 1995, Part 2, p 2.

7. *Statement on the Defence Estimates 1995*, Cm 2800 (London: HMSO, May 1995); and IISS, *Military Balance* (London: IISS, 1995).

8. IISS, *Military Balance*.

9. Ibid.

10. 'Kuwait's Defence Agreement with France', KUNA, 18 August 1992, in *BBC Survey of World Broadcasts*, ME/1464, 20 August 1992, p A/4.

11. 'Gulf Security: The Role of the West', *International Security Review* (London: RUSI, 1993), p 263.

12. Bernard Gray, 'Fears Grow on $4 bn Aircraft Order', *Financial Times*, 13 November 1995.

13. 'UK and the Middle East', *MEED Special Report,* 30 June 1995, p 12.

14. 'France and the Middle East', *MEED Special Report*, 13 September 1995, p 13.

15. Ibid, p 14.

16. International Monetary Fund, *Direction of Trade Statistics Yearbook 1995* (New York: IMF, 1995).

17. Ibid.

18. 'Germany and the Middle East,' *MEED Special Report,* 20 October 1995, p 10.

19. IMF, *Direction of Trade Statistics*.

20. Ibid.

21. Ibid.

22. 'France and the Middle East', p 14.

23. Excerpts from a press briefing given by Herve de Charette, Amman, 19 September 1995, in *France: Statements*, Service de Presse et d'Information, SAC/95/215, 28 September 1995, p 7.

24. 'Italy and the Middle East', *MEED Special Report*, 7 July 1995, p 8.

25. COM(95) 541, Brussels, 22 November 1995.

6. The Collape of the Soviet Union and Gulf Security

1. See, for example, Circular Telegram from Department of State to Certain Diplomatic Missions, 15 February 1955, *Foreign Relations of the US: 1955–57*, vol XII (Washington, DC: US Government Printing Office, 1991).

2. Ibid, p 130: US Department of State Position Paper, 14 July 1955.

3. See Valentin Rudenko's interview with Boris Kuzyk, 'Pravo byt' spetseksporterom – ne privilegiya' (A right not a privilege to special exports), *Krasnaya zvezda*, 29 July 1995.

4. See Robert V. Barylski, 'The Russian Federation and Eurasia's Islamic Crescent', *Europe-Asia Studies*, vol 46, no 3, 1994, pp 389–416.

5. *Foreign Relations*, p 185, National Intelligence Estimate: 30-4-55, 8 November 1955.

6. Ibid, p 374: Summary from US Secretary of Defense Wilson to President Eisenhower, 4 December 1956.

7. Yeltsin used the term 'triple alliance' when he called Soviet Minister of Defense Yevgeny Shaposhnikov to discuss his agreement with the leaders of Belarus and Ukraine on 8 December 1991. Shaposhnikov was disturbed by the ethno-political implications.

8. I discuss this more fully in Barylski, 'The Russian Federation and Eurasia's Islamic Crescent'; and 'Central Asia and the Post-Soviet Military System in the Formative Year: 1992', *Central Asia Monitor*, no 6, 1992, pp 18–29.

9. See Audrey L. Alstadt, *The Azerbaijani Turks: Power and Identity under Russian Rule* (Stanford, CA: Hoover Institution Press, 1992), pp 90–99.

10. See Mamed Emin Rasulzade, 'Vospominaniya O I. V. Stalin' (Remembrances of J. V. Stalin'), *Vostochnyi ekspress*, no 1, 1993. Mamed Emin Rasulzade was the DRA's primary leader.

11. See Yu. I. Polyakov and A. I. Chugunov, *Konets basmachestva* (Moscow, 1976).

12. See Yevgeny Dolgoplatov, *The Army and the Revolutionary Transformation of Society* (Moscow: Progress Publishers, 1981), p 96.

13. See David B. Nissman, *The Soviet Union and Iranian Azerbaijan: The Uses of Nationalism for Political Penetration* (Boulder, CO: Westview Press, 1987).

14. Russian security assessments address Turkish and Iranian efforts to expand influence in the Caucasus and Central Asia. See the report by Yevgeny Primakov, Director of Russia's Foreign Intelligence Service, which appeared in *Rossiiskaya gazeta*, 22 September 1994, Foreign Broadcast Information Service FBIS-SOV-94-185, p 1.

15. Russians complained that Turkey had abandoned the friendly policy towards Russia that Kemal Ataturk had instituted as a fundamental element in Turkish foreign policy. See Col. Viktor Kostenyuk, 'Turtsiya i konflikt v Zakavkazye' (Turkey and the Caucasian conflict), *Krasnaya zvezda*, 27 April 1993.

16. Russia has sold Turkey weapons and expanded trade even while complaining about pan-Turkism. Grachev visited Turkey in May 1993 to finalize arms sales and to discuss confidence-building measures. He even toured some Turkish regions near the former borders. See Aleksandr Sychev, 'Turtsiya pokupayet oruzhie u Rossii, no ne razdelyaet eye vzglyadov na polozhenie v goryachikh tochkakh' (Turkey buys Russian weapons but does not share her views on the situation in the hot spots), *Izvestiya*, 14 May 1993.

17. See Tadeusz Swietochowski, 'Azerbaijan's Triangular Relationship: The Land Between Russia, Turkey and Iran', in Ali Babuazizi and Myron Weiner (eds), *The New Geopolitics of Central Asia and Its Borderlands* (Bloomington, IN: Indiana University Press, 1994).

18. See Yuri Melnikov and Vladimir Frolov, 'Iran and Russian–US Relations', *International Affairs*, no 5, 1995, pp 12–19. The journal is published by Russia's Ministry of Foreign Affairs.

19. Ibid, p 18.

20. See Igor Melnikov, 'Russia and the Middle East', *International Affairs*, no 1, 1993, pp 61–9.

21. See Vladimir Zhirinovsky, *Poslednii brosok na yug* (The Final Thrust to the South) (Moscow: Liberal Democratic Party Press, 1993), p 72.

22. Ibid, p 136.

23. See Robert V. Barylski, 'The Caucasus, Central Asia, and the Near-Abroad Syndrome', *Central Asia Monitor*, vol 2, nos 5 and 6, 1993, pp 21–8 and 31–7.

24. See Vitaly Strugovets, 'Klan na klan poshel stenoyu' (Clan against clan), *Krasnaya zvezda*, 6 February 1996.

25. See M. T. Abasov (ed), *Chernyi Yanvar'* (Black January) (Baku: Azerneshr, 1990).

26. Ibid, pp 94–6. See Sheikh Ali Pasha-Zade's comments to Mikhail Gorbachev of 21 January 1990.

27. Agababa Rzaev (a senior constitutional lawyer and scholar) and G. Guseinov, 'Sushchestvuet li ugroza islamskogo fundamentalizma?' (Does an Islamic threat exist?), *Vozrozhdenie*, nos 7–9, 1991, pp 7–9, 65ff. *Vozrozhdenie* was the successor to *Kommunist Azerbaijana*.

28. See Andrei Kozyrev, 'Mirotvorchestvo stoit ne malo. No otkaz ot nego-esche dorozhe' (Peacekeeping is not cheap but rejecting it will cost us more), *Krasnaya zvezda*, 1 September 1993.

29. See Primakov's report, note 14.

30. See, for example, Melnikov: 'Russia and the Middle East', pp 61–9.

31. Boris Yeltsin, 'Obrashchenie Prezidenta Rossii k grazhdanam strany', *Krasnaya zvezda*, 5 November 1992.

32. Boris Yeltsin, cited in Tatyana Malkina, 'Candidate: Boris Yeltsin's Starting with Good Intentions', *Sevodnya*, 16 February 1996. Translated in *Current Digest of the Soviet Press* vol 48, no 7, 1996, p 2.

33. See Ravil Mustafin's report on Viktor Posuvalyuk's press conference, 'Est' takaya kontseptsiya', *Krasnaya zvezda*, 5 November 1993.

34. See Hafeez Malik, 'Tatarstan's Treaty with Russia: Autonomy or Independence', *Journal of South Asian and Middle Eastern Studies*, vol 18, no 2, 1994, pp 1–35.

35. See FBIS-SOV-94-196, p 50.

36. See, for example, Vadim Markushin's interview with Vladimir Zhurbenko, 'Rossiya dolzhna obezopasit' svoi flangi' (Russia must protect its flanks), *Krasnaya zvezda*, 7 December 1994.

37. Precisely 1928 military personnel. Ministry of Defence Information Service, 'Vypolnili voinskii dolg do kontsa', *Krasnaya zvezda*, 10 December 1995.

38. Russia was unwilling to meet Azerbaijan's demands regarding the Armenian military presence and occupation of some 25 per cent of its territory. The Armenian forces in Azerbaijan used Armenia as their rear base, and Armenia was Russia's ally.

39. Moscow also kept a third eye on Pakistan which was deeply interested in the civil war in Afghanistan. Moscow, Tehran and Delhi shared an interest in containing Pakistan.

40. See Vadim Markushin's analysis of Deputy Foreign Minister Viktor Posuvalyuk's press conference on the eve of Foreign Minister Kozyrev's trip to the Gulf, 'Blizhnyi Vostok: Rossiiskii MID menyaet stoiku' (Near East: Russian MFA changes position), *Krasnaya zvezda*, 3 August 1995.

41. See Deputy Foreign Minister Viktor Posuvalyuk's comments as reported by Mustafin: 'Est' takaya kontseptsiya'.

42. See 'O vizite Rossiiskoi voennoi delegatsii v Obyedinennye Arabskie Emiraty' (On the Russian military delegation's visit to the United Arab Emirates), *Krasnaya zvezda*, 6 January 1993.

43. See Vladimir Kosarev, 'Abu Dabi: shag na puti k rynku oruzhiya' (Abu Dhabi: a step towards the arms market), *Krasnaya zvezda*, 16 February 1991.

44. See Vladimir Kosarev, 'Vozvratitsya li Rossiya na mirovoi rynok oruzhiya ili nashi tanki tak i budut rzhavet' v Sibirskoi taige?' (Will Russia return to the world arms market or will our tanks continue to rust in the Siberian taiga?), *Krasnaya zvezda*, 2 March 1993.

45. Mikhail Pogorelyi, 'Rossiiskoe oruzhiye—na beregakh Persidskogo zaliva' (Russian arms on the shores of the Persian Gulf), *Krasnaya zvezda*, 7 April 1995.

46. Ibid.

47. See 'Vstrecha v ministerstve oborony' (Meeting at the Ministry of Defense), *Krasnaya zvezda*, 11 May 1995.

48. See 'Plans Advance for Caspian Crude Oil Pipeline', *Oil and Gas Journal*, 30 January 1995, pp 38–9.

49. See Valery Neverov and Aleksandr Igolkin, 'Neft v mirovoi politike' (Oil in world politics), *Krasnaya zvezda*, 22 September 1994.

50. See Michael Collins Dunn, 'Gulf Security: Past and Future' in Ibrahim Ibrahim (ed) *The Gulf Crisis: Background and Consequences* (Washington, DC: Center for Contemporary Arab Studies, Georgetown University, 1992).

51. See Elmar Guseinov, 'Russian–Iraqi Trade Agreement: Prestige in Exchange for Billions', *Izvestiya*, 15 September 1994. Translated in *Current Digest of the Soviet Press*, vol 46, no 37, 1994, pp 27–8.

52. See Irina Grudinina, 'Moscow Rejects Charge of "Duplicitous Diplomacy" Towards Persian Gulf Countries', *Sevodnya*, 16 September 1995. Translated in *Current Digest of the Soviet Press*, vol 46, no 37, 1994, p 28.

53. See Vladimir Abarinov, 'The Gulf: Kozyrev and Husayn Exchange Promises', *Sevodnya*, 15 October 1995. Translated in *Current Digest of the Soviet Press*, vol 46, no 41, 1994, pp 11–12.

54. *Baghdad INA*, 10 November 1994 (in Arabic). FBIS-NES-94-21-8, 10 November 1994, p 22.

55. *Tehran Voice of the Islamic Republic of Iran*, 20 November 1994 (in English); FBIS-NES-94-224, p 68.

56. Vladimir Lenin, 'Speech Closing the Congress, 16 March 1921', in V. I. Lenin, *Collected Works*, vol 32, December 1920–August 1921 (Moscow: Progress Publishers, 1965), p 266.

57. See Robert V. Barylski, 'Russia, the West, and the Caspian Energy Hub', *Middle East Journal*, spring 1995, pp 217–32.

58. See Georgii Bovt, 'Situation in Gulf Area', *Kommersant Daily*, 11 October 1994. FBIS-SOV-94-197, pp 1–2.

59. See Boris Yeltsin's State of the Federation Message (23 February 1996), *Krasnaya zvezda*, 11 March 1996.

60. See Viktor Ivanov, 'Nationalization is Taken Seriously – The Minister Explains His Plans', *Kommersant Daily*, 14 February 1996. Translated in *Current Digest of the Soviet Press*, vol 48, no 7, p 10. See the entire issue for a set of articles on the subject of General Kulikov's proposals.

7. Revolutionary Islamism and Gulf Security in the Twenty-first Century

1. The contemporary puritan concept of *bid'a* can be traced back to the great Hanbali jurist, Ibn Taymiyya, whose writings and teachings form the core of the Wahhabi doctrine of Tawhid (strict monotheism). The concept is based on the saying attributed to the Prophet, 'any manner or way which someone invents within this religion such that manner or way is not a part of this religion is to be rejected.' The textual authentication is surah 5:3 of the Quran, 'Today I have perfected your religion for you ... and I have chosen Islam as your religion.' The central idea is that it is reprehensible to suggest that there are ways to obtain God's pleasure that were not available to the Prophet. See Iftikhar Zaman, 'Bid'ah,' in John L. Esposito, ed, *The Encyclopedia of the Modern Islamic World*, vol 1 (New York and Oxford: Oxford University Press, 1995), pp 215–16.

2. Most Muslim scholars consider the pius ancestors to be the first three generations of Muslims – the Companions of the Prophet Mohammad, ending with Anas Ibn Malik (d. 710 or 712 AD); their disciples, (al-Tabi'un); and their disciples (Tabi'i al-Tabi'un) ending with Ahmad ibn Hanbal (d. 855 AD), founder of the Hanbali school of Sunni Islamic jurisprudence, the school generally associated with the Wahhabi puritan reform movement. Later Islamic scholars who are also considered Salafis include Taqi al-din Ahmad Ibn Taymiyyah (d. 1328 AD), whose teachings influenced the Wahhabi reform movement, and Muhammad ibn Abd al-Wahhab (d. 1792), the movement's founder. The Arabian Salafis associate themselves with these Salafis, the latter two in particular, and not with the more contemporary Salafiyya reform movement of Jamal al-Din al-Afghani and Muhammad Abduh in the nineteenth and early twentieth centuries.

3. John L. Esposito, 'Political Islam and Gulf Security.' Unpublished paper prepared for the Second Annual Conference of Emirates Center for Strategic Studies and Research, Abu Dhabi, UAE, 5–8 January 1996, p 1.

4. See David E. Long, 'The Impact of the Iranian Revolution on the Arabian Peninsula and the Gulf States,' in John L. Esposito, ed, *The Iranian Revolution: Its Global Impact* (Miami: Florida International University Press, 1990), pp 100–116.

5. 'Chronology,' *The Middle East Journal* 50, no 2 (Spring 1996), p 263.

6. Robin Wright, 'Experts Ask: Did Saudi Crackdown Light Fuse of Bomb?' *Los Angeles Times*, 15 November 1995.

7. *Washington Post*, January 26, 1996, p A1.

8. *Washington Post*, November 1, 1996, p A1.

9. See R. K. Ramazani, 'Iran's Export of the Revolution: Politics, Ends and Means,' in *The Iranian Revolution*, pp 54–6.

10. See Chapter 12, 'Population Growth, the Labor Market and Gulf Security' by Michael E. Bonine.

11. The following discussion is based in part on ideas developed in David E. Long, 'The U.S. Military Presence in the Gulf: Part of the Problem or Part of the Solution? A View from the Arabian Peninsula,' (unpublished paper delivered at a conference on Islamic Activism and US Interests in the Arabian Peninsula), sponsored by the Institute of National Strategic Studies, Washington, DC, 17 January 1996.

12. For an interesting analysis study of the role of the Saudi religious establishment in the politics of this period, see Joseph Kechichian, 'The Role of the Ulama in the Politics of an Islamic State,' *International Journal of Middle East Studies* 18 (February 1986), pp 53–71.

13. As quoted in Esposito, 'Political Islam and Gulf Security,' p 15. See Judith Caesar, 'Rumblings Under the Throne: Saudi Arabian Politics' *The Nation* 251, no 21, p 762. Hawali had been highly critical of the Western military presence during the Gulf War in the widely circulated 'the Hawali Tapes.'

14. Munira A. Fakhro, 'The Uprising in Bahrain: Future Prospects for the Gulf' (unpublished paper delivered at the Gulf 2000 International Conference held in Bellagio, Italy, July 25–7, 1995), p 8, cited in Esposito, 'Political Islam and Gulf Security,' p 23.

15. Ibid., p 9.

16. Ibid.

17. Ibid.

18. *Herald* (September 1990), p 30, quoted in Esposito, 'Political Islam and Gulf Security,' p 13.

8. Boundaries, Territorial Disputes and the GCC States

Maps 1 a and b, 2 and 3 were originally published in Richard Schofield (ed), *Territorial Foundations of the Gulf States* (London: UCL Press, 1994), pp 22–3, 46 and 58.

1. Since the oil reserves of the region will last by any reckoning well into the next century, this paper will take such an interest as given.

2. A. K. S. Lambton, *State and Government in Medieval Islam: An Introduction to the Study of Islamic Political Theory: the Jurists* (Oxford: Oxford University Press, 1981), p 13.

3. George Joffe, 'Concepts of Sovereignty in the Gulf Region', in Richard Schofield (ed), *Territorial Foundations of the Gulf States* (London: UCL Press, 1994), p 79.

4. John B. Kelly, *Eastern Arabian Frontiers* (London: Faber and Faber, 1964), p 17.

5. Donal Cruise O'Brien, 'The Message from Tripoli', *Guardian*, 6 August 1982.

6. Alasdair Drysdale and Gerald H. Blake, *The Middle East and North Africa: A Political Geography* (New York: Oxford University Press, 1985), p 149.

7. Richard Schofield, 'Mending Gulf Fences', *Middle East Insight* vol 12, no 2, 1996, p 36.

8. Ali Mohamed al-Damkhi, *Invasion: Saddam Hussein's Reign of Terror in Kuwait* (London: Kuwait Research and Advertising Co Ltd, 1992), p 3.

9. When discussing the thorny problem of a boundary delimitation between Kuwait and his Najdi kingdom in the period before Sir Percy Cox imposed his line late during 1922 at Uqair, Ibn Saud had reportedly commented more than once that the boundaries of Kuwait stop at Riyadh and the boundaries of Najd stop at the walls of Kuwait city.

10. Richard Schofield, 'Borders and Territoriality in the Gulf and the Arabian Peninsula During the Twentieth Century', in Richard Schofield (ed), *Territorial Foundations of the Gulf States* (London and New York: UCL Press and St Martin's Press, 1994), p 52–3.

11. Ibid, p 41.

12. Richard Schofield, *Kuwait and Iraq: Historical Claims and Territorial Disputes*, 2nd edn (London: Royal Institute of International Affairs, 1993).

13. The Baghdad media have often commented that Kuwait is the cork in the bottle that is Iraq. In the not too distant past, a prominent Kuwaiti minister also rather neatly likened Iraq to 'a big garage with a very small door'.

14. Richard Schofield, 'Britain and the Borders of Kuwait, 1902–1913', in B. J. Slot (ed), *Kuwait: the Development of Historic Identity* (forthcoming).

15. Schofield, *Kuwait and Iraq*, p 11.

16. Maps 1a and 1b show the evolution of territorial limits and claims in southern and south-eastern Arabia, 1903–55. Map 2 shows the evolution of delimited state territory in northern Arabia, 1913 to the present. Map 3 shows the current (1997) territorial framework in southern Arabia.

17. For a detailed historical background to this and the other examples given in this section of the chapter, see Schofield: 'Borders and Territoriality', pp 1–77.

18. See Schofield: *Kuwait and Iraq*, for a development of such arguments.

19. Schofield: 'Mending Gulf Fences', p 37.

20. US State Department, Bureau of Intelligence and Research, *Geographic Notes*, vol 13, March 1991, pp 2–4.

21. *Arab Times*, 10 April 1993.

22. It had earlier been registered by Saudi Arabia with the Secretariat of the Arab League in Cairo.

23. Having said this, the effect of the incident, ironically, was to persuade Saudi Arabia to release the text of the 1965 Saudi–Qatari boundary treaty to the public. Its precise content had previously only been guessed at. So, in the space of 18 months, the texts of Saudi Arabia's border treaties with Iraq (1975 and 1981), Oman (1990) and Qatar (1965) had been released to the public and registered at what the legal community believes to be the appropriate international institutions. Already, such developments were beginning to cast aspersions on the criticisms most typically made of Arabian boundaries and, more specifically, the agreements which have introduced them: that is, that they had not been concluded in a manner which was designed to render them final and permanent.

24. Following the 30 September 1992 Khafus border post incident, a copy of the 1965 treaty (or sections thereof) was published in early October (1992) in the *Saudi Gazette*.

25. See, for example, Zakki M. A. Farsi, *National Guide and Atlas of the Kingdom of Saudi Arabia* (Riyadh, 1989).

26. A tripartite statement issued by the Foreign Ministers of Qatar, Saudi Arabia and Egypt on 20 December 1992 announced the signature of an agreement (which has remained unpublished) to form a joint Qatari–Saudi committee which would 'draw the final borders [between the states] within a year'. The most important provisions of the tripartite statement were as follows: '(a) in implementation of the border agreement concluded between the Kingdom of Saudi Arabia and the State of Qatar on ... 4 December 1965, it was agreed to append a map showing the final border line to which both states shall be committed; (b) the formation of a joint Saudi–Qatari committee in accordance with article five of the agreement to be entrusted with the task of implementing the 1965 agreement with all of its provisions and articles and the contents of this joint statement.' The Qatari–Saudi joint committee was then required to demarcate the land border in accordance with the appended map. (*BBC SWB*, 29 December 1992.)

27. Foreign Broadcast and Information Service (hereafter: FBIS), FBIS-NES-95-123, 27 June 1995, p 25.

28. Richard Schofield, 'Border Disputes in the Gulf: Past, Present and Future' in Larry Potter and Gary Sick (eds), *The Gulf in the Next Millennium* (Boulder, CO: Westview Press, forthcoming).

29. See Rouhollah K. Ramazani and Joseph A. Kechichian, *The Gulf Co-operation Council: Record and Analysis* (Charlottesville: University of Virginia Press, 1988), p 126; Fred Lawson, *Bahrain: The Modernization of Autocracy* (Boulder, CO: Westview Press, 1989), pp 133–4.

30. This was, of course, also the identical response of the GCC, Arab League, United Nations and NATO to the Iraqi invasion of Kuwait on 2 August 1990.

31. See Richard Schofield, 'Disputed Territory, the Gulf Cooperation Council and Iran', *Iranian Journal of International Affairs*, vol 5, nos 3–4, autumn 1993–winter 1994, p 618.

32. Schofield: *Kuwait and Iraq*, pp 127–32.

33. John Duke Anthony, 'The Gulf Co-operation Council in the Postwar Period: Progress and Potential in Deterrence and Defense', paper presented at the annual conference of the Middle East Studies Association of North America, Washington, DC, 23–26 November 1991, p 14.

34. Yet there was no mention of the Hawar dispute in the GCC Supreme Council's final communiqué of 25 December 1990, *BBC SWB*, ME/0957/A/9, 29 December 1990.

35. Translated text of the declaration reproduced as an appendix in Bruce Maddy-Weitzman, 'Inter-Arab relations', in A. Ayalon (ed), *Middle East Contemporary Survey 1992* (Boulder, CO: Westview Press, 1994), pp 184–5.

36. Ibid.

37. See translated text of final communiqué in FBIS-NES-94-246, 22 December 1994, pp 10–13.

38. 'Minister views peace process, Qatar dispute' in FBIS-NES-95-030, 14 February 1995.

39. See David Pike, 'Cross-border Hydrocarbon Reserves', in Richard Schofield (ed), *Territorial Foundations of the Gulf States* (London and New York: UCL Press and St Martin's Press, 1994), pp 187–99.

40. See translated text of the final communiqué in FBIS-NES-94-246, 22 December 1994, pp 10–13.

41. FBIS-NES-95-111, 9 June 1995, p 35.

42. FBIS-NES-95-133, 12 July 1995, p 28.

43. For a full, translated text of the 1974 treaty and the annexed exchange of letters see *Middle East Economic Survey*, vol 38, no 38, 19 June 1995, pp D1–D3.

44. *BBC SWB*, ME/2150 MED/1, 11 November 1994.

45. 'In this regard, the Council considered the Republic of Iraq's recognition of the State of Kuwait's sovereignty and territorial integrity and international boundaries with the Republic of Iraq as stipulated by Resolutions 687 and 833 and viewed it as an important step towards Iraq's implementation of all relevant Security Council resolutions': extract from final communiqué of the Supreme Council of the GCC at the fifteenth annual summit in Manama, 21 December 1995. (FBIS-NES-94-246, 22 December 1994, p 10.)

46. See Richard Schofield, 'The Last Missing Fence in the Desert: The Saudi–Yemeni Boundary', *Geopolitics and International Boundaries*, vol 1, no 3, 1996.

47. Ibid. At least this was the first occasion upon which a San'a government had forwarded a territorial claim that could be depicted cartographically.

48. In so doing, it was trying to approximate the territorial extent of the Greater Yemen (Bilad al-Yemen) of seventeenth-century tradition.

49. Yemen formally applied for full membership of the GCC at the Doha summit in December 1996. Though the application has been temporarily shelved – with only Qatar expressing any enthusiasm for the proposal – its very occurrence led to speculation in the Gulf media that Yemeni membership of the GCC would be linked to its compliance with Saudi desiderata on the border question.

50. The December 1990 agreement actually stated that 'the two states' should refer the dispute to the ICJ should no progress result from continuing bilateral efforts to reach an out-of-court settlement. This would later become one of Bahrain's chief objections to Qatar unilaterally referring the dispute to the courts during the summer of 1991. Whether or not the 1990 agreement had committed Bahrain and Qatar to refer the case jointly to the courts would not be resolved by the ICJ until 1 July 1994. Then, by a majority vote, the ICJ dismissed Bahrain's argument, ruling that Qatar had been within its rights to refer the dispute unilaterally, even if its application had been 'incomplete'.

51. Unofficial communiqué no 91/21 issued by the International Court of Justice, 8 July 1991. Only on 15 February 1995, as the ICJ made its most recent ruling, the then Qatari Crown Prince (now Emir) Sheikh Hamad thanked King Fahd for his mediation efforts, 'which had led to the signing of the [December] 1990 accord'. (FBIS-NES-95-033, 17 February 1995.)

52. When Britain departed the Gulf politically in 1971, Saudi Arabia accepted responsibility for mediation of the Hawar dispute. Saudi mediation efforts have been channelled through the good offices of the GCC since its inception early in 1981, though successes in the decade thereafter were in controlling the dispute rather than in making any great strides towards solving it. During March 1982, for example, a meeting of the GCC Council of Ministers reviewed the Hawar dispute pursuant to conspicuous muscle-flexing in Doha and Manama. At this Bahrain and Qatar agreed to 'freeze the situation and not to cause an escalation of the dispute'. (Ramazani and Kechichian: *The Gulf Cooperation Council*, p 126.)

53. Zubara has retained an enduring symbolic significance for the ruling family in

Bahrain. This is because of its position as the ancestral home of the al Khalifah dynasty; its first ruler was buried here. From the 1870s onwards, Bahrain has claimed rather ill-defined rights to the locality, ranging from full sovereignty, to jurisdiction over Bahraini nationals in Qatar, to private law rights. The very terminology employed by the ICJ to describe Bahrain's concern with Zubara – 'historic interest' – suggests that there is no possibility whatsoever of any sovereign claim by the island state to the locality being entertained by the courts.

54. 'Qatar hopes that the efforts of King Fahd of Saudi Arabia will continue and is ready to withdraw its request to the International Court of Justice if an acceptable settlement is reached': translated comments of Crown Prince Sheikh Hamad bin Khalifah al Thani in FBIS-NES-95-033, 17 February 1995.

55. For a brief summary of the history of the dispute, see Schofield: 'Borders and Territoriality', pp 34–41. For a treatment sympathetic to Iran, see Pirouz Mojtahed-Zadeh, *The Islands of Tunb and Abu Musa: An Iranian Argument in Search of Peace and Co-operation in the Persian Gulf*, Occasional Paper 15 (London: Centre of Near and Middle Eastern Studies, SOAS, 1985). Also see Richard Schofield, *Unfinished Business: Iran, the UAE, Abu Musa and the Tunbs* (London: Royal Institute of International Affairs, forthcoming).

56. For text of MOU see Arab Research Centre, *Round Table Discussion on the Dispute Over the Gulf Islands* (London: Arab Research Centre, 1993), p 14.

57. Sharjah refused, even though the request was unexceptional in the realm of contemporary Gulf affairs, on the basis that this might turn out to be the thin end of the wedge; requests for security passes might soon be followed by requests for visas, and so on.

58. *Iran Focus*, November 1992, p 2.

59. Nowhere was this illustrated better than in the witty remark from Abbas Maleki, Minister of State at the Iranian Foreign Ministry: 'The volume of press coverage on Abu Musa is bigger than the island itself' (*Iran Focus*, November 1992, p 2).

60. *BBC SWB*, ME/1573/A/7, 29 December 1992.

61. Ibid.

62. *Middle East Economic Survey*, 11 January 1993, p C3.

63. Text reproduced in the *Gulf 2000* electronic library.

64. See comments of General Binford Peay, Commander of US Forces in the Middle East, before the Senate Armed Forces Committee in Washington, DC, as reported by Reuters (15 February 1995).

65. Anthony Cordesman, 'Defence: Spending Priorities', paper presented to 'Timewatch GCC: Economic Restructuring and Business Prospects', a conference organized by the Royal Institute of International Affairs, Queen Elizabeth II Conference Centre, London, 15 November 1995.

66. FBIS-NES-95-131, 10 July 1995, p 4.

67. For a more considered analysis, see Richard Schofield, *Unfinished Business: Iran, the UAE, Abu Musa and the Tunbs* (London: Royal Institute of International Affairs, forthcoming).

68. Schofield: 'Mending Gulf Fences', p 41.

9. The Greater Middle East Co-prosperity Sphere

1. Shimon Peres, *The New Middle East* (New York: Henry Holt, 1993).

2. Elsewhere I have distinguished between social or cultural Islamists on the one hand, and political Islamists on the other. The former are prevalent in the Muslim Brethren

organization and are primarily concerned with social and cultural issues, such as segregating the sexes, banning alcohol sales, and generally implementing Islamic law, or shari'a. Political Islamists emphasize a larger Third World discourse of imperialism and social justice, but give it an Islamic hue. Political Islamists are usually independents or belong to Muslim Brethren splinter groups. See Glenn E. Robinson, *Defensive Democratization in Jordan* (forthcoming).

3. A good statement of the nationalist vision, little heard in the West, can be found in Jamil Hilal, *Istratijiyat isra'il al-iqtisadiya l'il-sharq al-awsat* (Israel's economic strategy in the Middle East) (Beirut: Institute for Palestine Studies, 1995).

4. Michael Barnett, 'Regional Security After the Gulf War', paper presented at the conference on 'The Middle East: After the Guns Fell Silent', University of Utah, May 1995, p 22.

5. For the best statement of this theory, see Bruce Russett, *Grasping the Democratic Peace* (Princeton, NJ: Princeton University Press, 1993).

6. Interestingly, the democratic peace thesis is said to have played a decisive role in causing Israel – particularly Shimon Peres – to agree to a large Palestinian elected council. Instead of the actually constituted 88-seat body, Israel originally wanted a legislative council only a fraction of that size. In theory, a more democratic Palestine will naturally have less hostile relations with a democratic Israel, while an authoritarian Palestine would be more war-like.

7. The politics of the Palestinian Authority are analysed in Glenn E. Robinson, *Building a Palestinian State: The Incomplete Revolution* (Bloomington: Indiana University Press, 1997).

8. Ilan Peleg, 'The Peace Process and Israel's Political Culture: A *Kulturkampf* in the Making', paper presented at the annual meeting of the American Political Science Association, Chicago, 31 August 1995.

9. The figures in the following two paragraphs come from John Page, Chief Economist for the Middle East and North Africa Region at the World Bank, and are found in his work *Economic Prospects and the Role of Regional Development Finance Institutions, Regional Economic Development in the Middle East: Opportunities and Risks* (Washington, DC: Center for Policy Analysis on Palestine, December 1995).

10. For further analysis on this and related issues, see David Waldner, 'The Politics of Peace and Prosperity: Economic Interdependence and National Security in the Middle East' in Bahman Baktiari (ed), *Essays in Honor of R. K. Ramazani* (forthcoming).

11. Larry Diamond, Juan J. Linz and Seymour Martin Lipset (eds), *Democracy in Developing Countries*, 4 vols (Boulder, CO: Lynne Rienner, 1987–94).

12. Peter Smith, 'Crisis and Democracy in Latin America', *World Politics*, vol 43, July 1991, pp 608–34.

13. Steven Heydemann, 'Taxation without Representation: Authoritarianism and Economic Liberalization in Syria', in Ellis Goldberg, Resat Kasaba and Joel Migdal (eds), *Rules and Rights in the Middle East: Democracy, Law, and Society* (Seattle: University of Washington Press, 1993).

14. Immanuel Wallerstein, *The Modern World-System*, 3 vols (San Diego, CA: Academic Press, 1974–80).

15. For a further discussion on compradors, see Fernando Henrique Cardoso and Enzo Faletto, *Dependency and Development in Latin America* (Berkeley, CA: University of California Press, 1979).

10. Economics and Security in the Gulf

1. This calculation employs data obtained from the OPEC statistical bulletins for 1983, 1984 and 1986.

2. Proven reserve statistics are those provided by British Petroleum. Production figures are available in the *Asian Energy Yearbook* (London: Petroleum Economist Ltd, 1995).

3. Robert Mabro first articulated the OPEC control mechanism options. Consider also elaborations and qualifications in David J. Teece, 'OPEC Behavior: An Alternative View', in James M. Griffin and David J. Teece (eds), *OPEC Behavior and World Oil Prices* (London: George Allen, 1982), pp 64–93. But to explain what happened in 1985–86, one must resort to the dynamics of the administered price model in order to see how Saudi Arabia was able to punish price cheaters and drive marginal producers out of the market. See Charles F. Doran, *Myth, Oil, and Politics: Introduction to the Political Economy of Petroleum* (New York: Free Press, 1977), pp 138–41, for an early explication of how Saudi Arabia could exercise this leadership. Saudi Arabia, however, does not exercise judgement independent of opinion inside OPEC, or external to it as far away as Washington, DC, as ultimately became clear.

4. See Siamack Shojai (ed), *The New Global Oil Market: Understanding Energy Issues in the World Economy* (Westport, CT: Praeger, 1995); Geoffrey Heal and Graciela Chichilnisky, *Oil and the International Economy* (New York: Oxford University Press, 1991); and J. E. Hartshorn, *Oil Trade: Politics and Prospects* (Cambridge: Cambridge University Press, 1993).

5. Edward N. Krapels, 'The Fundamentals of the World Oil Market of the 1980s', in Wilfred L. Kohl (ed), *After the Oil Collapse: OPEC, the United States, and the World Oil Market* (Baltimore: Johns Hopkins University Press, 1991), pp 43–66.

6. Amory B. Lovins and L. Hunter Lovins, 'Drill Rigs and Battleships are the Answer! (But What was the Question?): Oil Efficiency, Economic Rationality, and Security', in Robert G. Reed III and Fereidun Feshariaki (eds), *The Oil Market in the 1990s: Challenges for the New Era* (Boulder, CO: Westview Press, 1989), pp 83–138.

7. John L. Kennedy, 'The Shape of World Oil Markets in the 1990s', in Shankar Sharma and Joseph L. H. Tan (eds), *Global Oil Trends: The Asia-Pacific Market in the 1990s* (Singapore: ASEAN Economic Research Unit, Institute of Southeast Asian Studies, 1991), pp 38–55.

8. See Fereidun Feshariaki and David T. Isaak, *OPEC, the Gulf, and the World Petroleum Market: A Study in Government Policy and Downstream Operations* (Boulder, CO: Westview Press, 1983). For one of the most informing discussions of the oil industry in the advanced industrial economy, consider Paul H. Frankel, 'The Changing Structure of the Oil Industry', in Reed and Feshariaki (eds), *The Oil Market in the 1990s.*

9. For these problems of indigenous development even in the largest and most sophisticated economies like that of the USA, see G. John Ikenberry, 'The Limits of State Building', in his *Reasons of State: Oil Politics and the Capacities of American Government* (Ithaca, NY: Cornell University Press, 1988), pp 104–37.

10. Alan Gelb and associates, *Oil Windfalls: Blessing or Curse?* (New York: World Bank/ Oxford University Press, 1988).

11. An excellent overview is Robert Z. Lawrence, 'Emerging Regional Arrangements: Building Blocks or Stumbling Blocks?', in Richard O'Brien (ed), *Finance and the International Economy 5: The AMEX Bank Review Prize Essays* (Oxford: Oxford University Press, 1991), pp 22–35.

12. Rodney Wilson, 'The Economic Relations of the Middle East: Toward Europe or Within the Region?', *Middle East Journal*, vol 48, no 2, 1994, pp 268–87; Mary Ann Tetreault and Haya al-Mughni, 'Modernization and its Discontents: State and Gender in Kuwait', *Middle East Journal*, vol 49, no 3, 1995, pp 403–17.

13. Joseph Wright Twinam, *The Gulf, Cooperation and the Council: An American Perspective* (Washington, DC: Middle East Policy Council, 1992), pp 173–89.

14. Rouhollah K. Ramazani and Joseph A. Kechichian, *The Gulf Cooperation Council: Record and Analysis* (with a Foreword by Sultan Bin Mohamed Al-Qasimi) (Charlottesville: University of Virginia Press, 1988).

15. 'Complex Legal and Bureaucratic Restraints on the Private Sector are Probably the Most Intractable Obstacles to the Development of Efficient Middle East Markets', *Middle East Economic Digest*, 6 January 1995, pp 2–3.

16. 'GCC Banks on the Offset Factor', *Middle East Economic Digest*, 7 April 1995, pp 4–5.

17. Rouhollah K. Ramazani, 'Iran's Foreign Policy: Both North and South', *Middle East Journal*, vol 46, no 3, 1992, pp 393–412; Phebe Marr, 'The United States, Europe, and the Middle East: An Uneasy Triangle', *Middle East Journal*, 48, no 2, 1994, pp 211–25; David E. Long, 'Saudi Arabia in the 1990s: Plus ça change … ', in Charles F. Doran and Stephen W. Buck (eds), *Gulf, Energy, and Global Security* (Boulder, CO: Lynne Rienner, 1991), pp 85–106.

18. Andrew W. Parasiliti, 'Origins of the Gulf War and the Iraq Cycle of Power and Role', unpublished PhD Dissertation. Johns Hopkins, SAIS, 1996.

19. Philip Robins, 'Can Gulf Monarchies Survive the Oil Bust?', *Middle East Quarterly*, vol 1, no 4, 1994, pp 13–22.

20. Vahan Zanoyan, 'After the Oil Boom', *Foreign Affairs*, vol 74, no 6, 1995, p 2.

21. 'Tremors', *The Economist*, 18 November 1995, p 46.

22. 'A Payments Surplus for Saudi Arabia?', *Middle East Economic Digest*, 25 June 1995, p 4.

23. *International Investor*, New York, September 1994.

24. 'Iran Puts Its Finances in Order', *Middle East Economic Digest*, 19 August 1994, pp 2–3.

11. Social Transformation, Changing Expectations and Gulf Security

1. See for example, John Duke Anthony, *Arab States of the Lower Gulf: People, Politics, Petroleum* (Washington, DC: Middle East Institute, 1975), p 220.

2. See Hazem Beblawi and Giacomo Luciani (eds), *The Rentier State* (London: Croom Helm, 1987).

3. On generations, see Dale F. Eickelman, 'Oman's Next Generation: Challenges and Prospects', in H. Richard Sindelar and J. E. Peterson (eds), *Crosscurrents in the Gulf* (London: Routledge, 1988); on the new middle class, see Manfred Halpern, *The Politics of Social Change in the Middle East and North Africa* (Princeton, NJ: Princeton University Press, 1963).

4. See, for example, Neil Hicks and Ghanim al-Najjar, 'The Utility of Tradition: Civil Society in Kuwait', in Augustus Richard Norton (ed), *Civil Society in the Middle East*, vol 1, (Leiden: E. J. Brill, 1995); and my 'Civil Society in the Arab Gulf States', in ibid, vol 2, (1996) both abstracted in Jillian Schwedler (ed), *Toward Civil Society in the Middle East? A Primer* (Boulder, CO: Lynne Rienner, 1995).

5. See Gregory Gause, *Oil Monarchies: Domestic and Security Challenges in the Arab Gulf States* (New York: Council on Foreign Relations Press, 1994); Mary Ann Tetreault, 'Civil Society in Kuwait: Protected Spaces and Women's Rights', *Middle East Journal*, vol 47, no 2, 1993; Mary Ann Tetreault and Haya al-Mughni, 'Modernization and Its Discontents: State and Gender in Kuwait', *Middle East Journal*, vol 49, no 3, 1995; Shafeeq Ghabra, 'Voluntary Associations in Kuwait: The Foundation of a New System?' *Middle East Journal*, vol 45, no 2, 1991; and Christian Koch's 'Interest Groups and Associational Life in the Political

Development of the State of Kuwait', PhD dissertation, University of Erlangen-Nurnberg (forthcoming).

6. Jill Crystal, *Oil and Politics in the Gulf: Rulers and Merchants in Kuwait and Qatar* (Cambridge: Cambridge University Press, 1995).

7. I make this argument at length in *Oil and Politics* and focus on it in the invasion and post-war period in ch 5 of *Kuwait: The Transformation of an Oil State* (Boulder, CO: Westview Press, 1989).

8. See Fuad Khuri, *Tribe and State in Bahrain: The Transformation of Social and Political Authority in an Arab State* (Chicago, IL: University of Chicago Press, 1980); Fred Lawson, *Bahrain: The Modernization of Autocracy* (Boulder, CO: Westview Press, 1989).

9. See Mary Ann Tetréault, *The Kuwait Petroleum Corporation and the Economics of the New World Order* (Westport, CT: Quorum, 1995).

10. See Haya al-Mughni, *Women in Kuwait: The Politics of Gender* (London: al-Saqi Books, 1993) who makes the argument very well using case-studies of different women's groups that often carry other interests, for example those of merchant families.

11. Of course, many argue that had the Assembly not been shut down prior to the invasion it might have affected the foreign policy decisions preceding and related to the invasion.

12. Importing foreigners was one issue; marrying them has now become another in several Gulf states. In Qatar, it has produced laws, apparently easily evaded, against such marriages in an effort to produce sufficient marriageable men for Qatari women. In Kuwait, it has resulted in a rather different pressure: a lobby by Kuwaiti women married to non-nationals demanding citizenship rights for their spouses and children.

13. Amnesty International reported that they were charged with creating an illegal organization and distributing pamphlets denouncing Oman for staging a conference that Israel attended. After the 1994 arrests of the Islamists, Omani authorities accused foreign parties of financing the militant group, the first ever dismantled in Oman. *Jordan Times*, 11 November 1995, p 2.

14. Indeed, on visiting Kuwait after the war, it was striking to witness to what extent the government has sought to wipe out any visible reminder of the occupation. No bombed out buildings have been saved as a memorial, no museum to the occupation built. The only indication that the ruling family wants the occupation remembered is a small memorial, in the form of a car, maintained by a member of the family who headed the Olympic Committee. On the other hand, the memory itself is not only quite alive but memorialized in little private museums, corners of buildings where memorabilia of the occupation (twisted charred objects) are retained. Thus, the memory of the occupation has been privatized, and has become a construct of civil society rather than the state.

15. Initially the majority of both the Jordanian and Palestinian expatriate communities in Kuwait, and both the government of Jordan and the leadership of the then Palestine Liberation Organization, were uncritical of the Iraqi invasion of Kuwait.

16. Interview with Dr Mohammed Hussein Gholum Ali, 19 September 1995, presently researching the bedouin migration, Sociology Department, Kuwait University.

17. *New York Times*, 15 April 1996, C1.

18. Amnesty International, *Report 1995*, pp 66–7.

19. Walt W. Rostow, *The Stages of Economic Growth: A Non-Communist Manifesto* (Cambridge: Cambridge University Press, 1967).

20. See Eickelman: 'Oman's Next Generation'.

21. See Jill Crystal, 'Authoritarianism and Its Adversaries in the Arab World', *World Politics*, vol 46, no 2, 1994.

22. See *Middle East International*, 14 April 1995, p 11.

23. See Gause: *Oil Monarchies*.

24. One author who makes a strong economic argument is Khaldun al-Naqeeb, *Society and State in the Gulf and Arab Peninsula: A Different Perspective* (London: Routledge, 1990). The following summary draws from my review of his book in *World Politics* (note 21). He grounds his explanation for authoritarianism, especially in the pre-oil period, in the economic and, to him, consequent political processes accompanying colonialism. State violence is a function of state position in the world economy; authoritarianism is the culmination of a centuries'-long economic transformation. Al-Naqeeb argues that each historical period of economic activity generates a particular political form. Unlike many authors whose histories of the area begin with oil (a point of departure appropriately criticized by, for example, Muhammad al-Rumaihi in *Beyond Oil: Unity and Development in the Gulf* [London: al-Saqi, 1983], al-Naqeeb's analysis links pre- and post-oil politics. He focuses on three periods. The first (lasting until the seventeenth century), was a flourishing economy based on speculative trade, linking coastal cities to interior tribes and to larger trade networks outside the Gulf. This trade carried Islam, creating a unified culture. Central political power, the Ottoman state, was weak, and this was why trade flourished: state power is stifling. Locally, desert and settled urban tribal leaders ruled in alliance, balanced against urban merchants. This economy was destroyed in the second, imperial, era when Britain, under the guise of eliminating piracy and the slave and arms trades, replaced regional trade networks with a pearl-based European trade which Britain could control. The political counterpart of this new economy was the fragmentation of the region into small units dominated by increasingly dynastic, familial leaders kept in place by treaties, by force, and by a new political instrument – borders – which linked sovereignty to places, not people. The coastal cities lost power to the tribal hinterlands where colonial penetration was weaker. Resistance to this new system flowed first from this hinterland (the Wahhabi movement), later from the cities as Arab nationalism, which Britain manipulated by creating borders, limiting the free movement of dissidents, historically an important check on ruling authority. The third period, giving rise to what he characterizes as contemporary authoritarianism, began with oil. Oil revenues concentrated power in the state. Initially this state was benignly bureaucratic but, as it expanded, absorbing independent social institutions, it created opposition among remnants of the old labor force, bedouin and pearl divers who had become educated middle-class bureaucrats. At first the state tried to depoliticize these groups by buying them off. When these efforts failed, rulers, perhaps because they had never been forced, owing to oil revenues, to develop other more subtle ways of dealing with opposition, increasingly resorted to terror. Although oil revenues can postpone the day of reckoning, al-Naqeeb argues that the limits inherent in dependent state capitalism and the necessarily stifling and wasteful bureaucratic control that dependency creates ultimately absorb even these massive oil revenues and inhibit growth. The exhaustion of oil revenues ushers in a new phase of limited growth which generates new political pressures. The regimes contain this new pressure with more violence, leaving them more dependent on the West for related technology. To al-Naqeeb, what he characterizes as authoritarianism in the Gulf belongs to a family of authoritarian outcomes that colonialism produces; however, the particular form that emerges in the Gulf is also particularly characteristic of oil economies. With this last observation he links the older dependency-based writing to the new and growing body of literature on the *rentier* state, a literature which argues that oil, by freeing rulers from their dependence on domestic revenue sources, frees them from the demands for democratic participation that accompany the provision of taxes. The result is a movement away from democracy: no taxation, hence no representation.

12. Population Growth, the Labor Market and Gulf Security

1. Nasra M. Shah, 'Structural Changes in the Receiving Country and Future Labor Migration: The Case of Kuwait', paper presented at the Annual Meeting of the Middle East Studies Association, Research Triangle Park, North Carolina, 11–14 November 1993, p 2.

2. Birks Sinclair and Associates Ltd (BSAL), 'GCC Market Report 1992' (Durham, England: Mountjoy Research Centre, 1992); BSAL, 'GCC and Kuwait Update' (Durham, England: Mountjoy Research Centre, 1992).

3. See Michael E. Bonine, 'Population and Labor After the Gulf War: Trends for the 1990s', *Middle East Insight*, vol 12, no 2, 1996, pp 37–40.

4. Ibid, pp 38–9.

5. Shah: 'Structural Changes', p 10.

6. Sharon Stanton Russell and Muhammad Ali Al-Ramadhan, 'Kuwait's Migration Policy Since the Gulf Crisis: Change or Continuity?', paper presented at the annual meeting of the Middle East Studies Association, Research Triangle Park, North Carolina, 11–14 November 1993.

7. BSAL, 'Kingdom of Saudi Arabia: 1992 Population Census, Note on the Preliminary Results' (Durham, England: Mountjoy Research Centre, 1992), p 1.

8. Ibid, p 2.

9. BSAL: 'GCC Market Report 1992', pp 89–107.

10. Ibid, p 90.

11. Ibid.

12. See also Bonine: 'Population and Labor After the Gulf War'.

13. BSAL: 'GCC Market Report 1992', p 92.

14. Ibid.

15. Ibid, p 106.

16. Ibid, pp 109–10.

17. Ibid, pp 60–61. However, if the November 1993 Omani census is correct (see text below), then the 537,060 non-nationals of the census means that BSAL's 1992 estimate of 380,003 expatriates is considerably too small, although the census figure is basically the same percentage as BSAL's estimate, 26.6 per cent compared to BSAL's 26.3 per cent.

18. Ibid, p 62.

19. For a brief overview, see Bonine: 'Population and Labor After the Gulf War'.

20. Russell and Al-Ramadhan: 'Kuwait's Migration Policy', pp 6–7.

21. Ibid, p 2.

22. Ibid, p 6, Table 1.

23. BSAL: 'GCC Market Report 1992', p 44.

24. Shah: 'Structural Changes', p 9.

25. Ibid, p 16.

26. BASL: 'GCC Market Report 1992', p 45.

27. Russell and Al-Ramadhan: 'Kuwait's Migration Policy', p 2.

28. Shah: 'Structural Changes', p 13.

29. Russell and Al-Ramadhan: 'Kuwait's Migration Policy', p 2.

30. *Arab Times*, 12 September 1993, cited in Shah: 'Structural Changes', p 16.

31. BASL: 'GCC Market Report 1992', pp 48–9.

32. Population Reference Bureau, *1995 World Population Data Sheet* (Washington, DC: Population Reference Bureau, 1995).

33. Note the rates for the countries of the Middle East in ibid. See also Michael E. Bonine, 'Population, Poverty, and Politics: Contemporary Middle East Cities in Crisis', in Michael E. Bonine (ed), *Population, Poverty, and Politics in Middle East Cities* (Gainesville, FL: University Press of Florida, forthcoming).

34. J. S. Birks and C. A. Sinclair, *Arab Manpower: The Crisis of Development* (London: Croom Helm, 1980), p 16.

35. J. S. Birks, 'The Demographic Challenge in the Arab Gulf', in B. R. Pridham (ed), *The Arab Gulf and the Arab World* (London: Croom Helm, 1988), p 145.

36. However, if BSAL is correct in its assertion of the underreporting of non-nationals in the 1992 Saudi census, then the non-national population would be even larger. See BSAL: 'Kingdom of Saudi Arabia'; and Birks Sinclair Ltd, 'Saudi Arabia to the 90s' (Durham, England: Mountjoy Research Centre, 1989). Since my mid-year 1996 estimates of the GCC total are 9.1 million more persons than BSAL's 1992 figure of 17.7 million, BSAL's estimates may certainly have been too conservative. My 1996 total reflects in particular extrapolations from the much larger populations enumerated in the September/October 1992 Kingdom of Saudi Arabia Population census (16.93 million), the November 1993 Omani census (2.02 million, and the December 1995 UAE census (2.38 million), as well as recent official estimates from the remaining states.

37. Shah: 'Structural Changes', p 14.

38. Ibid, p 20.

39. Ibid, p 17.

40. Birks and Sinclair: *Arab Manpower*, p 348.

41. Shah: 'Structural Changes', p 8.

13. Health, Education, Gender and the Security of the Gulf

1. See J. D. Latham, R. B. Sergeant and M. J. L. Young (eds), *Religion, Learning and Science in the Abbasid Period* (Cambridge: Cambridge University Press, 1990).

2. See Franz Rosenthal, *Science and Medicine in Islam: A Collection of Essays* (Aldershot, England: Gower, 1990). See also Ibn Qayyim al-Jawziyah Muhammad Ibn Abi Bakr, *Al-Tibb al-Nabawi* (Beirut: Dar al Kutub al Ilmiyah, 1988).

3. See Mai Yamani, 'Introduction' in Mai Yamani (ed), *Feminism and Islam: Legal and Literary Perspectives* (London: Ithaca Press, 1996).

4. See Mai Yamani, 'Formality and Propriety in the Hijaz', unpublished PhD dissertation, Oxford University, 1990.

5. See Mai Yamani 'You are What You Cook: Cuisine and Class in Mecca', in Richard Tapper and Sami Zubeida (eds), *The Culinary Cultures of the Middle East* (London: I.B.Tauris, 1994).

6. John C. Wilkinson, *Arabia's Frontiers: The Story of Britain's Boundary Drawing in the Desert* (London: I.B.Tauris, 1994).

7. A. Gargash, 'Prospects for Conflict and Cooperation: The Gulf Toward the Year 2000', paper presented at 'Gulf 2000: Future Prospects for the Gulf', 3rd International Conference, Bellagio, Italy, 25–27 July 1995.

8. R. Schofield, 'Border Disputes in the Gulf: Past, Present and Future', paper presented at 'Gulf 2000: Future Prospects for the Gulf', 2nd International Conference, Abu Dhabi, 1995.

9. The RUSI International Security Review, London, 1996.

10. F. Al-Mazidi, *The Future of the Gulf* (London: I.B.Tauris, 1993), p 39.

11. Ibid, p 57.

12. See M. Fakhro, 'The Uprising in Bahrain: An Assessment', paper presented at 'Gulf 2000: Future Prospects for the Gulf', 3rd International Conference, Bellagio, Italy, 25–27 July 1995.

13. During the first half of the century, slaves did household jobs. Slavery was abolished during the reign of King Faisal in 1965.

14. See Haya al-Mughni, *Women in Kuwait: The Politics of Gender* (London: al-Saqi Books, 1993).

15. The Middle East Executive Reports, vol 5, no 5, 1982, p 22.

16. See US Department of State Report, March 1996.

17. See N. Hijab, *Woman Power: The Arab Debate on Women and Work* (Cambridge: Cambridge University Press, 1988).

18. See 'Educational Development in Figures until 1410 A.H.', Saudi Arabian Ministry of Information, 1989.

19. See Ayman al-Yassini, *Religion and State in Saudi Arabia* (Boulder, CO: Westview Press, 1985), p 61.

20. See Fouad al-Farsy, *Saudi Arabia: A Case Study in Development* (London: KPI, 1986).

21. See Mai Yamani, 'Birth and Behaviour in a Hospital in Saudi Arabia', in British Society for Middle Eastern Studies (BRISMES) Bulletin 13, no 2, 1987.

22. See Peter Kandela, 'Primary Health Care in the Arab World: Book Reviews', Information Access Company, 5 September 1992.

23. Gareth Griffiths, 'Saudi Health Care Market Still Buoyant', *Financial Times*, 28 January 1983.

24. Brendan Keenan, 'Irish Group Wins $20 million Saudi Health Contract', *Financial Times*, 18 January 1985.

25. See 'Summit Health Signed a pact with Saudi Arabia', *Los Angeles Times*, 21 February 1995.

26. See Y. Al-Mazrua and S. Al-Shammari, 'Community Participation and Attitudes of Decision Makers Towards Community Involvement in Health Development in Saudi Arabia', *Bulletin of the World Health Organization*, vol 69, no 1, 1991, pp 43–9.

Bibliography

Abasov, M. T. (ed). *Chernyi Yanvar* (Black January) (Baku: Azerneshr, 1990).

Addleton, Jonathan S. *Undermining the Centre: The Gulf Migration and Pakistan* (New York: Oxford University Press, 1993).

Alaolmolki, Nozar. *The Persian Gulf Region in the Twenty-first Century: Stability and Change* (Lanham, MD: University Press of America, 1996).

Alnasrawi, Abbas. *The Economy of Iraq* (London: Greenwood Press, 1994).

Alstadt, Audrey L. *The Azerbaijani Turks: Power and Identity under Russian Rule* (Stanford, CA: Hoover Institution Press, 1992).

Anthony, John D. *Arab States of the Lower Gulf: People, Politics, Petroleum* (Washington, DC: Middle East Institute, 1975).

— 'The Gulf Co-operation Council in the Postwar Period: Progress and Potential in Deterrence and Defense', paper presented at the annual conference of the Middle East Studies Association of North America, Washington, DC, 23–26 November 1991.

Arab Research Centre. *Round Table Discussion on the Dispute over the Gulf Islands* (London: Arab Research Centre, 1993).

Asian Energy Yearbook (London: Petroleum Economist Ltd, 1995.

Ayoubi, Nazih. *Political Islam: Religion and Politics in the Arab World* (London: Routledge, 1991).

Bahgat, Gawdat. 'Regional Peace and Stability in the Gulf', *Security Dialogue*, vol 26, no 3 (New York: Sage Publications, 1995).

— 'The changing economic and political environment in the Gulf monarchies', *Journal of Social, Political and Economic Studies* 20, Fall 1995.

Bakhash, Shaul. *The Reign of the Ayatollahs: Iran and the Islamic Revolution* (New York: Basic Books, 1984).

Barnett, Michael. 'Regional Security after the Gulf War', paper presented at the conference on 'The Middle East: After the Guns Fell Silent', University of Utah, May 1995.

Barylski, Robert V. 'Central Asia and the Post-Soviet Military System in the Formative Year: 1992', *Central Asia Monitor*, no 6, 1992.

— 'The Caucasus, Central Asia, and the Near-Abroad Syndrome', *Central Asia Monitor*, vol 2, nos 5 and 6, 1993.

— 'The Russian Federation and Eurasia's Islamic Crescent', *Europe–Asia Studies*, vol 46, no 3, 1994.

— 'Russia, the West, and the Caspian Energy Hub', *Middle East Journal*, Spring 1995.

Beblawi, Hazem and Giacomo Luciani (eds). *The Rentier State* (London: Croom Helm, 1987).

Bhargava, Pradeep. *Political Economy of the Gulf States* (New Delhi: South Asian Publishers, 1989).

Bill, James A. 'Resurgent Islam in the Persian Gulf', *Foreign Affairs*, vol 63, no 5, 1984.

Birks, J. S. 'The Demographic Challenge in the Arab Gulf', in B. R. Pridham (ed), *The Arab Gulf and the Arab World* (London: Croom Helm, 1988).

Birks, J. S. and C. A. Sinclair. *Arab Manpower: The Crisis of Development* (London: Croom Helm, 1980).

Birks Sinclair and Associates Ltd. 'GCC and Kuwait Update' (Durham, England: Mountjoy Research Centre, 1992).

— 'GCC Market Report 1992' (Durham, England: Mountjoy Research Centre, 1992).

— 'Kingdom of Saudi Arabia: 1992 Population Census, Note on the Preliminary Results' (Durham, England: Mountjoy Research Centre, 1992).

— 'Saudi Arabia to the 90s' (Durham, England: Mountjoy Research Centre, 1989).

Bonine, Michael E. 'Population and Labor After the Gulf War: Trends for the 1990s', *Middle East Insight*, vol 12, no 2, 1996.

— (ed) *Population, Poverty, and Politics in Middle East Cities* (Gainesville, FL: University Press of Florida, forthcoming).

BP Annual Statistical Review (London: British Petroleum, 1995).

Builder, Carl H. and Theodore W. Karasik. *Organizing, Training and Equipping the Air Force for Crises and Lesser Conflicts* (Santa Monica, CA: Rand Corporation, 1995).

Caesar, Judith. 'Rumblings Under the Throne: Saudi Arabian Politics', *The Nation*, vol 251, 17 December 1990.

Cardoso, Fernando H. and Enzo Faletto. *Dependency and Development in Latin America* (Berkeley, CA: University of California Press, 1979).

Chubin, Shahram. *Security in the Persian Gulf: Domestic Political Factors* (Montclair, NJ: Allanheld Osman, 1981).

— *Iran's National Security Policy: Capabilities, Intentions, and Impact* (Washington, DC: Carnegie Endowment for International Peace, 1994).

— and Charles Tripp, *Iran–Saudi Arabia Relations and Regional Order*, Adelphi Paper 304 (Oxford: Oxford University Press, 1996).

Clawson, Patrick. 'Iran's Challenge to the West: How, When, and Why?' *Washington Institute Policy Papers*, no 33, 1993.

— 'U.S.–GCC Security Relations, II: Growing Domestic Economic and Political Problems', *Strategic Forum*, no 40, August 1995 (Washington, DC: National Defense University).

— 'U.S. Sanctions on Iran', *The Emirates Occasional Papers*, no 8, 1997 (Abu Dhabi: Emirates Center for Strategic Studies and Research).

Cordesman, Anthony H. *The Gulf and the West: Stategic Relations and Military Realities* (London: Mansell, 1988).

— *Iran and Iraq – The Threat from the Northern Gulf* (Boulder, CO: Westview Press, 1994).

— 'Iran and Iraq and Strategic Developments in the Gulf: A Graphic Summary' (Washington, DC: Center for Strategic and International Studies, October 1995) (unpublished).

— 'Defence: Spending Priorities', paper presented to 'Timewatch GCC: Economic Restructuring and Business Prospects', a conference organized by the Royal Institute of International Affairs, Queen Elizabeth II Conference Centre, London, 15 November 1995.

Crystal, Jill. *Kuwait: The Transformation of an Oil State* (Boulder, CO: Westview Press, 1992).

— *Oil and Politics in the Gulf: Rulers and Merchants in Kuwait and Qatar* (Cambridge: Cambridge University Press, 1990).

— 'Authoritarianism and Its Adversaries in the Arab World', *World Politics*, vol 46, no 2, 1994.

— 'Civil Society in the Arab Gulf States', in Augustus R. Norton (ed) *Civil Society in the Middle East*, vol 2 (Leiden: E. J. Brill, 1996).

Damkhi, Ali M. al-. *Invasion: Saddam Hussein's Reign of Terror in Kuwait* (London: Kuwait Research and Advertising Co Ltd, 1992).

Davies, Charles E. *Global Interests in the Arab Gulf* (Exeter: University of Exeter Press, 1992).

Dessouki, Ali E. H. (ed). *Islamic Resurgence in the Arab World* (New York: Praeger, 1982).

Diamond, Larry, Juan J. Linz and Seymour M. Lipset (eds). *Democracy in Developing Countries*, 4 vols (Boulder: Lynne Rienner, 1987–94).

Dolgoplatov, Yevgeny. *The Army and the Revolutionary Transformation of Society* (Moscow: Progress Publishers, 1981).

Doran, Charles F. *Myth, Oil, and Politics: Introduction to the Political Economy of Petroleum* (New York: Free Press, 1977).

— and Stephen W. Buck. *The Gulf, Energy and Global Security: Political and Economic Issues* (Boulder, CO: Lynne Rienner Publishers, 1991).

Drysdale, Alasdair and Gerald H. Blake. *The Middle East and North Africa: A Political Geography* (New York: Oxford University Press, 1985).

Dunn, Michael C. 'Gulf Security: Past and Future', in Ibrahim Ibrahim (ed), *The Gulf Crisis: Background and Consequences* (Washington, DC: Center for Contemporary Arab Studies, Georgetown University, 1992).

Economist Intelligence Unit (EIU). *Iraq: Country Profile 1994–1995* (London: EIU, 1995).

— *Iraq* (London: EIU, 2nd quarter 1995).

— *Iran* (London: EIU, 2nd quarter 1995).

Eelens, F., T. Schampers and J. D. Speckmann (eds). *Labour Migration to the Middle East: From Lri Lanka the Gulf* (London: Kegan Paul International, 1992).

Ehteshami, Anoushiravan, Gerd Nonnerman and Charles Tripp (eds). *War and Peace in the Gulf: Domestic Politics and Regional Relations into the 1990s* (Reading: Ithaca Press, 1991).

Eickelman, Dale F. 'Oman's Next Generation: Challenges and Prospects', in H. Richard Sindelar and J. E. Peterson (eds), *Crosscurrents in the Gulf* (London: Routledge, 1988).

Eisenstadt, Michael. 'Iraq's Military Capabilities: An Assessment' (Washington, DC: Washington Institute for Near East Policy, Policy Watch, October 1994).

Esposito, John L. (ed). *The Iranian Revolution: Its Global Impact.* (Gainesville: University of Florida Press, 1990).

— *Islam and Politics*, 3rd edn (Syracuse: New York University Press, 1991).

— *The Islamic Threat: Myth or Reality?* (rev edn, New York: Oxford University Press, 1995).

— 'Constitution of the Islamic Republic of Iran', *Middle East Journal*, vol 34, 1980.

— 'Islam in a World of Shattered Dreams: Islam, Arab Politics and the Gulf Crisis', *The World & I*, February 1991.

Fakhro, Munira A. *Women at Work in the Gulf: A Case Study of Bahrain* (Kegan Paul International, 1990).

— 'The Uprising in Bahrain: An Assessment', paper presented at 'Gulf 2000: Future Prospects for the Gulf', 3rd International Conference, Bellagio, Italy, 25–27 July 1995.

FAO Mission to Iraq. 'Executive Summary and Recommendations', July–August 1995 (unpublished).

Farsi, Zakki. M. A. *National Guide and Atlas of the Kingdom of Saudi Arabia* (Riyadh, 1989).

Farsy, Fouad al-. *Saudi Arabia: A Case Study in Development* (London: KPI, 1986).

Feshariaki, Fereidun and David T. Isaak. *OPEC, the Gulf, and the World Petroleum Market: A Study in Government Policy and Downstream Operations* (Boulder, CO: Westview Press, 1983).

Feste, Karen. 'The Iranian Revolution and Political Change in the Arab World', *The Emirates Occasional Papers*, no 4, 1996 (Abu Dhabi: Emirates Center for Strategic Studies and Research).

Foreign Relations of the US: 1955–57, vol XII (Washington, DC: US Government Printing Office, 1992).

Franke, Rend Rahim. 'Iraq: Race to the Finish Line' (unpublished paper) (Washington, DC: Iraq Foundation, 1994).

Fuller, Graham E. and Bruce Pirnie. *Iran's Destabilizing Potential in the Persian Gulf* (Santa Monica, CA: Rand Corporation Publications, 1996).

Gargash, Anwar. 'Prospects for Conflict and Cooperation: The Gulf Toward the Year 2000', paper presented at 'Gulf 2000: Future Prospects for the Gulf', 3rd International Conference, Bellagio, Italy, 25–27 July 1995.

Garnham, David. 'Deterrence Essentials. Keys to Controlling an Adversary's Behaviour', *The Emirates Occasional Papers*, no 3, 1995 (Abu Dhabi: Emirates Center for Strategic Studies and Research).

Gause, Gregory. *Oil Monarchies: Domestic and Security Challenges in the Arab Gulf States* (New York: Council on Foreign Relations Press, 1994).

Gelb, Alan and Associates. *Oil Windfalls: Blessing or Curse?* (New York: World Bank/Oxford University Press, 1988).

Ghabra, Shafeeq. 'Voluntary Associations in Kuwait: The Foundation of a New System?', *Middle East Journal*, vol 45, no 2, 1991.

Golan, Galia. *Moscow and the Middle East: New Thinking on Regional Conflicts* (London: Pinter, 1992).

Goldberg, J. 'The Shi'ia Minority in Saudi Arabia', in Juan R. I. Cole and Nikki R. Keddies (eds), *Shi'ism and Social Protest* (New Haven, CT: Yale University Press, 1986).

Graham Brown, Sarah. 'The Iraq Sanctions Dilemma', *Middle East Report*, vol 193, no 24, 1995.

Green, Jerrold D. *Revolution in Iran: The Politics of Countermobilization* (New York: Praeger, 1982).

— 'Terrorism and Politics in Iran', in Martha Crenshaw (ed), *Terrorism in Context* (University Park, PA: Pennsylvania State University Press, 1995).

— 'Gulf Security Without the Gulf States', *Harvard Journal of World Affairs*, vol 4, no 1, 1995.

Grimmett, Richard F. 'Conventional Arms Transfers to the Third World' (Washington, DC: Congressional Research Service, 1995).

Gunter, Michael. 'A *de facto* Kurdish State in Northern Iraq', *Middle East Journal*, vol 50, no 2, 1996.

Halpern, Manfred. *The Politics of Social Change in the Middle East and North Africa* (Princeton, NJ: Princeton University Press, 1963).

Hameed, Mazher A. *Arabia Imperiled: The Security Imperatives of the Arab Gulf States* (Washington, DC: Middle East Assessments Group, 1986).

Hardy, Roger. *Arabia after the Storm: Internal Stability of the Arab Gulf States* (London: Royal Institute of International Affairs, 1992).

Hartshorn, J. E. *Oil Trade: Politics and Prospects* (Cambridge: Cambridge University Press, 1993).

Hashim, Ahmad. *The Crisis of the Iranian State: Domestic, Foreign, and Security Policies in Post-Khomeini Iran.* Adelphi Paper no 296 (London: International Institute of Strategic Studies, 1995).

Hazelton, Fran (ed). *Iraq since the Gulf War: Prospects for Democracy* (London: Zed Books, 1994).

Heal, Geoffrey and Graciela Chichilnisky. *Oil and the International Economy* (New York: Oxford University Press, 1991).

Heard-Bey, Frauke. *From Trucial States to United Arab Emirates* (London: Addison-Wesley Longman International, 1996).

Heidenrich, John. G. 'The Gulf War: How Many Died?' *Foreign Policy*, no 90, 1993.

Herrmann, Richard K. 'Russian policy in the Middle East: stategic change and tactical contradictions', *Middle East Journal* 48, Summer 1994.

Hess, Andrew C. 'Peace and political reform in the Gulf: the private sector', *Journal of International Affairs* 49, Summer 1995.

Heydemann, Steven. 'Taxation without Representation: Authoritarianism and Economic Liberalization in Syria', in Ellis Goldberg, Resat Kasaba and Joel Midgal (eds), *Rules and Rights in the Middle East: Democracy, Law, and Society* (Seattle: University of Washington Press, 1993).

Hicks, Neil and Ghanim al-Najjar. 'The Utility of Tradition: Civil Society in Kuwait', in Augustus R. Norton (ed), *Civil Society in the Middle East*, vol 1 (Leiden: E. J. Brill, 1995).

Hijab, N. *Woman Power: The Arab Debate on Women and Work* (Cambridge: Cambridge University Press, 1988).

Hilal, Jamil. *istratijiyat isra'il al-iqtisadiya l'il-sharq al-awsat* (Israel's economic strategy in the Middle East) (Beirut: Institute for Palestine Studies, 1995).

Hiro, Dilip. *Iran Under the Ayatollahs* (London: Routledge and Kegan Paul, 1985).

— *Desert Shield to Desert Storm* (London: Routledge, 1992).

Hooglund, Eric. 'The Pulse of Iran Today', *Middle East Insight*, vol 11, no 5, 1995.

Hudson, Michael C. 'The Islamic Factor in Syrian and Iraqi Politics', in James P. Piscatori (ed), *Islam in the Political Process* (Cambridge: Cambridge University Press, 1983).

Human Rights Watch/Middle East. *Iraq's Crime of Genocide: The Anfal Campaign Against the Kurds* (New Haven, CT: Yale University Press, 1995).

Huntington, Samuel P. 'The Clash of Civilizations?' *Foreign Affairs*, vol 72, summer 1993.

Ibn Qayyim al-Jawziyah Muhammad Ibn Abi Bakr. *Al-Tibb al-Nabawi* (Beirut: Dar al Kutub al Ilmiyah, 1988).

Ikenberry, G. John. 'The Limits of State Building', in his *Reasons of State: Oil Politics and the Capacities of American Government* (Ithaca, NY: Cornell University Press, 1988).

International Monetary Fund. *Direction of Trade Statistics Yearbook 1995* (New York: IMF, 1995).

International Security Review. 'Gulf Security: The Role of the West' (London: RUSI, 1993).

Joffe, George. 'Concepts of Sovereignty in the Gulf Region', in Richard Schofield (ed), *Territorial Foundations of the Gulf States* (London: UCL Press, 1994).

Johar, Hasan and Gawdat Bahgat. 'Oil and democracy: the American dilemma in the Persian Gulf region', *Comparative Strategy* 14, April/June 1995.

Johnson, Douglas, V. II and Steven Metz. *American Civil–Military Relations: New Issues, Enduring Problems* (Carlisle, PA: US Army War College Strategic Studies Institute, 1995).

Johnson, Paul. 'The Myth of American Isolationism', *Foreign Affairs*, vol 74, no 3, 1995.

Kandela, Peter. 'Primary Health Care in the Arab World: Book Reviews', Information Access Company, 5 September 1992.

Karp, Aaron. 'The Demise of the Middle East Arms Race', *Washington Quarterly*, vol 18, no 4, 1995.

Katzman, Kenneth. 'Beyond Dual Containment', *The Emirates Occasional Papers*, no 6, 1996 (Abu Dhabi: Emirates Center for Strategic Studies and Research).

— *Persian Gulf Armed Forces*, Congressional Research Service Report 95-380F (Washington, DC: Library of Congress, March 1995).

Kazemi, Farhad. 'Models of Iranian Politics, the Road to the Islamic Revolution, and the Challenge to Civil Society', *World Politics*, vol 47, no 4, 1995.

Kechichian, Joseph A. 'The Role of the Ulama in the Politics of an Islamic State', *International Journal of Middle East Studies*, vol 18, February 1986.

— *Political Dynamics and Security in the Arabian Peninsula through the 1990s* (Santa Monica, CA: Rand Corporation Study MR-167-AF/A, 1993).

— *Oman and the World: The Emergence of an Independent Foreign Policy* (Santa Monica, CA: Rand Corporation Publications, 1995).

Keddie, Nikki R. *Iran and the Muslim World: Resistance and Revolution* (New York: Macmillan Press, 1995).

Kelly, John B. *Eastern Arabian Frontiers* (London: Faber and Faber, 1964).

— *Arabia, the Gulf and the West* (New York: Basic Books, 1991 reprint).

Kennedy, John L. 'The Shape of World Oil Markets in the 1990s', in Shankar Sharma and Joseph L. H. Tan (eds), *Global Oil Trends: The Asia-Pacific Market in the 1990s* (Singapore: ASEAN Economic Research Unit, Institute of Southeast Asian Studies, 1991).

Khalilzad, Zalmay. 'The United States and the Persian Gulf: Preventing Regional Hegemony', *Survival*, vol 37, no 2, 1995.

Khalizad, Zalmay, et al. *The Impact of the Arab–Israeli Conflict on Gulf Security* (1996).

Khuri, Fuad. *Tribe and State in Bahrain: The Transformation of Social and Political Authority in an Arab State* (Chicago, IL: University of Chicago Press, 1980).

Koch, Christian. 'Interest Groups and Associational Life in the Political Development of the State of Kuwait', PhD dissertation, University of Erlangen-Nurnberg (forthcoming).

Korb, Lawrence J. 'Our Overstuffed Armed Forces', *Foreign Affairs*, vol 74, no 6, 1995.

Krapels, Edward N. 'The Fundamentals of the World Oil Market of the 1980s', in Wilfred L. Kohl (ed), *After the Oil Collapse: OPEC, the United States, and the World Oil Market* (Baltimore: Johns Hopkins University Press, 1991).

Lake, Anthony. 'Debate: Confronting Backlash States', *Foreign Affairs*, vol 73, no 2, 1994.

Lambton, A. K. S. *State and Government in Medieval Islam: An Introduction to the Study of Islamic Political Theory: The Jurists* (Oxford: Oxford University Press, 1981).

Lane, Charles. 'Changing Iran: Germany's New Ostpolitik', *Foreign Affairs*, vol 74, no 6, November/December 1995.

Latham, John D., Robert B. Sergeant and M. J. L. Young (eds). *Religion, Learning and Science in the Abbasid Period* (Cambridge: Cambridge University Press, 1990).

Lawrence, Robert Z. 'Emerging Regional Arrangements: Building Blocks or Stumbling Blocks?', in Richard O'Brien (ed), *Finance and the International Economy: 5, The AMEX Bank Review Prize Essays* (Oxford: Oxford University Press, 1991).

Lawson, Fred. *Bahrain: The Modernization of Autocracy* (Boulder, CO: Westview Press, 1989).

Lelyveld, Michael S. 'Iran Extends Power in Region Via Trade Deals', *Journal of Commerce*, 14 September 1995.

Lenin, Vladimir. 'Speech Closing the Congress, 16 March 1921', in V. I. Lenin, *Collected Works*, vol 32, December 1920–August 1921 (Moscow: Progress Publishers, 1965).

Lewis, Bernard. 'Muslim Rage', *Atlantic Monthly*, June 1992.

Long, David E. 'Saudi Arabia in the 1990s: Plus ça change … ', in Charles F. Doran and Stephen W. Buck (eds), *The Gulf, Energy, and Global Security* (Boulder, CO: Lynne Rienner, 1991).

Looney, Robert E. *Manpower Policies and Development in the Persian Gulf Region* (Westport, CN: Praeger, 1994).

— 'The impact of defense expenditure on industrial development in the Arab Gulf', *Middle Eastern Studies* 30, April 1994.

Lovins, Amory B. and L. Hunter Lovins. 'Drill Rigs and Battleships are the Answer! (But What was the Question?): Oil Efficiency, Economic Rationality, and Security', in Robert G. Reed III and Fereidun Fesharaki (eds), *The Oil Market in the 1990s: Challenges for the New Era* (Boulder, CO: Westview Press, 1989).

McLachlan, Keith and Anne McLachlan. *Oil and Development in the Gulf* (London: John Murray, 1989).

McNaugher, Thomas. 'Iran's Military Posture: Whether "Hegemonic" or "Defensive," Iran's Force Buildup Complicates U.S. Defense Planning', *Middle East Insight* (special edition on Iran), vol 11, no 5, 1995.

Maddy-Weitzman, Bruce. 'Inter-Arab Relations', in A. Ayalon (ed), *Middle East Contemporary Survey*. Boulder, CO: Westview Press, 1992.

Malek, M. and J. Rasquinha. 'Socio-economic foundations of stability in the Gulf region', *Journal of Contemporary Asia* 23, no. 1, 1993.

Malik, Hafeez. 'Tatarstan's Treaty with Russia: Autonomy or Independence', *Journal of South Asian and Middle Eastern Studies*, vol 18, no 2, 1994.

Marr, Phebe. *The Modern History of Iraq* (Boulder, CO: Westview Press, 1985).

— 'Iraq's Future, Plus ça change … or Something Better?', in Ibrahim Ibrahim (ed), *The Gulf Crisis: Background and Consequences* (Washington, DC: Center for Contemporary Arab Studies, Georgetown University, 1992).

— 'The United States, Europe, and the Middle East: An Uneasy Triangle', *Middle East Journal*, vol 48, no 2, 1994.

— 'U.S.–GCC Security Relations, 1: Differing Threat Perceptions', *Strategic Forum*, no 39, August 1995 (Washington, DC: National Defense University).

Mazidi, Feisal Al-. *The Future of the Gulf* (London: I.B.Tauris, 1993).

Mazrua, Y. Al- and S. Al-Shammari. 'Community Participation and Attitudes of Decision Makers Towards Community Involvement in Health Development in Saudi Arabia', *World Health Organization Bulletin*, 1991.

Melnikov, Igor. 'Russia and the Middle East', *International Affairs*, no 1, 1993.

Melnikov, Yuri and Vladimir Frolov. 'Iran and Russian–US Relations', *International Affairs*, no 5, 1995.

Middle East Economic Digest (MEED) Special Report. 'UK and the Middle East', 30 June 1995.

— *Special Report*. 'Italy and the Middle East', 7 July 1995.

— *Special Report*. 'France and the Middle East', 13 September 1995.

— *Special Report*. 'Germany and the Middle East', 20 October 1995.

— *Special Report*. 'Italy and the Middle East', 7 July 1995.

Miller, Judith. 'Is Islam a Threat? Yes', *Foreign Affairs*, vol 72, no 2, 1993.

Moynihan, Joseph. 'Information Warfare: Concepts, Boundaries and Employment Strategies', *The Emirates Occasional Papers*, no 7, 1997 (Abu Dhabi: Emirates Center for Strategic Studies and Research).

Mozaffari, Mehdi. 'The "New" Balkanization of the Persian Gulf?', *Cambridge Review of International Affairs*, vol 8, no 2 and vol 9, no 1, 1994/95.

Mughni, Haya al-. *Women in Kuwait: The Politics of Gender* (London: al-Saqi Books, 1993).

Naqeeb, Khaldoun Al-. *Society and State in the Arab Gulf Peninsula: A Different Perspective*) London: Routledge, 1991).

Nissman, David B. *The Soviet Union and Iranian Azerbaijan: The Uses of Nationalism for Political Penetration* (Boulder, CO: Westview Press, 1987).

Ochsenwald, William. 'Saudi Arabia and the Islamic Revival', *International Journal of Middle East Studies*, vol 13, 1981.

Osama, Abdul Rahman. *The Dilemma of Development in the Arabian Peninsula* (London: Routledge, 1986.)

Page, John. *Economic Prospects and the Role of Regional Development Finance Institutions, Regional Economic Development in the Middle East: Opportunities and Risks* (Washington, DC: Center for Policy Analysis on Palestine, December 1995).

Palmer, Michael A. *Guardians of the Gulf: A History of America's Expanding Role in the Persian Gulf, 1833–1991* (New York: Free Press, 1992).

Parasiliti, Andrew W. 'Origins of the Gulf War and the Iraq Cycle of Power and Role', unpublished PhD dissertation, Johns Hopkins, SAIS, 1996.

Parsons, Anthony. 'Prospects for Peace and Stability in the Middle East', *Conflict Studies*, 262 (London: Research Institute for the Study of Conflict and Terrorism, 1993).

Peleg, Ilan. 'The Peace Process and Israel's Political Culture: A Kulturkampf in the Making', paper presented at the annual meeting of the American Political Science Association, Chicago, 31 August 1995.

Peres, Shimon. *The New Middle East* (New York: Henry Holt, 1993).

Peterson, J. E. *The Arab Gulf States: Steps Towards Political Participation* (New York: Praeger Publishers, 1988).

Petroleum Finance Company (PFC). *Country Report: Iraq* (Washington, DC: PFC, December 1994).

Pike, David. 'Cross-border Hydrocarbon Reserves', in Richard Schofield (ed), *Territorial Foundations of the Gulf States* (London and New York: UCL Press and St Martin's Press, 1994).

Pipes, Daniel and Patrick Clawson. 'Ambitious Iran, Troubled Neighbors', *Foreign Affairs* (America and the World 1992/93), vol 72, no 1, 1993.

Piscatori, James P. 'Ideological Politics in Saudi Arabia', in J. P. Piscatori (ed), *Islam in the Political Process* (Cambridge: Cambridge University Press, 1983).

Pollack, Johnathan. *Should the U.S. Worry About the Chinese–Iranian Security Relationship*, DRR-923-1-A (Santa Monica, CA: Rand Corporation, December 1994).

Polyakov, Yu. I. and A. I. Chugunov. *Konets basmachestva* (Moscow: 1976).

Population Reference Bureau. *1995 World Population Data Sheet* (Washington, DC: Population Reference Bureau, 1995).

Price, Richard. *Maritime Laws of Arabian Gulf Cooperation Council States* (Kluwer Academic Publishers, 1986).

Ramazani, Rouhollah K. 'Iran's Foreign Policy: Both North and South', *Middle East Journal*, vol 46, no 3, 1992.

— and Joseph A. Kechichian. *The Gulf Cooperation Council: Record and Analysis* (Charlottesville: University of Virginia Press, 1988).

Rasulzade, Mamed E. 'Vospominaniya O I. V. Stalin' (Remembrances of J. V. Stalin) *Vostochnyi ekspress*, no 1, 1993.

Reed, Robert G. III and Fereidun Feshariaki (eds). *The Oil Market in the 1990s: Challenges for the New Era* (Boulder, CO: Westview Press, 1989).

Ritcheson, Philip L. 'Iranian military resurgence: scope, motivations, and implications for regional security', *Armed Forces and Society* 21, Summer 1995.

Robins, Philip. 'Can Gulf Monarchies Survive the Oil Bust?', *Middle East Quarterly*, vol 1, no 4, 1994.

Robinson, Glenn. E. *Building a Palestinian State: The Incomplete Revolution* (Bloomington: Indiana University Press, 1997).

— *Defensive Democratization in Jordan* (forthcoming).

Rosenthal, Franz. *Science and Medicine in Islam: A Collection of Essays* (Aldershot, England: Gower, 1990).

Rostow, Walt W. *The Stages of Economic Growth: A Non-Communist Manifesto* (Cambridge: Cambridge University Press, 1967).

Rumaihi, Mohammad. *Beyond Oil: Unity and Development in the Gulf* (London: Saqi Books, 1986).

Russell, Sharon S. and Muhammad A. Al-Ramadhan, 'Kuwait's Migration Policy Since the Gulf Crisis: Change or Continuity?', paper presented at the annual meeting of the Middle East Studies Association, Research Triangle Park, North Carolina, 11–14 November 1993.

Russett, Bruce. *Grasping the Democratic Peace* (Princeton, NJ: Princeton University Press, 1993).

Rzaev, Agababa and G. Guseinov 'Sushchestvuet li ugroza islamskogo fundamentalizma?' (Does an Islamic threat exist?), *Vozrozhdenie*, nos 7–9, 1991.

Said Zahlan, Rosemarie. *The Making of the Modern Gulf States: Kuwait, Bahrain, Qatar, the United Arab Emirates and Oman* (London: Routledge, 1989).

Sani, Nasser. 'The Kuwaiti Power-sharing Experience', in Azzam Tamini (ed), *Power-Sharing Islam* (London: Grey Seal, 1993).

Sankari, Farouk A. 'Islam and Politics in Saudi Arabia', in Ali E. Hillal Dessouki (ed), *Islamic Resurgence in the Arab World* (New York: Praeger, 1982).

Schahgaldian, Nikola. B. *Iran and Postwar Security in the Persian Gulf* (Santa Monica, CA: Rand Corporation Publication MR-148-USDP, 1994).

Schofield, Richard. *Kuwait and Iraq: Historical Claims and Territorial Disputes* 2nd edn (London: Royal Institute of International Affairs, 1993).

— *Unfinished Business: Iran, the UAE, Abu Musa and the Tunbs* (London: Royal Institute of International Affairs, forthcoming).

— 'Disputed Territory, the Gulf Cooperation Council and Iran', *The Iranian Journal of International Affairs*, vol 5, nos 3–4, autumn 1993/winter 1994.

— 'Border Disputes in the Gulf: Past, Present and Future', paper presented at 'Gulf 2000: Future Prospects for the Gulf', 2nd International Conference, Abu Dhabi, 1995.

— 'Mending Gulf Fences', *Middle East Insight*, vol 12, no 2, 1996.

— 'The Last Missing Fence in the Desert: the Saudi–Yemeni Boundary', *Geopolitics and International Boundaries*, vol 1, no 3, 1996.

— 'Border Disputes in the Gulf: Past, Present and Future', in Larry Potter and Gary Sick (eds), *The Gulf in the Next Millennium* (Boulder, CO: Westview Press, forthcoming).

— 'Britain and the Borders of Kuwait, 1902–1913', in B. J. Slot (ed), *Kuwait: The Development of Historic Identity* (forthcoming).

— (ed). *Territorial Foundations of the Gulf States* (London and New York: UCL Press and St Martin's Press, 1994).

Schwedler, Jillian (ed). *Toward Civil Society in the Middle East? A Primer* (Boulder, CO: Lynne Rienner, 1995).

Shah, Nasra. M. 'Structural Changes in the Receiving Country and Future Labor Migration: The Case of Kuwait', paper presented at the Annual Meeting of the Middle East Studies Association, Research Triangle Park, North Carolina, 11–14 November 1993.

Shojai, Siamack (ed). *The New Global Oil Market: Understanding Energy Issues in the World Economy* (Westport, CT: Praeger, 1995).

Sick, Gary. 'Iran: The Adolescent Revolution', *Journal of International Affairs*, vol 49, no 1, summer 1995.

Smith, Peter. 'Crisis and Democracy in Latin America', *World Politics*, vol 43, July 1991.

Stevens, Paul. *Oil and Politics: The Post-War Gulf* (London: Royal Institute for International Affairs, 1992).

Suwaidi, Jamal S. al- (ed). *The Yemeni War of 1994. Causes and Consequences* (Abu Dhabi: Emirates Center for Strategic Studies and Research, 1995).

— (ed). *Iran and the Gulf. A Search for Stability* (Abu Dhabi: Emirates Center for Strategic Studies and Research,1996).

Swietochowski, Tadeusz. 'Azerbaijan's Triangular Relationship: The Land Between Russia, Turkey and Iran', in Ali Babuazizi and Myron Weiner (eds), *The New Geopolitics of Central Asia and Its Borderlands* (Bloomington: Indiana University Press, 1994).

Teece, David J. 'OPEC Behavior: An Alternative View', in James M. Griffin and David J. Teece (eds), *OPEC Behavior and World Oil Prices* (London: George Allen, 1982).

Tetreault, Mary A. *The Kuwait Petroleum Corporation and the Economics of the New World Order* (Westport, CT: Quorum, 1995).

— 'Civil Society in Kuwait: Protected Spaces and Women's Rights', *Middle East Journal*, vol 47, no 2, 1993.

Tetreault, Mary A. and Haya al-Mughni. 'Modernization and Its Discontents: State and Gender in Kuwait', *Middle East Journal*, vol 49, no 3, 1995.

Till, Julie. 'The GCC–EU Dialogue', *Gulf Report*, no 36, December 1993.

Twinam, Joseph W. *The Gulf, Cooperation and the Council: An American Perspective* (Washington, DC: Middle East Policy Council, 1992).

UN. *The United Nations and the Iraq–Kuwait Conflict, 1990–1996* (New York: UN Department of Public Information, 1996).

United States State Department, Bureau of Intelligence and Research, *Geographic Notes*, vol 13, March 1991.

Viorst, Milton. 'Changing Iran: The Limits of Revolution', *Foreign Affairs*, vol 74, no 6, 1985.

Voll, John O. *Islam: Continuity and Change in the Modern World*, 2nd edn (Syracuse: New York University Press, 1995).

Waldner, David. 'The Politics of Peace and Prosperity: Economic Interdependence and National Security in the Middle East', in Bahman Baktiari (ed), *Essays in Honor of R. K. Ramazani* (forthcoming).

Wallerstein, Immanuel. *The Modern World-System.* 3 vols (San Diego, CA: Academic Press, 1974–80).

Ware, Lew B., Strategic Studies Institute. *Terrorism: National Security Policy and the Home Front* (Carlisle, PA: US Army War College, May 1995).

Wilkinson, John C. *Arabia's Frontiers: The Story of Britain's Boundary Drawing in the Desert* (London: I.B.Tauris, 1994).

Wilson, Rodney. 'The Economic Relations of the Middle East: Toward Europe or Within the Region?' *Middle East Journal*, vol 48, no 2, 1994.

Yamani, Mai. (ed), *Feminism and Islam: Legal and Literary Perspectives* (London: Ithaca Press, 1996).

— 'Birth and Behaviour in a Hospital in Saudi Arabia', *British Society for Middle Eastern Studies (BRISMES) Bulletin*, vol 13, no 2, 1987.

— 'Formality and Propriety in the Hijaz', unpublished PhD dissertation, University of Oxford, 1990.

— 'You are What You Cook: Cuisine and Class in Mecca', in Richard Tapper and Sami Zubeida (eds), *The Culinary Cultures of the Middle East* (London: I.B.Tauris, 1994).

Yassini, Ayman al-. *Religion and State in Saudi Arabia* (Boulder, CO: Westview Press, 1985).

Zanoyan, Vahan. 'A Relevant Framework for Understanding the Global Crude Oil Market', in *Gulf Energy in the World: Challenges and Threats* (Abu Dhabi: Emirates Center for Strategic Study and Research, 1996).

— 'After the Oil Boom', *Foreign Affairs*, vol 74, no 6, 1995.

Index